Nirali's New Series

CONCISE STUDY SERIES

(50 Marks)

DIGITAL ELECTRONICS AND LOGIC DESIGN

Sem - I

S.E COMPUTER ENGINEERING

As per New Revised Syllabus of University of Pune

(Pattern 2012)

S. S. Kulkarni
M. E. (E & TC)
Associate Professor
Sinhgad Academy of Engineering
Kondhawa, Pune.

N 2812

DIGITAL ELECTRONICS AND LOGIC DESIGN (SE COMP.)

First Edition : June 2014

© :

The text of this publication, or any part thereof, should not be reproduced or transmitted in any form or stored in any computer storage system or device for distribution including photocopy, recording, taping or information retrieval system or reproduced on any disc, tape, perforated media or other information storage device etc., without the written permission of Authors with whom the rights are reserved. Breach of this condition is liable for legal action.

Every effort has been made to avoid errors or omissions in this publication. In spite of this, errors may have crept in. Any mistake, error or discrepancy so noted and shall be brought to our notice shall be taken care of in the next edition. It is notified that neither the publisher nor the authors or seller shall be responsible for any damage or loss of action to any one, of any kind, in any manner, therefrom.

Published By :
NIRALI PRAKASHAN
Abhyudaya Pragati, 1312, Shivaji Nagar,
Off J.M. Road, PUNE – 411005
Tel - (020) 25512336/37/39, Fax - (020) 25511379
Email : niralipune@pragationline.com

Printed at
Repro Knowledgecast Limited
India

DISTRIBUTION CENTRES
PUNE

Nirali Prakashan
119, Budhwar Peth, Jogeshwari Mandir Lane
Pune 411002, Maharashtra
Tel : (020) 2445 2044, 66022708, Fax : (020) 2445 1538
Email : bookorder@pragationline.com

Nirali Prakashan
S. No. 28/25, Dhyari,
Near Pari Company, Pune 411041
Tel : (022) 24690204 Fax : (020) 24690316
Email : dhyari@pragationline.com
bookorder@pragationline.com

MUMBAI
Nirali Prakashan
385, S.V.P. Road, Rasdhara Co-op. Hsg. Society Ltd.,
Girgaum, Mumbai 400004, Maharashtra
Tel : (022) 2385 6339 / 2386 9976, Fax : (022) 2386 9976
Email : niralimumbai@pragationline.com

DISTRIBUTION BRANCHES

NAGPUR
Pratibha Book Distributors
Above Maratha Mandir, Shop No. 3, First Floor,
Rani Jhanshi Square, Sitabuldi, Nagpur 440012,
Maharashtra, Tel : (0712) 254 7129

BENGALURU
Pragati Book House
House No. 1, Sanjeevappa Lane, Avenue Road Cross,
Opp. Rice Church, Bengaluru – 560002.
Tel : (080) 64513344, 64513355,
Mob : 9880582331, 9845021552
Email:bharatsavla@yahoo.com

JALGAON
Nirali Prakashan
34, V. V. Golani Market, Navi Peth, Jalgaon 425001,
Maharashtra, Tel : (0257) 222 0395
Mob : 94234 91860

KOLHAPUR
Nirali Prakashan
New Mahadvar Road,
Kedar Plaza, 1st Floor Opp. IDBI Bank
Kolhapur 416 012, Maharashtra. Mob : 9855046155

CHENNAI
Pragati Books
9/1, Montieth Road, Behind Taas Mahal, Egmore,
Chennai 600008 Tamil Nadu, Tel : (044) 6518 3535,
Mob : 94440 01782 / 98450 21552 / 98805 82331, Email : bharatsavla@yahoo.com

RETAIL OUTLETS
PUNE

Pragati Book Centre
157, Budhwar Peth, Opp. Ratan Talkies,
Pune 411002, Maharashtra
Tel : (020) 2445 8887 / 6602 2707, Fax : (020) 2445 8887

Pragati Book Centre
Amber Chamber, 28/A, Budhwar Peth,
Appa Balwant Chowk, Pune : 411002, Maharashtra,
Tel : (020) 20240335 / 66281669
Email : pbcpune@pragationline.com

Pragati Book Centre
676/B, Budhwar Peth, Opp. Jogeshwari Mandir,
Pune 411002, Maharashtra
Tel : (020) 6601 7784 / 6602 0855

PBC Book Sellers & Stationers
152, Budhwar Peth, Pune 411002, Maharashtra
Tel : (020) 2445 2254 / 6609 2463

MUMBAI
Pragati Book Corner
Indira Niwas, 111 - A, Bhavani Shankar Road, Dadar (W), Mumbai 400028, Maharashtra
Tel : (022) 2422 3526 / 6662 5254, Email : pbcmumbai@pragationline.com

Dear Students,

It gives us great pleasure to introduce a New Series "**C**oncise **S**tudy **S**eries" for Second Year Engineering students. These "**CSS**" books are written by Experienced and Eminent Professors of respective subjects.

The specialty of this new Series "**CSS**" is that it:

- ➢ *Covers full syllabus of University of Pune.*
- ➢ *Contains Matter written in Simple and Lucid language.*
- ➢ *Includes "To the Point" Topics and well arranged articles.*
- ➢ *Includes Most Likely Questions.*
- ➢ *Includes Previous Years University Question Papers.*
- ➢ *Available in all leading stores at Affordable Price.*

Happy Studying and Best of Luck!!!

Nirali Prakashan

SYLLABUS

Unit I : Number System & Logic Design Minimization Techniques :   8 Hrs.
Introduction: Binary, Hexadecimal numbers, octal numbers and number conversion. Signed Binary number representation: Signed Magnitude, 1's complement and 2's complement representation. Binary, Octal, Hexadecimal Arithmetic: 2's complement arithmetic. Algebra for logic circuits: Logic variables, Logic functions -NOT, AND, NOR, XOR, OR, XNOR, NAND Boolean algebra: Truth tables and Boolean algebra. Idealized logic gates and symbols. DeMorgan's rules Axiomatic definition of Boolean algebra, Basic theorems and properties of Boolean algebra Logic minimization : Representation of truth-table, SOP form, POS form, Simplification of logical functions, Minimization of SOP and POS forms, Don't care conditions Reduction techniques: K-Maps up to 4 variables and Quine-McClusky technique

Unit II : Logic Families   6 Hrs.
TTL: Standard TTL characteristics- Speed, power dissipation, fan-in, fan-out, current and voltage parameters, noise margin, operating temperature etc. Operation of TTL NAND gate. TTL Configurations- Active pull-up, Wired AND, totem pole, open collector. CMOS: CMOS Inverter, CMOS characteristics, CMOS configurations- Wired Logic, Open drain outputs Interfacing: TTL to CMOS and CMOS to TTL

Unit III : Combinational Logic   9 Hrs.
Codes:- BCD, Excess-3, Gray code , Binary Code and their conversion Arithmetic Operations: - Binary Addition, Subtraction, Multiplication, Division, BCD Addition Circuits: - Half- Adder, Full Adder, Half Subtract or, Full Sub tractor, BCD adder using and subtract using 7483, look ahead and carry, parity generator and checker using 74180, magnitude comparator using 7485. Multiplexers (MUX) : Working of MUX, Implementation of expression using MUX (IC 74153, 74151). Demultiplexers (DEMUX):- Implementation of expression using DEMUX, Decoder. (IC 74138).

Unit IV : Sequential Logic: 8Hrs
Introduction : Sequential Circuits. Difference between combinational circuits and sequential circuits Flip- flop: SR, JK, D, T; Preset & Clear, Master and Slave Flip Flops their truth tables and excitation tables, Conversion from one type to another type of Flip Flop. Application of Flip-flops: Bounce Elimination Switch, registers, counters. Registers: Buffer register; shift register; Counters: Asynchronous counter. Synchronous counter, ring counters, BCD Counter, Johnson Counter, Modulus of the counter (IC 7490), Pseudo Random Binary Sequence Generator, Sequence generator and detector

Unit V ASM & VHDL   9 Hrs
Algorithmic State Machines: ASM charts, notations, design of simple controller, multiplexer controller methodExamples: Sequence Generator, Types of Counter VHDL: Introduction to HDL, VHDL- Library, Entity, Architecture, Modeling Styles, Concurrent and Sequential Statements, Data Objects & Data Types, Attributes. Design Examples: VHDL for Combinational Circuits-Adder, MUX. VHDL for Sequential Circuits-Synchronous and Asynchronous Counter

Unit VI : PLDs   8 Hrs
PLD: PLA- Input, Output Buffers, AND, OR, Invert/ Non-Invert Matrix. Design Example: Any 4 Variables SOP function using PLDs, Study of basic Architecture of FPGA.

CONTENTS

Unit 1 : Number System and Logic Design Minimization Techniques   1.1-1.56

1.1	Number System	1.1
	1.1.1 Binary Number System	1.1
	1.1.2 Decimal Number System	1.1
	1.1.3 Octal Number System	1.2
	1.1.4 Hexadecimal Number System	1.2
1.2	Conversion of any Radix Numbers to Decimal number	
	1.2.1 Conversion of Binary to Decimal	1.3
	1.2.2 Conversion of Octal to Decimal	1.3
	1.2.3 Conversion of Hexadecimal Number to Decimal Number	1.3
1.3	Conversion from Decimal to other Number System	1.4
	1.3.1 Conversion of Decimal to Binary	1.4
	1.3.2 Conversion of Decimal to Octal	1.5
	1.3.3 Conversion of Hexadecimal to Decimal	1.5
1.4	Remaining radix conversion	1.6
	1.4.1 Conversion of Binary to Octal	1.6
	1.4.2 Converting Octal to Binary	1.6
	1.4.3 Converting of Hexadecimal to Binary	1.7
	1.4.4 Converting of Binary to Hexadecimal	1.7
	1.4.5 Converting Octal to Hexadecimal	1.8
	1.4.6 Converting Hexadecimal to Octal	1.8
1.5	Signed binary number representation	1.9
	1.5.1 Signed Magnitude	1.9
	1.5.2 One's Complement	1.10
	1.5.3 Two's Complement	1.10
1.6	Binary arithmetic	1.11
	1.6.1 Binary Addition	1.11
	1.6.2 Binary Subtraction	1.12
	1.6.3 Binary Multiplication	1.15
	1.6.4 Binary Division	1.15
1.7	Octal arithmetic	1.16
	1.7.1 Octal Addition	1.16
	1.7.2 Octal Subtraction using 8's Complement	1.16

1.8	Hexadecimal Arithmetic	1.18
	1.8.1 Hexadecimal Addition	1.18
	1.8.2 Hexadecimal Subtraction using 16's Complement	1.19
1.9	Basic Logic Gates	1.19
	1.9.1 NOT Gate (Inverter)	1.20
	1.9.2 AND Gate	1.21
	1.9.3 OR Gate	1.22
	1.9.4 NAND Gate	1.22
	1.9.5 NOR Gate	1.23
	1.9.6 Exclusive OR Gate	1.23
	1.9.7 Universal Gates – NAND and NOR	1.24
1.10	Boolean Algebra	1.25
	1.10.1 Axioms of Boolean Algebra	1.25
	1.10.2 Laws of Boolean Algebra	1.26
	1.10.3 Rules of Boolean Algebra	1.27
	1.10.4 DeMorgan's Theorems	1.27
1.11	Sum Of Products (SOP) Form	1.29
	1.11.1 Standard Terms and Standard (or Canonical) Forms	1.29
	1.11.2 Sum Term or Maximum Term (M)	1.29
	1.11.3 Product or Minimum Term (m)	1.31
	1.11.4 Standard (or Canonical) Forms	1.31
	1.11.5 Sum of Products (SOP) Form	1.31
1.12	Product of Sums (POS) Form	1.32
	1.12.1 Product-of-Sums (POS) Form	1.32
1.13	Reduction Techniques	1.33
	1.13.1 Boolean Algebra Simplification Technique	1.33
	1.13.2 Reduction of Boolean Equation using K-map	1.34
	1.13.3 Representing SOP Equation on K-map	1.35
	1.13.4 Representing POS Equation on K-map	1.36
	1.13.5 K-map Reduction Techniques	1.36
	1.13.6 Prime Implicant and Essential Prime Implicant	1.39
	1.13.7 Don't Care Condition	1.39
	1.13.8 Limitations of Karnaugh Map	1.41

1.14	Implementation of Boolean Function using Logic Gate	1.41
	1.14.1 Implementation of SOP	1.41
	1.14.2 Implementation of POS	1.42
	1.14.3 Implementation of Combinational Circuit	1.42
1.15	Introduction to Quine-MC Cluskey Method	1.45

Unit II : Logic Families 2.1-2.26

2.1	IC logic Families and Characteristics	2.1
	2.1.1 Introduction	2.1
	2.1.2 Packaging	2.1
	2.1.3 Classification of Logic Families	2.2
2.2	Characteristics of Digital ICs	2.2
	2.2.1 Fan–in	2.2
	2.2.2 Fan–out	2.2
	2.2.3 Propagation Delays	2.3
	2.2.4 Voltage and Current Parameters	2.3
	2.2.5 Current Sourcing and Current Sinking	2.4
	2.2.6 Noise Margin/Immunity	2.4
	2.2.7 Power Dissipation	2.5
	2.2.8 Figure of Merit	2.5
	2.2.9 Slew Rate	2.6
2.3	IC Logic Families	2.6
2.4	Transistor – Transistor logic (TTL)	2.6
	2.4.1 TTL NAND gate	2.7
	2.4.2 2 – input TTL NAND Gate (Totem pole output)	2.7
	2.4.3 3–input TTL NAND Gate	2.9
	2.4.4 Totem–Pole Output	2.9
	2.4.5 Open–collector Output	2.11
	2.4.6 Wired and Operation	2.11
	2.4.7 Tri–state Outputs	2.13
	2.4.8 Other TTL Characteristics	2.14
2.5	Complementary Metal-Oxide-Semiconductor (CMOS) Circuits	2.15
	2.5.1 CMOS Inverter	2.15
	2.5.2 CMOS NAND gate	2.16
	2.5.3 CMOS NOR gate	2.17

		2.5.4 CMOS Characteristics	2.19
2.6		CMOS and TTL interfacing	2.20
		2.6.1 TTL–to–CMOS Interfacing Techniques	2.20
		2.6.2 CMOS – to – TTL Interfacing Techniques	2.21
2.7		Different Logic Family Series	2.24
2.8		Comparison of CMOS and TTL	2.25
Unit III : Combinational Logic			**3.1-3.50**
3.1		Codes	3.1
3.2		BCD Code	3.2
		3.2.1 BCD Addition	3.3
		3.2.2 BCD Subtraction	3.4
3.3		Excess 3 code	3.6
3.4		Gray Code	3.8
		3.4.1 Application of Gray Code	3.9
		3.4.2 Advantages of Gray Code	3.10
		3.4.3 Converting Binary code to Gray code	3.11
		3.4.4 Converting Gray to Binary	3.11
3.5		Code Conversion	3.11
		3.5.1 Binary to BCD Conversion	3.12
		3.5.2 BCD to Binary Conversion	3.12
		3.5.3 BCD to Excess 3 Conversion	3.12
		3.5.4 Excess-3 to BCD Conversion	3.12
3.6		Half Adder And Full Adder	3.13
		3.6.1 Half-Adder	3.13
		3.6.2 Full-Adder	3.14
3.7		Half and Full Subtractor	3.16
		3.7.1 Half-subtractor	3.16
		3.7.2 Full-subtractor	3.17
3.8		Parallel Adder	3.19
3.9		Parallel Subtractor	3.19
3.10		Parallel Adder / Subtractor	3.20
3.11		Carry Look - ahead adder	3.20
3.12		BCD Adder	3.22
3.13		BCD Subtractor	3.25

	3.13.1 BCD subtraction using 9's complement	3.25
	3.13.2 BCD subtractor using 9's complement method	3.25
	3.13.3 BCD subtraction using 10's complement	3.27
	3.13.4 4-bit BCD subtraction using 10's complement method	3.27
3.14	Parity Generator and Checker	3.29
3.15	Magnitude Comparators	3.32
3.16	Multiplexers	3.34
	3.16.1 IC 74153 Dual 4 to 1 multiplexer	3.37
	3.16.2 IC 74151 Multiplexer	3.38
3.17	Demultiplexer	3.42
3.18	Decoder	3.46
	3.18.1 IC 74 138 (3 :8 decoder)	3.49

Unit IV : Sequential Logic   **4.1-4.98**

4.1	Sequential Circuits	4.1
4.2	Comparison of Combinational and Sequential Circuit	4.2
4.3	Sequential Circuit Types	4.3
4.4	One Bit Memory Cell (Basic Bistable Elements)	4.3
4.5	Latch vs Flip-Flop	4.4
4.6	Level Triggered and Edge Triggered	4.4
4.7	Latch	4.6
	4.7.1 SR Latch using NAND Gate	4.6
	4.7.2 SR Latch using NOR Gate	4.7
	4.7.3 D Latch	4.11
4.8	Clocked SR Flip Flop	4.12
4.9	Clocked S-R Flip Flop with Preset and Clear Inputs	4.14
4.10	JK Flip Flop	4.15
4.11	Master Slave JK (MS JK) Flip Flop	4.17
4.12	D Flip Flop	4.18
4.13	T Flip Flop	4.20
4.14	Different Representation of Flip Flop	4.21
4.15	Excitation Table of Flip Flop	4.21
	4.15.1 Excitation Table of S-R Flip-Flop	4.21
	4.15.2 Excitation Table of JK, D & T Flip Flop	4.22

4.16	Conversion of Flip Flops	4.25
	4.16.1 Convert S-R Flip Flop to JK Flip Flop	4.25
	4.16.2 Convert S-R flip flop to D flip flop	4.27
	4.16.3 Convert S-R Flip Flop into T Flip Flop	4.28
	4.16.4 Convert JK Flip Flop into T Flip Flop	4.28
	4.16.5 Convert JK Flip Flop into D Flip Flop	4.29
4.17	Applications of Flip-Flops	4.30
	4.17.1 Bounce Elimination Switch	4.30
4.18	Registers	4.32
4.19	Buffer register	4.32
4.20	Shift register	4.33
	4.20.1 Serial In Serial Out Shift Register	4.33
	4.20.2 Serial in Parallel Out Shift Register	4.35
	4.20.3 Parallel In Serial Out Shift Register	4.36
	4.20.4 Parallel In Parallel Out Shift Register	4.39
	4.20.5 Bi-directional Shift Register	4.39
	4.20.6 Universal Register	4.41
	4.20.7 4-bit Bidirectional Universal Shift Register (74HC194)	4.41
4.21	Counters	4.42
	4.21.1 Classification of Counters	4.42
4.22	Asynchronous (Ripple) Counters	4.43
	4.22.1 3-Bit Asynchronous Up (Ripple) Counter	4.44
	4.22.2 4-Bit Asynchronous Up Counter	4.46
	4.22.3 3-bit Asynchronous Down Counter	4.48
	4.22.4 4-bit Up / Down Ripple Counter	4.49
	4.22.5 MOD-N counter (Modulus of the counter)	4.50
	4.22.6 Frequency Division	4.52
	4.22.7 4 bit Asynchronous BCD Ripple Counter	4.54
	4.22.8 Drawbacks of Ripple Counter	4.55
4.23	Study of IC 7490	4.56
4.24	Synchronous Counter	4.60
	4.24.1 3-bit Synchronous Counter	4.61
	4.24.2 4-bit Synchronous Counter	4.63
	4.24.3 4-bit Up/Down Synchronous Counter	4.64

4.24.4	Modulo N Synchronous Counter	4.66
4.24.5	BCD Synchronous Counter	4.69
4.24.6	Ring Counter	4.71
4.24.7	Johnson Counter	4.73
4.24.8	Unused States and Lock Out Condition	4.75
4.25	Difference between Synchronous and Asynchronous Counters	4.78
4.26	Pseudo Random Sequence Generator	4.78
4.27	Sequence Generator	4.81
4.27.1	Sequence Generator using Shift Registers	4.81
4.27.2	Sequence Generator using Flip-Flops	4.85
4.28	The General form of a Sequential Circuit	4.87
4.28.1	Forms of Sequential Logic	4.87
4.29	Sequence Detector	4.88
4.29.1	Two Types of Sequence Detector	4.88

Unit V : ASM and VHDL 5.1-5.68

5.1	Introduction	5.1
5.2	ASM Chart Notations	5.1
5.3	Controller for ASM using multiplexers	5.7
5.4	Introduction to VHDL	5.15
5.5	VLSI Design	5.15
5.6	Comparison of VHDL and Verilog	5.16
5.7	Levels of Abstraction	5.16
5.8	Data Objects	5.18
5.9	VHDL Component	5.19
5.9.1	Entity	5.20
5.9.2	Architecture	5.23
5.10	Concurrent Statements	5.26
5.10.1	Concurrent Signal Assignment	5.26
5.10.2	Block Statement	5.29
5.10.3	Component Instantiation Statement	5.31
5.10.4	Generate Statement	5.33
5.10.5	Process Statement	5.35
5.11	Sequential Statements	5.39
5.11.1	If Statement	5.39

	5.11.2 Case Statement	5.40
	5.11.3 Null Statement	5.42
	5.11.4 Loop Statement	5.42
	5.11.5 Next Statement	5.43
	5.11.6 Exit Statement	5.44
	5.11.7 Report Statement	5.45
5.12	Styles of Modeling	5.49
	5.12.1 Data Flow Modeling	5.49
5.13	Package and Library	5.51
	5.13.1 Package	5.51
	5.13.2 Design Libraries	5.53
5.14	VHDL Codes	5.55
	5.14.1 Mux Code	5.55
	5.14.2 Binary Adder VHDL Code	5.57
	5.14.3 Counter VHDL Code	5.58
	5.14.4 Shift Register VHDL Code	5.63

Unit VI : Programmable Logic Devices   **6.1-6.34**

6.1	PLD overview	6.1
	6.1.1 SPLD (Simple PLD) Simple Logic Functions	6.2
	6.1.2 GAL (Generic Array Logic)	6.2
	6.1.3 Read only Memory (ROM) as a PLD	6.3
6.2	Programmable Logic Arrays (PLAs)	6.4
	6.2.1 Architecture of PLA	6.4
	6.2.2 Circuit Realization using PLA	6.14
6.3	Programmable Array Logic (PAL)	6.18
6.4	CPLD : Complex Programmable Logic Device	6.24
	6.4.1 XC9500 CPLD Family	6.25
6.5	FPGA : Field Programmable Gate Array	6.29
	6.5.1 Details of FPGA Architecture	6.30
6.6	Comparison of CPLD And FPGA	6.33

Unit - I

NUMBER SYSTEM AND LOGIC DESIGN MINIMIZATION TECHNIQUES

1.1 NUMBER SYSTEMS

Q. Explain different types of number systems?

- Binary Number System
- Decimal Number System
- Octal Number System
- Hexadecimal Number System

1.1.1 Binary Number System

- The binary number system is used in digital electronics. It has the following characteristics.

  Two digits : 0, 1

  Base : 2

  Weights : Powers of Base 2 (2^0, 2^1, 2^2, 2^3 ...) or (1, 2, 4, 8).

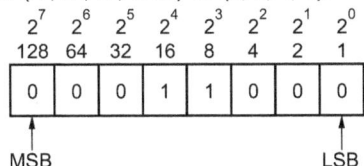

Fig. 1.1 : Binary number system

- In the binary system, 1's and 0's are arranged into columns.
- Each column is weighted. The first column on the right has a binary weight of 2^{10}. This equivalent to decimal 1 and is referred to as the Least Significant Bit (LSB).
- The number in the far left hand column is called Most Significant Bit (MSB).

1.1.2 Decimal Number System

- In decimal number system, we can express any decimal number in units, ten hundreds, thousands and so on.

e.g. 6597.8 this number can be represented as

$\qquad$ 6000 + 500 + 90 + 7 + 0.8 = 6597.8 = 6597.8_{10}

radix and base of decimal number system is 10.

	10^3	10^2	10^1	10^0		10^{-1}
In power of 10	6	5	9	7	•	8
	6×10^3	5×10^2	9×10^1	7×10^0	•	8×10^{-1}

Fig. 1.2

1.1.3 Octal Number System

- The octal number system consists of eight digits of decimal number system : 0, 1, 2, 3, 4, 5, 6 and 7. So its base is 8.

e.g. The octal number 8531.74 can be represented in power of 8 as shown in Fig. 1.3.

8^3	8^2	8^1	8^0		8^{-1}	8^{-2}
8	5	3	1	•	7	4
8×8^3	5×8^2	3×8^1	1×8^0	•	7×8^{-1}	4×8^{-2}

Fig. 1.3

1.1.4 Hexadecimal Number System

- The hexadecimal number system abase of 16 having 16 characters.

0, 1, 2, 3, 4, 5, 6, 7, 8, 9, A, B, C, D, E, F.

- It is easy to convert hexadecimal number to binary and vice versa.

e.g. 3FD. 48 can be represented in power of 16 as shown in Fig. 1.4 below.

16^2	16^1	16^0		16^{-1}	16^{-2}
3	F	D	•	4	8
3×16^2	$F \times 16^1$	$D \times 16^0$	•	4×16^{-1}	8×16^{-2}

Fig. 1.4

1.2 CONVERSION OF ANY RADIX NUMBERS TO DECIMAL NUMBER

- To convert from any radix r to Decimal. The formula for converting any Radix to Decimal.

$$N = A_{n-1} r^{n-1} + A_{n-2} r^{n-2} + \ldots + A_1 r^1 + A_0 r^0 + A_{-i} r^{-i} + \ldots + C_{-m} r^{-m} \quad \ldots(1)$$

where
- N = Number in decimal
- A = Digit
- r = Radix or base of number system number of digits
- m = The fractional part of the number
- n = The number of digit in the fractional part of the number

DIGITAL ELECTRONICS LOGIC DESIGN (S.E. COMP.)　　　　NUMBER SYSTEM AND LOGIC DESIGN

1.2.1 Conversion of Binary to Decimal

Q. Convert following number into decimal. $(10110.0101)_2$	[Dec. 07, 6 M]
Q. Perform the following operation $(1011.101)_2$	[Dec. 11, 8 M]
Q. Perform the following operation $(1001.10)_2 = (\ )_{10}$	[May 12, 2 M]

Example 1.1 : Convert binary number 1011.01 into its decimal equivalent.

Solution : Given binary number is 1011.01

Using formula given in equation 1.

$$(1011.01) = (1 \times 2^3 + 0 \times 2^2 + 1 \times 2^1 + 1 \times 2^0 + 0 \times 2^{-1} + 1 \times 2^{-2})$$

$$= 1 \times 8 + 0 \times 4 + 1 \times 2 + 1 \times 1 + 0 \times \frac{1}{2} + 1 \times \frac{1}{4}$$

$$= 8 + 0 + 2 + 1 + \frac{1}{4}$$

$$= (11.25)_{10}$$

1.2.2 Conversion of Octal to Decimal

Q. Convert the following octal number into its equivalent decimal.	
(a) (555) octal　(b) (777) octal	[May 07, 6 M]
Q. For a maximum 3-digit octal number obtain a equivalent decimal number.	[May 11, 1 M]
Q. Convert the following into its equivalent decimal numbers. $(327.4051)_8$	[Dec. 12, 2 M]

Example 1.2 :

$(321)_8 = (\ )_{10}$

Solution : Given number is $(321)_8$

Using formula given in equation 1.

$$(321)_8 = 3 \times 8^2 + 2 \times 8^1 + 2 \times 8^0 = 3 \times 64 + 2 \times 8 + 2 \times 1$$

$$= 192 + 16 + 2$$

$$(321)_8 = (210)_{10}$$

1.2.3 Conversion of Hexadecimal Number to Decimal Number

Q. Express following number in decimal. Show your step by step calculation. $(16.5)_{16}$	[May 07, 6 M]
Q. Convert the following :	
1. $(BF8)_{16} = (\ )_{10}$	[Dec. 11, 2 M]
2. $(1\ FFF)_{16} = (\ )_{10}$	[May 12, 2 M]
3. $(5A.FF)_{16} = (\ )_{10}$	[Dec. 12, 2 M]
4. $(3\ FFF)_{16} = (\ )_{10}$	[Dec. 12, 2 M]

Unit 1 | 1.3

Example 1.3 :

Convert hexadecimal number $(4D7.2)_{16}$ into its equivalent decimal number.

Solution : Given number is $(4D7.2)_{16}$

$$(4D7.2) = 4 \times 16^2 + 13 \times 16^1 + 7 \times 16^0 + 2 \times 16^{-1}$$

$$= 4 \times 144 + 13 \times 16 + 7 \times 1 + \frac{2}{16}$$

$$= 576 + 208 + 7 + 0.125$$

$$(4D7.2)_{16} = (791.125)_{10}$$

1.3 CONVERSION FROM DECIMAL TO OTHER NUMBER SYSTEM

- In this we need to first consider the given number having decimal point we need to separate integer part and fractional parts.
- Then convert each part different method and then combine for last answer.

1.3.1 Conversion of Decimal to Binary

Q.	Express the following numbers in binary		
(i)	$(1010.11)_{Decimal}$	(ii) $(428.10)_{Decimal}$	**[Dec. 10, 6 M]**
Q.	Express the following numbers in binary		
(i)	$(2948)_{10}$	(ii) $(11\ 01.11)_{10}$	**[Dec. 10, 6 M]**

Example 1.4 : Convert 125.12 decimal into binary number.

Solution : Integer part

Division	Remainder
125 ÷ 2 = 62	1
62 ÷ 2 = 31	0
31 ÷ 2 = 15	1
15 ÷ 2 = 7	1
7 ÷ 2 = 3	1
3 ÷ 2 = 1	1
1 ÷ 2 = 0	1

LSD ↑ MSD

$$(125)_{10} = (1111101)_2$$

Fractional part

```
  0.12         0.24         0.48         0.96
×  2         ×  2         ×  2         ×  2
-----        -----        -----        -----
  0.24         0.48         0.96         1.92
```

$$(0.12)_{10} = (0001)_2$$

∴ $(125.12)_{10} = (1111101.0001)_2$

1.3.2 Conversion of Decimal to Octal

Q. Convert the following number into octal form $(3287.51)_{10}$ [Dec. 12, 2 M]

Example 1.5 : Convert $(338.025)_{10}$ into octal.

Solution : Integer part

Division	Remainder
338 ÷ 8 = 42	2
42 ÷ 8 = 5	2
5 ÷ 8 = 0	5

LSD ↑ MSD

$(338)_8 = (522)_{10}$

Fractional part :

```
 0.025      0.200      0.600      0.800
×   8      ×   8      ×   8      ×   8
-----      -----      -----      -----
 0.200      1.600      4.800      6.400
   ↓          ↓          ↓          ↓
   0          1          4          6
```

$(0.025)_8 = (0146)_{10}$

∴ Final answer $(338.0.25)_8 = (522.0146)_{10}$

1.3.3 Conversion of Hexadecimal to Decimal

Q. Convert the following number into decimal number. [Dec. 11, May 12, 4 M]
  (i) $(1FFF)_{16}$ (ii) $(BF8)_{16}$

Q. Convert the following number into decimal number.
  (i) $(5A.FF)_{16}$ (ii) $(3FFF)_{16}$

Example 1.6 : Convert $(438)_{16}$ into decimal.

Solution : Integer part

Division	Remainder
438 ÷ 16 = 26	0
26 ÷ 16 = 1	1
10 ÷ 16 = 0	10 = A

LSD ↑ MSD

$(438)_{16} = (A10)$
$(438)_{16} = (A10)_{10}$

1.4 REMAINING RADIX CONVERSION

1.4.1 Conversion of Binary to Octal

Q. Convert the following octal number into octal. [Dec. 12, 2 M]

(i) $(11111001.1001100101)_2$

- Converting binary to octal is also a simple process. Break the binary digits into groups of three starting from the binary point and convert each group into its appropriate octal digit.
- For whole numbers, it may be necessary to add a zero as the MSB in order to complete a grouping of three bits. Note that this does not change the value of the binary number. Similarly, when representing fractions, it may be necessary to add a trailing zero in the LSB in order to form a complete grouping of three.

Example 1.7 : Converting $(010111)_2$ to Octal

111 = 7 (LSB)

010 = 2 (MSB)

Thus, $(010111)_2 = (27)_8$

Example 1.8 : Converting $(0.110111)_2$ to Octal

110 = 6 (MSB)

111 = 5 (LSB)

Thus, $(0.110101)_2 = (0.65)_8$

1.4.2 Converting Octal to Binary

Q. Convert the following octal number into binary.

(a) $(123456)_8$ (b) $(5726.34)_8$

(c) $(337)_8$ (d) $(0.53652)_8$

- The primary application of octal numbers is representing binary numbers, as it is easier to read large numbers in octal form that in binary form. Because each octal digit can be represented by a three-bit binary number (see Table 1.1, it is very easy to convert from octal to binary.
- Simply replace each octal digit with the appropriate three-bit binary number as indicated in the examples below.

Table 1.1 : Octal and binary numbers

Octal Digit	Binary Digit
0	000
1	001
2	010
3	011
4	100
5	101
6	110
7	111

$$13_8 = (001011)_2$$
$$(37.12)_8 = (011111.001010)_2$$

1.4.3 Converting of Hexadecimal to Binary

> Q. Convert the following hexadecimal to Binary numbers.
> (1) A72E (2) BD6.7 (3) 0.AF54 (4) DF (5) FF   [May 13, 10 M]

- Because each hexadecimal digit can be represented by a four-bit binary number it is very easy to convert from hexadecimal to binary. Simply replace each hexadecimal digit with the appropriate four-bit binary number as indicated in the examples below.

Example 1.9 :

$$A3_{16} = (10100011)_2$$
$$(37.12)_{16} = (00110111 . 00010010)_2$$

1.4.4 Converting of Binary to Hexadecimal

> Q. Convert $(11011011101)_2$ into hex. number.   [Dec. 12, 2 M]

- Converting binary to hexadecimal is another simple process. Break the binary digits into groups of four starting from the binary point and convert each group into its appropriate hexadecimal digit.

- For whole numbers, it may be necessary to add a zero as the MSB in order to complete a grouping of four bits. Note that this addition does not change the value of the binary number.

- Similarly, when representing fractions, it may be necessary to add a trailing zero in the LSB in order to form a complete grouping of four.

Example 1.10 :

(a) Converting $(1010111)_2$ to hexadecimal.

$$0111 = 7 \text{ (LSB)}$$
$$0101 = 5 \text{ (MSB)}$$

Thus, $(1010111)_2 = (57)_{16}$

(b) Converting $(0.00111111)_2$ to hexadecimal.

$$0011 = 3 \text{ (MSB)}$$
$$1111 = F \text{ (LSB)}$$

Thus, $(0.00111111)_2 = (0.3F)_{16}$

1.4.5 Converting Octal to Hexadecimal

Q. Convert the following octal numbers into its equivalent hex.	[May 10, 4 M]
(i) $(555)_{octal}$ (ii) $(777)_{octal}$	
Q. Convert $(36)_8$ into hexadecimal.	[May 12, 2 M]
Q. Convert $(377)_8$ into hexadecimal.	[Dec. 11, 2 M]

- To convert an octal number to hexadecimal follow the steps given below.

Step 1 : First convert octal to its binary.

Step 2 : Then convert binary number into hexadecimal.

Example 1.11 :

Convert $(777)_8$ into hex.

Step 1 : Convert $(777)_8$ into binary.

$$(777)_8 = (111111111)$$

Step 2 : For equivalent hexadecimal group the binary number into group of 4.

$$(777)_8 = (\underline{0001} \quad \underline{1111} \quad \underline{1111})$$
$$\quad \quad \quad \downarrow \quad \quad \downarrow \quad \quad \downarrow$$
$$\quad \quad \quad 1 \quad \quad F \quad \quad F$$

∴ $(777)_8 = (1FF)_{16}$

1.4.6 Converting Hexadecimal to Octal

Q. Convert hexadecimal numbers into octal numbers.	[May 13, 10 M]
(1) A72E (2) BD6.7 (3) 0.AF54 (4) DF (5) FF	

- To convert hexadecimal numbers into octal follow the below steps.

Step 1 : First write down given hexadecimal numbers into 4 group of binary numbers.

Step 2 : Then remove the group of four binary.

Step 3 : Make group of 3 binary bits starting from the LSB side.

Example 1.12 :

Convert hexadecimal numbers 5DB into octal.

Step 1 : Given number is 5DB.

Binary from of 5DB is = 01011.1011011

Step 2 : Rewrite number with removing group space.

$$= (\ 010\ \ 111\ \ 011\ \ 011\ )$$
$$\downarrow\ \ \ \downarrow\ \ \ \downarrow\ \ \ \downarrow$$
$$2\ \ \ 7\ \ \ 3\ \ \ 3$$

$(5DB)_6 = (2733)_8$

1.5 SIGNED BINARY NUMBER REPRESENTATION

Q. What do you mean by signed magnitude representation of a number ? **[Dec. 07, 2 M]**

Q. What are different ways of representing signed binary numbers ? Explain with examples ? **[Dec. 11, 6 M]**

- Signed Magnitude
- One's Complement
- Two's Complement

1.5.1 Signed Magnitude

- The simplest way to indicate negation is signed magnitude. In signed magnitude, the left-most bit is not actually part of the number, but is just the equivalent of a + / − sign.
- "0" indicates that the number is positive, "1" indicates negative. In 8 bits, 00001100 would be 12 (break this down into (1*2 ^3) + (1 * 2 ^2)). To indicate - 12, we would simply put a "1" rather than a "0" as the first bit : 10001100.
- The +ve or −ve signs are also represented in the binary form i.e. by using 0 or 1 so a 0 is used to represent the (+ve) sign and 1 is used to represent (−ve) sign.
- The most significant Bit (MSB) of binary number is used to represent the sign and the remaining bits are used for representing the magnitude.

e.g. 8 bit signed binary number show in Fig. 1.5

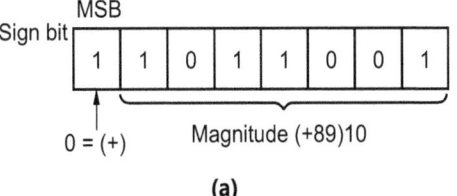

(a)

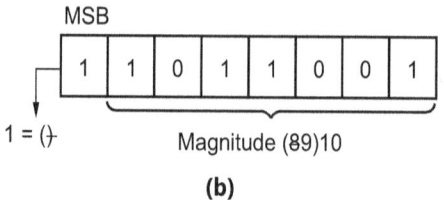

Fig. 1.5 : 8-bit signed binary numbers

This type of numbers is called number or signed magnitude number.

- For an 8 bit sign magnitude number the largest negative number is (–127) to largest positive, number is (127) i.e. from 0 to 255.

Advantages :

- We can easily find out the magnitude by deleting the sign bit.
- The simplicity of sign magnitude.

Disadvantage :

- Signed number require complicated circuits.

1.5.2 One's Complement

- In one's complement, positive numbers are represented as usual in regular binary. However, negative numbers are represented differently. To negate a number, replace all zeros with ones, and ones with zeros-flip the bits. Thus, 12 would be 00001100, and –12 would be 11110011.
- As in signed magnitude, the leftmost bit indicates the sign (1 is negative, 0 is positive). To compute the value of a negative number, flip the bits and translate as before.

1.5.3 Two's Complement

- Begin with the number in one's complement. Add 1 if the number is negative. Twelve would be represented as 00001100, and – 12 as 11110100. to verify this, let's subtract 1 from 11110100, to get 11110011. If we flip the bits, we get 00001100, or 12 in decimal.

Example 1.13 :

Represent the decimal numbers 25 and – 25 in the 8 bit signed magnitude 1's complement and 2's complement forms.

Solution :

Step 1 : (i) Representation of 25 signed magnitude

$$25 = 0 \quad 0011001$$
$$\quad\ \ \downarrow \qquad\quad \downarrow$$
$$\ \ \text{sign} \quad\ \ \text{Magnitude}$$

NUMBER SYSTEM AND LOGIC DESIGN

Step 2 : (ii) Representation of –25 in signed magnitude form.

$$25 = 1 \quad 0011001$$
$$\downarrow \qquad \underbrace{\qquad}$$
$$\text{sign} \quad \downarrow$$
$$\text{Magnitude}$$

Step 3 : (iii) Representation of – 25 in 1's complement form

$$25 = 00011001 \ldots \text{sign magnitude}$$
$$\downarrow$$
$$\text{invert all bits}$$
$$-25 = 11100110 \ldots \text{1's complement form}$$

Step 4 : (iv) Representation of – 25 in 2's complement form

$$25 = 00011001 \ldots \text{sign magnitude}$$
$$\text{invert all bits + add 1}$$
$$-25 = 11100111 \ldots \text{2's complement form}$$

1.6 BINARY ARITHMETIC

1.6.1 Binary Addition

Q. Perform addition of $(11001001)_2$ and $(10101111)_2$.

- The binary addition is the most basic operation of binary arithmetic. The two bit binary digit addition is shown in following table.

Table 1.2 : Truth table for half adder

Sr. No.	Operations	Sum	Carry
0	0 + 0	0	0
1	0 + 1	1	0
2	1 + 0	1	0
3	1 + 1	0	1

- The 3 bit (i.e. two significant bit and a previous carry) is called a full addition is shown in following table.

Table 1.3 : Truth table for full adder

Inputs			Outputs	
A	B	C_{in}	Sum	Cout
0	0	0	0	0
0	0	1	1	0
0	1	0	1	0
0	1	1	0	1
1	0	0	1	0
1	0	1	0	1
1	1	0	0	1
1	1	1	1	1

Binary addition method steps :

Step 1 : Add bits column wise from LSB with carry if any

Step 2 : If carry is generated write at the top of next column.

Step 3 : Write the sum at the bottom of the same column.

Example 1.14 : $(8)_{10}$ and $(12)_{10}$

Step 1 : First convert both number into binary.

$$(8)_{10} = (1000)_2$$
$$(12)_{10} = (1100)_2$$

Step 2 : Add bits column wise from the LSB with carry if any.

```
        1        ...carry
    + 1000       ...number 1
      1100       ...number 2
     _____
     10100
```
$= (10100)_2$

1.6.2 Binary Subtraction

- The subtraction for 2 bit procedure is given below in table 1.4.

Table 1.4

Sr. No.	Operations	Sub	Borrow
1	0-0	0	0
2	0-1	1	1
3	1-0	1	0
4	1-1	0	0

Subtraction method steps :

1. Subtract bits column wise starting from LSB with barrow if any.
2. Write borrow at the next column top.
3. Write difference bottom of the same column.

Example 1.15 :

Perform binary subtraction $(11101100)_2 - (00110010)_2$

Solution :

```
              10
         0 0 10  0 10
         1 1 1 0 1 1 0 0    ...number 1
       - 0 0 1 1 0 0 1 0    ...number 2
       _____
         1 0 1 1 1 0 1 0    Result
```

1.6.2.1 Binary subtraction using 1's complement method

Q. Perform binary subtraction using 1's complement form.

Steps :
1. First take 1's complement of second number.
2. Add first number and 1's complement of second number.
3. If the carry is generated then result is + ve and true form. Then add carry to the result to get final answer.
4. If the carry is not generated then result is –ve and in 1's complement form.

Example 1.16 :
Perform binary subtraction using 1's complement method.

$$(28)_{10} - (15)_{10}$$

Step 1 : First convert both numbers into binary.

$$(28)_{10} = (011100)_2$$
$$(15)_{10} = (001111)_2$$

Step 2 : Take 1's complement of second number i.e. $(15)_{10}$

$$(001111) = (15)_{10}$$
$$\downarrow \text{1's complement}$$
$$110000$$

Step 3 : Add first number and 1's complement of second number.

```
  011100
+ 110000
--------
 1001100
    ↓
  carry
```

Step 4 : Carry is generated so result is positive add carry to the result to get final result.

```
  001100
+      1
--------
  001101   final answer
```

$$001101 = (13)_{10}$$

1.6.2.2 Binary subtraction using 2's complement method

Q. Perform the following arithmetic's operations using 2's complement form
(i) 8 + 12 (ii) –8 + 12 (iii) 8 – 12 (iv) –8 – 12 **[May 05, 8 M]**

Q. Perform subtraction using 2's complement method.
(i) 96 – 78 (ii) 57 –77 (iii) 88 – 99

Steps:
1. First take 2's complement of second number.
2. Add first number to the 2's complement of second number.
3. If carry is generated then result number is positive and true form. Remove carry or ignore carry.
4. If carry is not generated then the result number is –ve and in the 2's complement form.

Example 1.17: Perform following substructure using 2's complement method

(a) $(4)_{10} - (9)_{10}$. [Dec. 06, 2 M]

Step 1: First write both number in the binary form.

$$(4)_{10} = 0100$$
$$(9)_{10} = 1001$$

Step 2: Obtain 2's complement of $(9)_{10}$

$(9)_{10}$ = 1001
↓ 2's complement
0111

Step 3: Add $(4)_{10}$ to 2's complement of $(9)_{10}$

```
      (4)₁₀                = 0100
           +
  2's complement of (9)₁₀  = 0111
                          0  1011
                          ↓   ↓
                    final carry  answer
```

zero shows the result is negative and in its 2's complement form.

Step 4: Convert the answer into true form

```
   Answer     1011
   Subtract –    1
              1010
              ↓ invert all bits
              0101   (answer in true form)
```

Thus the answer is – $(0101)_2$ i.e. $(-5)_{10}$.

(b) $(10011)_2 - (1101)_2$

Step 1: Take 2's complement of second number.

```
       01101
       ↓ invert all bits
       10010
       + 1
       10011
```

Unit 1 | 1.14

Step 2 : Add $(10011)_2$ to 2's complement of $(01101)_2$.

```
  10011      ...number 1
+ 10011      ...number 2 2's complement
  ──────
 100110
 |  result answer
 carry
```

Step 3 : Carry is 1 so number is positive discard carry.

final answer = 00110

1.6.3 Binary Multiplication

> **Q.** Perform the following operation without converting the numbers to decimal.
> (i) $(1000001)_2 \div (1101)_2$
> **[Dec. 04, 2 M]**

- Binary multiplication process for binary numbers is similar to decimal number. The two bit binary multiplication shown below

Table 1.5 : Rules for binary multiplication

Sr. No.	A	B	Ans.
1	0	0	0
2	0	1	0
3	1	0	0
4	1	1	1

Example 1.18 : $(1011)_2 \times (101)_2$

```
        1011    ...multiplicand
      × 101     ...multiplier
      ──────
        1011
    +  00000
    + 101100
      ──────
      110111    ...final answer
```

1.6.4 Binary Division

> **Q.** Perform following operation without converting the numbers to decimal.
> $11011011_2 \div 110_2$

The division process of binary number is same as the decimal number table 1.6 show the rules for binary 2 bit division.

Table 1.6 : Rules for binary division

Sr. No	Numbers		Division
	A	B	
1	0	1	0
2	1	1	1

Example 1.19 : 11011011_2 by 110_2

```
           11011011  by  110₂
             100100
       110) 11011011
            110
            ───────
            0001100
            110
            ───────
            00011
```

Quotient = $(100100)_2$, Reminder = $(11)_2$

1.7 OCTAL ARITHMETIC

1.7.1 Octal Addition

Q. Add the octal numbers [Dec. 12, 4 M]
$(777)_8 + (77)_8$ = ( )

- The sum of octal digit is same as decimal sum. If the decimal sum is greater than 8 or equal to 8, subtract 8, from the addition result to obtain the octal digit. A carry of 1 is produced when the decimal sum is in above condition.

Example 1.20 : Add $(634)_8$ and $(152)_8$

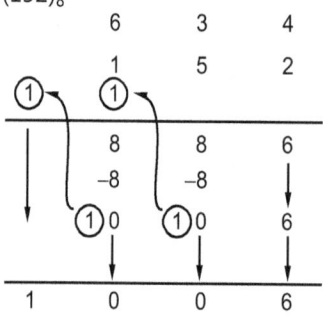

final answer = $(1006)_8$

1.7.2 Octal Subtraction using 8's Complement

Q. Perform subtraction using 8's complement form
(i) $(516)_8 - (413)_8$
(ii) $(316) - (451)_8$

Steps:

1. First take 8's complement of second number to take 8's complement, first take 7's complement of number then add 1 to 7's complement answer.
2. Add first number and second 8's complement number
3. If carry is produced in the addition it is ignored otherwise find 8's complement of sum as a result with negative sign.

Example 1.21 : Perform subtraction using 8's complement method.

$(516)_8 - (413)_8$

Step 1 : Subtract second number each digit of a number from 7 to get the 7's complement of the number and add 1 to answer to get 8's complement.

```
    777
  - 413
  -----
    364   7's complement
  +   1
  -----
    365   8s complement
```

Step 2 : Add first number to the 8's complement of second number.

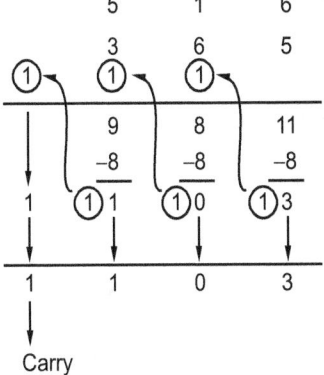

Step 3 : Carry is generated ignore carry.

final answer = $(103)_8$

Example 1.22 : $(316)_8 - (451)_8$

Step 1 : First take 8's complement of second number. i.e. $(451)_8$

```
    777
  - 451
  -----
    326   7's complement
  +   1
  -----
    327   8s complement
```

Step 2 : Add first number to 8's complement of second number.

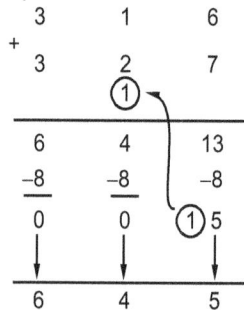

Step 3 : No carry generated hence take 8's complement of answer (645)

```
   777
 - 645
  ----
   132    7's complement
  + 1     add 1
  ----
   133    8s complement of (645)₈
```

$(316)_8 - (451)_8 = (-133)_8$

1.8 HEXADECIMAL ARITHMETIC

1.8.1 Hexadecimal Addition

Q. Perform the following operation. **[May 12, 4 M]**
(1) $(888)_{16} + (999)_{16} = ( )_{16}$
(2) $(658)_{16} + (975)_{16} = ?$

Rules:
- The sum of two hexadecimal digits is the same as their equivalent decimal sum, provided decimal equivalent is less that 16.
- If the sum is greater 16 or equal to 16, subtract 16 from the result and a carry of 1 is produced when the decimal sum is corrected to obtain final answer.

Example 1.23 : $(658)_{16} + (975)_{16} = ?$
Add given two numbers.

$$
\begin{array}{r}
(6)_{10}\ (5)_{10}\ (8)_{10} \\
+\ (9)_{10}\ (7)_{10}\ (5)_{10} \\
\hline
(15)_{10}\ (12)_{10}\ (13)_{10} \\
\downarrow\quad \downarrow\quad \downarrow \\
(F)_{16}\ (C)_{16}\ (D)_{16}
\end{array}
$$

∴ $(658)_{16} + (975)_{16} = (FCD)_{16}$

1.8.2 Hexadecimal Subtraction using 16's Complement

> Q. Perform form subtraction using 16's complement [May 10, 16 M]
>
> (i) $(ABC)_{16} - (CBA)_{16}$
>
> (ii) $(759)_{Hex.} - (975)_{Hex}$
>
> Q. Perform following operation [Dec. 09, 6 M]
>
> (i) $(387)_{Hex} - (2AC)_{Hex}$
>
> (ii) $(587)_{Hex} - (4EB)_{Hex}$

- The 16's complement of a hexadecimal number is found by adding a 1 to the least significant bit of the 15's complement of hexadecimal number.

Example 1.24 : $(587)_{Hex} - (4EB)_{Hex.}$

Step 1 : First take 16's complement of second number.

```
      15 15 15
    -  4  E  B
    ───────────
       B  1  4    15's complement
            + 1
    ───────────
       B  1  5    16's complement
```

Step 2 : Add first number to the 16's complement of second number

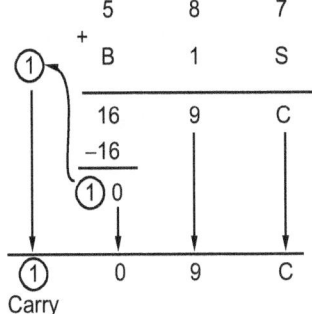

Step 3 : Discard carry

∴ $(587)_{Hex} - (4EB)_{Hex} = (09C)_{16}$

1.9 BASIC LOGIC GATES

- The term **Logic** refers to something which can be reasoned out. In many situations, the problem statements can be expressed in true or false and yes or no formats.
- Since, digital circuits also have two states or binary form, these kind of problem statements can be formulated using logic states or logic functions.

- Because the voltage levels in a digital circuit are assumed to be switched from one value to another, the digital circuits are called logic circuits or switching circuits.
- Logic gate is a logic circuit which obeys a certain set of logic rules. The manner in which a logic circuit responds to an input is referred to as the circuit's logic.
- The name logic gate is derived from the ability of such device to make decisions i.e. produce different outputs in response to different combinations of inputs.
- As mentioned earlier, logic gate is an electronic switching circuit.
- Semiconductor devices such as diode, BJT or MOSFET can be used to build logic gates.
- The inherent characteristics of these devices such as junction capacitance, uni- or bi-polar, diffusion capacitance decides the characteristics of logic gates.

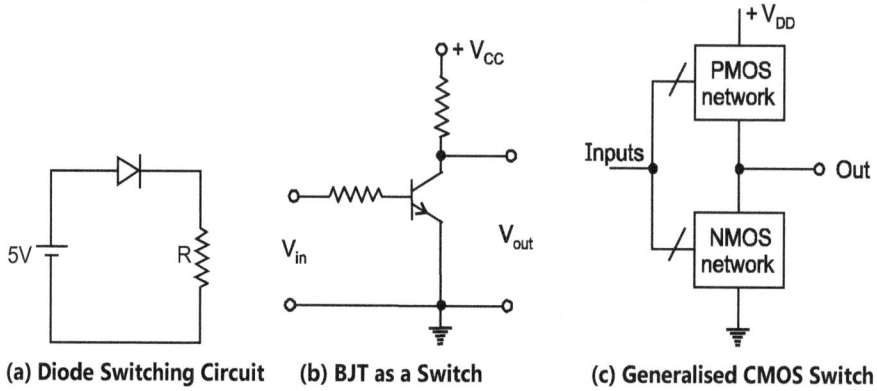

(a) Diode Switching Circuit (b) BJT as a Switch (c) Generalised CMOS Switch

Fig. 1.6 : Semiconductor devices as switches

The logic gates can be classified as below :

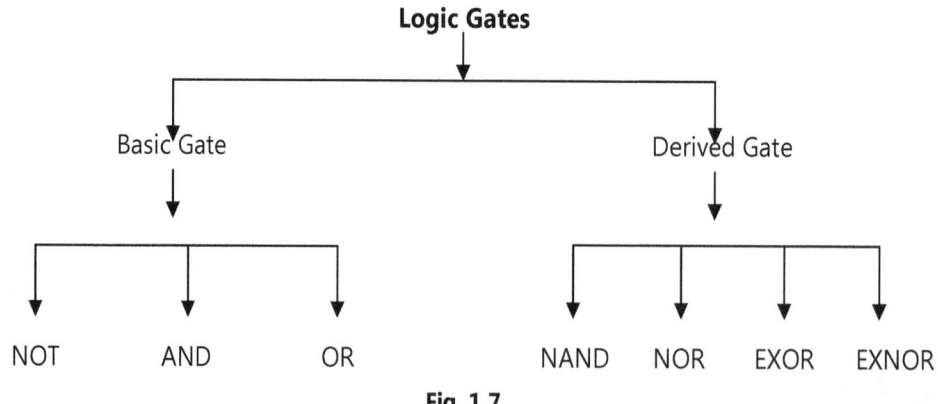

Fig. 1.7

1.9.1 NOT Gate (Inverter)

Logic Statement

- The output of a NOT circuit takes on the logic '1' state, if and only if the input does not take on the '1' state.

Truth Table of NOT

A	Y
0	1
1	0

Logic Symbol of NOT

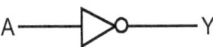

Fig. 1.8 : Logic symbol of NOT gate

- The bubble appearing at the output indicates inversion or negation.

Boolean Equation

$$Y = \bar{A}$$

- The bar above variable A represents the logical inversion operation.
- Some authors use ' ' ' symbol which is more appropriate.

i.e. $Y = A'$

1.9.2 AND Gate

Logic Statement

- The AND gate is an electronic logic circuit in which the output is in logic '1' state only and only when all the inputs are in logic '1' state.

Truth Table of AND

Inputs		Output
A	B	Y
0	0	0
0	1	0
1	0	0
1	1	1

Logic Symbol of AND

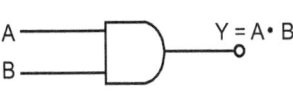
(a) Two Input AND Gate

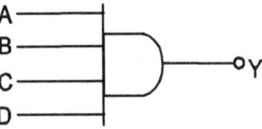
(b) Four Input AND Gate

Fig. 1.9 : Logic symbol of AND gate

Boolean Equation

$$Y = A \cdot B$$

The '·' operator is called logic AND operator.

1.9.3 OR Gate

Logic Statement

- The OR gate is an electronic circuit in which the output is in logic 1 state, when any one or more inputs are in logic 1 states.

Truth Table of OR

Input		Output
A	B	Y
0	0	0
0	1	1
1	0	1
1	1	1

Logic Symbol of OR

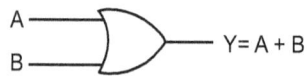

(a) Two Input OR Gate

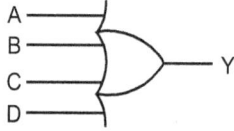

(b) Four Input OR Gate

Fig. 1.10 : Logic symbol of OR gate

Boolean Equation

$$Y = A + B$$

- The '+' operator is called logic OR operator.
- It must be noted that logical OR is not equal to addition.
  When A = B = 1 the logical OR gate gives '1' output whereas addition will give output as '0' and carry as '1'.

1.9.4 NAND Gate

Logic Statement

- The NAND gate is an electronic logic circuit in which the output is in logic 1 state, when both or any one of the inputs are in logic 0 state.

Truth Table of NAND

Inputs		Output
A	B	Y
0	0	1
0	1	1
1	0	1
1	1	0

Logic Symbol of NAND

(a) Two input NAND gate   (b) Four input NAND gate

Fig. 1.11 : Logic symbol of NAND gate

Boolean Equation

$$Y = \overline{(A \cdot B)}$$

1.9.5 NOR Gate

Logic Statement

- The NOR gate is an electronic logic circuit in which the output is in logic '1' state only when both or more inputs are in logic '0' states.

Truth Table of NOR

Input		Output
A	B	Y
0	0	1
0	1	0
1	0	0
1	1	0

Logic Symbol of NOR

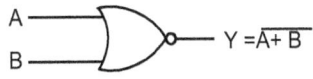
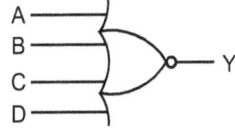

(a) Two input Nor gate   (b) Four input NOR gate

Fig. 1.12 : Logic symbol of NOR gate

Boolean Equation

$$Y = \overline{(A + B)}$$

1.9.6 Exclusive OR Gate

Logic Statement

- The XOR gate is an electronic logic circuit having two or more number of inputs and only one output which recognizes only inputs that have an odd number of logic 1 state.

Logic Symbol

Fig. 1.13 (a) : Logic symbol of EXOR gate

Boolean Equation

The Boolean equation for XOR gate is written as,

$$Y = \bar{A}B + A\bar{B}$$
or
$$Y = A \oplus B$$

Timing Diagram (Pulsed Operation)

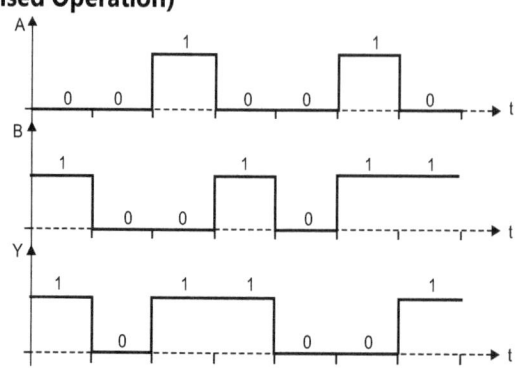

Fig. 1.13 (b) : Timing diagram for EXOR gate

1.9.7 Universal Gates – NAND and NOR

Q. Which gates are known as universal gates ? Justify using examples. **[May 12, 6 M]**

(a) NAND as an Universal Gate

- The NAND gate is an universal gate because all basic gates can be implemented using NAND gates.

Sr. No.	Gate	NAND Gate Implementation
1.	NOT gate	$Y = \bar{A}$
2.	AND gate	$Y = A \cdot B$
3.	OR gate	$Y = A + B$
4.	XOR gate	$\overline{\bar{A} \cdot B}$

Unit 1 | 1.24

- NOR and XNOR can be easily implemented by cascading NOT gate (using NAND) to the output of OR and XOR gates respectively.

(b) NOR as an Universal Gate

- NOR gate is also an universal gate as we can implement any basic gate using NOR gate.

Sr. No.	Gate	NOR Implementation
1.	NOT gate	$Y = \overline{A}$
2.	AND gate	$Y = A \cdot B$
3.	OR gate	$Y = A + B$
4.	XOR gate	$Y = A \oplus B$

- NAND and XNOR gates can be implemented by cascading NOT gate (using NOR) to the output of AND and XOR gates respectively.

1.10 BOOLEAN ALGEBRA

Q. State and prove any two theorem of Boolean algebra. [May 12, 4 M]

- The rules for manipulation of binary numbers developed by George Boole are known as Boolean algebra.
- A Boolean variable can only take binary values i.e. '1' or '0' just like ordinary algebra.
- Boolean algebra has also its own certain operators like AND (·), OR (+), NOT (−) and XOR (⊕).

1.10.1 Axioms of Boolean Algebra

- Axioms and postulates of Boolean algebra are a set of logical expressions that we accept without proof and upon which we can built useful theorems or laws.

- Axioms are nothing but logical expressions of the basic three gates i.e. AND, OR and NOT.

  Axiom 1 : 0.0 = 0   Axiom 6 : 0 + 1 = 1
  Axiom 2 : 0.1 = 0   Axiom 7 : 1 + 0 = 1
  Axiom 3 : 1.0 = 0   Axiom 8 : 1 + 1 = 1
  Axiom 4 : 1.1 = 1   Axiom 9 : $\overline{1}$ = 0
  Axiom 5 : 0 + 0 = 0   Axiom 10 : $\overline{0}$ = 1

1.10.2 Laws of Boolean Algebra

Sr. No.	Category of Law	Laws
1.	AND Laws	A · 0 = 0 A · 1 = A A · A = A A · $\overline{A}$ = 0
2.	OR Laws	A + 0 = A A + 1 = 1 A + A = A A + $\overline{A}$ = 1
3.	NOT or Inversion Laws	$\overline{\overline{A}}$ = A
4.	Commutative laws (allows change of position of variables)	A + B = B + A A · B = B . A
5.	Associative laws (allows grouping of variables)	A + (B + C) = (A + B) + C A · (B · C) = (A · B) · C
6.	Distributive Laws (allows factoring or distribution of terms)	A · (B + C) = A · B + A · C A + (B · C) = (A + B) · (A + C) A + ($\overline{A}$ · B) = A + B
7.	Impotence laws (means same value)	A · A = A A + A = A
8.	Identity laws	A · 1 = A A + 1 = 1
9.	Null laws	A · 0 = 0 A + 0 = A
10.	Absorption laws	A + (A · B) = A A (A + B) = A

1.10.3 Rules of Boolean Algebra

The rules that are followed in Boolean algebra are given below :
- Capital letters are used for representing variables and functions of variables.
- It will be assumed that the positive logic is used unless until the problem statement specifically mentions negative logic.
- The complement of a variable is represented by a "bar" (‾) over the variable letter.
- The logic AND function is shown by a "dot" (·) between the two variables, e.g. A · B. Many times, this dot is not written i.e. AB.
- Boolean addition is logical OR operation. It is different than mathematical addition. For example,

$$1 + 1 = 1 \text{ in Boolean algebra}$$
$$1 + 1 = 0 \text{ with carry 1 in mathematics}$$

1.10.4 DeMorgan's Theorems

> **Q.** What are DeMorgan's theorem ? How will define them in terms of your own words ?
> [Dec. 05, May 08, Dec. 09, 4 M]

- Boolean algebra was initially ignored by both mathematicians and technocrats. Bas Augustus DeMorgan was the first to put Boolean algebra to practice. DeMorgan discovered two important theorems which are known as DeMorgan's theorems.

The two theorems are,

1. $\overline{A + B} = \overline{A} \cdot \overline{B}$

2. $\overline{A \cdot B} = \overline{A} + \overline{B}$

1.10.4.1 DeMorgan's first theorem

- The statement of DeMorgan's first theorem goes like this, "Complement of a sum of variables is equal to the product of their individual complements".

$$\overline{A + B} = \overline{A} \cdot \overline{B}$$

Truth Table Proof :

A	B	$\overline{A}$	$\overline{B}$	A + B	L.H.S. = $\overline{A + B}$	R.H.S. = $\overline{A} \cdot \overline{B}$
0	0	1	1	0	1	1
0	1	1	0	1	0	0
1	0	0	1	1	0	0
1	1	0	0	1	0	0

Logic Diagram :

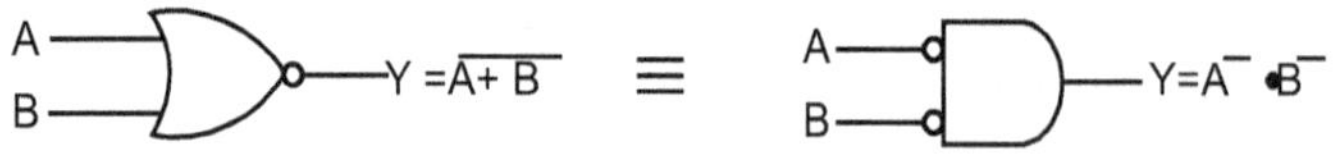

Fig. 1.14 : Logic diagram of DeMorgan's first theorem

Thus, NOR gate is equivalent to a bubbled AND gate.

1.10.4.2 DeMorgan's second theorem

- The statement of DeMorgan's second theorem goes like this, *"Complement of a product of variables is equal to the sum of their individual complements"*.

$$\overline{A + B} = \overline{A} \cdot \overline{B}$$

Truth Table Proof :

A	B	$\overline{A}$	$\overline{B}$	A·B	L.H.S. = $\overline{A \cdot B}$	R.H.S. = $\overline{A} + \overline{B}$
0	0	1	1	0	1	1
0	1	1	0	0	1	1
1	0	0	1	0	1	1
1	1	0	0	1	0	0

Logic Diagram :

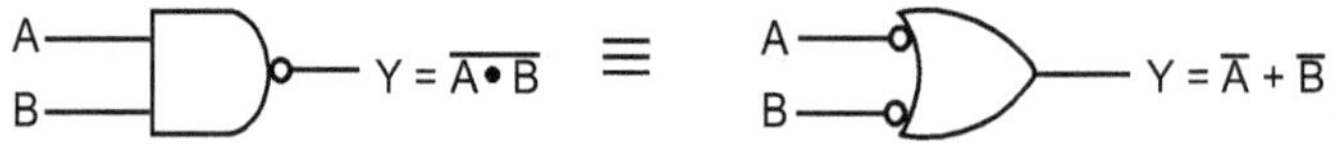

Fig. 1.15 : Logic diagram of DeMorgan's second theorem

- Thus, a NAND gate is equivalent to bubbled OR gate.

Example 1.25 :

Solution :

$$Y = (A + B)(A + C)$$

$Y = (A + B)(A + C)$

$= AA + AC + BA + BC$ \hfill (Distributive law)

$= A + AC + AB + BC$ \hfill ($\because$ AA = A)

$= A(1 + C) + AB + BC$

$= A + AB + BC$ \hfill ($\because$ 1 + C = 1)

$= A(1 + B) + BC$

$= A + BC$ \hfill ($\because$ 1 + B = 1)

1.10.4.3 Duality theorem

- The distinction between positive and negative logic gives rise to principle of duality.
- Because an OR gate is the positive logic system becomes AND gate in the negative logic system and vice-versa. Given a Boolean identity, we can produce a dual identity by changing '+' signs to '·' and vice-versa.

	Boolean Expression	Dual
1.	$A \cdot 0 = 0$	$A + 1 = 1$
2.	$A \cdot 1 = A$	$A + 0 = A$
3.	$A \cdot A = A$	$A + A = A$
4.	$A \cdot \overline{A} = 0$	$A + \overline{A} = 1$
5.	$A \cdot B = B \cdot A$	$A + B = B + A$

Example 1.26 : $(B + A)(B + D)(A + C)(C + D) = BC + AD$

Solution :

$$\begin{aligned}
LHS &= (B + A)(B + D)(A + C)(C + D) \\
&= (BB + BD + AB + AD)(AC + CC + AD + CD) \quad \because A \cdot A = A \\
&= (B + BD + AB + AD)(AC + AD + C + CD) \\
&= (B[1 + D + A] + AD)(C[1 + A + D] + AD) \quad \because A + 1 = 1 \\
&= (B + AD)(C + AD) \\
&= BC + BAD + CAD + AD \cdot AD \quad \because A \cdot A = A \\
&= BC + AD(B + C + 1) \\
&= BC + AD \quad \because A + 1 = 1
\end{aligned}$$

$$LHS = RHS$$

1.11 SUM OF PRODUCTS (SOP) FORM

Q. What is the sum of product form?

1.11.1 Standard Terms and Standard (or Canonical) Forms

- The object of a Boolean algebra is to describe the behaviour and logic structure.
- The behaviour of the logic circuit can be expressed in standard forms using standard terms.

1.11.2 Sum Term or Maximum Term (M)

- The output of OR gate is called **sum** term.
- In OR gate, the output is logic '1' for maximum number of combinations of inputs.
- So, the output of OR gate is also called Maximum term or Maxterm (M).
- A sum term of any 'n' variable functions containing all the 'n' literals is called a maxterm. The 'n' variables functions have 2^n maxterms.
- These are denoted as $M_0, M_1, M_2, \ldots M_n$.
- Each variables taking value '0' appears in uncomplemented form in maxterm and each variable taking '1' value appears in complemented form.

1.11.3 Product or Minimum Term (m)

- The output of AND gate is called product term.
- In AND gate, the output is logic '1' for minimum number of combinations of inputs. So, the output of AND gate is also called 'Minimum term or minterm (m).
- A product term of any 'n' variable functions containing all literals is called a minterm. The 'n' variable functions have 2^n minterms. These are denoted as $m_0, m_1, m_2, ..., m_n$.
- In minterms, each variables taking value '1' appears in uncomplemented form.

Table 1.7 : Maxterms and minterms of two-variables

Decimal Equivalent	Variables		Minterms		Maxterms	
	A	B	m_i	Notation	M_i	Notation
0	0	0	$\bar{A}\bar{B}$	m_0	$A + B$	M_0
1	0	1	$\bar{A}B$	m_1	$A + \bar{B}$	M_1
2	1	0	$A\bar{B}$	m_2	$\bar{A} + B$	M_2
3	1	1	AB	m_3	$\bar{A} + \bar{B}$	M_3

1.11.4 Standard (or Canonical) Forms

- If a function is expressed in such a way that each variable is present in each term.

1.11.5 Sum of Products (SOP) Form

- The output of AND gate is called product term.
- The output of OR gate is called sum term.
- The output of AND-OR gate circuit is called sum-of-products (SOP) form.
- Consider the equation,

$$Y = \bar{A}B + AB$$

- Each term in the equation is called the fundamental minterm. From table mentioned earlier, the output Y can be written as,

$$Y = m_1 + m_3 = \Sigma m_1, m_3$$
$$= \Sigma m_i$$

where, $i = 1, 3$
$$= \Sigma 1, 3$$

- The SOP form can be converted to standard SOP form by ANDing the terms in the expression with terms formed by ORing.
- The variable and its complement which are not present in that term.
- Following steps are followed to convert a given SOP form to standard SOP form :

   (i) Write down all the terms.

   (ii) If one or more variables are missing in any term, expand that term by multiplying it with the sum of each one of the missing variable and its complement.

   For example, $Y = AB + \bar{A}BC$

- The variable C is missing in first term. So, multiply the first term by $(C + \bar{C})$.

$$Y = AB(C + \bar{C}) + \bar{A}BC$$

(iii) Drop out the redundant terms.

Example 1.27 :

Convert $Y = \bar{A}B + A\bar{C} + B\bar{C}$ into standard SOP form.

Solution :

$$Y = \bar{A}B + A\bar{C} + B\bar{C}$$

$$= \bar{A}B(C + \bar{C}) + A\bar{C}(B + \bar{B}) + B\bar{C}(A + \bar{A})$$

$$= \bar{A}BC + \bar{A}B\bar{C} + A\bar{C}B + A\bar{C}\bar{B} + B\bar{C}A + B\bar{C}\bar{A}$$

$$= \underbrace{\bar{A}BC}_{} + \bar{A}B\bar{C} + A\bar{C}B + A\bar{C}\bar{B} + AB\bar{C} + \underbrace{\bar{A}B\bar{C}}_{}$$

Redundant terms

$$= \bar{A}BC + \bar{A}B\bar{C} + A\bar{C}B + A\bar{C}\bar{B} + AB\bar{C}$$

Example 1.28 :

Simplify $Y = \Sigma m\ (0, 1, 2, 3, 4, 5, 6, 7)$

Solution :

The given expression has all the minterms of a three variable table.

$$\therefore\ Y = \underline{\bar{A}\bar{B}\bar{C} + \bar{A}\bar{B}C} + \underline{\bar{A}B\bar{C} + \bar{A}BC} + \underline{A\bar{B}\bar{C} + A\bar{B}C} + \underline{AB\bar{C} + ABC}$$

$$= \bar{A}\bar{B}(C + \bar{C}) + \bar{A}B(\bar{C} + C) + A\bar{B}(\bar{C} + C) + AB(\bar{C} + C)$$

$$= \underbrace{\bar{A}\bar{B} + \bar{A}B}_{} + A\bar{B} + AB \qquad \therefore\ C + \bar{C} = 1$$

$$= \bar{A}\left(\bar{B} + B\right) + A\left(\bar{B} + B\right)$$

$$= \bar{A} + A$$

$$Y = 1$$

∴ The answer is always 'true' (1) because the given expression contains all possible minterms.

1.12 PRODUCT OF SUMS (POS) FORM

Q. What is the product of sum form?

1.12.1 Product-of-Sums (POS) Form

- The output of OR-AND gate circuit is called Product-Of-Sums (POS) form. Consider the equation,

$$Y = (A + B) \cdot (\bar{A} + B)$$
$$Y = M_0, M_2 = \pi\,(0, 2)$$

where, π stands for the product of maxterms.

- The POS form can be converted to standard POS form by ORing the terms in the expression with terms formed by ANDing the variable and its complement which are not present in that term.
- Following steps are followed to convert a POS form to standard POS form.

(i) Write down all the terms.

(ii) If one or more variables are missing in any sum terms, expand that term by adding the products of each of the missing term and its complement.

(iii) Drop out the redundant terms.

Example 1.29 :

Convert $Y = (A + B) \cdot (A + C) \cdot (B + \bar{C})$ into standard POS form.

Solution : $Y = (A + B) \cdot (A + C) \cdot (B + \bar{C})$

$$= (A + B + C \cdot \bar{C}) \cdot (A + B \cdot \bar{B} + C) \cdot (B + \bar{C} + A \cdot \bar{A})$$

We use $X + YZ = (X + Y) \cdot (X + Z)$ law to expand the equation.

$$= \underbrace{(A + B + C)}\,(A + B + \bar{C})\,(A + C + B)$$
$$(A + B + C)\,(B + \bar{C} + A)\,(B + \bar{C} + \bar{A})$$

$$= (A + B + C)\,(A + B + \bar{C})\,(A + \bar{B} + C)$$

$$(\bar{A} + B + \bar{C}) \qquad\qquad (\because \text{Redundant terms})$$

Example 1.30 :
Simplify the following three variable expression.
$$Y = \pi M (1, 3, 5, 7)$$

Solution :
The given Boolean expression is in POS from. From the table, we can rewrite the Boolean expression as

$$Y = \underbrace{(A + B + \bar{C})}_{N_1} \underbrace{(A + \bar{B} + \bar{C})}_{N_3} \underbrace{(\bar{A} + B + \bar{C})}_{N_5} \underbrace{(\bar{A} + \bar{B} + \bar{C})}_{N_7}$$

$$= (AA + A\bar{B} + A\bar{C} + BA + B\bar{B} + B\bar{C} + \bar{C}A + \bar{C}B + \bar{C}\bar{C})(\bar{A} + B + \bar{C})(\bar{A} + \bar{B} + \bar{C})$$

$$= (A + A\bar{B} + A\bar{C} + AB + 0 + B\bar{C})(\bar{A} + B + \bar{C})(\bar{A} + \bar{B} + \bar{C})$$

$$= (A + (1 + \bar{C}) + A(\bar{B} + B) + \bar{C}B)(\bar{A}(\bar{B} + B) + \bar{A}\bar{C} + \bar{C})$$

$$= (A + A + \bar{C}B)(\bar{A} + \bar{A}\bar{C} + \bar{C})$$

$$= (A + \bar{C}B)(\bar{A} + \bar{C}\bar{A})$$

$$= A\bar{A} + A\bar{C}\bar{A} + \bar{C}B\bar{A} + \bar{C}B\bar{C}\bar{A}$$

$$= 0 + 0 + \bar{C}B\bar{A} + \bar{C}B\bar{C}\bar{A} = \bar{A}B\bar{C} + \bar{A}B\bar{C}$$

$$Y = \bar{A}B\bar{C}$$

1.13 REDUCTION TECHNIQUES
1.13.1 Boolean Algebra Simplification Technique

Q. List out the reduction techniques.

- A good digital circuit must have minimum number of logic gates.
- Less number of gates means minimum propagation delay, skew, power dissipation.
- The number of logic gates can be reduced only if the number of terms in the Boolean expression can be reduced.
- There are four methods that are used to simplify or reduce the Boolean equations.
1. Algebraic (Boolean Laws, DeMorgan's Theorems).
2. Karnaugh (K) Map.
3. Variable Entered Mapping (VEM).
4. Quine-McClauskey (Q-M) Tabular Method.
- The K-map is the simplest and the most commonly used method.

1.13.2 Reduction of Boolean Equation using K-map

- The K-map method is a systematic approach for simplifying a Boolean expression.
- This method was proposed by Veitch and then modified by Karnaugh, hence it is called Karnaugh map.
- The basis of K-map method is graphical representation of minterms or maxterms in a chart called Karnaugh map (K-map). K-map contains cells.
- Each cell represents one of the 2^n possible product cells that can be formed from n variables.
- Thus, n-variable K-map has 4 cells, 3-variable k-map has 8 cells and 4-variable K-map has 16 cells.
- Product terms are assigned to the cells of a K-map by labelling each row and each column of the map with a variable, with its complements or with a combination of variables and complements. Fig. 1.16 depicts the 2-variable, 3-variable and 4-variable maps.

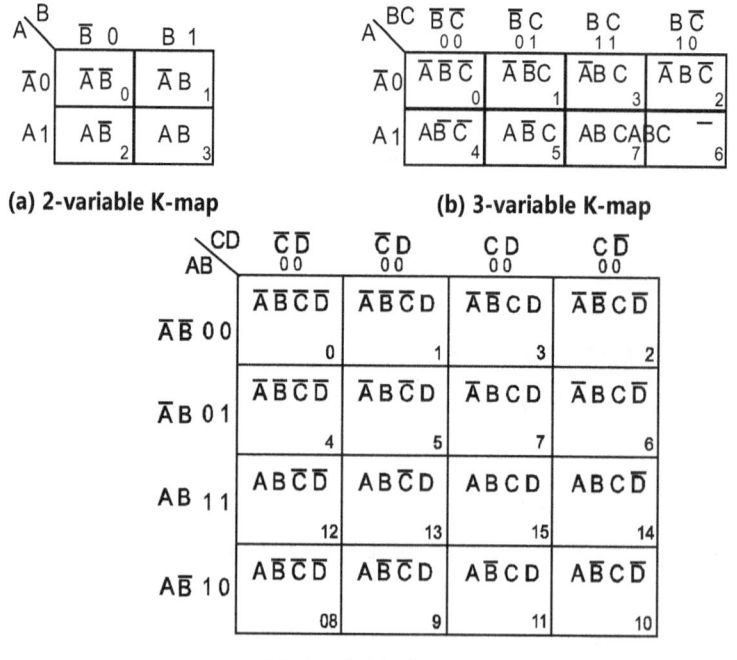

(a) 2-variable K-map (b) 3-variable K-map

(c) 4-variable K-map

Fig. 1.16

- It is important to note that only one variable changes, when we move from one cell to another along any row or any column.
- Therefore, the third column and the third row in a two-variable K-map have '11' binary representation instead of '10'.

- This peculiar arrangement of K-map has special significance as mentioned below.
- When two inputs change simultaneously then digital circuit output goes in a metastable state.
- Output can swing to either logic '1' or logic '0' state in metastable state.
- This state is to be avoided by prohibiting two inputs from switching simultaneously.
- We know that any logic function can be represented in SOP or POS form. The given Boolean expression can be used to fill entries in the truth table and truth table can be represented on K-map.
- With little practice, it is also possible to fill entries in k-map directly.

1.13.3 Representing SOP Equation on K-map

Example 1.31 :

Plot Boolean expression.

$$Y = \bar{A}\bar{B}CD + A\bar{B}\bar{C}\bar{D} + ABCD$$

Solution :

- The Boolean expression has four variables, so we use 4-variable k-map.
- Represent each product term by '1' in corresponding cell.
- Note that number of 1's in K-map is equal to the product terms in the given Boolean expression.
- Fill 0's in all other cells.

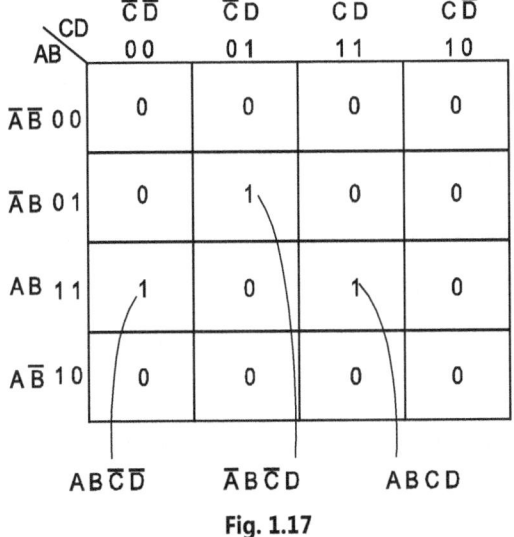

Fig. 1.17

1.13.4 Representing POS Equation on K-map

Example 1.32 :

Plot Boolean expression.

$$Z = (X + \overline{Y})(\overline{X} + \overline{Y})$$

Solution :

- The Boolean expression has two variables, so we use 2-variable K-map.

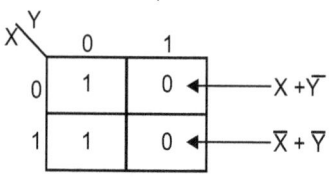

Fig. 1.18

- Represent each sum term by '0' in the corresponding cell.
- Note that number of '0's in K-map is equal to the sum terms in the given Boolean expression.
- Fill '1's in all other cells.

1.13.5 K-map Reduction Techniques

> **Q.** Simplify following logical expression using K-maps.
>
> $y = \overline{ABC} + \overline{AB}\overline{C} + \overline{A}B\overline{C} + A\overline{B}\overline{C} + AB\overline{C}$
>
> **Q.** Solve the following using minimization technique.
>
> $z = f(A, B, C, D) = \Sigma (0, 2, 4, 7, 11, 13, 15)$ [Dec. 09, 1 M]
>
> **Q.** Simplify the following function   [May 13, 4 M]
>
> $f_1 (A, B, C, D) = \Sigma m (0, 3, 5, 6, 9, 10, 12, 15)$

- In K-map minterms are represented by 1's and maxterms are represented by 0's.
- The objective of K-map reduction or simplification technique is to reduce the number of logic gates.
- Once the logic or Boolean expression is plotted on K-map, we use grouping technique to simplify the given Boolean expression as follows :

(a) Grouping Two Adjacent Ones (or Pair) :

- Consider a Boolean expression $Y = ABC + AB\overline{C}$.

  It can be seen from the given Boolean expression that we will require two three-input AND gates and one two-input OR gate to implement the logic equation.

- Now, if we plot the equation in a 3-variable K-map.

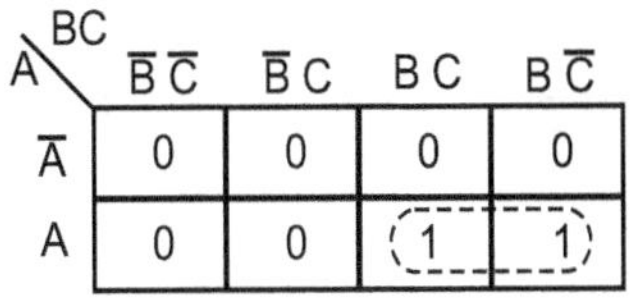
BC
A
$\bar{B}\bar{C}$ $\bar{B}C$ BC $B\bar{C}$
$\bar{A}$ 0 0 0 0
A 0 0 1 1

Fig. 1.19 : Grouping on two adjacent ones

- It can be noticed that when the two adjacent 1's are grouped then only one variable appears in its complemented and uncomplemented form i.e. C and $\bar{C}$.

$$Y = ABC + AB\bar{C}$$

$$= AB(C + \bar{C})$$

$$= AB \qquad (\because C + \bar{C} = 1)$$

- So, these two terms can be combined together to eliminate the variable C.
- Once this third variable is eliminated then it is possible to use two-input AND gate instead of three-input AND.

These adjacent 1's can be also in vertical or any other form as shown in Fig. 1.20.

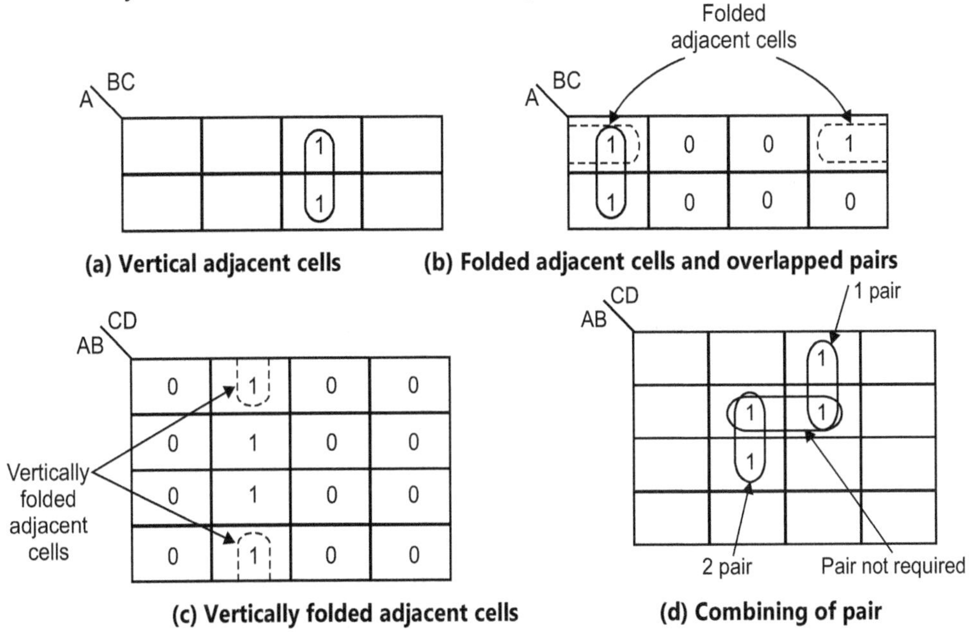
Folded
adjacent cells
BC
A
1
1
(a) Vertical adjacent cells
(b) Folded adjacent cells and overlapped pairs
CD
AB
Vertically
folded
adjacent
cells
(c) Vertically folded adjacent cells
1 pair
2 pair
Pair not required
(d) Combining of pair

Fig. 1.20 : Various combinations of 1 pairs

(b) Grouping of Four Adjacent Ones (Quad) :

- We can group four adjacent ones to eliminate two variables out of four variables.
- The several ways to form four adjacent ones or quads are shown in Fig. 1.21.

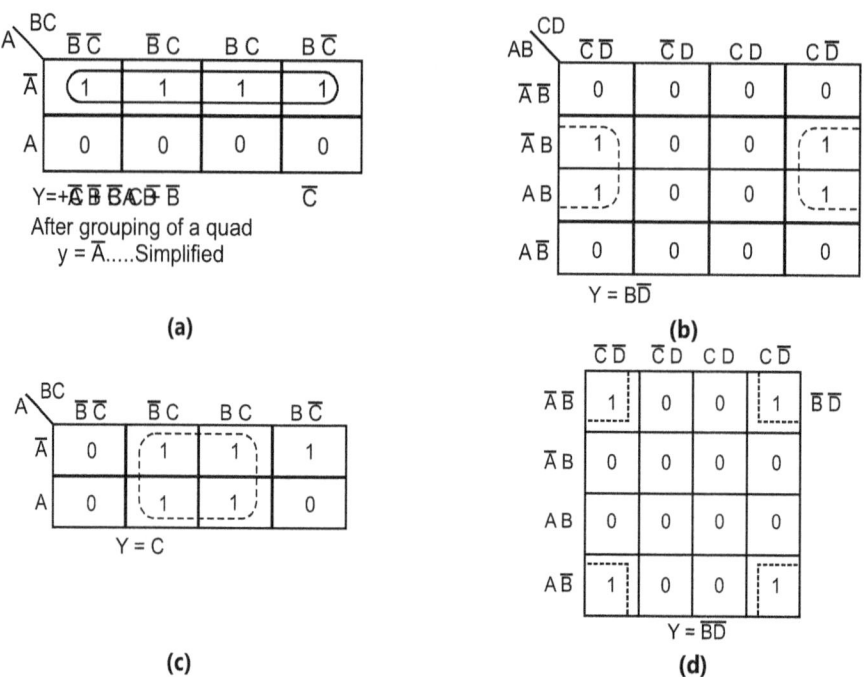

Fig. 1.21

(c) Grouping of Eight Adjacent Ones (octet)

- We can group four adjacent ones to eliminate three variables out of four variables.

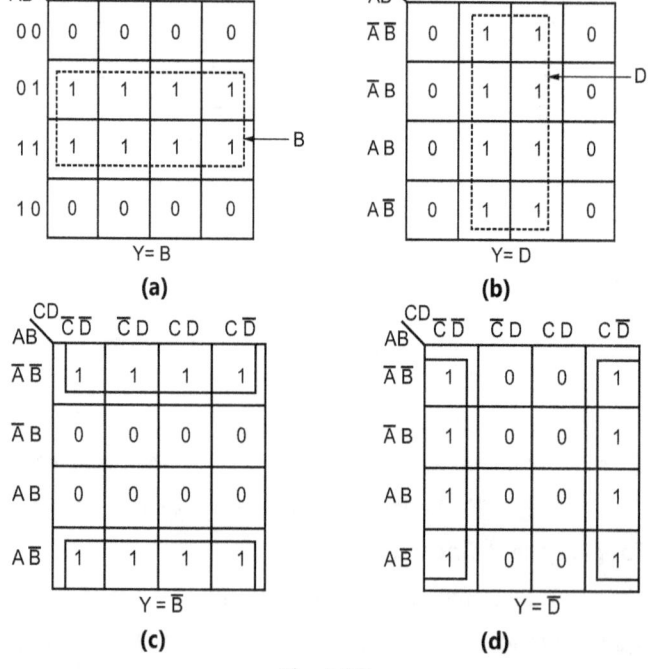

Fig. 1.22

1.13.6 Prime Implicant and Essential Prime Implicant

Q. What is prime implicant and essential prime implicant ?

- A group of one or more 1's which are adjacent and can be combined on a Karnaough Map is called an implicant.
- The process of simplication involves grouping of minterms and identifying prime implicants (PI) and essential prime implicants (EPI).
- A prime implicant is a group of minters that cannot be combined with any other minterm or groups. An essential prime implicant is a prime implicant in which one or more minterms are unique i.e. it contains at least one minterm which is not contained in any other prime-implicant.
- A prime implicant is a product term which cannot be further simplified by combination with other terms.

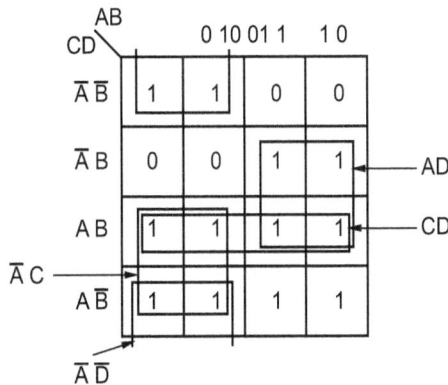

Fig. 1.23

Prime implicant = $\overline{AD}$ + $\overline{A}\overline{C}$ + $A\overline{D}$ + CD

Essential prime implicant = $\overline{AD}$

1.13.7 Don't Care Condition

- In some logic circuits, certain input conditions never occur or they are not possible. Therefore, the corresponding output never appears and the output level is not defined. It can be either HIGH or LOW. These output levels are represented as 'Don't Care Conditions' and are indicated by 'X'.
- Don't care conditions can be used to form groups and hence help in simplifying the Boolean expression. See the example below;

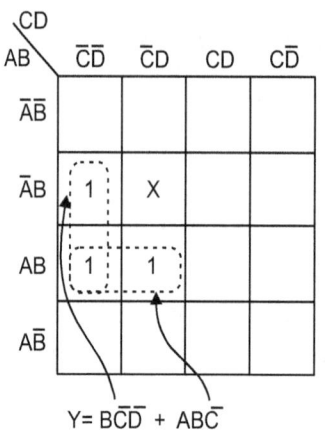
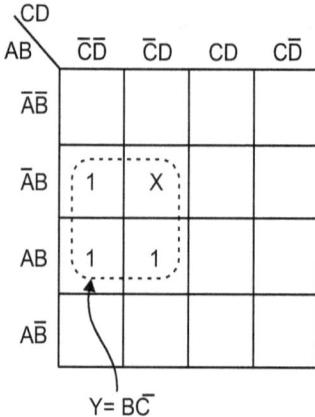

Y= B$\bar{C}\bar{D}$ + AB$\bar{C}$ Y= B$\bar{C}$

(a) Withoout Don't Care Condition   (b) With Don't Care Condition

Fig. 1.24 : Use of Don't Care Condition in simlifying the Boolean Expression

Example 1.33 :

Simplify the following Boolean expression

$$Y(A,B,C,D) = \Sigma m(1,3,7,11,15) + d(0,2,5)$$

Solution :

Representing all the minterms and don't care conditions on the K – map

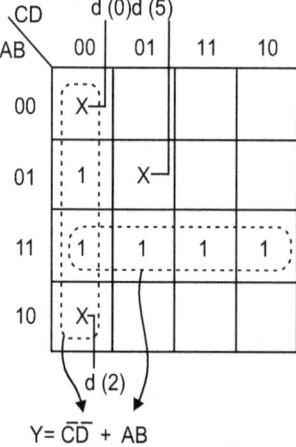

Y= $\bar{C}\bar{D}$ + AB

Fig. 1.25

Example 1.34 :

Simplify the Boolean expression $Y = \pi M(4,5,6,7,8,12) \cdot d(0,13,15,14)$

Solution :

Represent all the maxterms and don't care conditions in the K – map

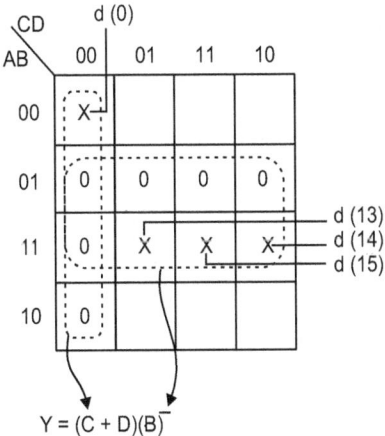

$$Y = (C + D)(\overline{B})$$

Fig. 1.26

1.13.8 Limitations of Karnaugh Map

Q. What is the limitation of K-map?

- The Map method of simplification is convenient as long as for the number of five and six variables. If the number of variables increases the difficultly to make combination of variables in k-map is increases.

1.14 IMPLEMENTATION OF BOOLEAN FUNCTION USING LOGIC GATE

Q. Show implementation of SOP and POS with the example.

- The Boolean algebra is used to express the output of any combinational network such a network can be implemented using logic gates.

1.14.1 Implementation of SOP

Consider the following expression.

$$F = A\overline{B} + \overline{C}D + BC$$

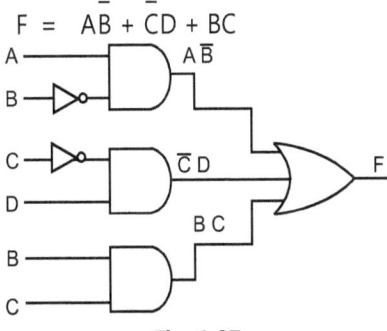

Fig. 1.27

In this expression, we have three product terms with 2 literals in each product term.

1.14.2 Implementation of POS

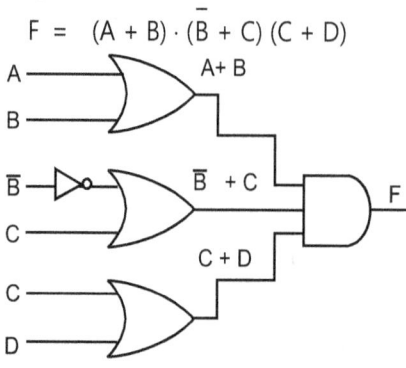

Fig. 1.28

In this expression we have three sum terms with 2 literals in two terms with 2 literals in two terms and 3 literals is one term.

Universal Gates :

The NAND and NOR gates are known as universal gate, since any logic function can be implemented using NAND or NOR gates.

1.14.3 Implementation of Combinational Circuit

- Logic gates are used to design a combinational circuit.
- For example, two AND gates and one OR gate can be used to build a combinational circuit to satisfy Boolean expression. Y = AB + CD as shown in Fig. 1.29.

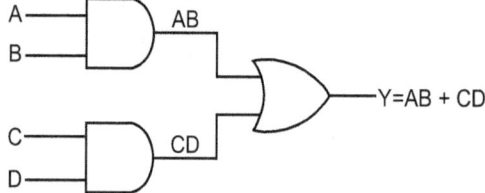

Fig. 1.29 : Combinational circuit for Y = AB + CD

Any combinational circuit can be built using four logics.

(i)   AND-OR (Use of inverters allowed).

(ii) OR-AND (Use of inverters allowed).

(iii) NAND-NAND (Inverters implemented using NAND).

(iv) NOR-NOR (Inverters implemented using NOR).

(i) AND-OR Logic :

- When the given Boolean expression is represented by Sum Of Product (SOP) terms then AND-OR logic is used.

- For example,

$$P = QR + ST$$

with product terms indicated.

- This can be implemented in AND-OR as shown in Fig. 1.30.

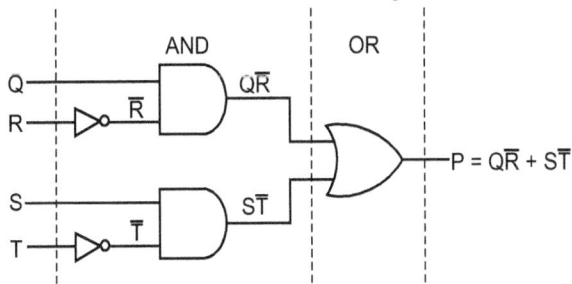

Fig. 1.30 : AND-OR logic

(ii) OR-AND Logic :
- When the Boolean expression is represented by product of sum (POS) terms then OR-AND logic is used.
- For example,

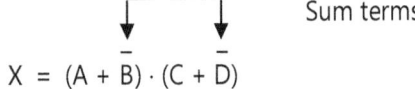

$$X = (\overline{A} + B) \cdot (C + \overline{D})$$

- This can be implemented in OR-AND as shown in Fig. 1.31.

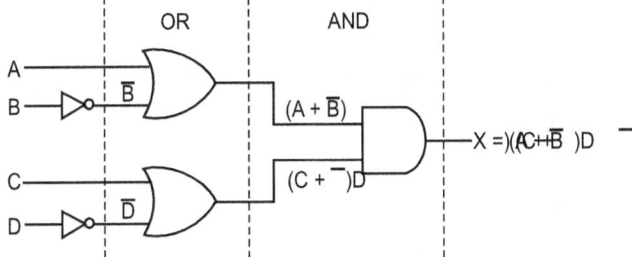

Fig. 1.31 : OR-AND logic

(iii) NAND-NAND Logic :

Q. Minimize $F(A, B, C, D) = \Sigma m(0, 2, 5, 6, 7, 13) + d(8, 10, 15)$ implement using NAND gates. **[May 07, 8 M]**

Q. Simplify the following 4 variable function using Kmap and represent using NAND gate only.

$$F(A, B, C, D) = (\overline{A}\overline{B}\overline{C}D + \overline{A}\overline{B}C\overline{D} + \overline{A}B\overline{C}D + \overline{A}BC\overline{D} + \overline{A}BCD + AB\overline{C}D) +$$

$$d(\overline{A}\overline{B}\overline{C}\overline{D} + \overline{A}\overline{B}CD + \overline{A}BCD + A\overline{B}\overline{C}\overline{D} + A\overline{B}\overline{C}D + A\overline{B}C\overline{D})$$

[May 08, 8 M]

Q. Minimize the following equation using K-map and realize it using NAND gates only.

$$Y = \Sigma m(0, 12, 3, 5, 7, 8, 9, 11, 14)$$ **[Dec. 11, 10 M]**

- We have already studied that NAND and NOR are universal gates.
- So, any Boolean expression that can be expressed in AND-OR (SOP) or OR-AND (POS) logic can be converted to NAND-NAND or NOR-Nor logic by replacing the basic gates by NAND or NOR gates.
- Following example, shows converting AND-OR logic to NAND-NAND logic. See Fig. 1.32 (a).

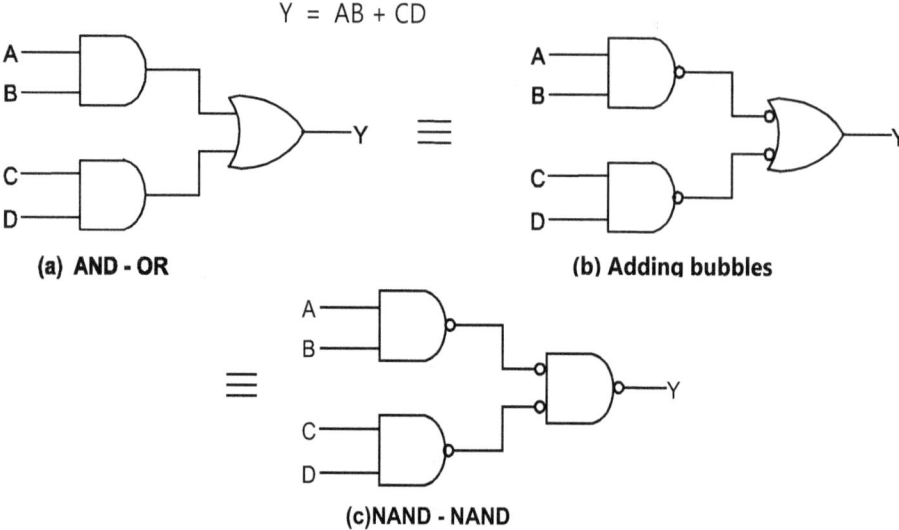

Fig. 1.32 (a) : Converting AND-OR logic to NAND-NAND logic

Rules to convert AND-OR to NAND-NAND :
- Simplify the Boolean expression.
- Express it in Sum-Of-Product (SOP) form.
- Add bubbles on the outputs of each AND and on the inputs to all OR. Draw a nand gate for each product term.
- Draw a single nand gate at the second level.

(iv) NOR-NOR Logic :

> Q. Minimize the function using Kmap and implement using only NOR gates.
> $$f(\omega, x, y, z) = \text{TTM} (1, 3, 5, 7, 13, 15)$$ [Dec. 05, 6 M]
>
> Q. Minimize the function using Kmap and implement using only one type gate.
> $$f(A, B, C, D) = \text{TTM} (0, 3, 5, 6, 10) \cdot d (1, 2, 11, 12)$$ [Dec. 06, 6 M]
>
> Q. Minimize function using Kmap and implement using NOR gate. [Dec. 07, 6 M]
> $$f(A, B, C, D) = \text{TTM} (1, 4, 5, 6, 7, 8, 12) + d (3, 9, 11, 14)$$

- Any OR-AND logic can be converted into NOR-NOR logic. For example, refer Fig. 1.32 (b).

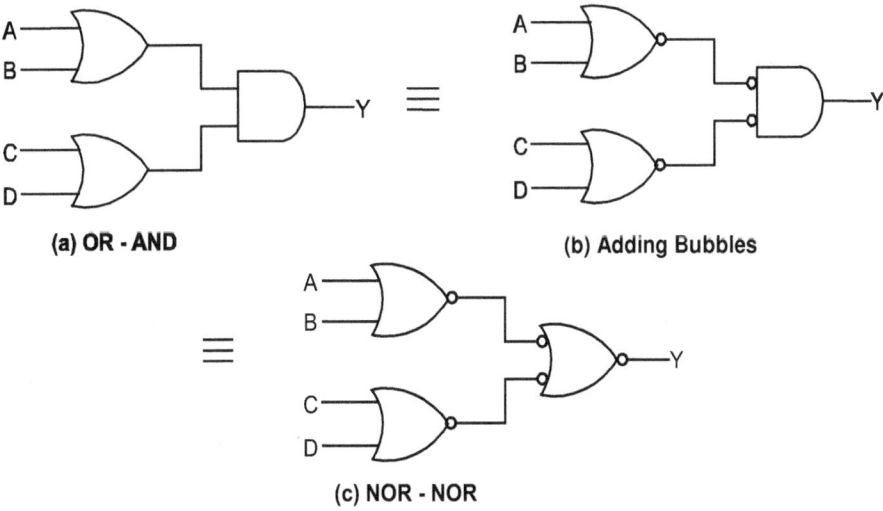

(a) OR - AND

(b) Adding Bubbles

(c) NOR - NOR

Fig. 1.32 (b) : Converting OR-AND logic to NOR-NOR logic

1.15 INTRODUCTION TO QUINE-MC CLUSKEY METHOD

Introduction :

The Quine-McCluskey method is an exact algorithm which finds a minimum cost sum-of-products implementation of a Boolean function. This section introduces the method and applies it to several examples.

There are four main steps in the Quine McCluskey algorithm :

1. Generate Prime Implicants
2. Construct Prime Implicant Table
3. Reduce Prime Implicant Table
   (a) Remove Essential Prime Implicants
   (b) Row Dominance
   (c) Column Dominance
4. Solve Prime Implicant Table.

Note : In step 1, the prime implicants of a function are generated using an iterative procedure. In step 2, a prime implicant table is constructed. The columns of the table are the prime implicants of the function. The rows are minterms of where the function is 1, called ON-set minterms. The goal of the method is to cover all the rows using a minimum of prime implicants.

The reduction step (Step 3) is used to reduce the size of the table. This step has three sub-steps which are iterated until no further table reduction is possible. At this point, the reduced table is either empty or non-empty. If the reduced table is empty, the removed essential prime implicants form a minimum cost solution. However, if reduced table is not empty, the table must be "solved" (Step 4). The table can be solved using either "Petrick's method" or the "branching method". This section focuses on Petrick's method which is used more frequently.

Column Dominance :

- Consider the following Karnaugh map of 4-input Boolean function :
- There are 5 prime implicants, each of which covers 2 ON-set minterms. First, we note that two implicants are essential prime implicants : A'C'D and ACD. These implicants must be added to the final cover. There are 3 remaining prime implicants. We must pick a minimum subset of these to cover the uncovered ON-set minterms.
- Here is the prime implicant table for the Karnaugh map. The 5 prime implicants are listed as columns, and the 6 ON-set minterms are listed as rows.

	A'C'D (0, 4)	A' BC' (4, 5)	BC'D (5, 13)	ABD (13, 15)	ACD (11, 15)
0	X				
4	X	X			
5		X	X		
11					X
13			X	X	
15				X	X

- We cross out columns A'C'D and ACD and mark them with asterisks, to indicate that these are essential. Each row intersected by one of these columns is also crossed out, because that minterm is now covered. At this point, prime implicant BC'D covers 2 remaining ON-set minterms (5 and 13). However, prime implicant A'BC' covers only one of these (namely, 5), as does ABD (namely, 13). Therefore, we can always use BC'D instead of either A'BC or ABD, since it covers the same minterms. That is BC'D **column-dominates** A'BC, and BC'D **column-dominates** ABD. The dominated prime implicants can be crossed out, and only column BC'D remains.

Row Dominance :

- Consider the following Karnaugh map of a 4-input Boolean function :

There are 4 prime implicants : A'B', C'D, A'D and A'C. None of these is an essential prime implicant. We must pick a minimum subset of these to cover the 5 ON -set Karnaugh. Here is the prime implicants table for the Karnaugh map. The 4 prime implicants are listed as columns, and the 5 ON-set minterms are listed as rows.

DIGITAL ELECTRONICS LOGIC DESIGN (S.E. COMP.) NUMBER SYSTEM AND LOGIC DESIGN

	A'B' (1, 2, 3)	C'D (1, 5)	A'D (1, 3, 5, 7)	A'C (2, 3, 7)
1	X	X	X	
2	X			X
3	X		X	X
5		X	X	
7			X	X

- Note that row 3 is contained in three columns : A'B', A'D, and A'C. Row 2 is covered by two of these three columns : A'B' and A'C, and row 7 is also covered by two of these three columns : A'D and A'C. In this case, any prime implicant which contains row 2 also contains row 3.
- Similarly, any prime implicant which contains row 7 also contains row 3. Therefore, we can ignore the covering of row 3 : it will always be covered as long as we cover row 2 or row 7. To see this, note that row 3 row dominates row 2, and row 3 **row dominates** row 7. The situation is now the reverse of column dominance : we cross out the dominating (larger) row. In this case, row 3 can be crossed out; it no longer needs to be considered.
- Similarly, row 1 row dominates row 5. Therefore, row 1 can be crossed out. We are guaranteed that row 1 will still be covered, since any prime implicants which covers row 5 will also cover row 1.

Example 1.35 :
Minimize the given Boolean expression
$$F(A, B, C, D) = \Sigma m (0, 2, 5, 6, 7, 8, 10, 12, 13, 14, 15)$$

Solution :
Step 1 : Generate Prime Implicants :

List Minterms

Column I	
0	0000
2	0010
8	1000
5	0101
6	0110
10	1010
12	1100
7	0111
13	1101
14	1110
15	1111

Combine Pairs of Minterms from Column I :

A check (√) is written next to every minterm which can combined with another minterm. Two minterms can be combined if there is a change in bit value of only column. Rest all the three columns should have the same bit value. Start with first minterm i.e. '0' and compare it with every other minterm. After comparing it can be seen that '0' can be combined with '2' and '8'. Repeat the same for all other minterms.

Column I				Column II	
0	0000	√		(0, 2)	00–0
2	0010	√		(0, 8)	– 000
8	1000	√		(2, 6)	0 – 10
5	0101	√		(2, 10)	– 010
6	0110	√		(8, 10)	10 –0
10	1010	√		(8, 12)	1–00
12	1100	√		(5, 7)	01 – 1
7	0111	√		(5, 13)	– 101
13	1101	√		(6, 7)	011 –
14	1110	√		(6, 14)	– 110
15	1111	√		(10, 14)	1–10
				(12, 13)	110–
				(12, 14)	11–0
				(7, 15)	– 111
				(13, 15)	11 – 1
				(14, 15)	111–

Combine Pairs of Products from Column II

Column I			Column II			Column III	
0	0000	√	(0, 2)	00–0	√	(0, 2, 8, 10)	–0–0
2	0010	√	(0, 8)	–000	√	(0, 8, 2, 10)	–0–0
8	1000	√	(2, 6)	0–10	√	(2, 6, 10, 14)	– 10
5	0101	√	(2, 10)	–010	√	(2, 10, 6, 14)	–10
6	0110	√	(8, 10)	10–0	√	(8, 10, 12, 14)	1–0

Unit 1 | 1.48

10	1010	√	(8, 12)	1–00	√	(8, 12, 10, 14)	1–0
12	1100	√	(5, 7)	–101	√	(5, 7, 13, 15)	–1–1
7	0111	√	(5, 13)	1–01	√	(5, 13, 7, 15)	–1–1
13	1101	√	(6, 7)	011–	√	(6, 7, 14, 15)	–11–
14	1110	√	(6, 14)	–110	√	(6, 14, 7, 15)	–11–
15	1111	√	(10, 14)	1–10	√	(12, 13, 14, 15)	11–
			(12, 13)	110 –	√	(12, 14, 13, 15)	11–
			(12,14)	11–	√		
			(7, 15)	–111	√		
			(13, 15)	11–1	√		

- Column III contains a number of duplicate entries, e.g. (0, 2, 8, 10) and (0, 8, 2, 10). Duplicate entries appear because a product in Column III can be formed in several ways. For example, (0, 2, 8, 10) is formed by combining products (0, 2) and (8, 10) from column II, and (0, 8, 2, 10) (the same product) is formed by combining products (0, 8) and (2, 10).
- Duplicate entries should be crossed out. The remaining unchecked products cannot be combined with other products. These are the prime implicants : (0, 2, 8, 10), (2, 6, 10, 14), (5, 7, 13, 15), (6, 7, 14, 15), (8, 10, 12, 14) and (12, 13, 14, 15); or, using the usual product notation : B'D', CD', BD, BC, AD' and AB.

Step 2 : Construct Prime Implicant Table :

	B'D' (– 0–0)	CD' (– – 10)	BD (– 1– 1)	BC (– 11 –)	AD' (1 – – 0)	AB (11 – –)
	(0, 2, 8, 10)	(2, 6, 10, 14)	(5, 7, 13, 15)	(6, 7, 14, 15)	(8, 10, 12, 14)	(12, 13, 14, 15)
0	X					
2	X	X				
5			X			
6		X		X		
7			X	X		
8	X				X	
10	X	X			X	
12					X	X
13			X			X
14		X		X	X	X
15			X	X		X

Step 3 : Reduce Prime Implicant Table :
Iteration 1
(i) Remove Primary Essential Prime Implicants :

	B'D' (*)	CD'	BD (*)	BC	AD'	AB
	(0, 2, 8, 10)	(2, 6, 10, 14)	(5, 7, 13, 15)	(6, 7, 14, 15)	(8, 10, 12, 14)	(12, 13, 14, 15)
(0)0	X					
2	X	X				
(0)5			X			
6		X		X		
7			X	X		
8	X				X	
10	X	X			X	
12					X	X
13			X			X
14		X		X	X	X
15			X	X		X

* Indicates an essential prime implicant
(0) Indicates a distinguished row, i.e. a row covered by only 1 prime implicant

- In step 1, primary essential prime implicants are identified. These are implicants which will appear in any solution. A row which is covered by only 1 prime implicant is called a distinguished row. The prime implicant which covers it is an essential prime implicant. In this step, essential prime implicants are identified and removed. The corresponding column is crossed out. Also, each row where the column contains an X is completely crossed out, since these minterms are now covered. These essential implicants will be added to the final solution. In this example, B'D' and BD are both primary essentials.

(ii) Row Dominance : The table is simplified by removing rows and columns which were crossed out in step (i). (Note : you do not need to do this, but it makes the table easier to read. Instead, you can continue to mark up the original table)

	CD'	BC	AD'	AB
	(2, 6, 10, 14)	(6, 7, 14, 15)	(8, 10, 12, 14)	(12, 13, 14, 15)
6	X	X		
12			X	X
14	X	X	X	X

Row 14 dominates both row 6 and row 12. That is, row 14 has an "X" in every column where row 6 has an "X" (and, in fact, row 14 has "X"s in other columns as well).

Similarly, row 14 has an "X" in every column where row 12 has an "X". Rows 6 and 12 are said to be dominated by row 14.

- A dominating row can always be eliminated. To see this, note that every product which covers row 6 also covers row 14. That is, if some product covers row 6, row 14 is guaranteed to be covered. Similarly, any product which covers row 12 will also cover row 14. Therefore, row 14 can be crossed out.

(iii) Column Dominance :

	CD' (2, 6, 10, 14)	BC (6, 7, 14, 15)	AD' (8, 10, 12, 14)	AB (12, 13, 14, 15)
6	X	X		
12			X	X

- Column CD' dominates column BC. That is, column CD, has an "X" in every row where column BC has an "X". In fact, in this example, column BC also dominates column CD', so each is dominated by the other. (Such columns are said to co-dominate each other.) Similarly, columns AD' and AB dominate each other, and each is dominated by the other.
- A dominated column can always be eliminated. To see this, note that every row covered by the dominated column is also covered by the dominating column. For example : C'D covers every row which BC covers. Therefore, the dominating column can always replace the dominated column, so the dominated column is crossed out. In this example, CD' and BC dominate each other, so either column can be crossed out (but not both) Similarly, AD' and AB dominate each other, so either column can be crossed out.

Iteration 2 : (i) Remove Secondary Essential Prime Implicants

	CD' (**) (2, 6, 10, 14)	AD' (* *) (8, 10, 12, 14)
(0) 6	X	
(0) 12		X

** Indicates a secondary essential prime implicant
(0) Indicates a distinguished row

- In iteration 2 and beyond, secondary essential prime implicants are identified. These are implicants which will appear in any solution, given the choice of column-dominance used in the previous steps (if 2 columns co-dominated each other in a previous step, the choice of which was deleted can affect what is an "essential" at this step). As before, a row which is covered by only 1 prime implicant is called a distinguished row. The prime implicant which covers it is a (secondary) essential prime implicant.

- Secondary essential prime implicants are identified and removed. The corresponding columns are crossed out. Also, each row where the column contains an X is completely crossed out, since these minterms are now covered. These essential implicants will be added to the final solution. In this example, both CD' and AD' are secondary essentials.

Step 4 : Solve Prime Implicant Table.

No other rows remain to be covered, so no further steps are required. Therefore, the minimum-cost solution consists of the primary and secondary essential prime implicants B'D', BD, CD' and AD' :   F = B'D' + BD + CD' + Ad'

Example 1.36 :

Minimize the given Boolean expression

$$F(A, B, C, D) = \Sigma m\ (0, 2, 3, 4, 5, 6, 7, 8, 9, 10, 11, 12, 13)$$

Solution :

Step 1 : Generate Prime Implicants.

Use the method described in earlier example.

Step 2 : Construct Prime Implicants Table.

	A'D'	B'D'	C'D'	A'C	B'C	A'B	BC	AB'	AC'
0	X	X	X						
2	X	X		X	X				
3				X	X				
4	X		X			X	X		
5						X	X		
6	X			X		X			
7				X		X			
8		X	X					X	X
9								X	X
10		X			X			X	
11					X			X	
12			X				X		X
13							X		X

Step 3 : Reduce Prime Implicant Table.

Iteration 1

(i) Remove Primary Essential Prime Implicants :

There are no primary essential prime implicants : each row is covered by at least two products.

(ii) Row Dominance:

	A'D'	B'D'	C'D'	A'C	B'C	A'B	BC'	AB'	AC'
0	X	X	X						
2	X	X		X	X				
3				X	X				
4	X		X			X	X		
5						X	X		
6	X			X		X			
7					X	X			
8		X	X					X	X
9								X	X
10		X		X				X	
11					X			X	
12			X				X		X
13							X		X

There are many instances of row dominance. Row 2 dominates 3, 4 dominates 5, 6 dominates 7, 8 dominates 9, 10 dominates 11, 12 dominates 13. Dominating rows are removed.

(iii) **Column Dominance :**

	A'D'	B'D'	C'D'	A'C	B'C	A'B	BC'	AB'	AC'
0	X	X	X						
3				X	X				
5						X	X		
7					X	X			
9								X	X
11					X			X	
13							X		X

Columns A'D', B'D' and C'D' each dominate one another. We can remove any two of them.

Iteration 2

(i) Remove Secondary Essential Prime Implicants

	A'D'**	A'C	B'C	A'B	AC'	AB'	AC'
(0)0	X						
3		X	X				
5				X	X		
7		X		X			
9						X	X
11			X			X	
13					X		X

** indicates a secondary essential prime implicant (0) indicates a distinguished row
Product A'D' is a secondary essential prime implicant; it is removed from the table.

(ii) Row Dominance :
No further row dominance is possible.

(iii) Row Dominance :
No further column dominance is possible.

Step 4 : Solve Prime Implicant Table.

	A'C	B'C	A'B	BC'	AB'	AC'
3	X	X				
5			X	X		
7	X		X			
9					X	X
11		X			X	
13				X		X

There are no additional secondary essential prime implicants, and no further row-or column-dominance is possible. The remaining covering problem is called a cyclic covering problem. A solution can be obtained using gone of two methods : (i) Petrick's method or (ii) the branching method. We use Petrick's method below :

Petrick's Method :

- In Petrick's method, a Boolean expression p is formed which describes all possible solution of the table. The prime implicants in the table are numbered in order, from 1 to 6.

$p_1 = A'C$, $p_2 = B'C$, $p_3 = A'B$, $p_4 = BC'$, $p_5 = AB'$, $p_6 = AC'$.

For each prime implicant p_i, a Boolean variable p_i is used true whenever prime implicant p_i is included in the solution. Note the difference ! : p_i is an implicant, while p_i is a corresponding.

- Boolean proposition (i.e. true/false statement) which has a true (1) or false (0) value. $p_i = 1$ means "I select prime implicant p_i for inclusion in the cover," while $p_1 = 0$ means "I do not select prime implicant p_i for inclusion in the cover.

- Using these p_i variables, a larger Boolean expression p can be formed, which captures the precise conditions for every row in the table to be covered. Each clause in p is a disjunction (OR) of several possible column selections to cover a particular row. The conjunction (AND) of all of these clauses is the Boolean expression p, which describes precisely the conditions to be satisfied for all rows are covered.

- For the above prime implicant table, the covering requirements can be captured by the Boolean equation:

$$p = (p_1 + p_2)(p_3 + p_4)(p_1 + p_3)(p_5 + p_6)(p_2 + p_5)(p_4 + p_6)$$

- If Boolean variable $p = 1$, each of the disjunctive clauses is satisfied (1), and all rows are covered. In this case, the set of p'_is which are 1 indicate a valid cover using the corresponding selection of primes p'_is (columns). If $p = 0$, then at least one disjunctive clause is not satisfied (0), meaning that at least one row is not covered. In this case, the set of P'_1s which are 1 correspond to a set of selected primes p_i which do not form a valid cover. Note that the above equation is simply a rewriting of the prime implicant table as a Boolean formula : the clasues correspond to the rows.

- In the right expression, the sum $(p_1 + p_2)$ describes the covering requirement for row 3 : product p_1 or p_2 must be included in the solution, in order to cover row 3. Similarly, the sum $(p_3 + p_4)$ describes the covering requirement for row 5 : product p_3 or p_4 must be included to cover row 5. Each sum corresponds to a different row of the table. These, sums are ANDed together, since all such requirement must be satisfied.

Since p is a Boolean expression, it can be multiplied out into sum of products form :

$$p = p_1 p_4 p_5 + p_1 p_3 p_5 p_6 + p_2 p_3 p_4 p_5 + p_2 p_3 p_5 p_6$$
$$+ p_1 p_2 p_4 p_6 + p_1 p_2 p_3 p_6 + p_2 p_3 p_4 p_6 + p_2 p_3 p_6$$

- Each product describes a solution for the table. Only two products have 3 Boolean variables; the remainder has 4 variables. These two products, $p_1\ p_4\ p_5$ and $p_2\ p_3\ p_6$ describe two minimal solutions. The first product describes a solution which includes prime implicants p_1, p_4 and p_5 that is A'C, BC' and AB'. The second product describes a solution using prime implicants p_2, p_3 and p_6; that is B'C, A'B and AC'.

- Both solutions have a minimal number of prime implicants, so either can be used. With either choice, we must include the secondary essential prime implicant, A'D', identified earlier.

- Therefore, the two minimum -cost solutions are :

$$F = A'D' + A'C + BC' + AB'$$
$$F = A'D' + B'C + A'B + AC'$$

Unit - II

LOGIC FAMILIES

2.1 IC LOGIC FAMILIES AND CHARACTERISTICS

2.1.1 Introduction

> Q. What are ICs? How are they categorized ?
> Q. What is the basic difference between unipolar IC and bipolar IC ?

- ICs are miniature, low – cost electronic circuits whose components are fabricated on a single, continuous piece of semiconductor material to perform a high – level function.
- Usually referred to as a monolithic IC.
- First introduced in 1958
- Categorized as digital or linear ICs or according to the level of complexity of the IC.

Category		Number of Gates
Small scale integration	SSI	< 12
Medium scale integration	MSI	12 to 99
Large scale integration	LSI	100 to 9999
Very Large Scale Integration	VLSI	10,000 or more

- Digital IC can be categorized into bipolar or unipolar IC. Bipolar ICs are devices whose active components are current controlled while unipolar ICs are devices whose active components are voltage controlled.

2.1.2 Packaging

> Q. Why good packaging of an IC is necessary?

- Protects the chip from mechanical damage and chemical contamination.
- Provides a complete unit large enough to handle.
- It is made large enough so that electrical connections can be made.
- Material is molded plastic, epoxy, resin or Silicon. Ceramic is used if higher thermal dissipation capabilities are required. Metal/glass is used in special cases.

Three most common packages for ICs are
(a) Dual-in-line ((DIPs) most common)
(b) Flat pack
(c) Axial lead (TO5)

2.1.3 Classification of Logic Families

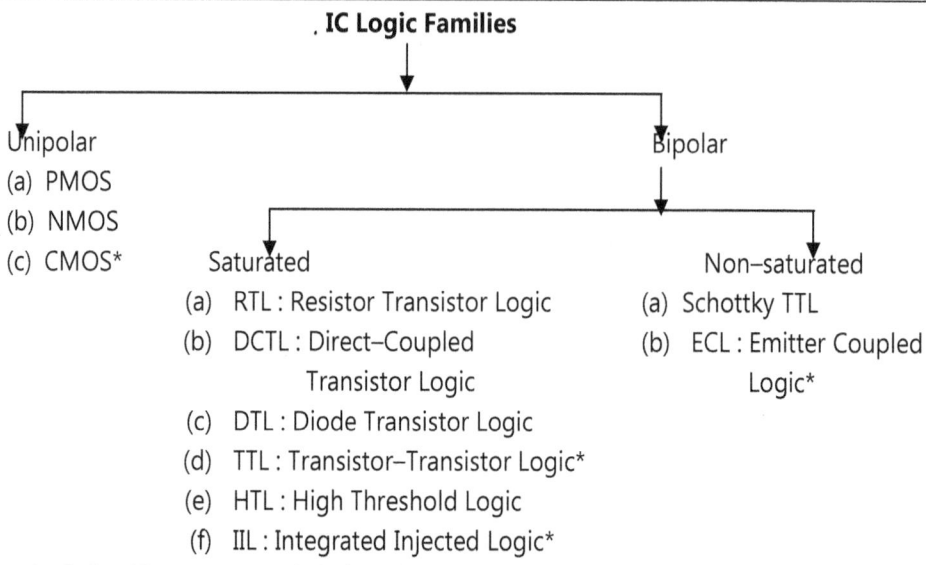

- These logic families are currently being used and others are obsolete.
- Complementary MOS or CMOS is very popular as it consumes less power.

CMOS and IIL logic families are suitable for Very Large Scale Integration (VLSI) technology.

2.2 CHARACTERISTICS OF DIGITAL ICs

Q. Define the following parameters of digital IC families fan-in and fan-out.
[Dec. 06, 10, 11, 2 M]

Q. Define and explain fan out.
[May 07, Dec. 08, 12, 2 M]

2.2.1 Fan-in

- Fan – in (input load factor) is the number of input signals that can be connected to a gate without causing it to operate outside its intended operating range.
- Expressed in terms of standard inputs or units loads (ULs)

Example : A fan-in of 8 means that 8 unit loads can be safely connected to the gate inputs.

2.2.2 Fan-out

Fan – out (output load factor) is the maximum number of inputs that can be driven by a logic gate. A fan-out of 10 means that 10 unit loads can be driven by the gate while still maintaining the output voltage within specifications for logic levels 0 and 1.

2.2.3 Propagation Delays

> **Q.** Define the following parameters of digital IC families : propagation delay
> **[Dec. 06, 10, 2 M]**
>
> **Q.** Define and explain : propagation delay.
> **[Dec. 08, 12, 2 M]**

The delay before a change in the input is reflected at the output is known as propagation delay.

t_{PHL} : delay time in going from logic 1 to logic 0 (turn – off delay)

t_{PLH} : delay time in going from logic 0 to logic 1 (turn – on delay)

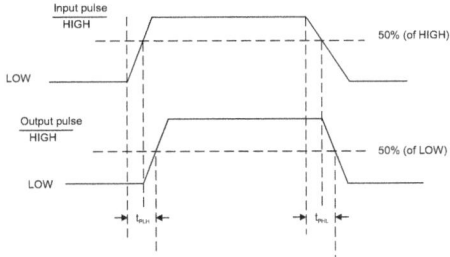

Fig. 2.1

$$\text{Total delay} = \frac{t_{PLH} + t_{PHL}}{2}$$

2.2.4 Voltage and Current Parameters

- Theoretically, the input voltage levels are 0V and +5V(TTL) for logic 0 and logic 1 respectively.
- Practically, it is impossible to maintain these perfect voltage levels. Hence, there is a need to define the worst case input and output voltage levels to consider whether the input or output should be considered as logic 0 or logic 1.

Voltage Parameters (Refer to Fig. 2.2)

1. $V_{IL(max)}$: Maximum low level input voltage. It is the maximum input voltage which is considered as a logic 1. If the input voltage is higher than $V_{IL(max)}$, then it is not considered as logic 0 level.

2. $V_{IH(min)}$: Minimum high level input voltage. It is the minimum input voltage which is considered as logic 1 level. If the input voltage is lower than $V_{IH(min)}$, then it is not considered as logic 1 level.

3. $V_{OH(min)}$: Minimum high level output voltage. It is the minimum output voltage which is considered as logic 1 level.

4. $V_{OL(max)}$: Maximum low level output voltage. It is the maximum output voltage which is considered as logic 0 level. If the input voltage is higher than $V_{OL(max)}$, then it is not considered as logic 0 level.

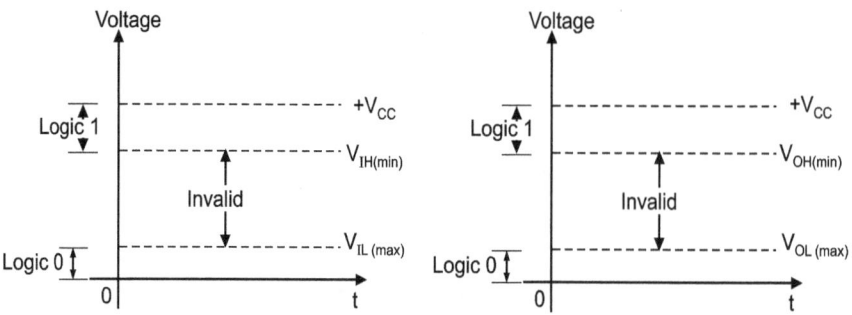

Fig. 2.2 : Voltage parameter

Current Parameters :

- I_{IL} : Low level input current – It is the current flowing in an input terminal when the input voltage corresponds to logic 0.
- I_{IH} : High level input current – It is the current flowing in an input terminal when the input voltage corresponds to logic 1.
- I_{OH} : High level output current – It is the current flowing from the output when the output voltage corresponds to logic 1.
- I_{OL} : Low level output current – It is the current flowing from an output when the output voltage corresponds to logic 0.

2.2.5 Current Sourcing and Current Sinking

- **Current Sourcing :** A device output is said to source current when current flows from the power supply, out of the device output and through the load to ground. Refer Fig. 2.3 (a)
- **Current Sinking :** Current sinking is when current flows from the power supply, to the load and through the device output to ground. Refer Fig. 2.3 (b).

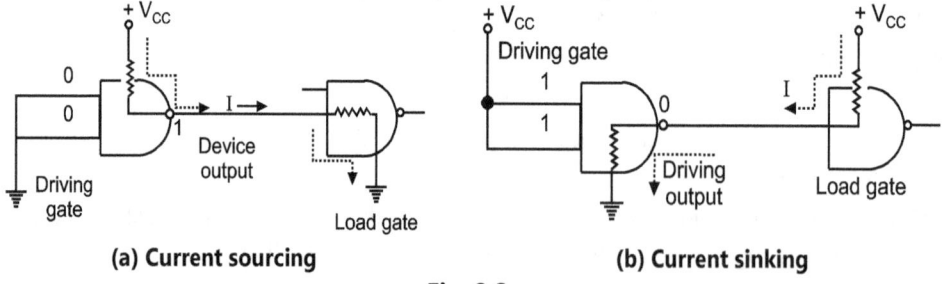

(a) Current sourcing   (b) Current sinking

Fig. 2.3

2.2.6 Noise Margin/Immunity

> **Q.** Define the following parameters of digital IC families : Noise margin.
> **[Dec. 06, 10, 11, May 07 2 M]**
>
> **Q.** Explain the following characteristics of CMOS logic family : Noise margin.
> **[May 12, 2 M]**

- Any unwanted electrical signal which can induce some voltage in the wires used in between the gates or load is known as Noise.
- The ability of a device or a circuit to tolerate noise such that there is no unwanted change in the output.
- A quantitative measure of noise immunity is called as Noise Margin.
- The voltage levels $V_{OH(min)}$ and $V_{IH(Min)}$ are adjusted to different levels with some difference between them so that the effect of noise voltage are minimized.

$$\therefore \quad V_{NH} = V_{OH(min)} - V_{IH(min)}$$
$$V_{NL} = V_{IL(max)} - V_{OL(max)}$$

Where V_{NH} – is the high level noise margin and V_{NL} – is the low level noise margin

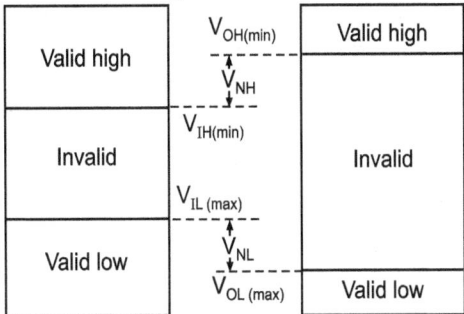

Fig. 2.4 : Noise Margins

2.2.7 Power Dissipation

Q. Define and explain power dissipation. [Dec. 08, 2 M]

- The amount of energy (in milliWatts) that the IC dissipates in the form of heat is known as power dissipation.
- Due to excessive temperature, the IC can get damaged. So, care should be taken so that power dissipation is not much and loading on power supplies is reduced.

Operating Temperature
- For consumer and industrial applications, the acceptable temperature range is 0° to 70° and for military applications it is –55°C to 125°C.

2.2.8 Figure of Merit

- Also known as Speed Power Product (SPP).
- It is defined as the product of power dissipation and propagation delay where speed is in seconds and power is specified in Watts.
- Mathematically,
  Figure of merit = Propagation delay × Power dissipation
- Figure of merit is constant. So, if power dissipation is decreased, propagation delay increases and vice versa.
- Practically, the value of figure of merit should be as low as possible.

2.2.9 Slew Rate

> **Q.** Define Slew rate.

- Slew Rate is defined as the ratio of output voltage swing to propagation delay. Its unit is V/ns. The slew rate determines the overall delay in the digital circuit. The larger the slew rate better is the speed of the digital IC. Smaller slew rate may cause the set-up and hold time violations leading to malfunctioning of the digital IC function.

2.3 IC LOGIC FAMILIES

So far, we have specified the logic level as either 0 or 1, or HIGH or LOW. In circuit implementation, we will have to specify the actual voltage/current levels that constitute a HIGH or a LOW. These standardized voltage/current levels are grouped in families of digital ICs so that ICs belonging to the same family will have the same characteristics.

Common families are

- RTL : Resistor – Transistor Logic
- DTL : Diode – Transistor Logic
- TTL : Transistor – Transistor Logic
- ECL : Emitter Coupled Logic
- IIL : Integrated Injection Logic.

CMOS ICs : Complementary metal – oxide – semiconductor ICs

2.4 TRANSISTOR – TRANSISTOR LOGIC (TTL)

- Transistor –Transistor Logic, or TTL refers to the technology for designing and fabricating digital integrated circuits that employ logic gates consisting primarily of bipolar transistors. It overcomes the main problem associated with DTL, i.e., lack of speed.

Most popular and widely used IC logic family.

- Introduced by Texas Instruments in 1964.
- Operates from a + 5V power supply.
- Standardized labeling system starting with 54 or 74. For example 7400, 7401, 74121 etc.
- A HIGH is normally + 5V while a LOW is normally 0V or GROUND.

To provide greater flexibility with regard to speed and power dissipation considerations, the following sub-families have been developed :

7400 Standard series.

74L00 low-power series

74H00 high-speed series

74S00 Schottky series

74LS00 low-power Schottky series.

2.4.1 TTL NAND gate

> Q. Draw and explain the working of 2–input TTL NAND gate.   [Dec. 05, 06, 08, 6 M]
>
> Q. Draw and explain working of TTL NAND gate.
>
> Q. Explain with neat diagrams and compare different types of output configurations in case of family.   [Dec. 04, 12 M]

Concept of Multi– emitter transistor :

Consider a transistor with not one emitter but three emitters, one base and one collector as shown in Fig. 2.5(a) below.

- Its equivalent circuit can be drawn with two diodes as shown in the Fig. 2.5 (b).

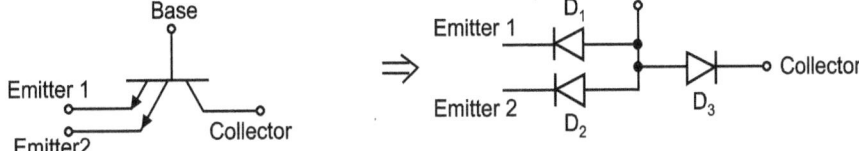

(a) Multi emitter transistor (b) Equivalent circuit

Fig. 2.5 : Multi emitter transistor

2.4.2 2 – input TTL NAND Gate (Totem pole output)

- Let A and B be the input terminals. Therefore, for 2 inputs, four combinations are possible as shown in the truth table.
- The inputs or outputs are ideally 0V or +5V for logic 0 and 1 respectively.

Table 2.1 : Truth table

Input		Output
A	B	Y
0	0	1
0	1	1
1	0	1
1	1	0

Fig. 2.6 (a) shows a two – input TTL NAND gate

Fig. 2.6 (b) shows the equivalent circuit of transistor T_1.

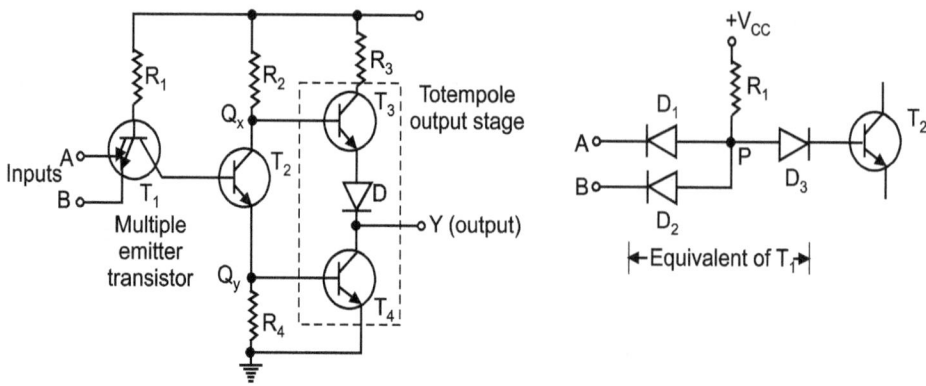

(a) Two input TTL NAND gate **(b) Equivalent circuit of transistor T_1**

Fig. 2.6 : 2-Input TTL NAND gate

Case 1 : When A = 0 B = 0

- When both the inputs are low, then both the diodes D_1 and D_2 conduct, and voltage at point P is pulled to 0.7V.
- Hence T_2 stops conducting (or is turned OFF) as the base–emitter junction of T_2 is not forward biased.
- When T_2 is turned OFF, the collector voltage at Q_x rises to V_{cc}.
- Since, base–emitter junction of T_3 is forward biased, output Y is pulled up to a high voltage ($\therefore$ Y =1)

Case 1 : When A = 0 B = 1 or A = 1 B = 0

- If either of the inputs are low, then the voltage at point P will again be pulled down to 0.7V.
- This voltage is again not sufficient to switch ON T_2 and hence the whole working is same as that in the previous case.
- So, the output is Y = 1

Case 2 : A = 1 and B = 1

- If A = 1 and B = 1, then both the diodes D_1 and D_2 are not conducting.
- Hence, because of V_{cc}, D_3 starts conducting, which forward biases the base–emitter function of T_2 and T_2 is turned ON.
- When T_2 is turned ON, voltage at Q_x drops down and T_3 is turned OFF.
- Due to this, voltage at Q_y increases so as to turn ON T_4 and T_4 goes into saturation.
- Therefore, the output voltage Y is pulled down to a low voltage.
  Hence Y = LOW

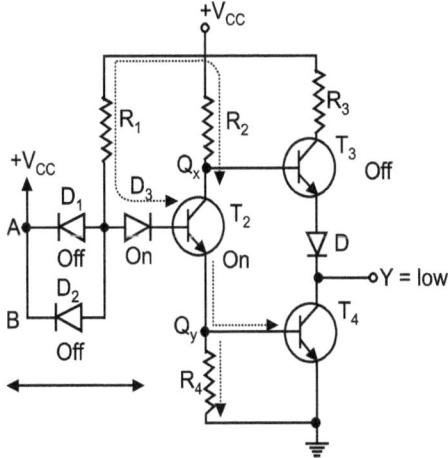

Fig. 2.7 : Equivalent circuit for A = B = 1

2.4.3 3-input TTL NAND Gate

- Fig. 2.8 given below shows a 3 – input TTL NAND gate.
- The working of a 3 – input TTL NAND gate is the same as that of a 2– input TTL NAND gate except that the transistor T_1 has 3 emitters.

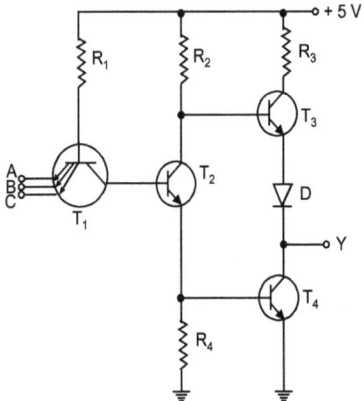

Fig. 2.8 : 3–input TTL NAND gate

2.4.4 Totem–Pole Output

| Q. Explain the advantages of Totem pole output in TTL. [May 06, 2 M] |
| Q. Explain with neat diagrams and compare the different types of output configuration in case of TTL family. [Dec. 12, 3 M] |

- The schematic of a typical TTL 7400 NAND gate is shown in Fig. 2.9.
- In this diagram, observe that the output stage consists of two active elements, T_3 and T_4.
- This circuit is designed such that the operation of T_3 and T_4 are complementary, that is when one transistor is ON the other is OFF.

- This configuration with T_4 stacked on top of T_3 is referred to as a **totem – pole** output.

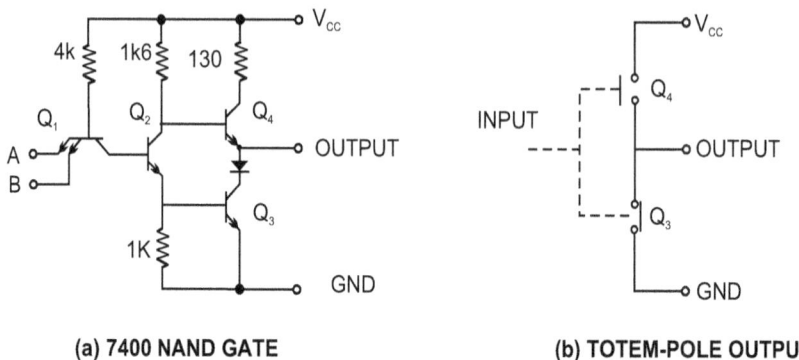

(a) 7400 NAND GATE   (b) TOTEM-POLE OUTPUT

Fig. 2.9 : Schematic of a typical TTL gate

- Also shown in Fig. 2.9 (b) is a simplified schematic of the operation of the totem–pole output. Transistors T_3 and T_4 behave as switches controlled by the INPUT.

- At any time, only one of the two switches is closed while the other is open. In other words, when T_3 is closed, T_4 is open.

- Conversely, when T_3 is open, T_4 is closed. By analyzing this circuit you can follow how the output changes from 0 to 5 volts.

Advantages of Totem – Pole Output

- The main advantage of the totem pole arrangement is that it offers low –output impedance in either of output states (Y = LOW , or Y = HIGH)

- Therefore , any stray capacitance at the output can be charged or discharged very rapidly through this low impedance and hence transitions from one state to the other is very quick at the output.

- Suppose , in the absence of T_3, the collector terminal of T_4 would be connected to $+V_{cc}$ through R_3. As a result , T_4 would need to conduct a fairly large current.

Disadvantages of Totem – Pole output

- The main disadvantage of this type of arrangement is its switching speed.

Explanation

- The transistor T_4 switches OFF slowly than the transistor T_3.

- On account of this , there is a fraction of time (in nanoseconds) , that both the transistor T_3 and T_4 are conducting and therefore, draw a heavy current (30 to 40 mA) from the power supply.

2.4.5 Open-collector output

- Fig. 2.10 (a) shows the schematic of a typical TTL gate with open – collector output, for example, a 7403 NAND gate.
- Observe here that the circuit elements associated with T_4 in the totem–pole circuit is missing and the collector of T_3 is left open – circuited, hence the name **open–collector**.

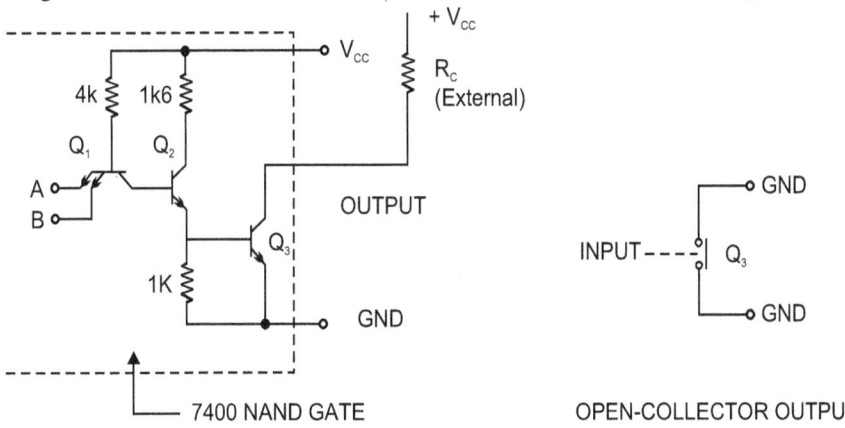

Fig. 2.10 (a) : Open collector output

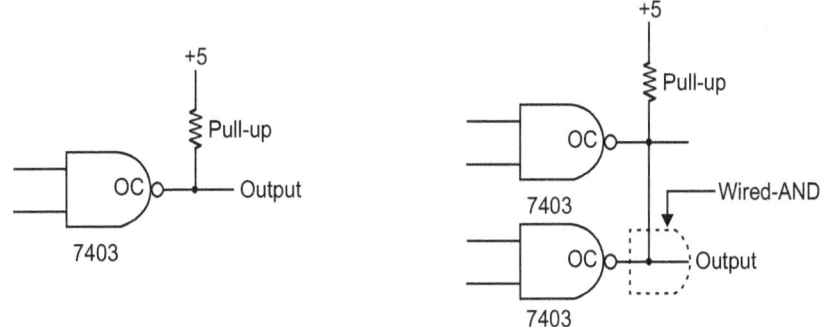

Open-Collector wired-AND Function

Fig. 2.10 (b) : Open collector wired OR function

- An open–collector output has **current sinking** capabilities, that is, it can present a logic–LO output. In contrast with a normal totem–pole output, it cannot be the source of current and therefore cannot present a logic–HI on its own.
- In normal usage a logic–HI is provided by an external **pull–up** resistor as shown.

2.4.6 Wired AND operation

| Q. Define wired AND connection, | [May 05, 2 M] |
| Q. Define and explain wired ANDing. | [May 07, Dec. 08, 2M] |

Fig. 2.11 (a) shows NAND gates being used to perform AND operation.

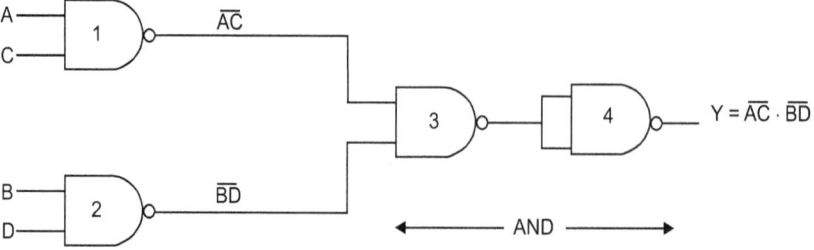

Fig. 2.11 (a) "AND"ing NAND gates

- Therefore, the final Boolean expression is

$$Y = \overline{AC} \cdot \overline{BD}$$

- The same Boolean expression can be obtained by replacing NAND gates 3 and 4 by shorting the $\overline{AC}$ and $\overline{BD}$ signals together.

- When two or more outputs ($\overline{AC}$ and $\overline{BD}$ in this example) are tied together then if any one of the outputs goes to low the common output point goes to low. This happens because the transistor T_4 (see Fig. 1.29 (c)) gets grounded. The common output will be high only when all outputs are high.

- This is called "wired – AND " ing or outputs. This is shown in Fig. 2.12 (b).

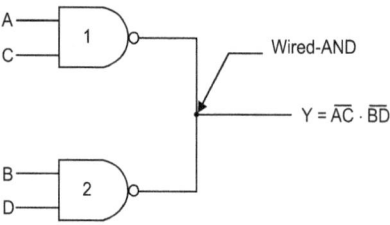

Fig. 2.12 (b) "Wired – AND" ing outputs

- Wired–AND operation is not possible with TTL gates having totem–pole output circuits.
- The wired–And operation of two totem pole TTL gates are shown in Fig. 2.12 (c). Let us assume that the output of gate X is high and gate Y is low. The transistor Q_{4Y} acts as a low resistive load on the transistor Q_{3X}.
- Therefore, the current through Q_{4Y} can be very high (755 mA). The sink current of Q_4 transistor is 16mA. The excess current through Q_{4Y} may damage it. The current through Q_{3X} will be go on increasing where more than two TTL outputs are wired–AND ed.

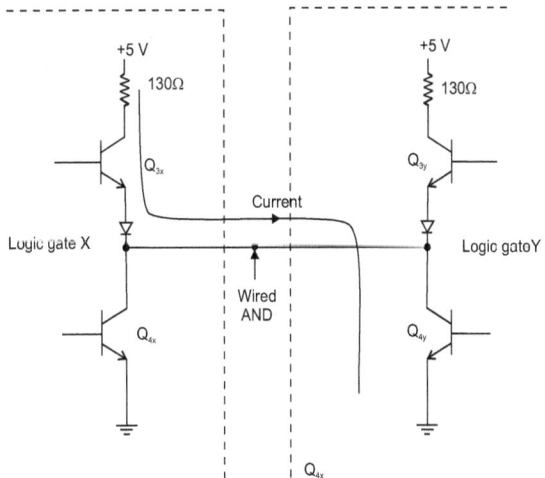

Fig. 2.12 (c) : Wired–AND ing of totem pole outputs

The main advantage of wired– AND operation is that it requires less number of gates.

Open–collector Buffer / Drivers :

- Any logic circuit that is called a *buffer*, a *driver*, or a *buffer/driver* is designed to have a greater output current and /or voltage capability than an ordinary logic circuit. Buffer/driver ICs are available with totem–pole outputs and with open–collector outputs.

- The 7406 is a popular open–collector buffer/driver IC that contains six INVERTERs with open–collector outputs that can sink up to 40 mA in the LOW state. In addition, the 7406 can handle output voltages up to 30 V. This means that the output transistor can be connected to a voltage greater than 5 V.

2.4.7 Tri–state Outputs

Q. What do you mean by tristate logic ? Define and explain tristate logic.
Q. Explain the concept of tristate logic.

- Boolean logic is based on a binary system whereby an output can have one of two states, ON or OFF. What is meant by **tri–state** or **3– state** outputs ? Let us examine the typical totem–pole output once again.

T4	T3	OUTPUT
OFF	ON	0
ON	OFF	1
OFF	OFF	HI – Z
ON	ON	DAMAGING

- Consider all possibilities for T_3 and T_4. The first two conditions show the normal totem-pole operation. If both T_3 and T_4 are ON, maximum current will flow from V_{cc} to GND, possibly damaging the device.
- If both T_3 and T_4 are OFF, the output pin appears to be disconnected from the circuit. The voltage at the output pin is indeterminate and is said to be **floating**. This called the **high impedance** or **Hi-Z state**.

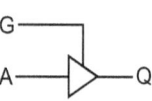

G	A	Q
0	0	HI – Z
0	1	HI – Z
1	0	0
1	1	1

Fig. 2.13 : 74126 Bus Driver with 3-state output

2.4.8 Other TTL Characteristics

Q. What should be done with the unused inputs of a TTL-NAND gate ?
Q. What should be done with the unused inputs of a TTL-NOR gate ?

- **Unused Inputs : NAND :** If the input is unused i.e. left disconnected then it acts as logic high input. The unconnected input may act as antenna and pick up noise. Hence, it is a good practice to connect unused inputs to V_{cc} through a 1 kΩ resistor. It is also possible to tie the unused input to a used input.
NOR : The unused inputs have to be connected to ground.

Fig. 2.14 : Unused TTL inputs

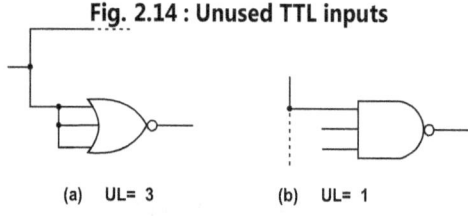

(a) UL= 3   (b) UL= 1

Fig. 2.15

- **Tied-Together Inputs :** When two or more TTL- gate inputs are tied together then the common input will generally have an input loading factor (UL) that is the sum of the input loading factors for each input.
For example NOR gate in the Fig. 2.15 above has 3 UL.

2.5 COMPLEMENTARY METAL-OXIDE-SEMICONDUCTOR (CMOS) CIRCUITS

- The drawbacks of P – MOS and N – MOS families are overcome by the CMOS family.
- The CMOS logic family has both p – channel and n – channel MOSSFETs in the same circuit.
- It is fabricated by connecting a p – channel in series with an n – channel MOSFET.

2.5.1 CMOS Inverter

| Q. Explain CMOS Inverter. | [May 05, 07, 3 M] |
| Q. Explain the operation of CMOS inverter. | [Dec. 08, 3 M] |

- Fig. 2.16 (a) given below shows a CMOS inverter and its equivalent.

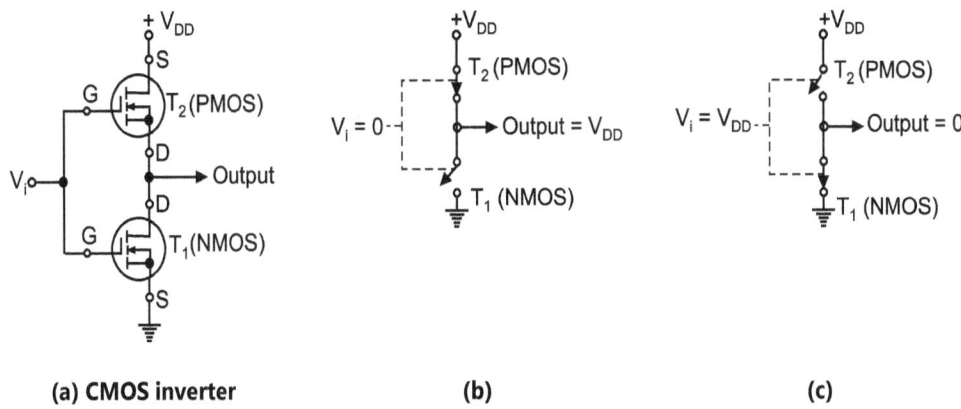

(a) CMOS inverter   (b)   (c)

Fig. 2.16

- Observe that the drains of both the PMOS transistor and NMOS transistor are tied together and the output is taken from the common drain.
- The gates are tied together and the input is given through the common gate.

Case 1 : When V_{in} = 0V (Low)

- When input voltage = 0V, then V_{GS} of transistor T_1 (NMOS) will be 0 volts. Therefore it will not conduct and will be OFF. Fig. 1.4 (b) shows the equivalent circuit.
- V_{GS} of transistor T_2 will be equal to $-V_{DD}$. So, T_2 will be conducting or ON.
- Therefore output Y = HIGH or $V_{out} = V_{DD}$.

Case 2 : When V_{in} = 5V (HIGH)

- When input V_{in} = +5V (HIGH), V_{GS} of T_2 = 5V and hence it would be OFF. Fig. 1.33 (c) shows the equivalent circuit.
- V_{GS} of T_1 = +5V, So, T_1 is ON and conducting. Therefore output (Y = 0) or V_{out} = 0V.

Thus, the above circuit acts as an inverter.

2.5.2 CMOS NAND gate

Q. Explain with a neat circuit diagram the working of 2-input CMOS NAND gate.
[Dec. 04, 09, May 06, 3 M]

Q. Explain with neat diagram, CMOS NAND gate. [May 05, 2 M]

Q. Draw CMOS circuit for NAND gate.

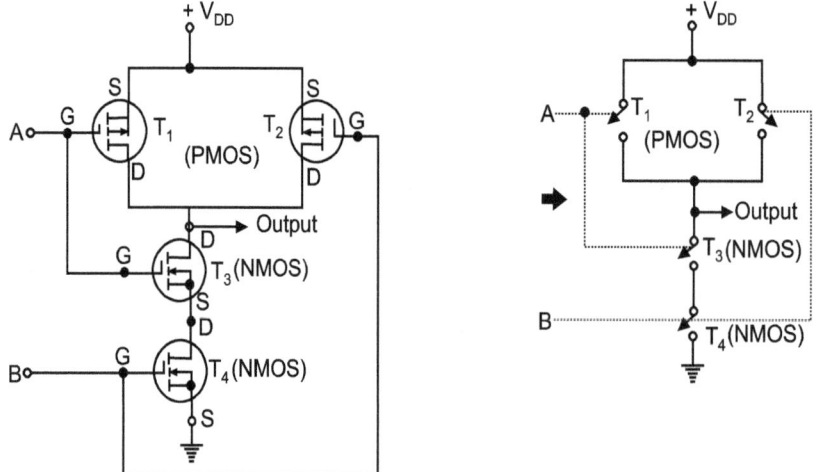

Fig. 2.17 (a) : Shows a CMOS two – input NAND and its equivalent circuit.

Case 1 : A = 0, B = 0 (Fig. 2.18 (a))

- $V_{GS1} = V_{GS2} = -V_{DD} = -5V$, $V_{GS3} = V_{GS4} = 0V$
- Therefore T_1 = ON, T_2 = ON, T_3 = OFF, T_4 = OFF
- ∴ Output Y = 1 or V_{out} = +5V

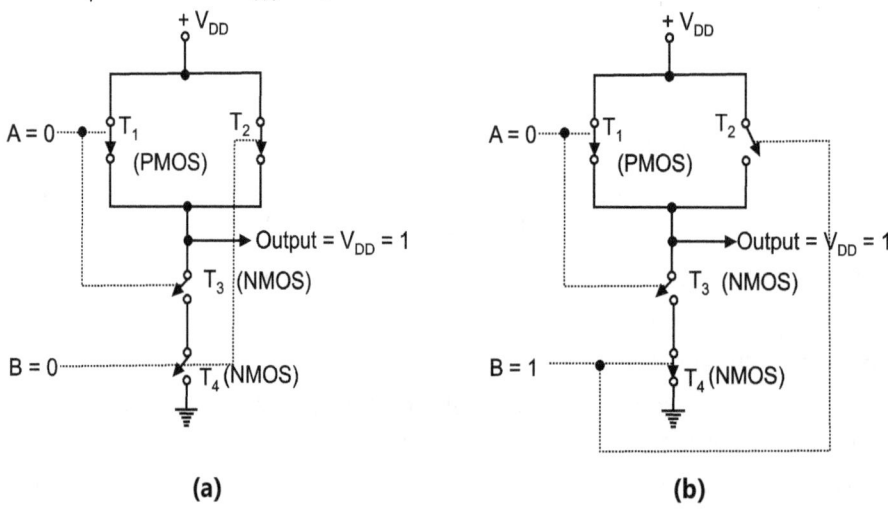

(a)   (b)

Fig. 2.18

Case 2 : A = 0 , B = 1 (Fig. 2.18 (b))
- $V_{GS1} = -5V$, $V_{GS2} = 0V$, $V_{GS3} = 0V$, $V_{GS4} = +5V$
- ∴ Output Y = 1 or V_{out} = +5V.

Case 3 : A = 1 , B = 0 (Fig. 2.18 (c))
- $V_{GS1} = 0V$, $V_{GS2} = -5V$, $V_{GS3} = +5V$, $V_{GS4} = 0V$.
- So , T_1 is OFF T_3 is ON, T_2 is ON and T_4 is OFF.
  - ∴ Y =1 or V_{out} = +5V

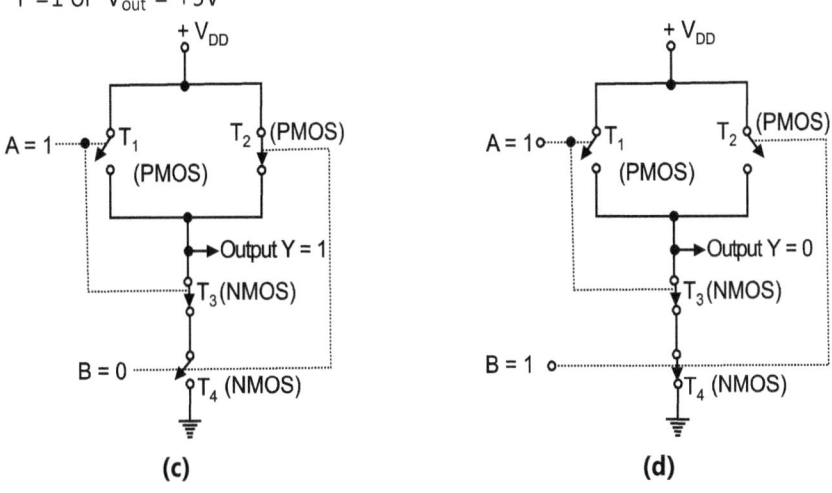

Fig. 2.18

Case 4 : A = 1 , B = 1 Fig. 2.18 (d)
- $V_{GS1} = V_{GS2} = 0V$, $V_{GS3} = V_{GS4} = 5V$
- So , T_1 is OFF , T_3 is ON , T_2 is OFF and T_4 is ON.
  - ∴ Y =0 or V_{out} = 0V

Summary of Operations :

A	B	T_1	T_2	T_3	T_4	V_{out}
0 V	0 V	ON	ON	OFF	OFF	5 V
0 V	5 V	ON	OFF	OFF	ON	5 V
5 V	0 V	OFF	ON	ON	OFF	5 V
5 V	5 V	OFF	OFF	ON	ON	0 V

2.5.3 CMOS NOR gate

> **Q.** Draw and explain briefly the working of 2-input CMOS NOR gate.
>
> [Dec. 04, 05, 06, 07, 08, 12 May 07, 11, 8 M]
>
> **Q.** Explain with neat diagram CMOS NOR gate.   [May 05, 10, 5 M]
>
> **Q.** Draw CMOS circuit for NOR gate.   [Dec. 11, 4 M]

- Fig. 1.36 shows a CMOS 2 – input NOR gate and its equivalent circuits.
- NMOS transistor T_3 and T_4 are connected in parallel and PMOS T_1 and T_2 are connected in series.

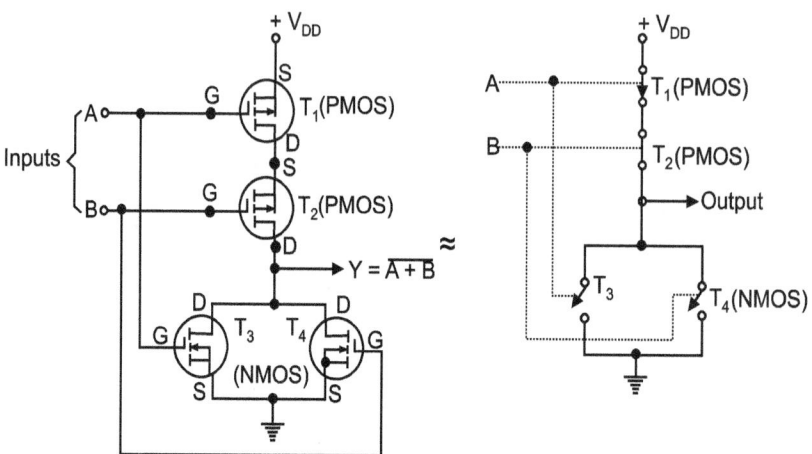

Fig. 2.19

Case 1 : A = 0 , B = 0

- Whenever both the inputs are 0 , then both NMOS are in OFF condition.
- $V_{GS1} = V_{GS2} = -5V$, $V_{GS3} = V_{GS4} = 0V$
- ∴ $T_1 = T_2 =$ ON $T_3 = T_4 =$ OFF $Y = 1$ or $V_{out} = +5V$.

Case 2 : A = 0 , B = 1

- $V_{GS1} = -5V$, $V_{GS2} = 0V$, $V_{GS3} = 0V$ and $V_{GS4} = +5V$ So , T_1 and T_4 are ON , and T_2 and T_3 are OFF.
- Thus , output Y=0 , $V_{out} = 0V$
- Similarly , for the next states (A = 1 , B = 0 and A = 1 , B = 1) either of the NMOS or both the NMOS are ON.
- This provides short circuit path between output Y and ground terminal and the output becomes logic LOW.

For summary of transistor operations refer to the Truth table below.

A	B	T_1	T_2	T_3	T_4	V_{out}
0 V	0 V	ON	ON	OFF	OFF	5 V
0 V	5 V	ON	OFF	OFF	ON	0 V
5 V	0 V	OFF	ON	ON	OFF	0 V
5 V	5 V	OFF	OFF	ON	ON	0 V

2.5.4 CMOS Characteristics

> Q. Explain power dissipation, fan-out of a CMOS IC.
> Q. Why CMOS inputs should never be left floating ?
> Q. How can static charge damage a CMOS IC ?

1. **Supply Voltage :** The 4000 and 74C series can operate with V_{DD} values ranging from 3 to 15 volts. The 74HC and 74HCT series can operate with voltage values ranging from 2 to 6 volts.

2. **Voltage Levels :** The output of a CMOS is approximately 0V for LOW state and close to 5V for HIGH state.

Generally, the input voltage levels are expressed as percentage of VDD (power supply).

For example
$$V_{IL(max)} = 30\% \text{ of } V_{DD} \text{ and}$$
$$V_{IH(min)} = 70\% \text{ of } V_{DD}$$

3. **Power Dissipation :**
   - For a dc input, power dissipation is extremely low.
   - But for a switching circuit, power dissipation increases.
   - If V_{DD} = 5V, the dc power dissipation is 2.5 nW per gate.

   But if V_{DD} = 10V, then it increases (10nW), which is still too small compared to TTL gates where P_D = 10mW
   - Therefore, CMOS devices are preferred for battery operated systems.
   - Hence, for low operating frequencies, power dissipation is low and for higher frequencies, power dissipation increases.

4. **Fan Out :**
   - The maximum fan – out of a CMOS family is 50 for operating frequency below 1 MHz ($\leq$1MHz).
   - This fan – out is limited to 50 as it depends on the propagation delay of each of the gates at the output.

5. **Switching Speed**
   - With increase in V_{DD}, the speed of the CMOS gate increases.
   - The less the propagation delay, more is the speed of the gate.
   - For example :

   For 4000 series – Average t_{pd} = 50ns (V_{DD} = 5V)

   Average t_{pd} = 25ns (V_{DD} = 10V)

   For 74 HC series – t_{pd} = 8ns (V_{DD} = 5V)

   74 AC/ACT series – t_{pd} = 4.7ns (V_{DD} = 5V)

6. Noise Margins
- We know that the noise margins are calculated using –

$$V_{NH} = V_{OH(min)} - V_{IH(min)}$$
$$V_{NL} = V_{IL(max)} - V_{OL(max)}$$

- CMOS ICs are preferred to TTL for operation in noisy environment.
- We know that, if the supply voltage is increased the noise margins in CMOS increases.

7. Unused Inputs
- CMOS inputs should never be left unconnected or floating.
- It there are any unused inputs, they have to be either tied to 0V or V_{DD} power supply or connected to other inputs.
- This is done so that the unused inputs do not get induced voltages due to noise or static charges.
- Such induced voltages may cause overheating and damage the IC permanently.

8. Susceptibility to Static Charge :
- The CMOS gates are prone to static charges because of high input resistance.
- This static charge may induce a high voltage and damage the dielectric insulation between the MOSFET gate and the channel.
- Now – a – days Zener diodes are included on each input to protect the IC from static damage.

2.6 CMOS AND TTL INTERFACING

2.6.1 TTL–to–CMOS Interfacing Techniques

> Q. Explain with neat diagram, interface of TTL gate driving CMOS gate.
> Q. Draw and justify TTL driving CMOS. **[Dec. 07, 10, 2 & 4 M]**
> Q. Explain with neat diagrams, interface of TTL gate driving CMOS gate.
> **[May 06, Dec. 06, 08, 09, May 11, Dec. 12, 4 M]**

- There are instances wherein the output of a TTL logic gate needs to be used for driving the input of a CMOS gate. Since the voltage–current characteristics and requirements of a TTL gate differ from those of a CMOS gate, it is good practice to use proper interfacial components between them when connecting them to each other. Below are some common techniques used in connecting a TTL gate to a CMOS gate.

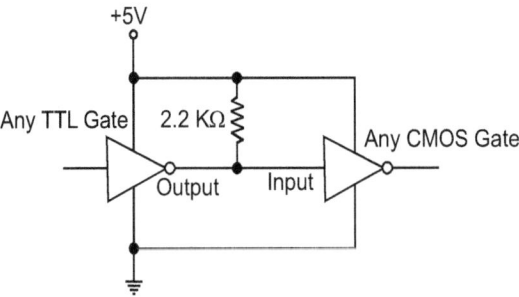

Fig. 2.20 (a) : Interfacing any TTL gate to any CMOS gate using the same power supply (5V)

- When the CMOS gate, that the TTL gate will drive, also uses the same 5-V supply used by the TTL gate, the simple interfacing technique shown in Fig. 2.20 (a) may be employed. Here, a pull-up resistor is just placed between the TTL output and the 5-V supply.

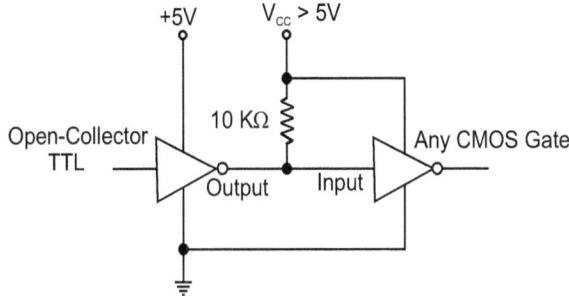

Fig. 2.20 (b) : Interfacing an Open-Collector TTL gate to any CMOS gate using different power supplies

- When the CMOS gate that the TTL gate will drive has a supply voltage that's different from the 5-V supply used by the TTL gate and if the TTL gate has an open collector, the simple interfacing technique shown in Fig. 2.20 (b) may be employed. Here, a 10-K pull-up resistor is just placed between the TTL output and the CMOS gate's supply.

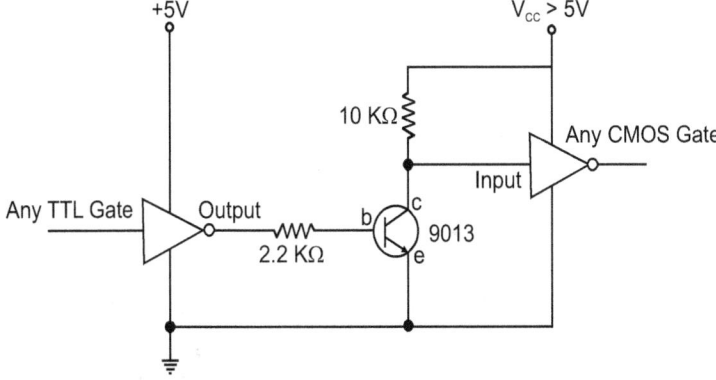

Fig. 2.20 (c) : Interfacing any TTL gate to any CMOS gate using different power supplies

- When the CMOS gate that the TTL gate will drive has a supply voltage that's different from the 5-V supply used by the TTL gate and if the TTL gate does not have an open collector, it would be good to use an NPN transistor to translate the TTL output voltage level to a correct CMOS input voltage level as shown in Fig. 2.20 (c) so as not to overstress the TTL gate.

Important Tips for TTL to CMOS interfacing :
- TTL output thresholds are inconsistent with 74HC, 74C and 40' CMOS inputs.
- When CMOS is run with V_{CC} = 5 V.
- Use an open collector buffer with pullup to 5 V.
- When CMOS uses V_{CC} = 3.3 V (Usually 74HC only)
- Direct connection from TTL to CMOS possible.
- When CMOS uses V_{CC} > 5 V (Usually 4000 or 74C series < use level shifter buffer chip 40109, LTC1045, 14504 or use open collector buffer with pullup to 5 V.

2.6.2 CMOS – to – TTL Interfacing Techniques

Q. Explain with neat diagrams, interface of driving CMOS gate to TTL gate.
  [May 06, Dec. 06, 09, 12, May 11, 4 M]

Q. Draw and justify CMOS driving TTL. [Dec. 07, 2M, Dec. 10, 4 M]

- There are instances wherein the output of a CMOS logic gate needs to be used for driving the input of a TTL gate. Since the voltage–current characteristics and requirements of a CMOS gate differ from those of a TTL gate, it is good practice to use proper interfacial components between them when connecting them to each other. Below are some common techniques used in connecting a CMOS gate to a TTL gate.

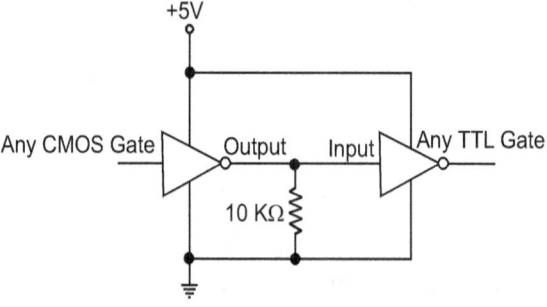

Fig. 2.21 (a) : Interfacing any CMOS gate to any TTL gate using the same power supply (5V)

- When the CMOS gate that will drive the TTL gate also uses the same 5-V supply used by the TTL gate, the simple interfacing technique shown in Fig. 2.21a) may be employed. Here, a pull-down resistor is just between the CMOS gate output and ground.

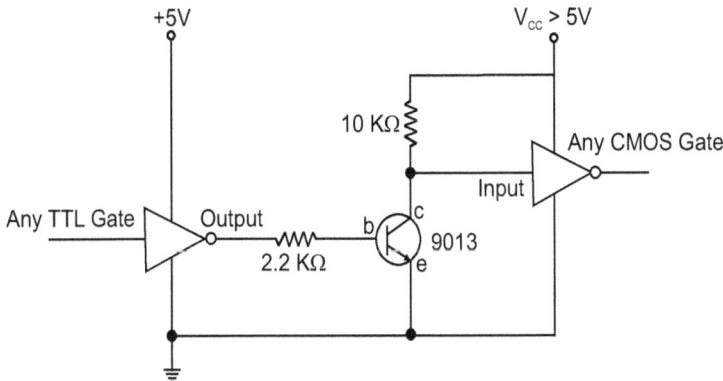

Fig. 2.21 (b) : Interfacing an Open-Collector TTL gate to any CMOS gate using different power supplies

- When the CMOS gate that will drive the TTL gate has a supply voltage that's different from the 5-V supply used by the TTL gate, it would be good to use an NPN transistor to translate the CMOS output voltage level to correct TTL input voltage level as shown in Fig. 2.21 (b).
- Note that the transistor uses the 5V TTL supply for its V_{CC}.
- As an alternative to the technique shown in Fig. 2.21 (b) the technique shown in Fig. 2.21 (c) may be employed to connect a CMOS gate to a TTL gate.
- Instead of a transistor, a CMOS buffer (inverting or non-inverting) may be used as long as it is supplied from the 5-V TTL supply. The example in Fig. 2.21 (c) is an inverting buffer, so the input to the TTL gate is an inverted logic of the CMOS output.

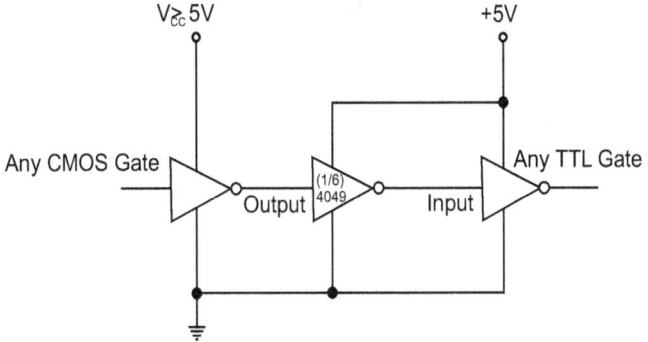

Fig. 2.21 (c) : Interfacing any TTL gate to any CMOS gate using different power supplies

Important Tips for Interfacing CMOS to TTL
- If V_{CC} is + 5V, then one CMOS output can drive one LS TTL input
- CMOS logic levels are close to 0 V or 5 V, so no threshold incompatibility
- If CMOS is run at $V_{CC} \sim 3.3$ V, thresholds are still compatible with TTL
- Sometimes 4000 series or 74 C chips are run at $V_{CC} > 5$ V for improved speed
- Need level-shifter chip to interface to TTL, for example 4049/50, 74C901/2.

2.7 DIFFERENT LOGIC FAMILY SERIES

74AC : A high speed CMOS logic family with CMOS input switching levels and buffered CMOS outputs that can drive ± 24 mA of I_{OH} and I_{OL}.

74ACT : A high speed CMOS logic family with the same buffered CMOS outputs that can drive ± 24 mA of I_{OH} and I_{OL}. This family has a TTL–to–CMOS input buffer stage. The inputs will interface with TTL outputs operating at 5 volts with V_{OH} = 2.4 volts and V_{OL} = 0.4 volts. The devices have the same output buffered structures as the AC family.

74LCX : These devices have a mixed 3 volts–to–5 volts capability for use with applications that have both 3 volts and a 5 volts devices which interface with one another.

74LVX : This family consists of low cost devices with 5 volts tolerant inputs. The devices can receive and output 3 volts or 5 volts.

74LVQ : This family consists of low cost devices designed for 3.3 volts only applications.

74LVT : This family has both high speed and a high output drive. These devices have a + 64 mA / – 32 mA output drive currents. The chips are 5 volts tolerant and are designed to be used with applications that have both 3 V and 5 V devices which interface with one another.

74ALCX : This devices are about the same as the LVT family with out the high drive currents.

74xx : The first TTL family developed. The 74xx family offers a wide variety of logic functions. There are a number of other TTL logic families which offer either higher speed or lower power.

74LXX : This is the Low power version of the TTL family above. The value of the internal device resistors have been increased by a factor of 10x. The family offers 1/10 the power consumption as the previous family, but operates at 1/3 the speed.

74LSXX : This devices adds a Schottky diode between the Base and Collector of the transistor. The Schottky diode prevents the transistor from going into full saturation. So the 74LS family operates at the same speed as the 74 family [10nS] with only 2mW of power dissipation compared to 10mW for 74xx or 1mW for the 74L family [at 33nS].

74SXX : This gains its speed using the same Schottky diode as the 74LS family, but the value of the internal device resistors have been decreased by half the original values of the 74XX family. So, the speed increases [3 nS] and the power consumption also increases [20 mW].

74ALSXX : The advanced LS family offers near same high speed as the 74Sxx family at 4 nS at a power dissipation of only 1mW. Except for the 74SXX family, the 74ALS family out performs the other three TTL families listed. If the design calls for a TTL family which needs to operate at 3 nS, this is the family to use.

74ASXX : If the design needs to operate faster than 3 nS then the 74 AS family should be use. This family is twice as fast as the 74ALS family with a propagation delay of only 1.5 nS. The price is a 7 mW power dissipation.

2.8 COMPARISON OF CMOS AND TTL

Q. Compare TTL and COMS logic families with respect to :
1. Power dissipation per gate
2. Propagation delay
3. Figure of merit
4. Fan out. **[Dec. 05, 06, 8 M]**

Q. Compare COMS and TTL logic families on the basis of :
1. Noise margin
2. Fan out
2. Basic gate
3. Unconnected inputs.
4. Power supply voltage
6. Figure of merit **[May 07, 4 M, May 11, 8 M]**

Sr. No	Parameter	CMOS	TTL
1.	Device used	N – Channel MOSFET and P – channel MOSFET	Bipolar junction transistor
2.	$V_{IH(min)}$	3.5 V (V_{DD} = 5 V)	2 V
3.	$V_{IL(max)}$	1.5 V	0.8 V
4.	$V_{OH(min)}$	4.95 V	2.7 V
5.	$V_{OL(max)}$	0.05 V	0.4 V
6.	Low level noise margin	V_{NL} = 1.45 V	0.4 V
7.	High level noise margin	V_{NH} = 1.45 V	0.4 V
8.	Noise immunity	Better than TTL	Less than CMOS
9.	Propagation delay	105 ns (Metal gate CMOS)	10 ns. (Standard TTL)
10.	Switching speed	Less than TTL	Faster than CMOS
11.	Power dissipation per gate.	P_D = 0.1 mW. Hence used for battery backup applications	10mW

12.	Speed power product.	10.5pJ	100pJ
13.	Dependence of P_D on frequency	P_D increases with increase in frequency.	P_D does not depend on frequency.
14.	Fan out	Typically 50.	10
15.	Unconnected inputs	Unused inputs should be returned to GND or V_{DD}. They should never be left floating.	Inputs can remain floating. The floating inputs are treated as logic 1s.
16.	Component density	More than TTL since MOSFETs need smaller space while fabricating an IC.	Less than CMOS since BJT needs more space.
17.	Operating areas	MOSFETs are operated as switches. i.e. in the ohmic region or off region.	Transistors are operated in saturation or cut off regions.
18.	Power supply voltage	Flexible from 3 V to 15 V.	Fixed equal to 5 V.

Unit - III

COMBINATIONAL LOGIC

3.1 CODES

Q. What are the different types of codes used in digital systems ? Explain them.

- The codes are used to represent the given digital information in particular format.
- The codes are used to store and transmit the data efficiency. All codes are represented finally as '0' and '1' which computers can understand. There are various types of codes which are enlisted below.

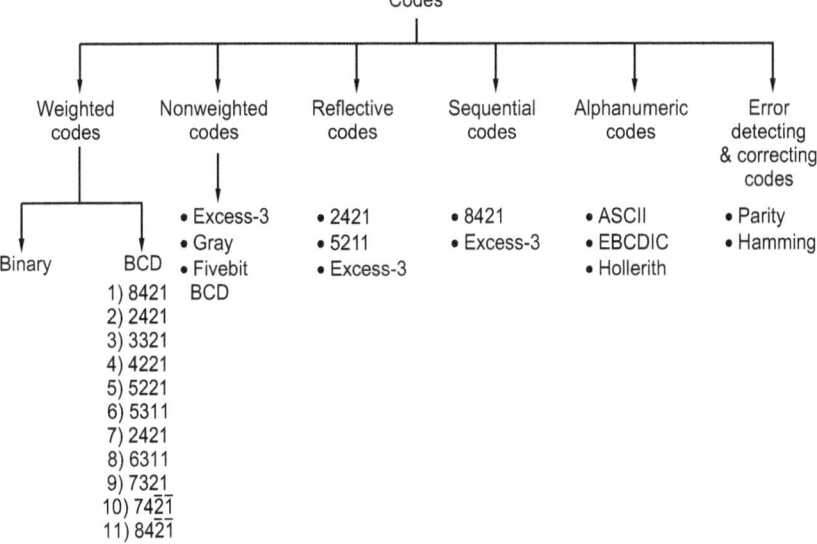

Fig. 3.1

- **Weighted codes :** The weight of digit or bit depends on its position e.g. the weight of 6 in 647 is 600, 4 is 0 and 7 is 1.
- **Non weighted codes :** Non weighted codes are not assigned with any weight to each digit position i.e. each digit position within the number is not assigned fixed value excess-3 and gray codes are the non weighted codes.
- **Reflective codes :** A code is said to be reflective when the code for 9 is the complement for 0, the code for 8 is complement for 1, 7 for 2, 6 for 3 and 5 for 4.

  e.g.　　　　2 + 4 + 2 + 1
  code for 9　 1　1　1　1
  　　　　　　↓ complement
  code for 0　 0　0　0　0

- **Sequential codes :** In this codes each succeeding code is one binary number greater than its preceding code. This type of codes mainly used in mathematical manipulation. The 8421 and excess – 3 are sequential codes.
- **Alphanumerical Code :** The binary codes of alphabets, number and special symbols are known as alpha numerical codes. e.g. ASCII (American Standard Code for Information Interchange) code.
- **Error detecting and Correcting Codes :** Special types of codes like parity or Hamming codes are used to detect errors when digital data is transmitted over long distance.

Thus, codes are used to represent binary information and reliable communication. In this chapter we will study three important codes Viz. BCD (Binary Coded Decimal), Gray and seven segment code.

3.2 BCD CODE

Q. Write short note on BCD code ? [3 M]

- Each digit of decimal number is represented by four bits. For example digit '5' is represented as '0101'. The BCD code is also called as 8-4-2-1 code where 8,4,2 and 1 represent weights of binary symbol in the respective positions. The examples of BCD codes are given below ;

Decimal	4	2	8	6	3
BCD	0100	0010	1000	0110	0011

- BCD code for 0 to 9 digits are given as;

Decimal digit	BCD code
0	0 0 0 0
1	0 0 0 1
2	0 0 1 0
3	0 0 1 1
4	0 1 0 0
5	0 1 0 1
6	0 1 1 0
7	0 1 1 1
8	1 0 0 0
9	1 0 0 1

The remaining 4 digit binary representations i.e. 1010, 1011, 1100, 1101, 1110 and 1111 are invalid BCD codes.

BCD Arithmetic : The arithmetic of BCD code is complex. It can be used to perform addition and subtraction.

Rules :

1. If four bits sum is equal to or less than 9, no correction is needed. The sum is in proper BCD form.
2. If the four bit sum is greater than of 9 or if a carry is generated from the four bit sum, the sum is invalid.
3. To correct the invalid sum add 6 $(0110)_2$ to the four bit sum. If carry results from this addition, add it to the next higher order BCD digit.

3.2.1 BCD Addition

- In BCD addition, each digit of decimal number is first represented using it's four - bit BCD equivalent numbers.
- The addition of two BCD numbers is carried out using simple binary addition. After the binary addition the result may be invalid or valid BCD.
- If the result is invalid BCD then the it is converted into the valid BCD by adding $(0110)_2$ or $(06)_{10}$. If carry is generated after the addition of $(0110)_2$ then it is added to next bit.

Example 3.1 :

$(569)_{10} + (687)_{10}$

Step 1 :

```
        (569)₁₀  =  0101   0110   1001
      + (687)₁₀  =  0110   1000   0111
                   ─────────────────────
                    0111   1111   0000
```

           invalid invalid valid BCD
         BCD number BCD with carry 1

Step 2 : Add $(6)_{10}$ to each one

```
   1011  1111  0000
 + 0110  0110  0110
   ──────────────────
  10010  0101  0110
↓
  1  2    5     6    ...final answer
```

$(569)_{10} + (687)_{10} = (1256)_{10}$

3.2.2 BCD Subtraction

- Subtraction is nothing but addition of a signed number i.e. A − B = A + (−B). The negative BCD number can be expressed by taking the 9's or 10's complement of the BCD number which is to be subtracted.

3.2.2.1 BCD subtraction using 9's complement

- The 9's complement is obtained by subtracting the given number from 9. Thus 9's Complement of 3 is 6 (9 − 3 = 6).

Steps to perform BCD subtraciton using 9's complement.

- Find the 9's complement of subtractor.
- Perform the BCD addition of the first number and 9's complement of second number.
- If carry is generated, then result is positive. Add the carry into the result to get the correct result.
- If carry is not generated then result is negative and it is in 9's complement form.

Example 3.2 :

Subtract 4 from 8 in BCD (8 − 4 − 2 − 1) using 9's complement of subtraction.

Solution :   8 − 4 = 8 + 5   where 5 is 9's complement of 4

Step 1 :

```
       1000      ← BCD code of 8
  +
       0101      ← BCD code of 5
       ─────
       1101      ← Invalid BCD answer
       0110      ← add (0110)₂
         11      ← Carry
       ─────
      10011
```

Because carry is generated, the answer is positive

Step 2 : Add carry into answer

```
       0011
  +
          1
       ─────
          1
       0100      ← valid BCD answer
```

3.2.2.2 BCD subtraction using 10's complement

The 10's complement of a number is obtained by adding '1' into 9's complement.

Step to perform BCD subtraction using 10's complement.
- Find the 10's complement of the subtraction.
- Perform the BCD addition.
- If carry is not generated then the result is negative and it is in 10's complement form.
- If carry is generated then the result is positive. Discard the carry.

Example 3.3 : Perform 8 – 3 using 10's complement.

Solution :   8 – 3 = 8 + 7   where 7 is 10's complement of 3 i.e. [(9 – 3) + 1 = 7]

```
   1000        ← BCD code of 8
 + 0111        ← BCD code of 7
   ----
   1111        ← Invalid BCD code

   0110        ← add (0110)₂
     11        ← Carry
  -----
  10101
```

The carry is generated. ∴ The result is positive. Discarded the carry

∴ The answer is (5).

Example 3.4 : Represent $(7)_{10}$ using all the weighted 4-bit BCD codes

1. 3321 code

$$(7)_{10} = 3\ 3\ 2\ 1$$
$$\downarrow \downarrow \downarrow \downarrow$$
$$1\ 1\ 0\ 1$$
$$= (1101)_{3221\ BCD}$$

2. 4221 code

$$(7)_{10} = 4\ 2\ 2\ 1$$
$$\downarrow \downarrow \downarrow \downarrow$$
$$1\ 0\ 1\ 1$$
$$= (1011)_{4221\ BCD}$$

3. 5211 code

$$(7)_{10} = 5\ 2\ 2\ 1$$
$$\downarrow \downarrow \downarrow \downarrow$$
$$1\ 1\ 0\ 0$$
$$= (1100)_{5211\ BCD}$$

4. 5311 code

$$(7)_{10} = 5\ 3\ 1\ 1$$
$$\downarrow\downarrow\downarrow\downarrow$$
$$1\ 0\ 1\ 1$$
$$= (1011)_{5311\ BCD}$$

5. 5421 code

$$(7)_{10} = 5\ 4\ 1\ \cancel{1}$$
$$\downarrow\downarrow\downarrow\downarrow$$
$$1\ 0\ 1\ 0$$
$$= (1011)_{5421\ BCD}$$

6. 6311 code

$$(7)_{10} = 6\ \cancel{3}\ \cancel{1}\ 1$$
$$\downarrow\downarrow\downarrow\downarrow$$
$$1\ 0\ 0\ 1$$

7. 7421 code

$$(7)_{10} = 7\ \cancel{4}\ \cancel{2}\ \cancel{1}$$
$$1\ 0\ 0\ 0$$
$$= (1000)_{7421\ BCD}$$

8. $74\bar{2}\bar{1}$ code

$$(7)_{10} = 7 + 4 - \bar{2} - \bar{1}$$
$$\downarrow\ \ \downarrow\ \ \downarrow\ \ \downarrow$$
$$1\ \ 0\ \ 0\ \ 0$$
$$= (1000)_{74\bar{2}\bar{1}\ BCD}$$

3.3 EXCESS 3 CODE

Q. With the help of suitable example, explain the meaning of self complementing code.

[Dec. 03, 08, 3 M]

- Excess – 3 wide is derived from the natural BCD code by adding 3 to each coded number.
- It is non-weighted code.
- Table 3.1 shows excess-3 codes to represent single digit.
- The excess – 3 codes are obtained as follows

$$\text{Decimal number} \longrightarrow 8421\ \text{BCD number} \xrightarrow{\text{add}\ 0011} \text{Excess-3 code.}$$

Table 3.1

Decimal Number	BCD 8 4 2 1	Excess – 3
0	0 0 0 0	0 0 1 1
1	0 0 0 1	0 1 0 0
2	0 0 1 0	0 1 0 1
3	0 0 1 1	0 1 1 0
4	0 1 0 0	0 1 1 1
5	0 1 0 1	1 0 0 0
6	0 1 1 0	1 0 0 1
7	0 1 1 1	1 0 1 0
8	1 0 0 0	1 0 1 1
9	1 0 0 1	1 1 0 0

The excess-3 is also called as sequential code, because each succeeding code is one binary number than its preceding code.

The excess-3 is also known as self complementary because we get the 9's complement of number just complete of number just complement of each bit by means replacing ???

Example 3.5 : What is Excess-3 code of binary number ?

0010 B, 0110 B and 0111 B

(a) 0010 B

    add (0011) to the number

      0010

+   0011

    ─────

      0101

(b) 0010 B

    add (0011) to each number

      0110

+   0011

    ─────

      1001

(c) 0111 B

    add (0011) to the given number

      0111

+   0011

    ─────

      1010

3.4 GRAY CODE

Q. Prepare a table 4 bit gray code along with relationship with binary code.
[May 06, 2 M]

Q. What will be the gray code 4-bit binary number ?
[Dec. 06, 6 M]

Q. What is Gray code covert binary number.
1100B, 0111B and 1101 B into gray number.

- Gray is a non-weighted code.
- The feature of gray code is that the only one bit will change, each time the decimal number is incremented this is shown in table 3.2.

Table 3.2

Decimal Code	Binary code	Gray code
0	0000	0000
1	0001	0001
2	0010	0011
3	0011	0010
4	0100	0110
5	0101	0111
6	0110	0101
7	0111	0100
8	1000	1100
9	1001	1101
10	1010	1111
11	1011	1110
12	1100	1010
13	1101	1011
14	1110	1001
15	1111	1000

- Gray code also exhibits the reflective property.
- The two least significant bits for decimal 4 to 7 are the mirror images of those for decimal 3 to 0.
- The three least significant bits for decimal 8 through 15 are mirror images of those for decimal 7 through 0.

3.4.1 Application of Gray Code

> Q. What are the advantages of gray code over pure binary code ?
> Q. State the applications of gray code or How gray codes are useful in digital system ?
>
> [May 06, 12, 2 M]

- Gray code is mostly used in the shaft position encoders.
- A shaft position encoder produces a code coordinate which represents the angular position of the shaft. The shaft position encoder consist of alight source, an optical disc and alight detector as shown in Fig. 3.2 (a).

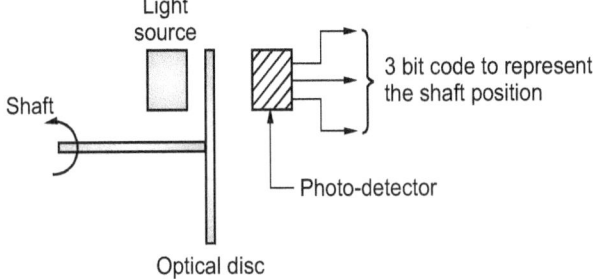

Fig. 3.2 (a) : Shaft position encoder

- Patterns of opaque and transparent segments is etched out on the optical disc. So corresponding to the black position. The photo detector produces a "1" and corresponding to the transparent portion a "0" is produced.
- The patterns on the disc are according to the code required to be produced at the detector output.
- Fig. 3.2 (b) shows the patterns for binary code and Fig. 3.2 (c) shows the pattern for producing gray code.

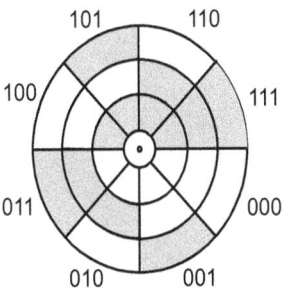

(b) Pattern for binary code

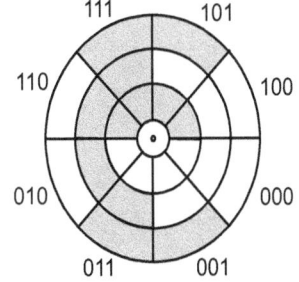

(c) Pattern for gray code

Fig. 3.2

3.4.2 Advantages of Gray Code

- The advantage of Gray code over straight binary code is that Gray code changes by only 1 bit as it sequences from one number to the next.
- The 3-bit Gray code representations for number 0 through 7 are listed below. Design a decoder to convert a 3-bit binary number into a Gray code number. Your decoder should have three inputs and three outputs and it should convert a binary number, say 011 (decimal 3), to a Gray code number, 010 for all the eight decimal numbers 0 to 7.

Table 3.3

Decimal	Binary b_2, b_1, b_0	Gray g_2, g_1, g_0
0	000	000
1	001	001
2	010	011
3	011	010
4	100	110
5	101	111
6	110	101
7	111	100

3.4.3 Converting Binary code to Gray code

Q. Find gray codes for the following binary number.
(i) 11001100 (ii) 01011110   [Dec. 08, 2M]

Q. Explain rule for any sequence binary to gray code conversion.   [May 12, 2 M]

A binary number can be converted in gray by following steps :

Step 1 : First take MSB as it is.

Step 2 : Add this MSB bit to the next position bit, recording the sum and neglecting any carry.

Step 3 : Take successive sums until complete.

Example 3.6 : Convert binary 11001100   [Dec. 08, 1 M]

Given binary number

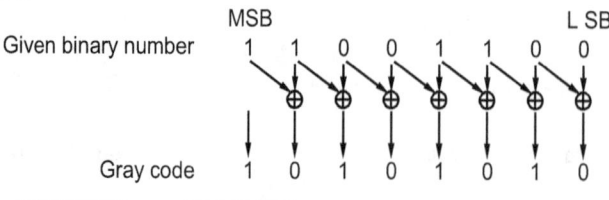

$\therefore \quad (11001100)_2 = (10101010)_{gray}$

In general from the conversion of binary to gray takes place as follows

G_3 (MSB) = B_3 (MSB) $G_2 = B_3 \oplus B_2$

$G_1 = B_2 \oplus B_1$ (LSB) $G_0 = B_1 \oplus B_3$

3.4.4 Converting Gray to Binary

Q. Explain rule for any sequence gray to binary code conversion.

For gray to binary conversion, follows the steps given below.

Step 1 : The MSB of gray and binary are same. So write it directly.

Step 2 : Add binary MSB to the next bit of gray code. Record the result and ignore the carriers.

Step 3 : Continue above process till the LSB is reached.

Example 3.7 : Convert 11101 gray to binary.

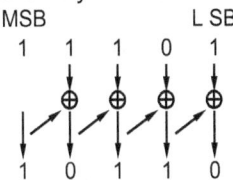

∴ $(11101)_{gray} = (1011)_2$

In general we can say that the conversion below 4-bit gray number $G_3G_2G_1G_0$ into a 4-bit binary number $B_3B_2B_1B_0$ it takes places as below

B_3 (MSB) = G_3 (MSB) $B_2 = B_3 \oplus G_2$

$B_1 = B_2 \oplus G_1$ $B_0 = B_1 \oplus G_0$

3.5 CODE CONVERSION

3.5.1 Binary to BCD Conversion

For the binary to BCD conversion two steps to be followed are as shown below :

(i) First write binary number into decimal number.

(ii) the from decimal number convert into BCD.

Example 3.8 : Convert $(1101)_2$ into BCD.

Step 1 : Write given number into decimal number

$(1101)_2 = 1 \times 2^3 + 1 \times 2^2 + 0 \times 2^1 + 1 \times 2^0$

$= 8 + 4 + 0 + 1$

$= (13)_{10}$

Step 2 : Convert 13 into BCD.

∴ $(13)_{10} = (0001\ 0011)_{BCD}$

3.5.2 BCD to Binary Conversion

Q. Represent 37 into BCD.

Step 1 : Convert BCD to decimal number
Step 2 : Convert BCD to decimal number to binary number
Example 3.9 : Convert $(0101\ 0101)_{BCD}$ into binary number
Step 1 : Convert given BCD to decimal number
$$(0101.0101)_{BCD} = (55)_{10}$$
Step 2 : Convert $(55)_{10}$ to binary
$$(55)_{10} = (110011)_2$$
$\therefore \quad (0101\ 0101) = (110011)_2$

3.5.3 BCD to Excess 3 Conversion

For BCD to excess-3 conversion steps are given below.
Step 1 : First convert BCD to decimal.
Step 2 : Add $(3)_{10}$ to this decimal number
Step 3 : Convert into binary to get the excess-3 code

Example 3.10 : Convert $(1001)_{BCD}$ to excess – 3
Step 1 : Convert BCD to decimal
$$(1001)_{BCD} = (9)_{10}$$
Step 2 : Add $(3)_{10}$ to decimal number

$\therefore \quad$ 9
$+ \quad$ 3
$\overline{\quad\ 12}$ ...Answer

Step 3 : Convert answer to binary number
$$(12)_{10} = (1100)$$
$\therefore \quad (1001)_{BCD} = (1100)_{Excess-3}$

3.5.4 Excess-3 to BCD Conversion

The same procedure like BCD to excess-3 only change is subtract $(3)_{10}$ from decimal number

Example 3.11 : $(10011010)_{excess-3}$ convert into BCD.
Solution :

```
     11   111      ...carry
    1001 1010    ...Excess-3
  − 0011 0011    ...(03)10
    ─────────
    0110 0111    ...BCD answer
```

3.6 HALF ADDER AND FULL ADDER

Q. Design a half-adder and full-adder circuits using K-maps. **[May 07, 6 M]**

- Addition is the most basic arithmetic operation in digital circuit.
- The simple addition of two bits has the following truth table.

Table 3.4 : Truth Table

A	B	Sum	Carry
0	0	0	0
0	1	1	0
1	0	1	0
1	1	0	1

- Note that when both the inputs are 1's then 'sum' is '0' and one carry is generated, similar to decimal addition.

3.6.1 Half-Adder

- The half-adder has two inputs (A, B) and two outputs (sum, carry).
- The block diagram of half-adder is shown in Fig. 3.3.

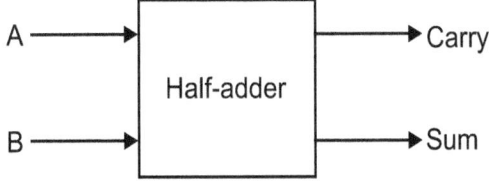

Fig. 3.3

- When the circuit has two or more outputs, one K-map is plotted for each output.
- The K-maps for half adder are :

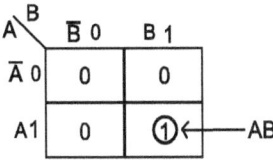

Fig. 3.4 : K-map for carry

∴ Carry output = AB

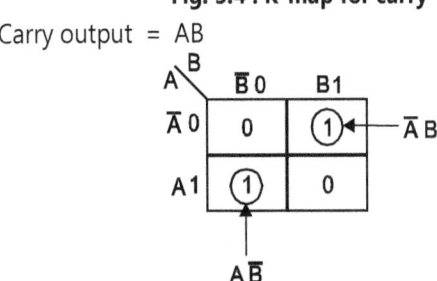

Fig.3.5 : K-Map for sum output

∴ Sum = $\bar{A}B + A\bar{B}$
= $A \oplus B$
↑
XOR

Half-Adder Circuit :

The half-adder circuit based on above K-map simplifications is shown in Fig. 3.6.

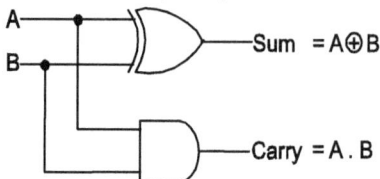

Fig. 3.6 : Half adder logic diagram

3.6.2 Full-Adder

- Full-adder has an additional input of previous carry in.
- Full-adder is a combinational circuit that forms the arithmetic sum of three input bits i.e. A, B, Cin and produces two outputs, sum, C_{out}.
- The logic block diagram of full adder is shown in Fig. 3.7.

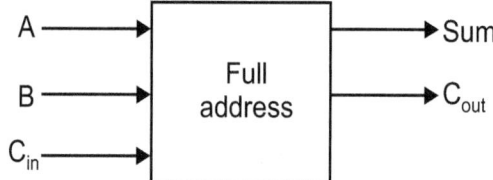

Fig. 3.7 : Block diagram of full-adder

The truth table of full-adder

Table 3.5

Inputs			Outputs	
A	B	C_{in}	C_{out}	Sum
0	0	0	0	0
0	0	1	0	1
0	1	0	0	1
0	1	1	1	0
1	0	0	0	1
1	0	1	1	0
1	1	0	1	0
1	1	1	1	1

- Full-adder truth table is plotted on two K-maps corresponding to two outputs, C_{out} and sum.

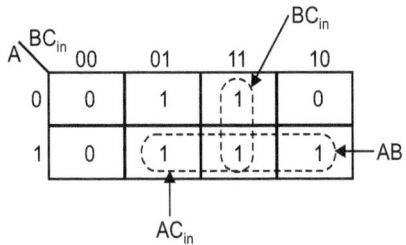

Fig. 3.8 : K-map for C_{out}

$$C_{out} = AB + AC_{in} + BC_{in}$$

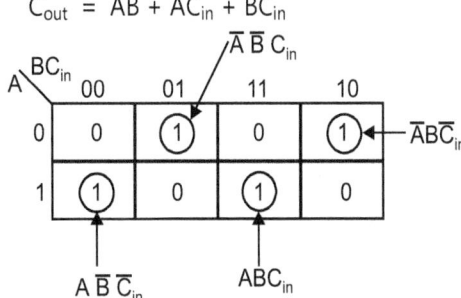

Fig. 3.9 : K-Map for Sum

$$\text{Sum} = \bar{A}\bar{B}C_{in} + \bar{A}B\bar{C}_{in} + AB C_{in} + A\bar{B}\bar{C}_{in}$$

$$\text{Sum} = \bar{A}\bar{B}C_{in} + A\bar{B}\bar{C}_{in} + AB C_{in} + \bar{A}B\bar{C}_{in}$$

$$= C_{in}(\bar{A}\bar{B} + AB) + \bar{C}_{in}(A\bar{B} + \bar{A}B)$$

$$= C_{in} \oplus (A \oplus B)$$

- The sum is the XORed output of A, B and Cin inputs.

Full-Adder Circuit :

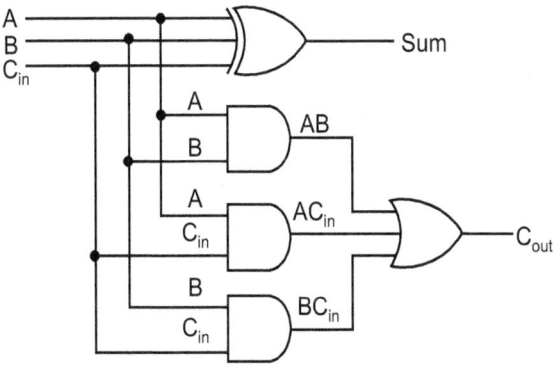

Fig. 3.10 : Full-adder logic diagram

Full-Adder Circuit using Half-Adder :

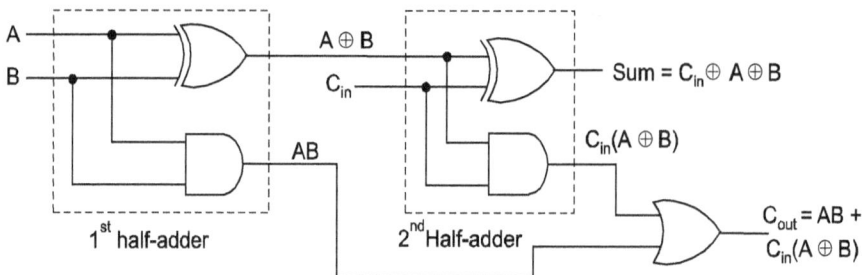

Fig. 3.11 : Full-adder using half adder

For K-map simplification :

$$C_{out} = AB + AC_{in} + BC_{in}$$
$$= AB + C_{in}(A + B)$$
$$= AB + C_{in}(A\bar{B} + \bar{A}B)$$
$$= AB + C_{in}(A \oplus B)$$

Therefore, the C_{out} is produced by ORing the carry output of the first adder (AB) with sum of output of the first adder (A ⊕ B).

3.7 HALF AND FULL SUBTRACTOR

Q. Design a half and full subtractor circuit using K-map.

Subtractor : The subtraction of two binary numbers is performed by combinational circuits called as half-subtractor and full-subtractor.

3.7.1 half-subtractor

Half-subtractor is a combinational logic circuit which subtracts two one-bit binary numbers. The truth table and the K-maps for corresponding outputs are as shown in Fig. 3.12 below :

Table 3.6 : Truth Table

Inputs		Outputs	
A (Minuend)	B (Subtrahend)	D (Difference)	C (Borrow)
0	0	0	0
0	1	1	1
1	0	1	0
1	1	0	0

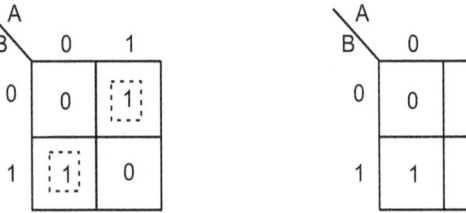

(a) k-map for D (difference) (b) k-map for C (borrow)

Fig. 3.12: Truth Table and K-maps of half-subtractor

- From the K-maps for the boolean expressions for the outputs are written as;

$$D = A\bar{B} + \bar{A}B = A \oplus B$$

$$C = \bar{A}B$$

- Therefore, the logic circuit for half subtractor is drawn as;

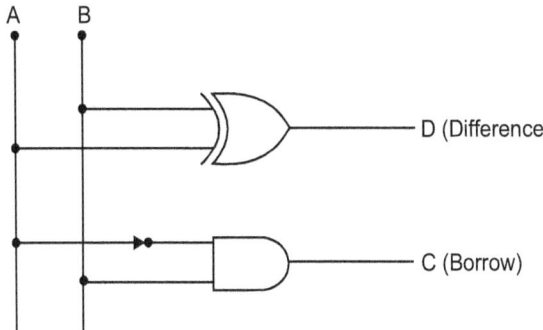

Fig. 3.13 : Half-subtractor

3.7.2 Full-subtractor

Full-subtractor allows to subtract a borrow which may be generated from lower order bit subtraction. A simple block schematic of full subtractor is shown in Fig. 3.14 below :

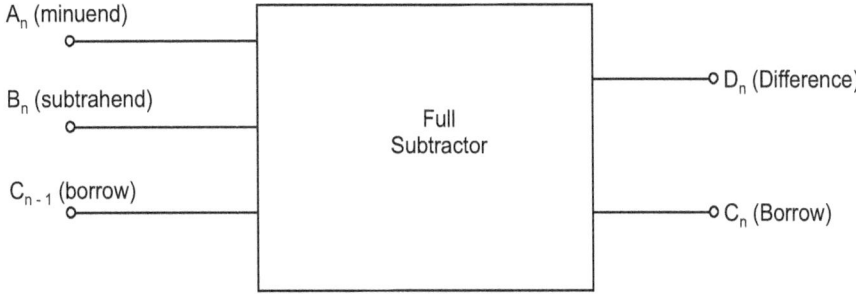

Fig. 3.14

- The truth table and k-maps for the corresponding outputs are shown in Fig. 3.15 below

Table 3.7 : Truth Table

Inputs			Outputs	
A_n	B_n	C_{n-1}	D_n	C_n
0	0	0	0	0
0	0	1	1	1
0	1	0	1	1
0	1	1	0	1
1	0	0	1	0
1	0	1	0	0
1	1	0	0	0
1	1	1	1	1

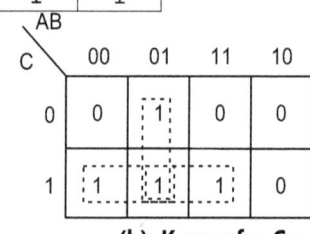

(a) K-map for Dn (b) K-map for Cn

Fig. 3.15

- Therefore, the boolean expression for Dn is ≈ B

$$D_1 = \overline{A}_n \overline{B}_n C_{n-1} + A_n B_n C_{n-1} + \overline{A}_n B_n \overline{C}_{n-1} + A_n \overline{B}_n \overline{C}_{n-1}$$

Which becomes exoring of the three inputs after simplification.

$$D_1 = C_{n-1} \oplus A \oplus B$$

The boolean expression for C_n is

$$C_1 = \overline{A}_n B_n + \overline{A}_n C_{n-1} + B_n C_{n-1}$$

- There are two boolean expressions can be used to design a combinational logic circuit for full-subtractor as shown in Fig. 3.16 below :

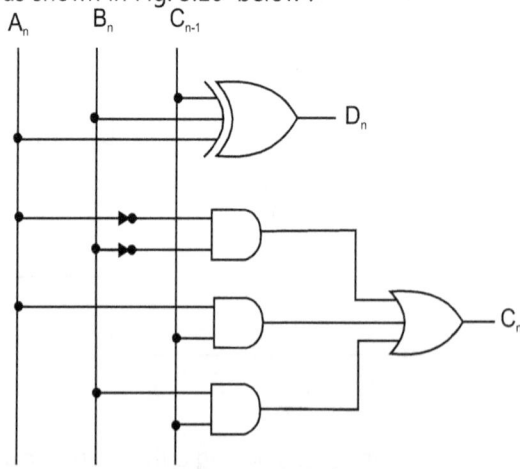

Fig. 3.16 : Full-subtractor

3.8 PARALLEL ADDER

Q. Design a 4-bit parallel adder using full-adders.

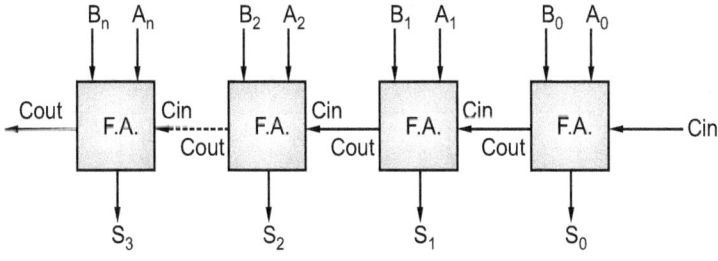

Fig. 3.17 : Block diagram of n-bit parallel adder

- A single full adder is capable of adding two one bit numbers and input carry. In order to add binary numbers with more than one bit, additional full adders must be employed. A 3 bit full adder can be constructed using number of full adder circuit connected in parallel.

- Fig. 3.17 shows the arrangement of parallel adder in that output of one adder i.e. connected to the carry input of the next higher order adder.

3.9 PARALLEL SUBTRACTOR

- The subtraction of binary numbers can be done must conveniently by means of complements. i.e. subtraction A-B can be done by taking 2's complement of B and adding it to A.

- The 2's complement can be obtained by taking 1's complement can be obtained by taking 1's complement and adding 1 to LSB in 1's complement of number.

- Logically it can be implemented with inverter of second bit and a one can be added to the sum through the input carry as shown in Fig. 3.18.

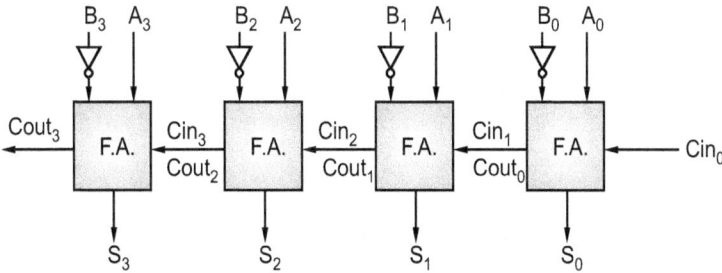

Fig. 3.18 : 4-bit parallel subtractor

3.10 PARALLEL ADDER / SUBTRACTOR

- The addition and subtraction operations can be combined into one circuit with one common binary adder. This is done by including an exclusive OR gate with each full adder as shown in Fig. 3.19.

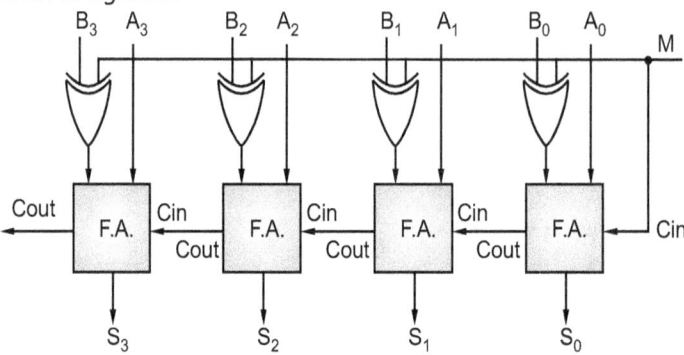

Fig. 3.19 : 4-bit adder subtractor

- The ripple adder is ripple carry adder in which the carry output of each full adder stage is connected to the carry input (C_{in}) of the next higher order stage. Therefore the sum and carry outputs of any stage cannot be produced until the input carry occurs, this leads to a time delay in addition process. This delay is known as carry propagation delay.
- One method of speeding up this process by eliminating inter stage carry delay is called look ahead carry addition.

3.11 CARRY LOOK - AHEAD ADDER

- The delay generated by an N - bit adder is proportional to the length N of the two numbers X and Y that are added because the carry signals have to propagate from one full-adder to the next. For large values of N, the delay becomes unacceptably large so that a special solution needs to be adopted to accelerate the calculation of the carry bits.
- This solution involves a "look- ahead carry generator" which is a block that simultaneously calculates all the carry bits involved. Once these bits are available to the rest of the circuit, each individual three-bit addition ($X_1 + Y_1$ + carry - in_i) is implemented by a simple 3 - input XOR gate.
- The design of the look ahead carry generator involves two Boolean functions named Generate and Propagate. For each input bits pair these functions are defined as :

$$Gi = Xi \cdot Yi$$
$$Pi = Xi + Yi$$

- The carry bit c-out(i) generated when adding two bits Xi and Yi is '1' if the corresponding function Gi is '1' or if the C-out (i-1) = '1' and the function Pi = '1' simultaneously. In the first case, the carry bit is activated by the local conditions (the values for Xi and Yi).

- In the second, the carry bit is received from the less significant elementary addition and is propagated further to the more significant elementary addition. Therefore, the carry out bit corresponding to a pair of bits Xi and Yi is calculated according to the equation :

$$\text{carry\_out (i)} = G_i + P_i \cdot \text{carry\_in (i-1)}$$

- For a four-bit adder the carry-outs are calculated as follows

$$\text{carry\_out0} = G_0 + P_0 \cdot \text{carry\_in}_0$$

$$\text{carry\_out1} = G_1 + P_1 \cdot \text{carry\_out}_0 = G_1 + P_1 G_0 + P_1 P_0 \cdot \text{carry\_in}_0$$

$$\text{carry\_out2} = G_2 + P_2 G_1 + P_2 P_1 G_0 + P_2 P_1 P_0 \cdot \text{carry\_in}_0$$

$$\text{carry\_out3} = G_3 + P_3 G_2 + P_3 P_2 G_1 + P_3 P_2 P_1 G_0 + P_3 P_2 P_1 \cdot \text{carry\_in}_0$$

- The set of equations above are implemented by the circuit below and a complete adder with a look-ahead carry generator is next. The input singnals need to propagate through a maximum of 4 logic gate in such an adder as opposed to 8 and 12 logic gates.

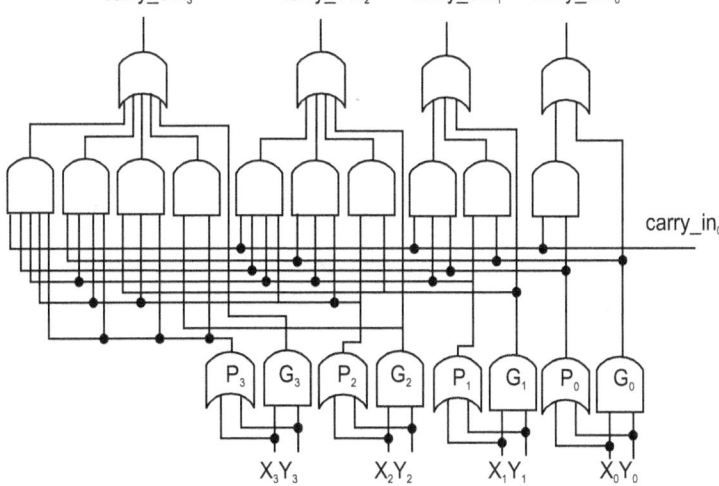

Fig.3.20: Carry look-ahead adder – carry output

- Sums can be calculated from the following equations, where carry_out is taken from the carry calculated in the above circuit.

$$\text{sum\_out}_0 = X_0 \oplus Y_0 \oplus \text{carry\_out}_0$$

$$\text{sum\_out}_1 = X_1 \oplus Y_1 \oplus \text{carry\_out}_1$$

$$\text{sum\_out}_2 = X_2 \oplus Y_2 \oplus \text{carry\_out}_2$$

$$\text{sum\_out}_3 = X_3 \oplus Y_3 \oplus \text{carry\_out}_3$$

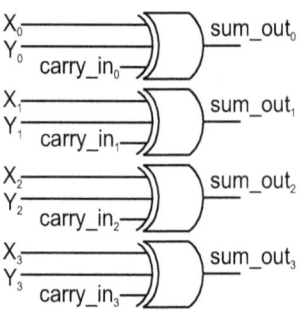

Fig. 3.21 : Carry look-ahead adder – sum output

3.12 BCD ADDER

Q. Explain with suitable example rules for BCD addition and design 1-digit BCD adder using IC 74LS83. **[Dec. 05, 6 M]**

Q. Draw and explain the basic IC 7483. How will you make two digit BCD adder ? Explain the logic of the circuit. **[May 05, 8 M]**

Q. Draw and explain 4-bit BCD adder using IC 7483. Explain any two BCD addition operations.

Q. How to convert 4-bit binary adder to BCD adder ? Explain with the help of circuit diagram. **[Dec. 06, May 07, 6 M]**

Q. How will make 3-digit BCD adder using 4-bit binary adder as a basic building block ? Explain with the help of suitable diagram. **[May 08, 8 M]**

Q. Draw and explain 4-bit BCD adder using IC 7483. Also explain with reference to your design addition of $(9 + 5)_{BCD}$ and $(7 + 2)_{BCD}$. **[Dec. 10, 8 M]**

Q. Draw and explain 4-bit BCD adder using IC 7483. Also explain with example addition of numbers with carry. **[Dec. 12, 8 M]**

- The digital systems handle the decimal number is the form of binary coded decimal numbers (BCD) A BCD adder is a circuit that adds two BCD digits and produces a sum digit also in BCD.

To implement BCD adder we require

1. 4 bit binary adder for initial condition.
2. logic circuit to detect sum greater than 9 and one more 4-bit adder to add 0110_2 in the sum if sum is greater than g or carry is 1.

Table 3.8

Input				Output
S_3	S_2	S_1	S_0	Y
0	0	0	0	0
0	0	0	1	0
0	0	1	0	0
0	0	1	1	0
0	1	0	0	0
0	1	0	1	0
0	1	1	0	0
0	1	1	1	0
1	0	0	0	0
1	0	0	1	0
1	0	1	0	1
1	0	1	1	1
1	1	0	0	1
1	1	0	1	1
1	1	1	0	1
1	1	1	1	1

- BCD adders can be cascaded to add numbers several digits long by connecting the carry out of a stage to the carry in of the next stage.
- The logic circuit to detect sum greater than 9 can be determined by simplifying the Boolean expression of given truth table Y = 1 indicates sum is greater than 9 we can put one more term C_{out} in the above expression to check whether carry is one. It any one condition is satisfied we need to add (0110) in the sum.

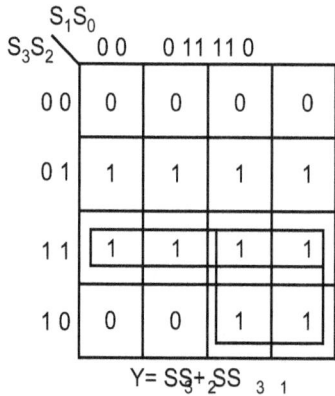

$Y = S_3S_2 + S_2S_1$

(a) K-map simplification

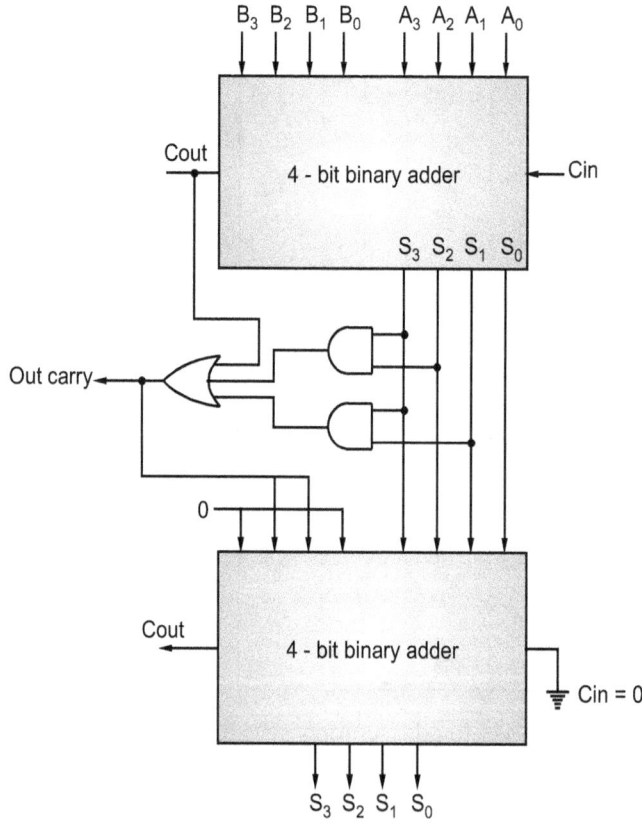

(b) Block diagram of BCD adder

Fig. 3.22

3.13 BCD SUBTRACTOR

- BCD subtraction can be performed using 9's and 10's complement.

3.13.1 BCD Subtraction using 9's Complement

The steps for 9's complement method :

- Find the 9's complement of negative number.
- Add two number using BCD addition.
- If carry is generated add carry to the result otherwise find 9's complement of the result.

Example 3.12 :

Subtract $(2)_{10}$ from $(7)_{10}$ in BCD.

Step 1 : Obtain 9's complement of $(2)_{10}$

$$\begin{array}{r} 9 \\ -\ 2 \\ \hline 7 \end{array}$$

Step 2 : Add 7 into 9's complement of 3.

```
              7
           + 7      ...9's complement of 2
          -----
end around... 1 4    ...sum
           + 1      ...add carry
          -----
              5     ...final result
```

3.13.2 BCD Subtractor using 9's Complement Method

Q. Draw and explain 4-bit BCD subtractor using IC 7483.

Q. What is the use of 7483 chip ? Draw and explain 9's complement used in BCD subtractor using 7483.

DIGITAL ELECTRONICS LOGIC DESIGN (S.E. COMP.)   COMBINATIONAL LOGIC

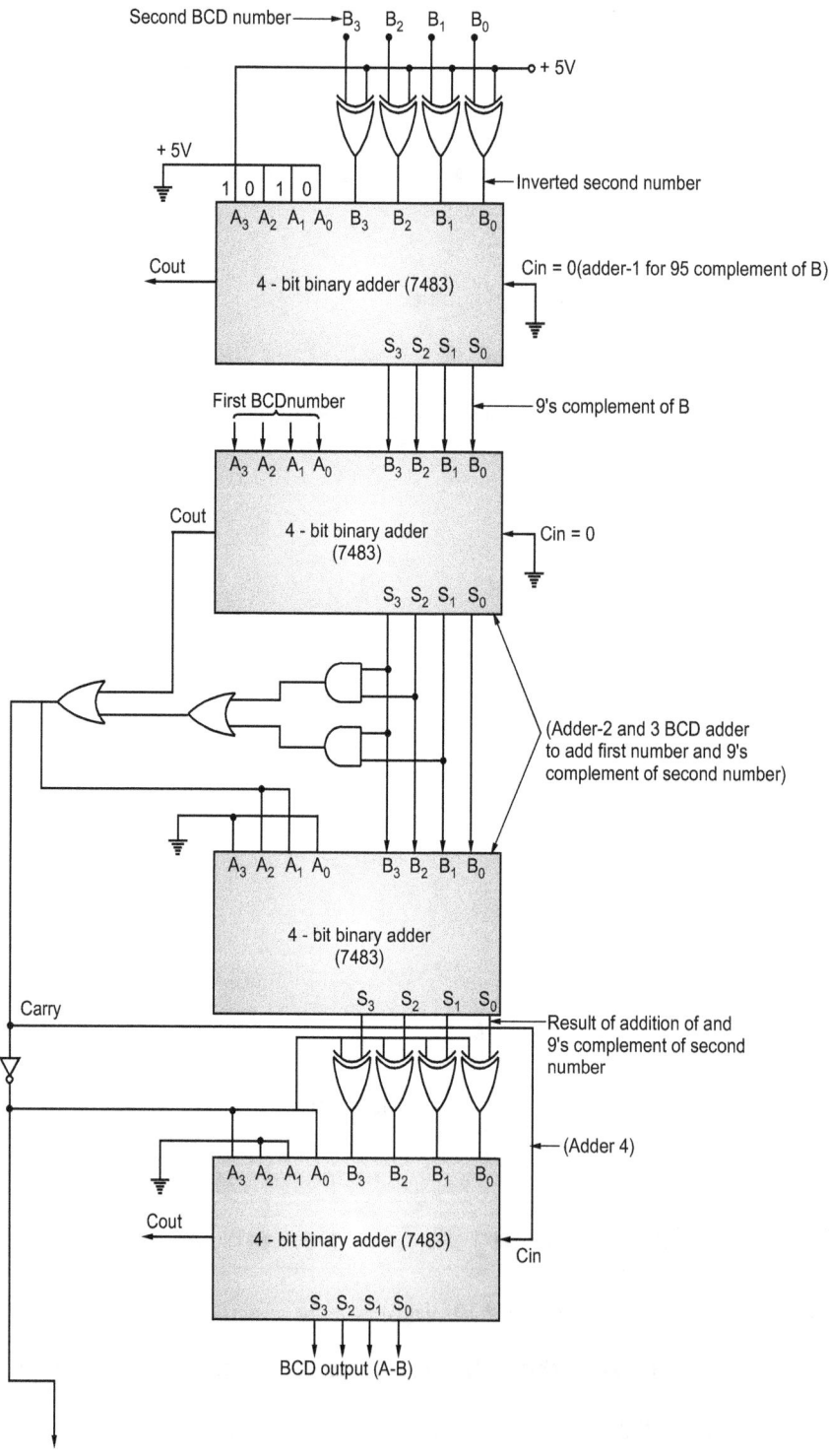

Fig. 3.23

Fig. 3.23 shows the circuit diagram of 4-bit BCD subtractor. It consists of four binary parallel adder (IC 7483).
- Adder 1 is to obtains the 9's complement of second number.
- Adder 2 and 3 are used for the normal 4-bit BCD adder with a facility to add 6 for correction.
- Adder 2 adds the first number with the 9's complement of second number B and adder 3 will correct the sum by adding six (0110) if necessary.
- The output of combinational circuit is used further as a carry. At the output of adder – 3 we get the correct BCD sum of first number and as complement of second number.
- Adder – 4 is used to either add 1 to the output of adder – 3 or take the 9's complement of the output of adder – 3 depending on the status of carry.
- If carry = 1 ; then add 1 to the sum output of adders
  If carry = 0; take as complement of sum output of adder 3.

3.13.3 BCD Subtraction using 10's Complement

The 10's complement is obtained by adding 1 to the 9's complement
Steps for 10's complement BCD subtraction given below :
- Obtain the 10's complement of second number
- Add first number with 10's complement of second number.
- Discard is card carry. If carry is 1 then the answer is positive and in its true form
- If carry is not produced the answer is negative so take 10's complement to get final answer.

Example 3.13 : Perform the subtraction $(9)_{10} - (4)_{10}$ in BCD using the 10's complement.

Step 1 : Obtain the 10's complement of $(4)_{10}$

$$\begin{array}{r} 9 \\ -4 \\ \hline 5 \\ +1 \\ \hline 6 \end{array} \quad \text{...9's complement}$$

...10's complement

Step 2 : Add $(9)_{10}$ and 10's complement of second number

$$(9)_{10} \rightarrow \quad 1001$$
$$(6)_{10} \rightarrow \quad 0110$$
$$\overline{\quad\quad\quad\quad 1111} \leftarrow \text{invalid BCD number}$$

Step 3 : add $(6)_{10}$ to invalid BCD number

$$\begin{array}{r} 1111 \\ 0110 \\ \hline \end{array}$$

Discard final carry → $\boxed{1}\;0101$ ← true BCD form

3.13.4 4-bit BCD Subtraction using 10's Complement Method

Q. Draw and explain 4-bit BCD subtractor using IC 7483.

DIGITAL ELECTRONICS LOGIC DESIGN (S.E. COMP.) — COMBINATIONAL LOGIC

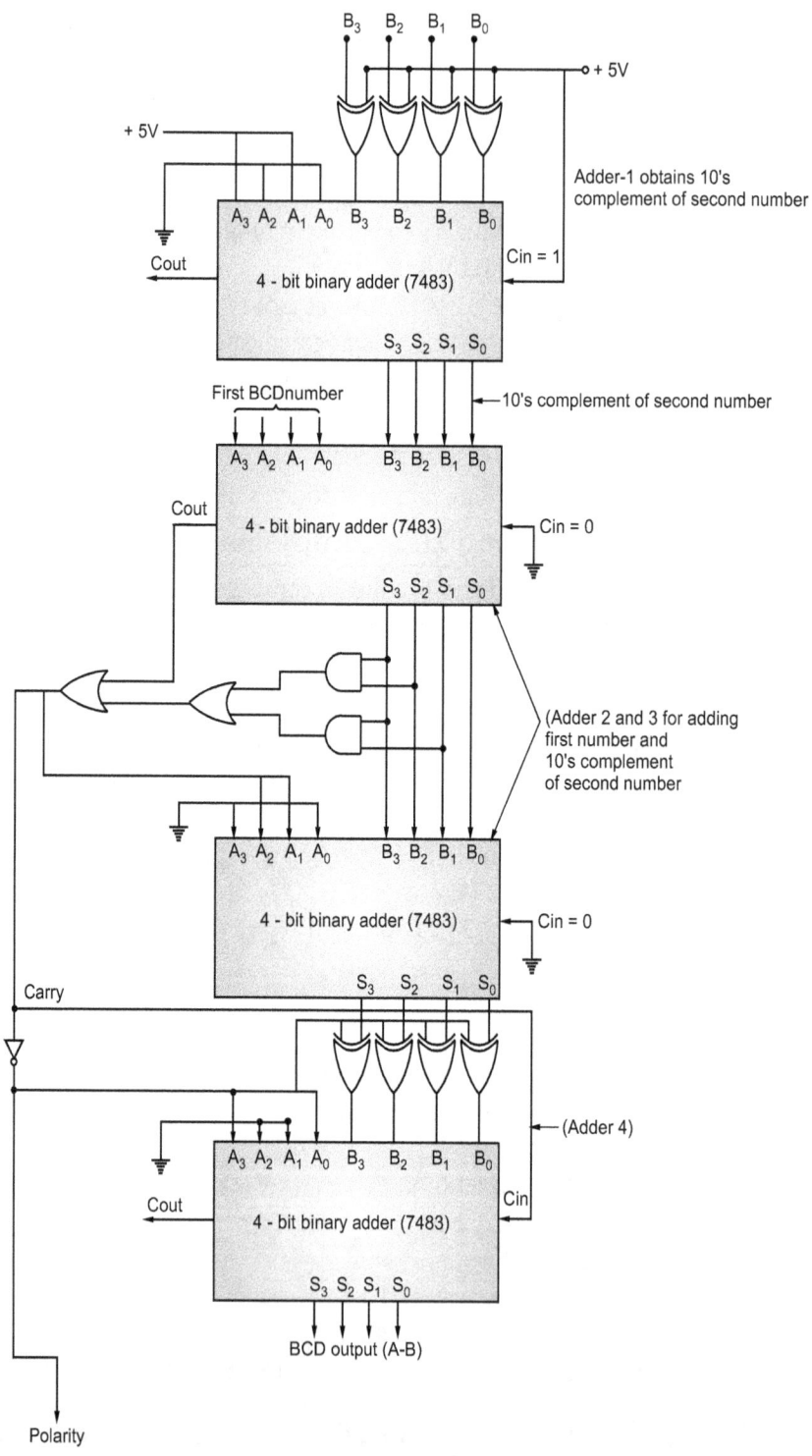

Fig. 3.24

The circuit consist of 4 adders. (See Fig. 3.24)

1. Adder 1 :

Performs the 10's complement of second number. The second numbers inverted using the EX-OR gates and then $C_{in} = 1$ is added to it to obtain 2's complement of second number.

- $A_3\ A_2\ A_1\ A_0 = 1010$ i.e. $(10)_{10}$ adder 1 adds 1010 and 2's complement of number B. i.e. adder 1 performs subtraction to obtain 10's complement of B.
- In that way we get 10's complement of second number.

2. Adder 2 and 3 :

- Adder 2 and 3 together forms the addition of BCD number. Adder 2 adds number A to 10's complement of B.
- If the correction is necessary adder 3 adds 6 (0110) to BCD answer.
- The output of the combinational circuit is treated as a carry and it passed to adder 4.

3. Adder 4 :

- If carry = 0 then due to inverter used $A_3\ A_2\ A_1\ A_0 = 1010$ i.e. $C(10)_{10}$ and carry input $C_{in} = 1$. Also the EXOR gates will acts as inverter.
- It carry = 1 then adder 4 will pass the adder – 3 output unchanged.

3.14 Parity Generator and Checker

Q. Explain the significance of parity bit. [May 07, 2 M]

Parity bit is an extra bit included along with the binary information to detect the errors which might occur during the transmission of the binary information. The combinational logic circuits which generate the parity bit (either even or odd) is called as **'parity generator'**. The total number of ones in the binary information is either even (if even parity generator is used) or odd (if odd parity generator is used). Parity generator circuit is used at the transmission side of the communication channel.

At the receiving end of the communication channel 'parity checker' circuit is used to check the parity of the received information. Parity checker circuit detects whether the received message is corrupted i.e. whether it has error.

IC 74180 is a popular nine input parity generator/checker. It can be used as a parity generator or checker. Its block representation is shown in Fig. 3.25 below :

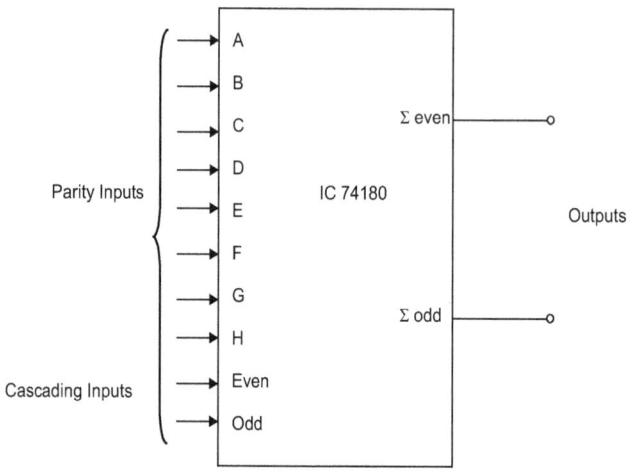

Fig. 3.25

The truth table for IC74180 is given below :

Parity inputs	Cascading Inputs		Outputs	
	Even	Odd	Even	Odd
Even	1	0	1	0
Odd	1	0	0	1
Even	0	1	0	1
Odd	0	1	1	0
X	1	1	1	0
X	0	0	0	0

The working of IC 74180 can be explained with the help of following input conditions.

(a) User wants even parity coding in the message :

\# Therefore cascading input, "even" should be '1'

\# If the number of 1's in the input message i.e. in parity inputs (A to H) is even then the IC 74180 will generate a '1' output at it's "Σ even" terminal.

\# If the number of 1's in the input message (A - H) is odd then the IC 74180 will generate a '1' output at its "Σ even" terminal.

(b) User wants odd parity coding in the message :

\# Therefore cascading input, "odd" should be '1'.

\# If the number of 1's in the input message i.e. in parity inputs (A–H) is even then the IC 74180 will generate a '1' at it's "Σ even" terminal output.

If the number of 1's in the input message i.e. in parity inputs (A–H) is odd then the IC74180 will generate a '1' output at its "Σ even" terminal.

A golden rule to understand the working of IC74180 is

Number of 1's in parity inputs (A to H)	Cascading input	Output
Even e.g. (01101100)	'Even' is set to '1'	'Σeven' output will be set '1'
Odd e.g. (00010000)	'Odd' is set to '1'	'Σeven' output will be set '1'
Odd e.g. (01100010)	'Even' is set to '1'	'Σodd' output will be set '1'
Even e.g. (11111111)	'Odd' is set to '1'	'Σodd' output will be set '1'

Example 3.14 :
Design a 9-bit odd parity generator using IC 74180.

Solution :
Since the user wants odd parity generator hence the cascading input 'odd' should be set to '1' and 'even' input should be reset to '0'.

The logic diagram for 9-bit odd parity generator using IC74180 is shown in Fig. 3.26 below :

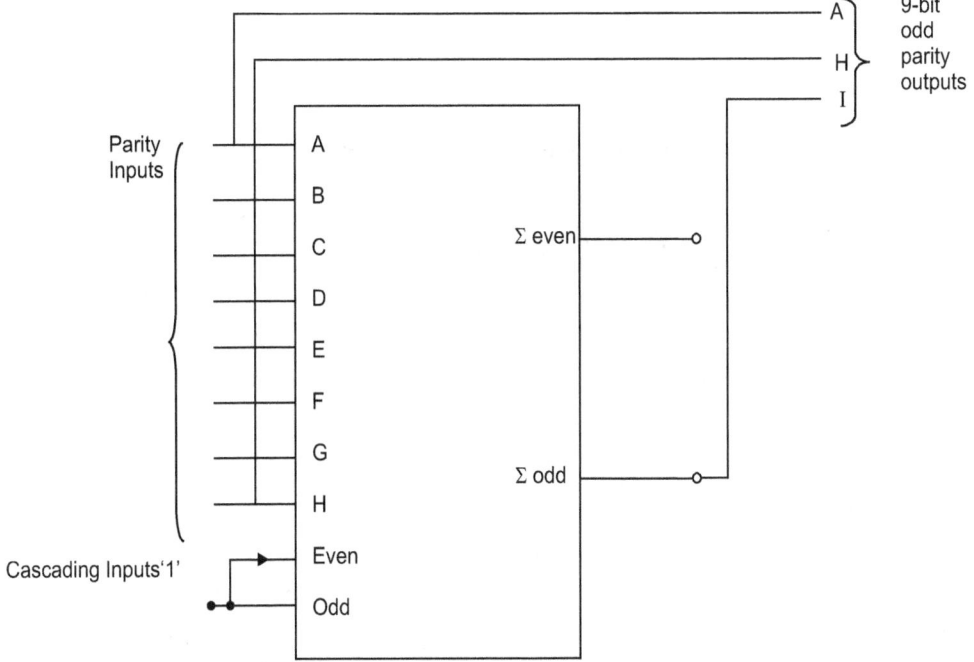

Fig. 3.26 : 9-bit odd parity generator

If the number of 1's in parity inputs (A – H) is even then the output 'Σodd' will be '1'. Thus, total number of 1's in the 9-bit outputs (A – I) will be odd.

If the number of 1's in parity inputs (A – H) is odd then the output 'Σodd' will be '0'. Thus, again total number of 1's in the 9-bit outputs (A – I) will be odd.

Example 3.15 :
Design a 9-bit even parity checker using IC 74180.
Solution :
Since the user wants even parity checker the cascading input 'even' will be connected to 'I' and the cascading input 'odd' will be connected to 'I'.

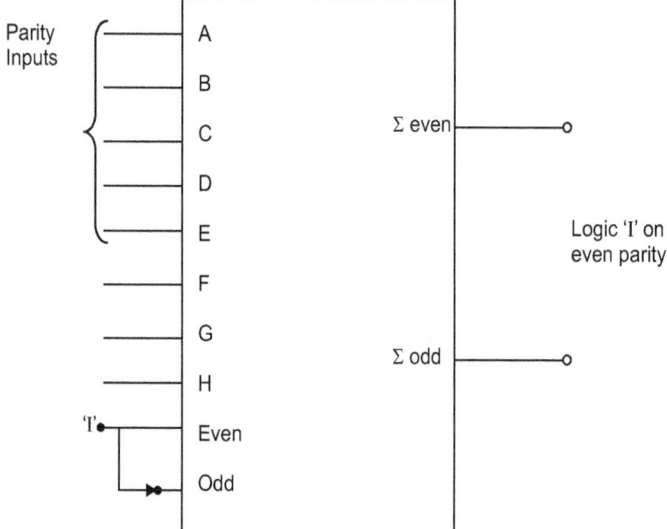

Fig. 3.27 : 9-bit Even Parity Checker

3.15 MAGNITUDE COMPARATORS

As well as comparing individual bits, multi – bit comparators can be constructed to compare whole binary or BCD words to produce an output if one word is larger, equal to or less than the other. A very good example of this is the 4 - bit **Magnitude Comparator.** Here, two 4 - bit words ("nibbles") are compared to produce the relevent output with one word connected to inputs A and the other to be compared against connected to input B as shown below.

4 - bit Magnitude Comparator :

Some commercially available Magnitude Comparators such as the 7485 have additional input terminals that allow more individual comparators to be "cascaded" together to compare words larger than 4 - bits with magnitude comparators of "n" - bits being produced. These cascading inputs are connected directly to the corresponding outputs of the previous comparator as shown to compare 8, 16 or even 32 - bit words.

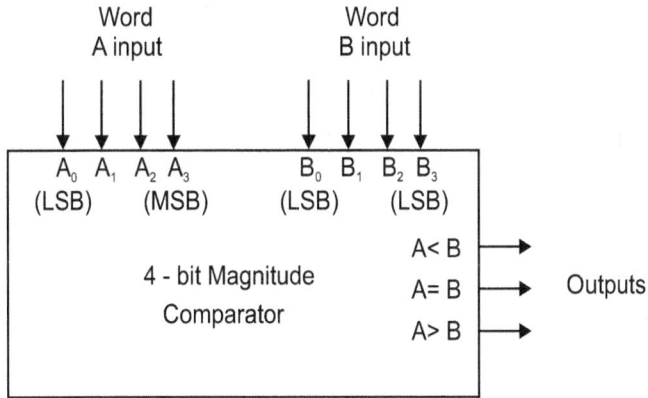

Fig. 3.28 : 4-bit Magnitude Comparator

8 - bit Word Comparator :

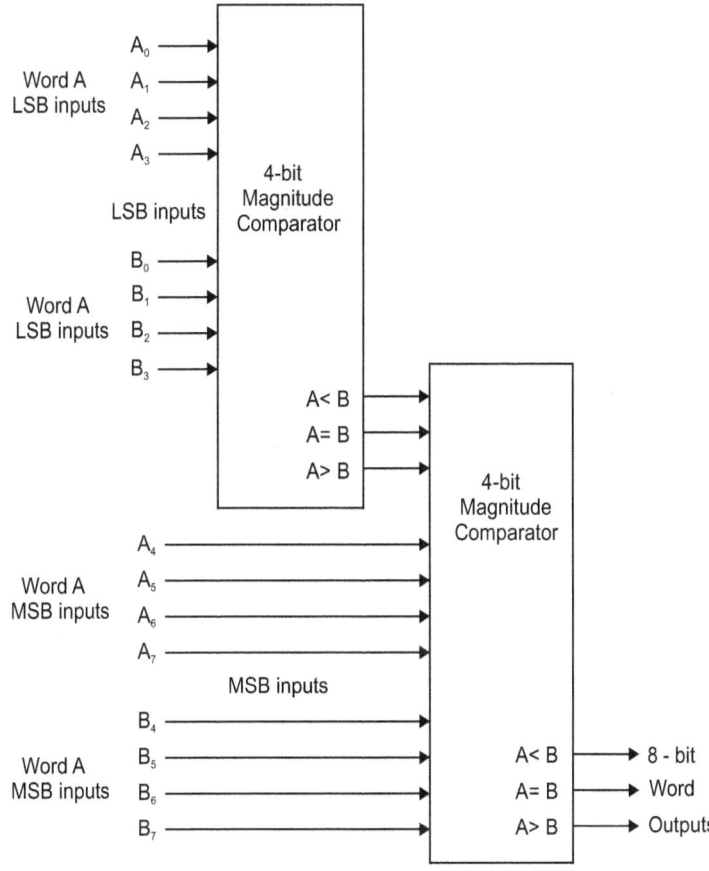

Fig. 3.29 : 8-bit word comparator

3.16 MULTIPLEXERS

Q. Design 16 : 1 multiplexer using 4 : 1 multiplexers. **[May 11, 8 M]**
Q. Design 14 : 1 mux using 4 : 1 mux (with enable input) **[May 10, 11, 8 M]**
Q. Design 28 : 1 mux using 8 : 1 mux. **[Dec. 10, 8 M]**
Q. Implement the following expression using 8 : 1 multiplexer.
  $f(A, B, C, D) = \Sigma m (2, 4, 6, 7, 9, 10, 11, 12, 15)$

- The literal meaning of word 'multiplex' is 'many into one'. A multiplexer circuit may have several inputs and only one output.
- Multiplexer is a special combinational logic circuit which accepts many inputs and allows only one of them to get through to the output at any instance of time.
- Therefore, multiplexer output is a particular data input which is selected with the help of control signal called 'select'.
- Multiplexers are important block of many important digital circuits such as microprocessor and microcontroller. The symbolic representation of multiplexer is shown in Fig. 3.30.

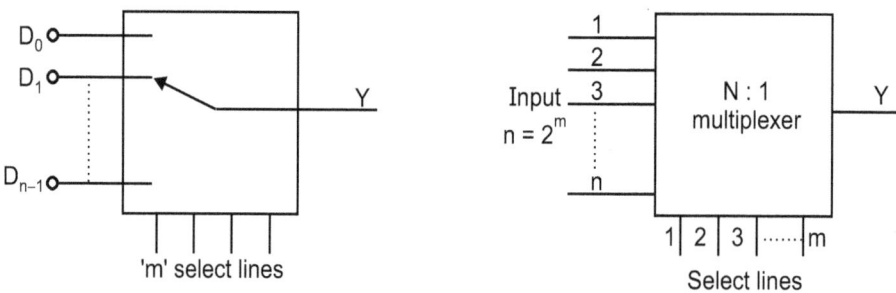

Fig. 3.30 : Symbolic representation of N : 1 multiplexer

2 : 1 Multiplexer :

- There are two data inputs D_0 and D_1 in 2 : 1 multiplexer.
- It has only one output. The number of select lines (m) is equal to 1.
- Every multiplexer has one more additional input called 'Enable' or 'Strobe' which is an active low input. This input is always kept at ground potential or logic '0'.
- Table shows truth table and logic circuit diagram of 2 : 1 multiplexer.

Table 3.9 : Truth Table of 2 : 1 multiplexer

S_0	Y
0	D_0
1	D_1

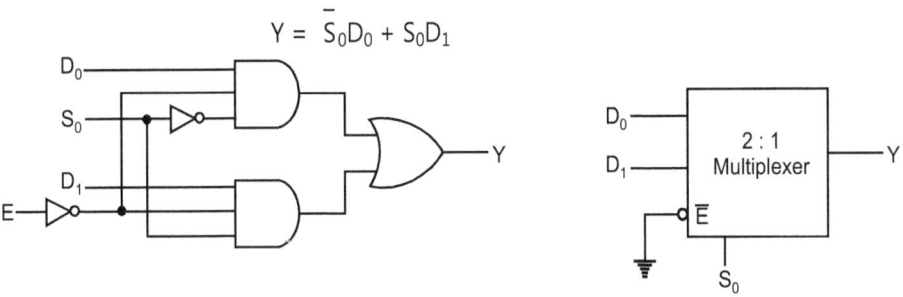

Fig. 3.31 : Logic circuit of 2 : 1 multiplexer   Fig. 3.32 : Logic symbol of 2 : 1 mux.

4 : 1 Multiplexer :

- 4 : 1 Multiplexer circuit has four data inputs and one output.
- The number of select lines required to control four data inputs is two.
- These two select lines are called S_0 and S_1.
- The Boolean expression for Y output is,

$$Y_1 = \bar{S_1}\bar{S_0}D_0 + \bar{S_1}S_0D_1 + S_1\bar{S_0}D_2 + S_1S_0D_3$$

Table shows truth table and logic circuit diagram of 4 : 1 multiplexer.

Table 3.10 : Truth table of 4 : 1 multiplexer

Inputs		Output
S_1	S_0	Y
0	0	D_0
0	1	D_1
1	0	D_2
1	1	D_3

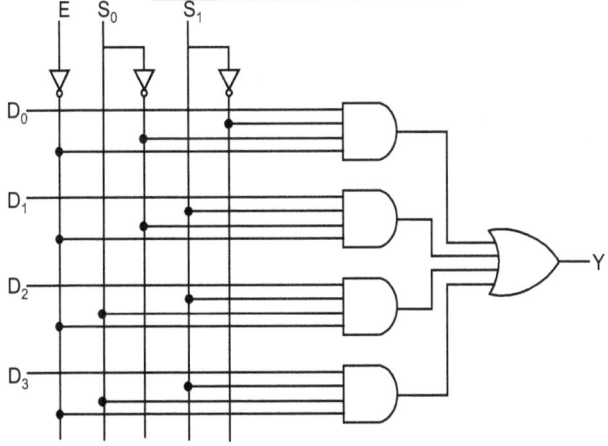

Fig. 3.33 (a) : Logic Circuit Diagram of 4 : 1 Multiplexer

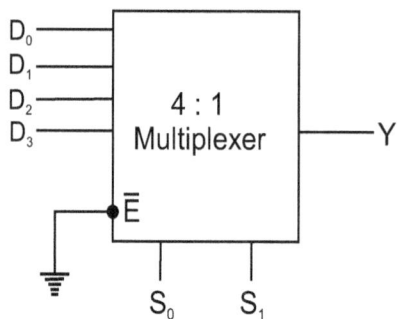

Fig. 3.33 (b) : Logic block diagram of 4 : 1 multiplexer

Multiplexer ICs

- The list of popular and commercially available multiplexer ICs.

Table 3.11

IC No.	Description	Output/Input
74150	16 : 1 Multiplexer	Inverted input
74151A	8 : 1 Multiplexer	Complementary output
74152	8 : 1 Multiplexer	Inverted input
74153	Dual 4 : 1 Multiplexer	Same as input
74157	Quad 2 : 1 Multiplexer	Same as input
74158	Quad 2 : 1 Multiplexer	Inverted input
74352	Dual 4 : 1 Multiplexer	Inverted input

Multiplexer Tree :

Fig. 3.34 shows design of 8 : 1 multiplexer using two 4 : 1 multiplexers and one 2 : 1 multiplexer.

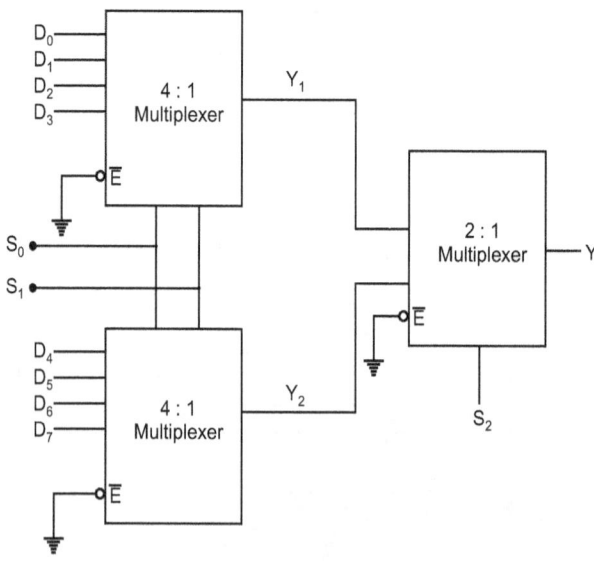

Fig. 3.34 : 8 : 1 multiplexer

3.16.1 IC 74153 Dual 4 to 1 multiplexer

IC 74153 is dual 4 to 1 multiplexer fig. 3.3 shows the symbol of IC 74153. It contains two identical and independent 4 to 1 multiplexers. Each multiplexer has separate enable inputs. The table 3.12 shows the truth table for IC 74153.

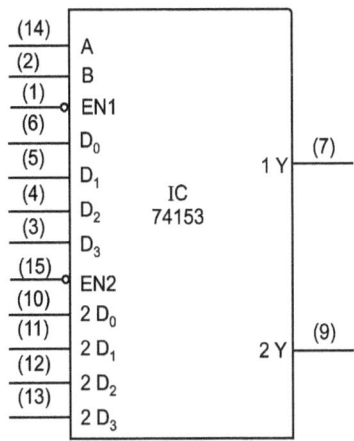

Fig. 3.35 : Logic symbol for 74153

Table : 3.12 Truth table for (74153 dual multiplexer)

Inputs				outputs	
EN1	EN2	B	A	Y	2Y
0	0	0	0	D_0	D_0
0	0	0	1	D_1	D_1
0	0	1	0	D_2	D_2
0	0	1	1	D_3	D_3
0	1	0	0	D_0	0
0	1	0	1	D_1	0
0	1	1	0	D_2	0
0	1	1	1	D_3	0
1	0	0	0	0	D_0
1	0	0	1	0	D_1
1	0	1	0	0	D_2
1	0	1	1	0	D_3
1	1	X	X	0	0

3.16.2 IC 74151 Multiplexer

IC 74151 is a 8 to 1 multiplexer. It has eight inputs. It provides two outputs one is active high and other is active low. Fig. 3.36 shows the logic symbol for IC 74151. As shown in the logic symbol there are three select inputs C,B and which select one of the eight inputs. IC 74151 is provided with active low enble input.

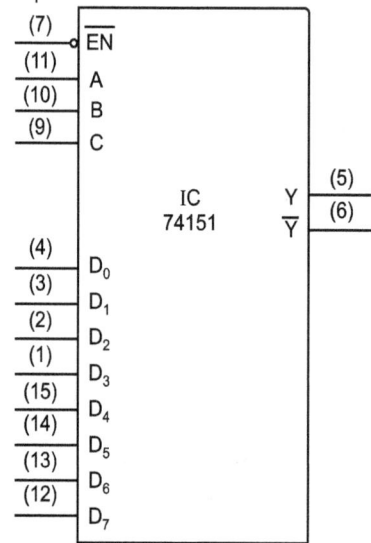

Fig. 3.36 : Logic symbol for 74151 8 to 1 multiplexer.

The truth table 3.13 shown below.

Table 3.13

Input Select			Enable	Outputs	
C	B	A	$\overline{EN}$	Y	$\overline{Y}$
X	X	X	1	0	1
0	0	0	0	D_0	$\overline{D_0}$
0	0	1	0	D_1	$\overline{D_1}$
0	1	0	0	D_2	$\overline{D_2}$
0	1	1	0	D_3	$\overline{D_3}$
1	0	0	0	D_4	$\overline{D_4}$
1	0	1	0	D_5	$\overline{D_5}$
1	1	0	0	D_6	$\overline{D_6}$
1	1	1	0	D_7	$\overline{D_7}$

Example 3.16 :

Implement the following expression using a multiplexer

(a) $\qquad Y = \Sigma m (0, 1, 2, 6, 7)$.

Solution :

Given : Boolean expression is,

$$Y (A, B, C) = \Sigma m (0, 1, 2, 6, 7)$$

It is a three-variable Boolean function and hence a multiplexer will require three select inputs. The inputs of multiplexer corresponding to given minterms are connected to V_{CC}. Other inputs are grounded.

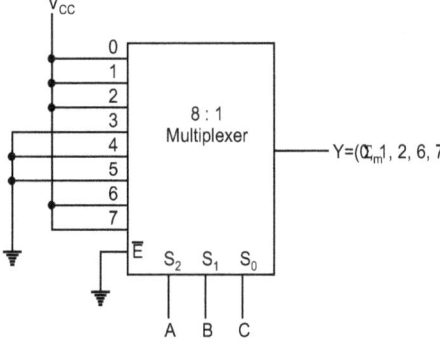

Fig. 3.37

Application of Multiplexer

- They are used in time multiplexing system.
- They are used infrequency multiplexing systems.
- It is also used implement combinational logic circuit.
- They are used in data acquisition systems.

Example 3.17 : Implement the following expression using a multiplexer

$$Y (A, B, C) = \pi M (0, 1, 4, 5)$$

Solution : Given Boolean function is a three variable function expressed in terms of maxterms.

The inputs of multiplexer corresponding to given maxterms are connected to ground and other inputs are connected to Vcc. The enable input is grounded.

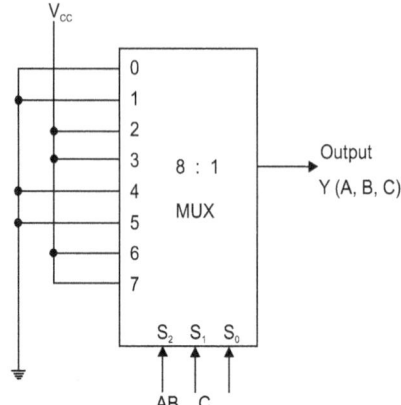

Fig. 3.38 : Multiplexer based circuit design

Example 3.18 :

Implement the following Boolean expression $Y = (A + B)(\bar{A} + B + C)(A + \bar{B})$ using multiplexer

Solution : Convert the given Boolean expression into standard POS form

$$\therefore \quad Y = (A + B + C\bar{C})(\bar{A} + B + C)(A + \bar{B} + C\bar{C})$$
$$= (A + B + C)$$

$$(A + B + \bar{C})(\bar{A} + B + C)(A + \bar{B} + C)(A + \bar{B} + \bar{C})$$

But
$$A + B + C = 000 = 0$$
$$A + B + \bar{C} = 001 = 1$$
$$\bar{A} + B + C = 100 = 4$$
$$A + \bar{B} + C = 010 = 2$$
$$A + \bar{B} + \bar{C} = 011 = 3$$

∴ The Boolean expression becomes $Y(A, B, C) = \pi M (0, 1, 2, 3, 4)$

Therefore, the inputs corresponding to given maxterms are connected to ground. Other inputs are connected to Vcc. The enable pin is grounded.

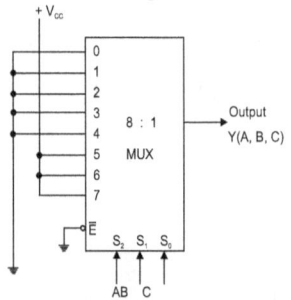

Fig. 3.39

Example 3.19 :

Implement following using multiplexer
(a) Half-adder
(b) Half-subtractor

Solution :

(a) Half - adder : The truth table for half adder is given below

Inputs		Outputs	
A	B	S	C
0	0	0	0
0	1	1	0
1	0	1	0
1	1	0	1

Therefore, Boolean expressions for the outputs are;

$$\text{Sum (A, B)} = \Sigma m (1, 2)$$
$$\text{Carry (A, B)} = \Sigma m (3)$$

Hence the logic diagram of half adder using two 4 : 1 multiplexers is;

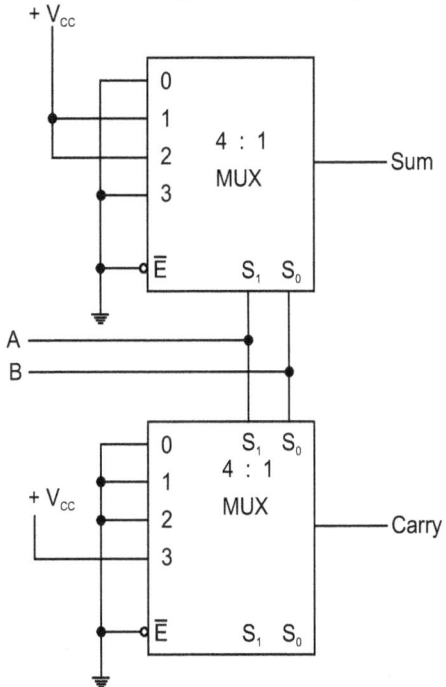

Fig. 3.40 : Half-adder using 4 : 1 multiplexer

(b) Half-Subtractor : The truth table for half subtractor is

Inputs		Outputs	
A	B	S	C
0	0	0	0
0	1	1	1
1	0	1	0
1	1	0	0

The Boolean expressions are

$\therefore$ D (A, B) = Σ m (1, 2)

C (A, B) = Σ m (1)

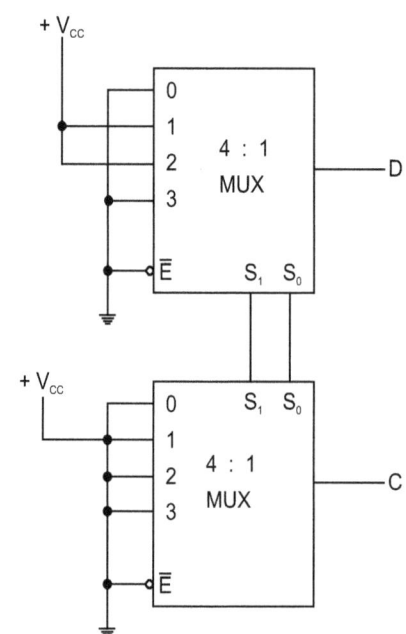

Fig. 3.41 : Half Subtractor using 4 : 1 Multiplexer

3.17 DEMULTIPLEXER

Q. Implement the following functions using demultiplexer.

f_1 (A, B, C) = Σm (1, 5, 7) , f_2 (A, B, C) = Σm (3, 6, 7)

Q. Implement two bit comparator using 1 : 16 demultiplexer (active low output). Draw the truth table of two bit comparator. **[Dec. 11, 8 M]**

- Demultiplexer is a combinational logic circuit having one input and several outputs.

- Demultiplexer means 'One into many'.

- It accepts a single input and sends it to one of the output lines.
- The output line is selected by control or select signals. For n-output demultiplexer, number of select lines is m, where $n = 2^m$.
- Fig. 3.42 depicts 1 : n demultiplexer.

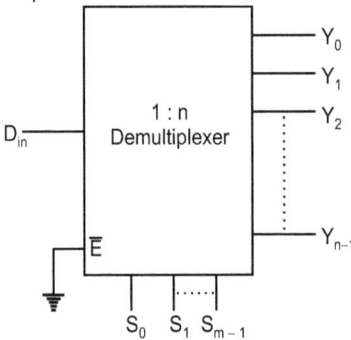

Fig. 3.42 : Block Diagram of 1 : n Demultiplexer

- This 1 : n demultiplexer is also known as binary-to-decimal decoder with binary inputs applied at the select lines, and the decoded output will be obtained on the output line.
- Consider an example 1 : 4 demultiplexer.
- The number of select input lines is 2.
- The truth table of 1 : 4 demultiplexer is given below :

Table 3.14

Select Inputs		Outputs			
S_0	S_1	Y_0	Y_1	Y_2	Y_3
0	0	1	0	0	0
0	1	0	1	0	0
1	0	0	0	1	0
1	1	0	0	0	1

- The logic expression for different outputs can be written as,

$$Y_0 = \bar{S_0}\bar{S_1},\ Y_1 = \bar{S_0}S_1,\ Y_2 = S_0\bar{S_1},\ Y_3 = S_0 S_1$$

- The logic circuit diagram of 1 : 4 demultiplexer is shown in Fig. 3.43.

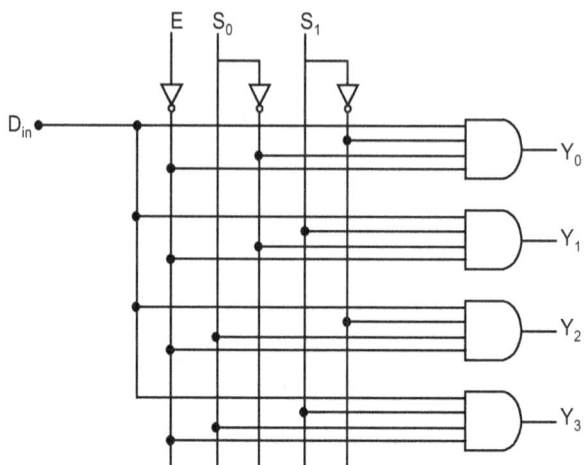

Fig. 3.43 : 1 : 4 Demultiplexer

Demultiplexer Tree :

- Demultiplexer tree can be built hierarchically by lower hierarchial demultiplexer.
- Many commercially available demultiplexer ICs are listed below.

IC	Description	Output/Input
74139	Dual 1 : 4	Inverted input
74138	Dual 1 : 8	Inverted input
74154	Dual 1 : 16	Same as input

- Let us consider example of implementing 1 : 8 demultiplexer using two 1 : 4 demultiplexers.

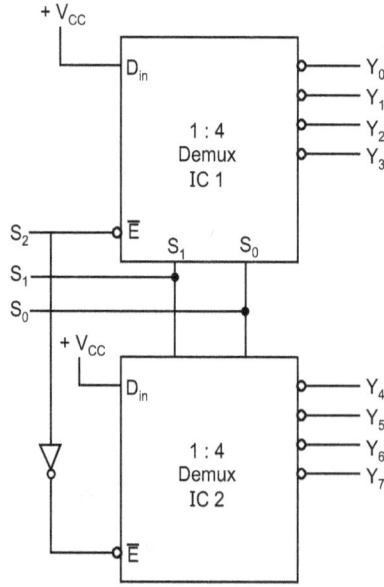

Fig. 3.45 : 1 : 8 Demultiplexer

- Note that 1 : 4 demultiplexer has inverted output. Whenever S_2 is logic '0', the IC_1 is selected and IC_2 is disabled. Depending upon the status of S_1 and S_0 lines the data in will be fed to one of the outputs Y_0, Y_1, Y_2 or Y_3.
- To send the output on Y_4 or Y_5 or Y_6 or Y_7 line, the status of pin S_2 is to be made high. Based on the logic status of S_0 and S_1 the data in will be fed to corresponding output line.
- The truth table of the above 1 : 8 multiplexer circuit having initial inverted input is given below.

Example 3.20 : Implement the following function using demultiplexer :

$$f_1 (A, B, C) = \Sigma m (0, 3, 7)$$
$$f_2 (A, B, C) = \Sigma m (1, 2, 5)$$

It can be implemented using 1 : 8 Demux.

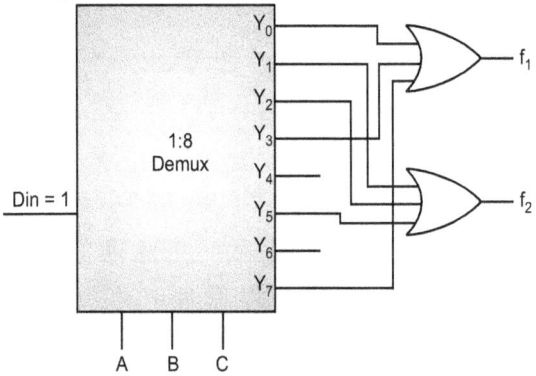

Fig. 3.45

Example 3.21 :
Design full - adder using 3 : 8 decoder
Solution : The truth table of full - adder is

Inputs			Outputs	
A	B	C_{n-1}	S_n	C_n
0	0	0	0	0
0	0	1	1	0
0	1	0	1	0
0	1	1	0	1
1	0	0	1	0
1	0	1	0	1
1	1	0	0	1
1	1	1	1	1

Therefore, the expressions for S_n and C_n are

$$S_n = \Sigma m (1, 2, 4, 7)$$
$$C_n = \Sigma m (3, 5, 6, 7)$$

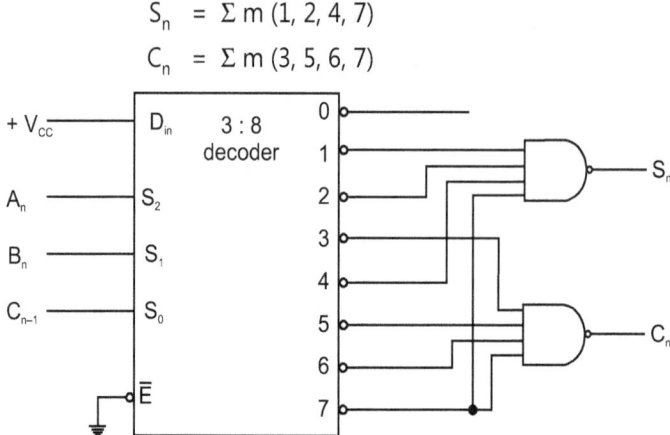

Fig. 3.46 : Full-adder using 3 : 8 decoder

3.18 DECODER

Q. Design and Implement a full adder circuit using 3 : 8 decoder. **[May 11, Dec. 11, 4 M]**
Q. Implement the logic circuit for full subtractor using decoder. **[May 10, Dec. 10, 4 M]**
Q. Explain decoder (1 : 8) as a binary to gray code converter. **[May 11, 8 M]**

- A decoder is multiple input, multiple output logic circuit which converts coded inputs into coded outputs, where the input and output codes are different.

Fig. 3.47 shows the structure of the decoder circuit.

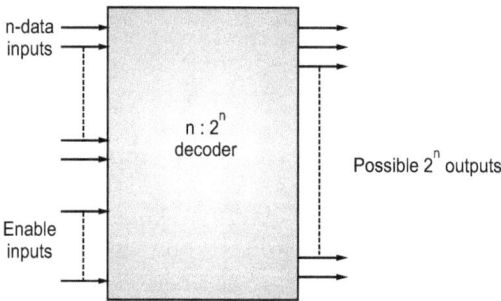

Fig. 3.47 : Structure of decoder

- As shown in Fig. 3.47 the encoded information is presented as n inputs producing 2^n possible outputs. The 2^n output values are from 0 through $2^n - 1$.
- A decoder is provided with enable inputs to activate decoded output based on data inputs. When any one enable input is unasserted, all outputs of decoder are disabled.

Table 3.15

Inputs			Selected IC	Outputs							
S_2	S_1	S_0		Y_7	Y_6	Y_5	Y_4	Y_3	Y_2	Y_1	Y_0
0	0	0	IC1	1	1	1	1	1	1	1	0
0	0	1	IC1	1	1	1	1	1	1	0	1
0	1	0	IC1	1	1	1	1	1	0	1	1
0	1	1	IC1	1	1	1	1	0	1	1	1
1	0	0	IC2	1	1	1	0	1	1	1	1
1	0	1	IC2	1	1	0	1	1	1	1	1
1	1	0	IC2	1	0	1	1	1	1	1	1
1	1	1	IC2	0	1	1	1	1	1	1	1

Example 3.22 :

Design 1 : 16 demultiplexer using

(a) 1 : 8 demultiplexer

(b) 1 : 4 demultiplexer

Solution : 1 : 8 demultiplexer is also known as 3 : 8 decolder. The MSB input S_3 of 4 - bit input i.e. S_3 S_2 S_1 S_0 is used to select one of these two 3 : 8 decoders. S_3 is connected to enable pin.

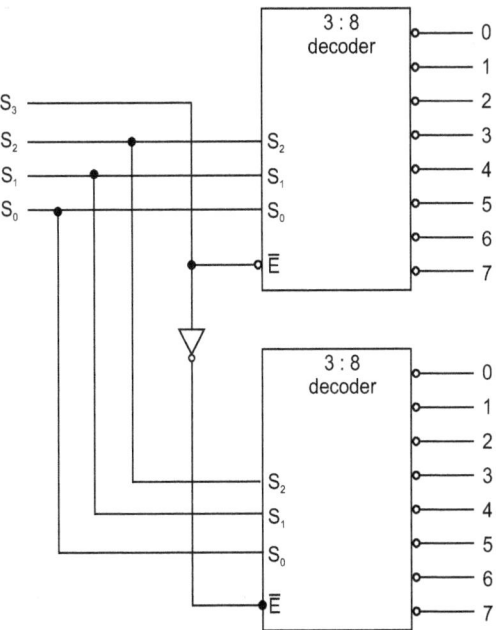

Fig. 3.48 : Demultiplexer using two 1 : 8 demultiplexers

(b)

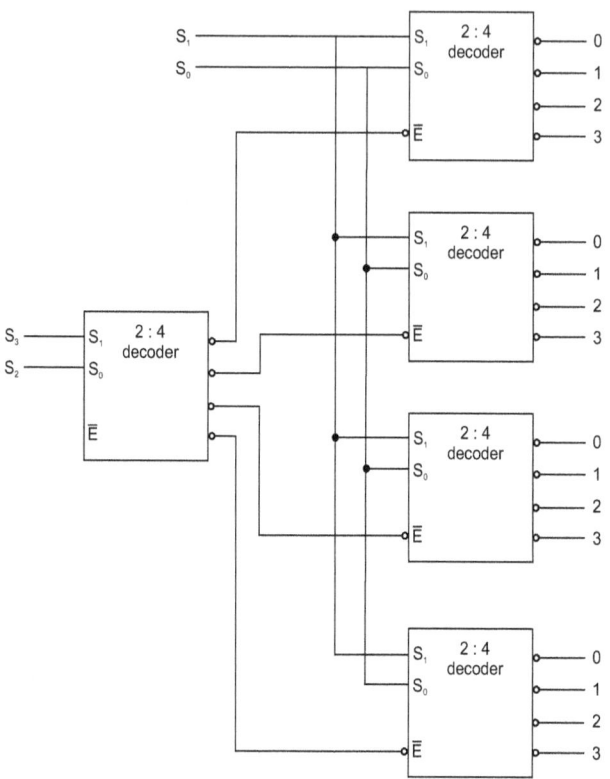

Fig. 3.49

Example 3.23 :

(a) Implement the following using 3 : 8 decoder

$$Y_0 (A, B, C) = \Sigma m (0, 1, 2, 4)$$
$$Y_1 (A, B, C) = \Sigma m (1, 3, 5, 7)$$
$$Y_2 (A, B, C) = \Sigma m (4, 5, 6, 7)$$

(b) Design some using NAND gates

Solution :

(a) Since the expressions for Y are in terms of minterms, we use OR gates. Because the outputs of decoder are active low, the inputs to OR gates are inverted.

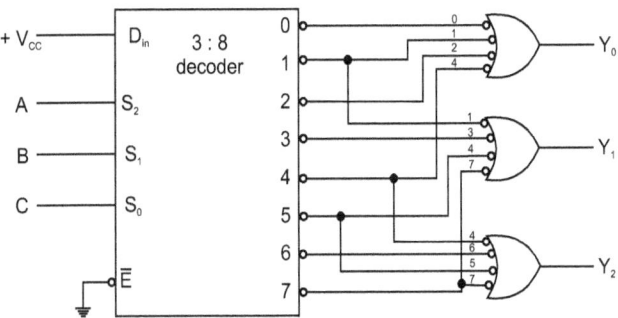

Fig. 3.50

(b) Inverted input OR gate is equivalent to NAND gate.

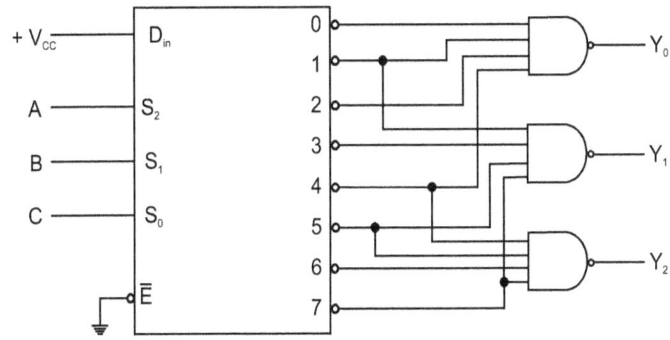

Fig 3.51

3.18.1 IC 74138 (3 :8 decoder)

IC 74138 is commercial IC for 3 to 8 decoder. It accepts three binary inputs (A, B and C) and when enabled provides eight individual active low outputs (Y_0-Y_7). The device has three enable inputs two active low ($\overline{G_2}$, $\overline{G_3}$) and one active high (G_1). Fig. 3.52 shows logic symbol of 74138 and function table also shown in table 3.16.

Inputs						Outputs							
G_3	G_2	G_1	C	B	A	$\overline{Y_7}$	$\overline{Y_6}$	$\overline{Y_5}$	$\overline{Y_4}$	$\overline{Y_3}$	$\overline{Y_2}$	$\overline{Y_1}$	$\overline{Y_0}$
1	X	X	X	X	X	1	1	1	1	1	01	1	1
X	1	X	X	X	X	1	1	1	1	1	1	1	1
X	1	0	X	X	X	1	1	1	1	1	1	1	1
0	0	1	0	0	0	1	1	1	1	1	1	1	0

0	0	1	0	0	1	1	1	1	1	1	1	1	0	1
0	0	1	0	1	0	1	1	1	1	1	1	0	1	1
0	0	1	0	1	1	1	1	1	1	0	1	1	1	1
0	0	1	1	0	0	1	1	1	0	1	1	1	1	1
0	0	1	1	0	1	1	1	0	1	1	1	1	1	1
0	0	1	1	1	0	1	0	1	1	1	1	1	1	1
0	0	1	1	1	1	0	1	1	1	1	1	1	1	1

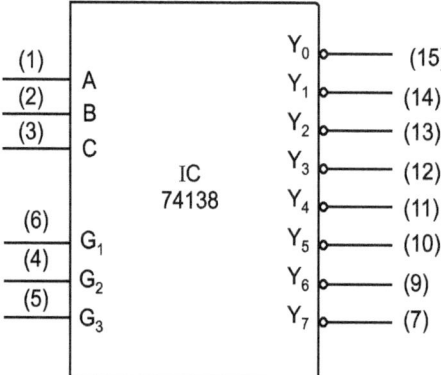

Fig. 3.52 : Logic symbol

Unit - IV

SEQUENTIAL LOGIC

4.1 SEQUENTIAL CIRCUITS

Q. Explain sequential circuit?

- In many applications it is required to generate digital outputs in accordance with the sequence in which the input signals are applied.
- Thus, these applications require that the outputs to be generated are not only dependent on present input conditions. The outputs also depend upon the past history of these inputs.
- The past history is provided by storing it in memory elements and providing a feedback from the output back to the input. Such circuits are known as sequential circuits
- Block diagram of a sequential circuit is shown in Fig. 4.1.

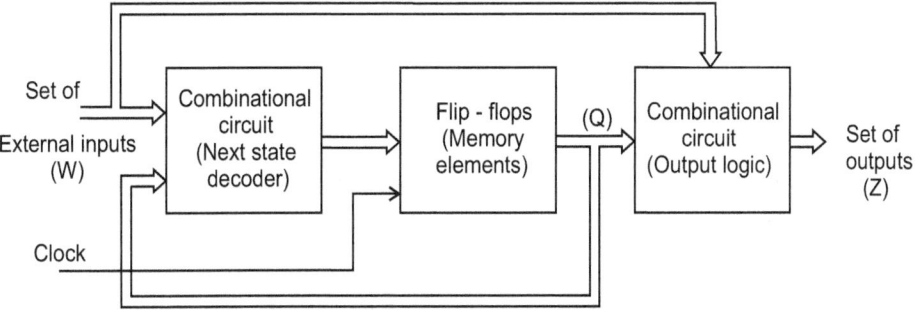

Fig. 4.1 : Block diagram of sequential circuit

- As shown in above Fig. 4.1, the circuit accepts a set of external inputs W and produces a set of outputs Z.
- The values of the outputs of the flip–flops are known as the state Q of the circuit.
- Upon application of clock pulse, the flip flop outputs change their state (circuit goes to next state).
- As shown in Fig. 4.1 the next state of the circuit is decided by the combinational circuit (next state decoder) that provides the inputs to the flip–flops.
- The combinational logic that provides the inputs to the flip–flops, derives its input from two sources (1) set of external inputs (W) and (2) the present state Q of the circuit (outputs of the flip–flops).

- Thus, changes in state depend upon the external inputs as well the present state of the circuit.
- As shown in Fig. 4.1, the outputs of the sequential circuit are generated by another combinational circuit (output logic). The outputs are generated from the present state Q of the circuit and the set of primary inputs W.
- Sequential circuits are also known as finite state machines (FSMs) as the functional behaviour of these circuits can be represented using finite number of states.
- Sequential circuits are broadly classified into two categories:

    (1) Moore type sequential circuits and (2) Mealy type sequential circuits.

4.2 COMPARISON OF COMBINATIONAL AND SEQUENTIAL CIRCUIT

Q. Explain difference between combinational and sequential circuit. **[Dec. 09, 4 M]**

Combinational Circuit	Sequential Circuit
1. The outputs depend on the combination of inputs.	1. The outputs depend on the past history of inputs as well as the present input states.
2. Memory is not required.	2. Memory is required to store previous states of the inputs.
3. The delay between outputs and inputs is less, so the combinational circuit is faster.	3. Sequential circuit is slower due to propagational delay of additional memory element.
4. Combinational circuits are concurrent in nature.	4. Sequential circuit is not entirely concurrent.
5. Easier to design.	5. Complex to design. Timings can be critical.
6. Block diagram : Input → [Combinational Logic circuit (gates)] → Output Fig. 4.2 (a)	6. Block diagram : Inputs → [Combinational logic cicuit] → Outputs, with feedback from/to Memory Fig. 4.2 (b)

4.3 SEQUENTIAL CIRCUIT TYPES

(A) Synchronous Circuit :

- The change in inputs can affect memory element upon the activation of clock signal.
- Memory elements are clocked flip-flops.
- The maximum operational speed of synchronous circuit is governed by the clock speed, which in turn, is decided by the propagation delays of the logic gates.

(B) Asynchronous Circuit :

- The change in inputs can occur at any instant of time.
- Memory elements are unclocked flip-flops or time delay elements.
- Asynchronous circuits can operate faster than synchronous circuits because the clock is absent.

4.4 ONE BIT MEMORY CELL (BASIC BISTABLE ELEMENTS)

- One bit memory cell, as the name suggests can store 'one' bit (logic 0 or logic 1) information.
- It can be built using NAND or NOR gates.
- A one bit memory cell using NAND gates is as shown in Fig. 4.3.

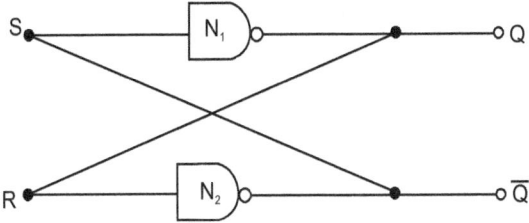

Fig. 4.3 : One bit memory cell

- The above circuit is also known as 'S-R' (Set-Reset) latch.
- This circuit has two stable states : '1 state' (Output Q = 1) and '0 state' (output $\overline{Q}$ = 0).
- The '1 state' is also called as 'set state' and the '0 state' is known as 'reset state'.
- The digital information gets locked or latched in this circuit. Therefore it is known as S-R i.e. set-reset latch.

Operation of the circuit :

- Two NAND gates (N_1 & N_2) are used as inverters. The output of N_1 is connected to the input of N_2 (R) and the output of N_2 is connected to the input of N_1 (S).

- Let us assume that the output of N_1 is logic 1 (Q = 1). This is the input of N_2 i.e. R=1. Therefore the output of N_2 becomes logic 0 ($\bar{Q}$ = 0).
- The output of N_2 is the input of N_1 i.e. S become 0 and consequently output of N_1 become 1 (Q=1), which confirms our assumption.
- Let us now assume that the output of N_1 is logic 0 (Q = 0). This is the input of N_2 i.e. R = 0. Therefore the output of N_2 becomes logic 1 ($\bar{Q}$ = 1).
- The output of N_2 is the input of N_1 i.e. S becomes 1 and consequently output of N_1 becomes 0 (Q = 0) which confirms our assumption.

Drawback :

- In the above circuit there is no way to enter the desired digital information. When the power is turned on, the circuit switches to one of the stable states i.e. 1 state or 0 state and it is not possible to predict it.
- To overcome this drawback, a modified circuit with 2 input NAND gates and two additional inverters are used. The desired digital information can be entered in this circuit.

4.5 LATCH VS FLIP-FLOP

Q. Explain difference between Latch and Flip flop.

- The main difference between latches and flip-flops is the method used for changing their state.
- Latches are controlled by enable signal, and they are level triggered, either positive level triggered or negative level triggered.
- Flip-flops are pulse or clock edge triggered instead of level triggered.

4.6 LEVEL TRIGGERED AND EDGE TRIGGERED

Q. Explain different type of level triggered and edge triggered?

(A) Level triggered : In level triggering the output state change according to input (s) when active level (i.e. positive or negative) is maintained at the enable input.

Two types of level triggered

1. **Positive level triggered :** The output of flip flop respond to the input changes when its enable input is 1 (high).

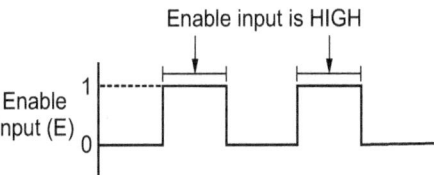

Fig. 4.4(a) : Positive level triggered

2. **Negative level triggered :** The output of flip-flop respond to the input changes when its input is 0 (low).

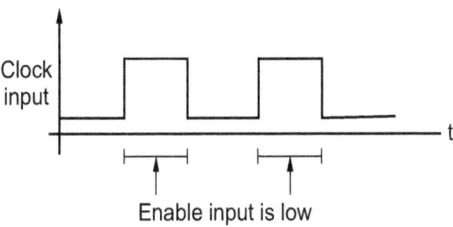

Fig. 4.4(b): Negative level triggered

- S-R flip flop and JK flip flop are known as level triggered flip flops as their output changes according to applied inputs as long as clock is present.
- As these flip flops respond when CLK=1 they are further called as positive level triggered flip flops.
- We know that level triggered JK flip flop has the drawback of race around condition. And to overcome that drawback we use master slave JK flip flop which is called as pulse triggered flip flop.
- In a pulse triggered flip flop like MS JK flip flop, output changes according to applied inputs, when a pulse is applied at the clock input. The state of this flip flop changes at the negative transition of the clock.
- Thus, in MS JK flip flop the race around condition is eliminated as the fed back output is blocked at the master when the CLK = 0.
- But in certain systems there is a possibility that the inputs of flip flop may change during the presence of the clock pulse. This causes uncertainty in the output of flip flop. This uncertainty can be eliminated by using edge triggered flip flops.

(B) Edge Triggered : In edge triggered flip flops output changes according to applied inputs only at the positive or negative edge of the clock pulse.

- Based on the type of edge there are two types of edge triggered flip flops : (1) positive edge triggered and (2) negative edge triggered.

- In case of positive edge triggered flip flop output changes only when the clock pulse changes from 0 to 1. While in case of negative edge triggered flip flop output responds only when the clock pulse changes from 1 to 0. The positive and negative edge of the clock is shown in Fig. 4.5.

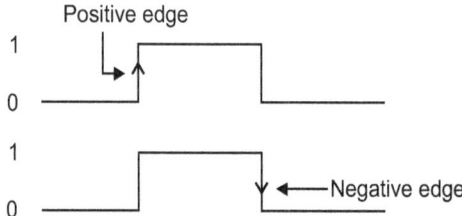

Fig. 4.5 : Positive & negative edge of the clock

- Thus, the state of the flip flop changes during very short interval of time in which clock changes from 0 to 1 or 1 to 0 and the uncertainty in the output gets completely eliminated.
- The logic symbol of positive edge triggered and negative edge triggered JK flip flop is shown in Fig. 4.6.

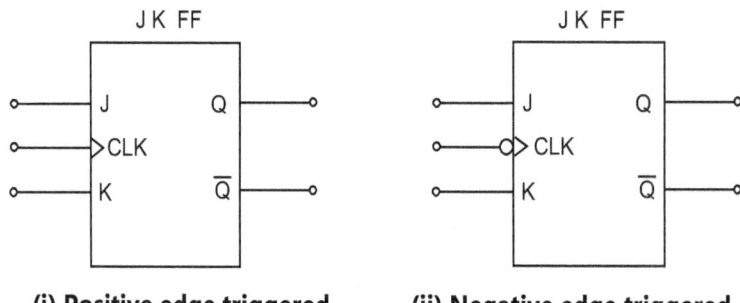

(i) Positive edge triggered   **(ii) Negative edge triggered**

Fig. 4.6 : Edge triggered JK flip flop

- Note that the logic symbol of negative edge triggered JK flip flop is same as that of MS JK flip flop without preset and clear inputs.
- Also in case of positive edge triggered JK flip flop bubble is absent.

4.7 LATCH

Q. Explain what is mean by latch?

- This circuit is with 2 input NAND gates N_1 and N_2; two additional inverters N_4 and N_4 is as shown in Fig. 4.7.

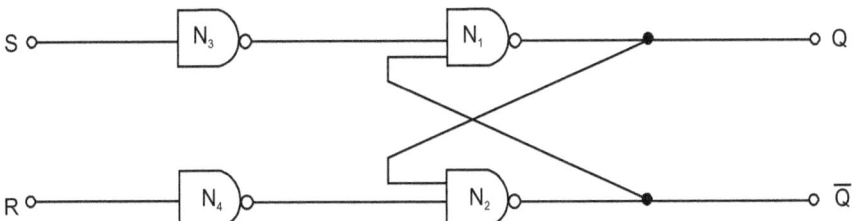

Fig. 4.7 : Memory cell with provision for entering data

- If S = R = 0, the circuit will behave exactly as the previous circuit shown in Fig. 4.7.
- If S = 1 & R = 0 then the output of N_4 will be 0 and the output of N_4 will be 1. As one of the inputs of N_1 is 0, its output will be certainly 1 (Q = 1).
- When Q become 1, both inputs of N_2 become 1 causing its output to go low ($\bar{Q}$ = 0). This is known as 1 state or set state of the circuit, which is achieved with the input pattern S = 1 and R = 0.
- If S = 0 and R = 1, then the output of N_4 will be 0 and the output of N_4 will be 1. As one of the inputs of N_2 becomes 0, its output will be certainly 1 ($\bar{Q}$ = 1).
- When $\bar{Q}$ becomes 1, both inputs of N_1 become 1 causing its output to go low (Q = 0). This is known as 0 state or reset state of the circuit which is achieved with the input pattern S = 0 and R = 1.
- In this way, user can enter desired information in the one bit memory cell.
- Uptil now we have seen that the outputs Q and $\bar{Q}$ are always complementary. If we apply the input S = 1 and R = 1, then the output of N_4 and N_4 become 0. This makes one input of both N_1 and N_2 as 0, which in turn cause both outputs Q and $\bar{Q}$ to become 1.
- Both Q and $\bar{Q}$ getting same state is not allowed and therefore the condition of inputs S = R = 1 is prohibited.

4.7.1 SR Latch using NAND Gate

Q. Explain SR latch using NAND gate?

- The simplest way to make any basic single bit set-reset SR latch is to connect together a pair of cross-coupled 2-input NAND gates as shown, to form a set-reset bistable also known as an active low SR NAND gate latch, so that there is feedback from each output to one of the other NAND gate inputs.

- This device consists of two inputs, one called the Set, S and the other called the Reset, R with two corresponding outputs $\bar{Q}$ and its inverse or complement $\bar{Q}$ (not-$\bar{Q}$) as shown below in Fig. 4.8.

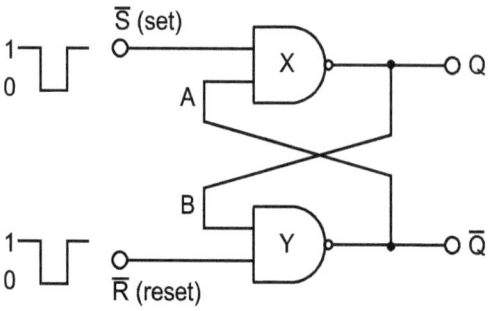

Fig. 4.8 : SR Latch using NAND gate

- **When S = 0, R = 0 :**
  The input R is at logic level "0" (R = 0) and input S is at logic level "1" (S = 1), the NAND gate Y has at least one of its inputs at logic "0" therefore, its output $\bar{Q}$ must be at a logic level "1" (NAND Gate principles). Output $\bar{Q}$ is also fed back to input "A" and so both inputs to NAND gate X are at logic level "1", and therefore its output Q must be at logic level "0".

- **When S = 1, R = 1 :**
  The NAND gate Y inputs are now R = "1" and B = "0". Since one of its inputs is still at logic level "0" the output at $\bar{Q}$ still remains HIGH at logic level "1" and there is no change of state. Therefore, the flip-flop circuit is said to be "Latched" or "Set" with $\bar{Q}$ = "1" and Q = "0".

- **When S = 0, R = 1 :**
  $\bar{Q}$ is at logic level "0", ($\bar{Q}$ = "0") its inverse output at Q is at logic level "1", ($\bar{Q}$ = "1"), and is given by R = "1" and S = "0". As gate X has one of its inputs at logic "0" its output $\bar{Q}$ must equal logic level "1" (again NAND gate principles). Output $\bar{Q}$ is fed back to input "B", so both inputs to NAND gate Y are at logic "1", therefore, $\bar{Q}$ = "0".

- **When S = 1, R = 1 :**
  If the set input, S now changes state to logic "1" with input R remaining at logic "1", output $\bar{Q}$ still remains LOW at logic level "0" and there is no change of state. Therefore, the flip-flop circuits "Reset" state has also been latched and we can define this "set/reset" action in the following truth table 4.1.

Table 4.1 : Truth table of latch using NAND gate

State	S	R	Q	Q̄	Description
Set	1	0	0	1	Set Q » 1
	1	1	0	1	no change
Reset	0	1	1	0	Reset Q » 0
	1	1	1	0	no change
Invalid	0	0	1	1	Invalid Condition

- It can be seen that when both inputs S = "1" and R = "1" the outputs Q̄ and Q̄ can be at either logic level "1" or "0", depending upon the state of the inputs S or R before this input condition existed. Therefore the condition of S = R = "1" does not change the state of the outputs Q̄ and Q̄.

- The input state of S=0 and R=0 is an undesirable or invalid condition and must be avoided. The condition of S = R = "0" causes both outputs Q̄ and Q̄ to be high together at logic level "1" when we would normally want Q̄ to be the inverse of Q̄. The result is that the flip-flop looses control of Q̄ and Q̄, and if the two inputs are now switched "high" again after this condition to logic "1", the flip-flop becomes unstable and switches to an unknown data state based upon the unbalance as shown in the following switching diagram.

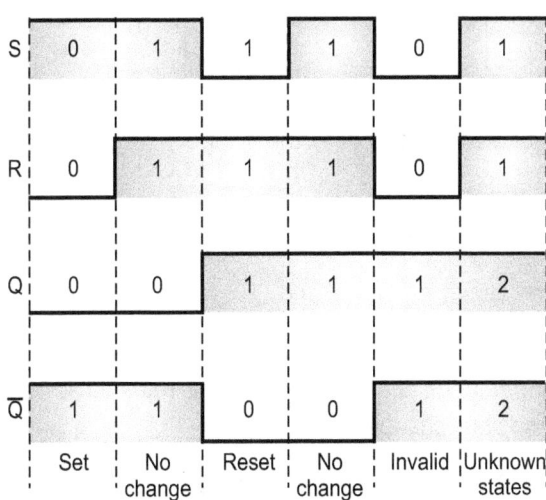

Fig. 4.9 : S-R latch using NAND gate Switching Diagram

- Then, a bistable SR flip-flop or SR latch is activated or set by a logic "1" applied to its S input and deactivated or reset by a logic "1" applied to its R. The SR flip-flop is said to be in an "invalid" condition (Meta-stable) if both the set and reset inputs are activated simultaneously.

4.7.2 SR Latch using NOR Gate

Q. Explain SR latch using NOR gate?

- RS latch have two inputs, S and R. S is called set and R is called reset.
- The S input is used to produce HIGH on Q (i.e. store binary 1 in flip-flop). The R input is used to produce low on Q (i.e. store binary 0 in flip-flop). $\bar{Q}$ is Q complementary output, so it always holds the opposite value of Q.
- The output of the S-R latch depends on current as well as previous inputs or state, and its state (value stored) can change as soon as its inputs change. The circuit and the truth table of RS latch is shown below.

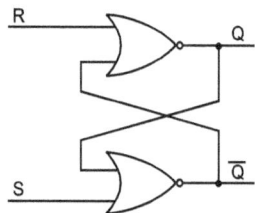

Fig. 4.10

Table 4.2 : Truth table SR latch using NOR gate

S	R	Q	Q+
0	0	0	0
0	0	1	1
0	1	X	0
1	0	X	1
1	1	X	0

- The operation has to be analyzed with the 4 inputs combinations together with the 2 possible previous states.

- **When S = 0 and R = 0 :** If we assume Q = 1 and $\bar{Q}$ = 0 as initial condition, then output Q after input is applied would be Q = 1 and $\bar{Q}$ = 0. Assuming Q = 0 and $\bar{Q}$ = 1 as initial condition, then output Q after the input applied would be Q = 0 and $\bar{Q}$ = 1. So it is clear that when both S and R inputs are low, the output is retained as before the application of inputs. (i.e. there is no state change).

- **When S = 1 and R = 0 :** If we assume Q = 1 and $\bar{Q}$ = 0 as initial condition, then output Q after input is applied would be Q = 1 and $\bar{Q}$ = 0. Assuming Q = 0 and Q = 1 as initial condition, then output Q after the input applied would be $\bar{Q}$ = 1 and $\bar{Q}$ = 0. So in simple words when S is HIGH and R is low, output Q is high.

- **When S = 0 and R = 1 :** If we assume Q = 1 and $\bar{Q}$ = 0 as initial condition, then output Q after input is applied would be Q = 0 and $\bar{Q}$ = 1. Assuming Q = 0 and $\bar{Q}$ = 1 as initial condition, then output Q after the input applied would be Q = = 0 and $\bar{Q}$ = 1. So in simple words when S is LOW and R is HIGH, output Q is LOW.

- **When S = 1 and R =1 :** No matter what state Q and $\bar{Q}$ are in, application of 1 at input of NOR gate always results in 0 at output of NOR gate, which results in both Q and $\bar{Q}$ set to LOW (i.e. Q = $\bar{Q}$). LOW in both the outputs basically is wrong, so this case is invalid.
- The waveform below shows the operation of NOR gates based RS Latch.

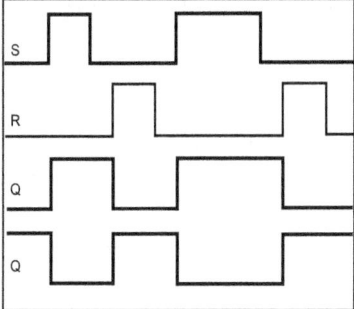

Fig. 4.11 : Waveform of SR latch using NOR gates

4.7.3 D Latch

Q. What is D latch?

- The SR latch seen earlier contains ambiguous state; to eliminate this condition we can ensure that S and R are never equal. This is done by connecting S and R together with an inverter.
- Thus we have D Latch this is same as the RS latch, with the only difference that there is only one input, instead of two (R and S). This input is called D or Data input.
- D latch is called D transparent latch for the reasons explained earlier. Delay flip-flop or delay latch is another name used. Below is the truth table and circuit of D latch.

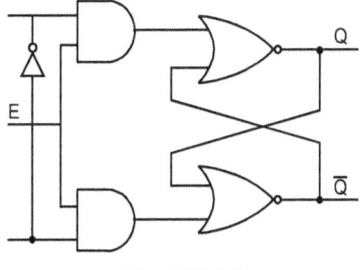

Fig. 4.12 (a)

Table 4.3 : Truth table of D latch

D	Q	Q+
1	X	1
0	X	0

- Below is the D latch waveform, which is similar to the RS latch one, but with R removed.

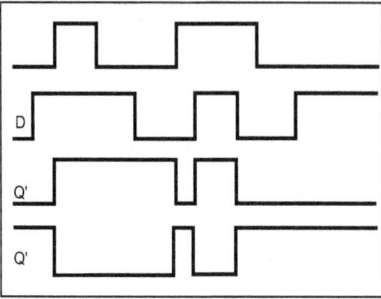

Fig. 4.12 (b) : D latch waveform

4.8 CLOCKED S-R FLIP-FLOP

Q. Explain clocked SR flip flop?

- It is often required to enter the desired digital information in the memory cell, in synchronism with a train of pulses known as clock. The circuit of clocked S-R flip flop is as shown in Fig. 4.13.

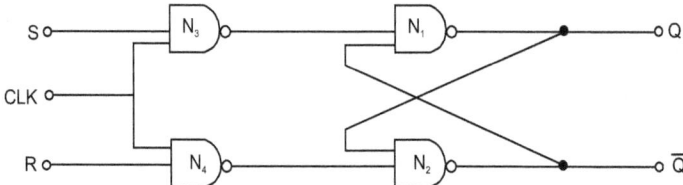

Fig. 4.13 : Clocked S-R flip flop

- In above circuit, when CLK = 0, output of both N_4 and N_4 is certainly 1. In this case, both S and R inputs have no effect on output Q.
- When CLK = 1, the operation of this circuit is exactly the same as that of SR latch.
- For S = R = 0, then output Q does not change i.e. if it is 0 it remains 0 and if it is 1, it remains 1. Thus, there is no change in the output for this input condition.
- For S = 1 and R = 0, the output Q becomes 1 in SR latch. This is known as the set state of the circuit.
- For S = 0 and R = 1 the output Q becomes 0 in SR latch. This is known as the reset state of the circuit.
- For S = R = 1, both the outputs Q and $\bar{Q}$ try to become 1 which is not allowed and therefore this input condition is prohibited.

- Thus, the above circuit responds to S and R inputs, only when CLK = 1.
- The operation of the circuit for CLK = 1 can be tabulated as shown in table 4.4.

Table 4.4 : Truth table of clocked SR flip-flop

Inputs		Output
S	R	Q
0	0	No change
0	1	0 (Reset)
1	0	1 (Set)
1	1	Prohibited

- If we represent Q_n as the output of present state of the circuit and S_n, R_n as the inputs of the present state, then Q_{n+1} becomes the output of the next state of the circuit.
- The above table 4.4 can be redrawn in terms of present state and next state as table 4.5.

Table 4.5 : Truth table of S-R flip flop

Inputs		Output
S_n	R_n	Q_{n+1}
0	0	Q_n
0	1	0
1	0	1
1	1	Prohibited

- The table 4.5 is the truth table of clocked S-R flip flop.
- The truth table of a flip flop is also referred to as the characteristic table as it specifies the operational characteristic of the flip flop.
- Logic symbol of clocked S-R flip flop is as shown in Fig. 4.14.

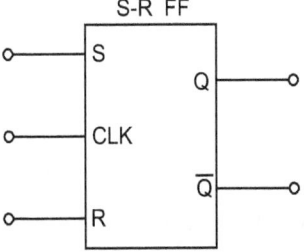

Fig. 4.14 : Logic symbol of clocked S-R flip flop

4.9 CLOCKED S-R FLIP FLOP WITH PRESET AND CLEAR INPUTS

Q. Explain SR flip flop with preset and clear inputs?

- The circuit of clocked S-R flip flop shown in Fig. 4.15 switches to either set state or reset state when the power is turned on i.e. the state of the circuit is uncertain.
- In many applications it is required to define the initial state of the flip flop when the power is turned on.
- This is accomplished by using the preset and clear inputs.
- Preset and clear inputs are known as asynchronous inputs as they do not work in synchronism with the clock.
- Clocked S-R flip flop with preset and clear inputs can be obtained by using N_1 and N_2 NAND gates as 4 input gates as shown in Fig. 4.15.

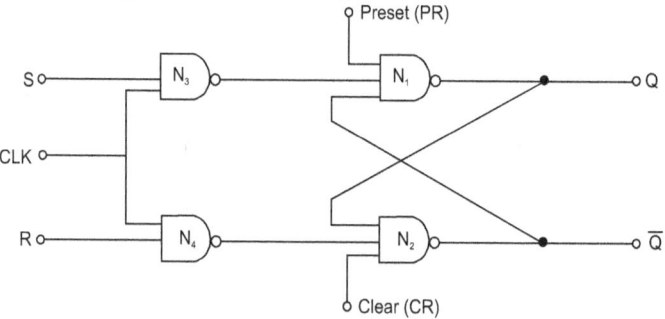

Fig 4.15 : Clocked S-R flip flop with preset and clear inputs.

- In When PR = CR = 1, above circuit operates in accordance with the truth table of clocked S-R flip flop given in table 4.5.
- When CR = 0 and PR = 1, one of the inputs of N_2 is 0, therefore its output is certainly high ($\bar{Q}$ = 1). Consequently all three inputs of N_1 are high which make Q = 0. Thus, CR = 0 resets or clears the flip flop.
- Similarly when CR = 1 and PR = 0, one of the inputs of N_1 is 0, therefore its output is certainly high (Q = 1). Consequently all three inputs of N_2 are high which make $\bar{Q}$ = 0. Thus, PR = 0 sets the flip flop.
- Both preset & clear inputs are known as active low inputs as they perform the intended operation of setting or clearing the flip flop, when they are low.
- Once the desired initial state of the flip flop is achieved using preset & clear inputs, these inputs are connected to logic 1 while the normal operation of the flip flop takes place.
- The condition PR = CR = 0 must not be used, since this leads to an uncertain state.

- The logic symbol of this flip flop is as shown in Fig. 4.16. Preset and clear inputs are shown as bubbled inputs indicating that they are active low inputs.

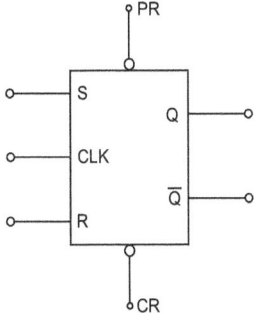

Fig 4.16 : Logic symbol of clocked S-R flip flop with preset and clear inputs.

4.10 JK FLIP FLOP

Q. What is race around condition? Explain with the help of timing diagram how it is removed in basic flip-flop circuit. **[May 05, 8 M]**

Q. Compare race and race around condition. How will you avoid race around condition? Explain? **[Dec. 05, 8 M]**

Q. Draw neat diagram of JK flip-flop using SR flip-flop. Write the truth table and explain what happens if both the inputs are 1 (J = K = 1). **[Dec. 04, 6 M]**

Q. How the race around condition is avoided? **[Dec. 08, 09, 4 M]**

- We know that in case of clocked S-R flip flop, for the input condition S = R = 1 both the outputs Q and $\bar{Q}$ try to become 1, which is not allowed and therefore this input condition is prohibited.
- This drawback can be eliminated by converting S-R flip flop into a JK flip flop.
- The data input J is ANDed with $\bar{Q}$ to obtain S input and the data input K is ANDed with Q to obtain R input as shown in Fig. 4.17.

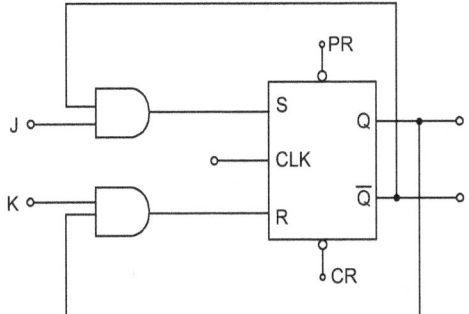

Fig. 4.17 : JK flip flop constructed using S-R flip flop

- When J = K = 0, output of both AND gates is 0. Therefore, S and R both become 0. So next state output Q_{n+1} remains same as that of present state output Q_n.

- When J = 0 & K = 1, the output of upper AND gate is 0, so S = 0. If the present state output Q_n = 0, the output of lower AND gate is also 0 & R becomes 0.

- For the input condition S = R = 0 the next state output remains unchanged. But if the present state output Q_n = 1, the output of lower AND gate becomes 1 i.e. R becomes 1.

- With S = 0 and R = 1 input combination the next state output Q_{n+1} is reset. Thus for J = 0 & K = 1 input condition, irrespective of the present state Q_n, the next state output Q_{n+1} be is 0 i.e. the flip flop is reset.

- Similarly for J = 1 and K = 0 input condition, the next state output Q_{n+1} is certainly 1 i.e. the flip flop is set.

Race around condition

- The race around condition occurs for the input combination J = K = 1.

- Let us assume that initially the output Q is 0. With this the output of lower AND gate becomes 0 and upper AND gate becomes 1. Therefore S becomes 1 & R becomes 0. This input combination of S-R causes output Q to become 1.Thus the output changes from 0 to 1 after the time interval Δt equal to the propagation delay through AND gate and S-R flip flop. Now we have J = K = 1 and output Q = 1.

- After another time interval Δt, the output Q will change back to 0 and the cycle repeats till CLK=1.

- At the end of the clock pulse the output Q is uncertain and this situation is known as race around condition. It is shown in Fig. 4.18.

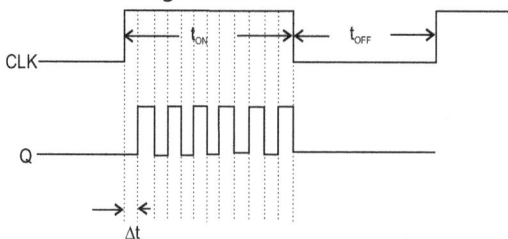

Fig. 4.18 : Timing diagram showing race around condition

- The race around condition can be eliminated if t_{ON} is made smaller than the propagation delay Δt.

- It can also be eliminated using the master slave JK (MS JK) flip flop.

- The operation of JK flip flop can be expressed with the truth table 4.6.

Table 4.6 : Truth table of JK flip flop

Inputs		Output
J_n	K_n	Q_{n+1}
0	0	Q_n
0	1	0
1	0	1
1	1	$\bar{Q}_n$

- The logic symbol of JK flip flop is shown in Fig. 4.19.

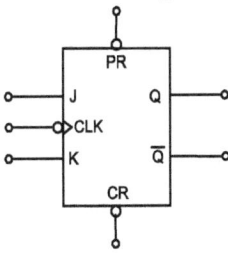

Fig. 4.19 : Logic symbol of JK flip flop

4.11 MASTER SLAVE JK (MS JK) FLIP FLOP

Q. What is the advantage of MS JK flip-flop ? Also explain working of MS JK flip-flop.
[Dec. 10, 8 M]

Q. What do you mean by master slave JK flip-flop. Explain the advantages of this flip-flop draw suitable circuit diagram and timing diagram. **[Dec. 06, 10 M]**

- Master slave JK flip flop is a cascade of two S-R flip flops as shown in Fig. 4.20.
- As shown in Fig. 4.20, outputs of slave are fed back to the inputs of master. Also clock is directly applied to the master while it is inverted and then applied to the slave.
- When CLK=1, the master is enabled and the slave is disabled. The outputs of master Q_m and $\bar{Q}_m$ respond to the inputs J and K according to the table 4.6. As long as CLK=1, Q & $\bar{Q}$ outputs do not change as the slave is disabled and therefore the fed back inputs of master also do not change.

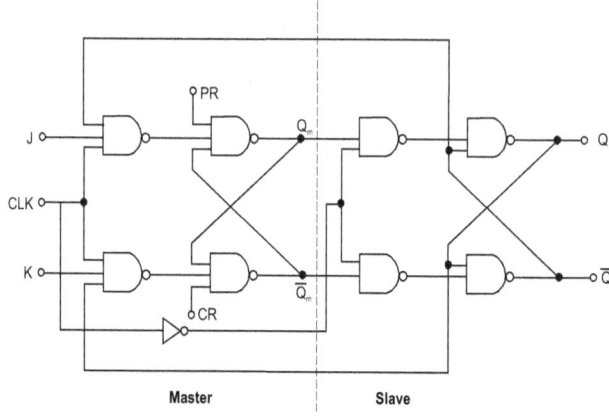

Fig. 4.20 : Master slave JK flip flop

- When CLK= 0, the slave is enabled and the master gets disabled. The outputs Q and $\bar{Q}$ change according to the outputs of the master Q_m and $\bar{Q}_m$. As long as CLK = 0, Q_m and $\bar{Q}_m$ outputs do not change as the master is disabled and therefore Q and $\bar{Q}$ outputs also retain their new values. Thus the race around condition gets eliminated.
- The state of the master slave JK flip flop shown in Fig. 4.21, changes at the negative transition of the clock pulse.
- The logic symbol of master slave JK flip flop is shown in Fig. 4.21.

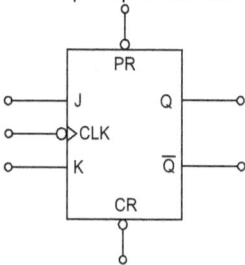

Fig. 4.21 : Logic symbol of MS JK flip flop

- The symbol '>' at the CLK input indicates that output changes when the clock makes a transition.
- The bubble indicates that the output changes when there is a negative transition of the clock (i.e. when the clock changes from 1 to 0).

4.12 D FLIP FLOP

Q. Explain D flip flop with preset and clear input?

- It has only one input called as data input (D).
- It is also known as data flip flop or delay flip flop.

- If we use only middle two rows of the truth table of S-R flip flop or JK flip flop we obtain D flip flop.
- The middle two rows of both truth tables indicate that the two inputs S, R or J, K are always complement of each other.
- Thus a D flip flop can be constructed from S-R flip flop or JK flip flop by connecting a NOT gate in between the two inputs as shown in Fig. 4.22.

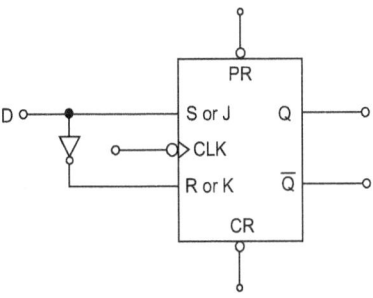

Fig. 4.22 : D flip flop using S-R flip flop or JK flip flop

- The truth table of D flip flop is as shown in table 4.7.

Table 4.7 : Truth table of D flip flop

Input	Output
D_n	Q_{n+1}
0	0
1	1

- Here D_n represents the present state input and Q_{n+1} represents the next state output.
- From truth table, it is clear that output is same as that of input therefore it is known as 'data' flip flop.
- The input data appears at the output at the end of the clock pulse. Thus transfer of data from input to the output is delayed by clock pulse and hence it is also called as 'delay' flip flop.
- The logic symbol of D flip flop is shown in Fig. 4.23.

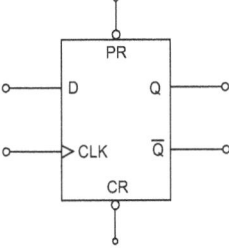

Fig. 4.23 : Logic symbol of D flip flop

4.13 T FLIP FLOP

Q. Explain D flip flop with preset and clear input? [May 07, 2 M]

- It has only one input called as toggle input (T). It is known as toggle flip flop.
- A T flip flop can be constructed from JK flip flop, just by connecting J and K input terminals together as shown in Fig. 4.24.

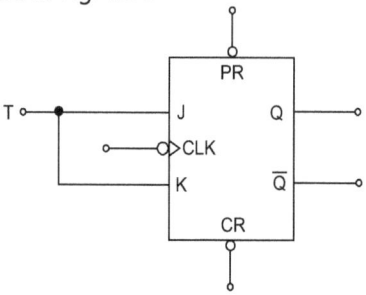

Fig. 4.24 : T flip flop using JK flip flop.

- The truth table of T flip flop is as below.

Table 4.8 : Truth table of T flip flop

Input	Output
T_n	Q_{n+1}
0	Q_n
1	$\overline{Q}_n$

- Here T_n represents the present state input, Q_n represents the present state output and Q_{n+1} represents the next state output.
- From truth table it is clear that, for T = 1, it acts as toggle switch. The output Q changes for every active transition of the clock signal. Therefore it is called as toggle flip flop.
- S-R flip flop can not be converted into T flip flop since S = R = 1 input condition is not allowed.
- The logic symbol of T flip flop is shown in Fig. 4.25.

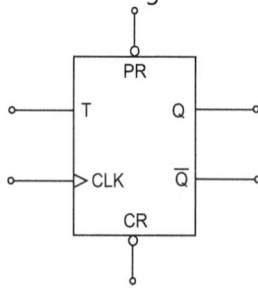

Fig. 4.25 : Logic symbol of T flip flop

4.14 DIFFERENT REPRESENTATION OF FLIP FLOP

- There are various ways in which a flip flop represented. Each represented type is used for a different application.
- Different types of representation of flip flop are :
  1. Characteristics equations.
  2. Flip flop as finite state machine.
  4. Excitation tables

4.15 EXCITATION TABLE OF FLIP FLOP

Q. What is excitation table of flip flop? [May 07, 2 M]

- In the design of sequential circuits, it is often required to find input conditions so that desired next state of the circuit is obtained from the present state of the circuit.
- These input conditions can be obtained using the excitation table of a flip flop.
- The truth table of a flip flop specifies its operational characteristic while the excitation table of a flip flop gives an idea regarding the present input conditions along with present state, to obtain the desired next state.
- Construction of excitation table is discussed below.

4.15.1 Excitation Table of S-R Flip-Flop

- Let the present state of the S-R flip flop be $Q_n = 0$ and the desired next state be $Q_{n+1} = 0$.
- As there is no change in the state of the flip flop (present state & next state is same), from the first row of the truth table of S-R flip flop we obtain the input condition as $S_n = 0$ and $R_n = 0$.
- Similarly from the third row of the truth table of S-R flip flop, it is clear that whatever may be the present state, the next state of the flip flop is certainly 0 for the input condition $S_n = 0$ and $R_n = 1$.
- By combining these two input conditions we conclude that, S_n input must be 0 while R_n input can be 0 or 1 i.e. R_n input can be X (don't care), to obtain next state $Q_{n+1} = 0$ from the present state $Q_n = 0$. This gives first row of the excitation table of S-R flip flop.
- Similarly input conditions can be found for remaining three combinations of present state & next state. The excitation table is given in table 4.9.

Table 4.9 : Excitation table of S-R flip flop

Present State	Next State	Flip flop inputs	
Q_n	Q_{n+1}	S_n	R_n
0	0	0	X
0	1	1	0
1	0	0	1
1	1	X	0

4.15.2 Excitation Table of JK, D & T Flip Flop

- In the similar manner excitation table of JK, D & T flip flops can be prepared by using their truth tables. Table 4.10, table 4.11 and table 4.12 are the excitation table of JK, D & T flip flop respectively.

Table 4.10 : Excitation table of JK flip flop

Present State	Next State	Flip flop input	
Q_n	Q_{n+1}	S_n	R_n
0	0	0	X
0	1	1	X
1	0	X	1
1	1	X	0

Table 4.11 : Excitation table of D flip flop

Present State	Next State	Flip flop input
Q_n	Q_{n+1}	D_n
0	0	0
0	1	1
1	0	0
1	1	1

Table 4.12 : Excitation table of T flip flop

Present State	Next State	Flip flop inputs
Q_n	Q_{n+1}	T_n
0	0	0
0	1	1
1	0	1
1	1	0

Example 4.1 :

Prepare the truth table for the circuit shown in Fig. 4.26 and show that it acts as T type flip flop. **[May 2004, 4 M]**

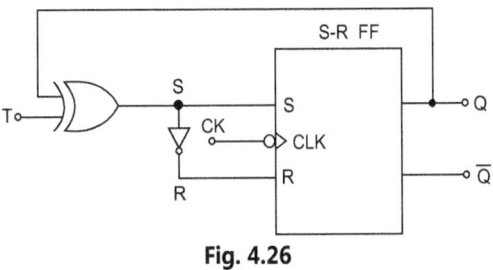

Fig. 4.26

Solution :

- Let us assume that initially Q=0 & T=0. Therefore output of EX-OR is also 0- which leads S=0 & R=1. From the truth table of S-R flip flop, for this input condition, next state output is 0. This gives first row of the truth table for the circuit.
- Now let us assume that Q=1 and T=0.Therefore output of EX-OR is 1 which leads S = 1 & R = 0. From the truth table of S-R flip flop for this input condition, next state output is 1. This gives second row of the truth table for the circuit.
- Proceeding in a similar manner, we can obtain the remaining two rows of the truth table. The complete truth table is given in table 4.13.

Table 4.13

Data Input	Present State	Next State
T	Q_n	Q_{n+1}
0	0	0
0	1	1
1	0	1
1	1	0

- From the first two rows of the table 4.13, it is clear that when T=0, the next state output Q_{n+1} is same as that of present state output Q_n. From the last two rows of the table 4.13, it is clear that, when T=1, the next state output Q_{n+1} is complement of the present state output Q_n. this can be represented in a tabular form as shown in table 4.14.

Table 4.14

Data input	Next state output
T_n	Q_{n+1}
0	Q_n
1	$\bar{Q}_n$

- The table 4.14 is the truth table of T type flip flop. Thus, the given circuit is same as that of T type flip flop.

Example 4.2 :

Analyze the circuit shown in Fig. 4.27 and prove that it is equivalent to T flip flop.

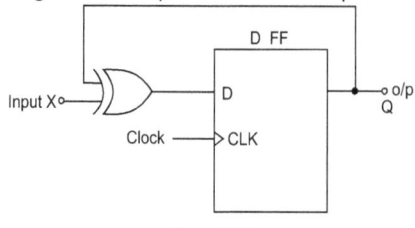

Fig. 4.27

Solution :

- Let us assume that initially X=0 & Q=0. Therefore output of EX-OR gate is also 0 which leads D=0. From the truth table of D flip flop, for this input condition next state output is 0. This gives first row of the truth table for the circuit.
- Now let us assume that Q=1 & X=0. Therefore, output of EX-OR gate is 1 which leads D=1. From the truth table of D flip flop, for this input condition next state output is 1. This gives second row of the truth table for the circuit.
- Proceeding in a similar manner we can obtain the remaining two rows of the truth table. The complete truth table is given table 4.15.

Table 4.15

Data input X	Present state Q_n	Next state Q_{n+1}
0	0	0
0	1	1
1	0	1
1	1	0

- From the first two rows of the above table, it is clear that when X=0 the next state output Q_{n+1} is same as that of present state output Q_n.
- From the last two rows of the above table it is clear that, when X=1, the next state output Q_{n+1} is complement of the present state output Q_n. This can be represented in tabular form as shown in table 4.16.

Table 4.16

Data input X_n	Next state output Q_{n+1}
0	Q_n
1	$\bar{Q}_n$

- The table 4.16 is the truth table of T-type flip flop. Thus the given circuit is equivalent to T type flip flop.

4.16 CONVERSION OF FLIP FLOPS

Q. Convert SR flip-flop (SR FF) into D FF.	[May 12, 2 M]
Q. Convert JK flip-flop into TFF. Show the truth table.	[Dec. 09, 4 M]
Q. How will you convert JK flip-flop into T-flip-flop. Explain application of T flip-flop in sequential circuit.	[May 06, 4 M]
Q. Convert SR flip-flop into T-flip-flop.	[May 12, 2M]
Q. Convert SR FF into JK FF.	[May 12, 2M]
Q. Convert JK FF into D FF	[Dec. 09, 4 M]

- Conversion of Flip flops is based upon the block diagram as shown in Fig. 4.28.

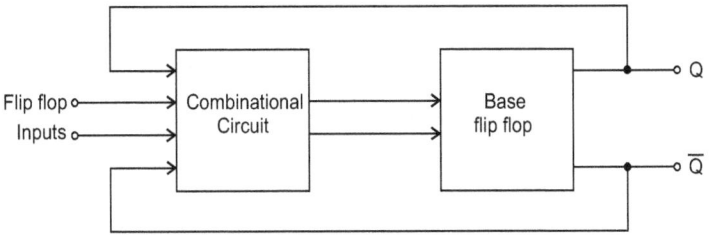

Fig. 4.28 : Block diagram used for flip flop conversion.

- Base flip flop shown in the Fig. 4.28 is the flip flop to be converted. Here we need to design a combinational circuit for converting the base flip flop into desired one.
- For designing the combinational circuit we have to use the excitation tables of both, base flip flop & desired flip flop. From that we construct a truth table with desired flip flop data inputs, present state Q, as inputs and base flip flop data inputs as outputs.
- Then we write separate K-maps for individual outputs and obtain the simplified expressions. Based on these expressions we get the combinational circuit required for conversion.

4.16.1 Convert S-R Flip Flop to JK Flip Flop

Q. Convert SR flip-flop into JK flip-flop.	[May 12, 2M]

- Here the base flip flop is S-R & desired flip flop is JK.
- We first construct a truth table in which inputs are - desired flip flop data inputs i.e. J, K and present state Q. In the truth table outputs are - based flip flop data inputs i.e. S,R.
- Using the excitation table of both flip flops we construct the truth table 4.17.

- The first row of excitation table of JK flip flop for Q=0 is JK=0X. Therefore in the truth table for first two rows we get inputs as JK=00 and JK=01 for Q=0.
- The first row of excitation table of S-R flip flop for Q=0 is S-R=0X. Therefore in the truth table for first two rows we get the outputs as S-R=0X.
- Proceeding in this manner we obtain the truth table 4.17.
- In this table cell number for the K-map is also written so that it becomes easy while representing the truth table in the K-map.
- Fig. 4.29 in the right bottom corner of K-map cell indicates the cell numbers.

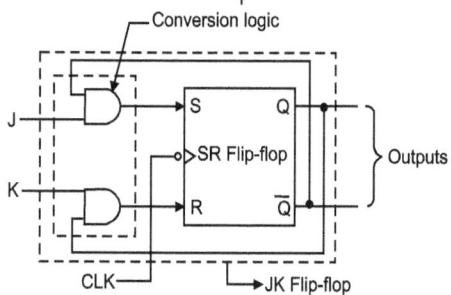

Fig. 4.29 : S-R to JK conversion

Table 4.17 : Truth table for S-R to JK conversion

Cell no.	Desired FF data inputs		Present state	Base FF data inputs	
	J	K	Q	S	R
0	0	0	0	0	x
2	0	1	0	0	x
4	1	0	0	1	0
6	1	1	0	1	0
4	0	1	1	0	1
7	1	1	1	0	1
1	0	0	1	x	0
5	1	0	1	x	0

- Now we write separate K-maps for S & R outputs according to the cell numbers.

(1) For S ⇒

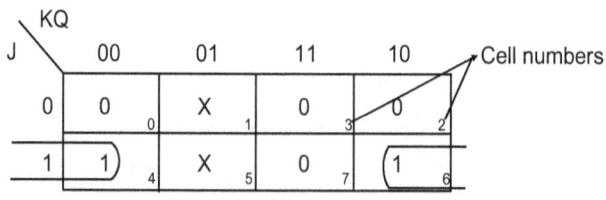

$$\therefore \quad S = J\bar{Q} \quad \ldots 4.1$$

(2) For R ⇒

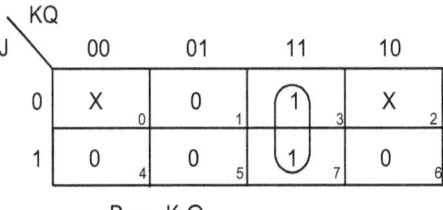

∴   R = KQ   ...4.2

- The resulting conversion diagram is as shown in Fig. 4.29.

4.16.2 Convert S-R flip flop to D flip flop

Q. Convert SR flip-flop (SR FF) into D FF.   [May 12, 2 M]

- Using the directions given for S-R to JK conversion we construct the truth table 4.18 for S-R to D conversion.

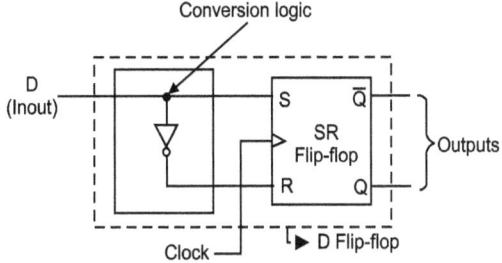

Fig. 4.30 : S-R to D conversion

Table 4.18 : Truth table for S-R to D conversion

Cell No	Desired FF data input	Present State	Base FF Data inputs	
	D	Q	S	R
0	0	0	0	×
2	1	0	1	0
1	0	1	0	1
4	1	1	×	0

- K map for S ⇒

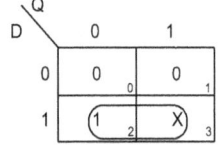

∴   S = D   ...4.4

- K map for R ⇒

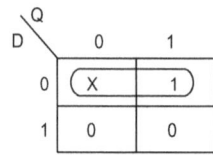

∴ R = $\bar{D}$ ...4.4

- The resulting conversion diagram is as shown in Fig. 4.40.

4.16.3 Convert S-R Flip Flop into T Flip Flop

Q. Convert SR flip-flop into T-flip-flop. [May 12, 2M]

- Converting SR flip flop to T flip flop is same as SR to D flip flop conversion.

4.16.4 Convert JK Flip Flop into T Flip Flop

Q. Convert JK flip-flop into T flip-flop. [May 12, 2M]

- We construct the truth table 4.19 for JK to T conversion.

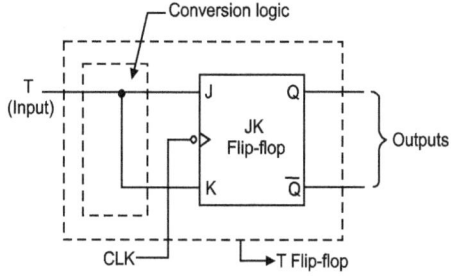

Fig. 4.31 : JK to T flip flop conversion

Table 4.19 : Truth table for JK to T conversion

Cell No	Desired FF data input	Present State	Base FF data input	
	T	Q	J	K
0	0	0	0	×
2	1	0	1	×
4	1	1	×	1
1	0	1	×	0

- K maps for J ⇒

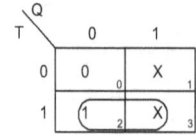

∴ J = T ...4.5

- K maps for K ⇒

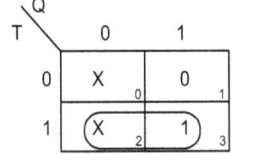

∴ K = T ...4.6

- The resulting conversion diagram is as known in Fig. 4.31.

4.16.5 Convert JK Flip Flop into D Flip Flop

Q. Convert JK flip-flop into D flip-flop. [May 12, 2M]

- Using the directions given in JK to T flip flop conversion we construct the truth table 4.20 for JK to D conversion.

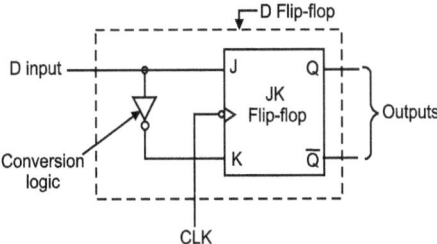

Fig. 4.32 : JK to D flip flop conversion

Table 4.20 : Truth table for JK to D conversion

Cell No	Desired FF Data Input	Present State	Base FF Data Input	
	D	Q	J	K
0	0	0	0	X
2	1	0	1	X
1	0	1	X	1
4	1	1	X	0

- k map for J=>

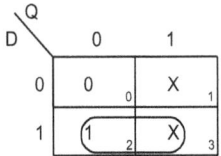

∴ J = D ...4.7

- k map for K=>

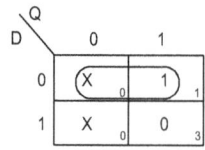

∴ $K = \bar{D}$ ...4.8

- . The resulting conversion diagram is as shown in Fig. 4.32.

4.17 APPLICATIONS OF FLIP-FLOPS

Q. List the applications of flip flops?

Q. Write short note on bounce elimination switch?

4.17.1 Bounce Elimination Switch

- Mechanical switches are used as a means to give input to any digital circuit.
- These switches are associated with a problem that when the arm of the switch is thrown from one position to another, it chatters many times initially. Then it comes to rest in the position of contact. This problem is known as switch bouncing or switch chattering.
- The bouncing of the switch causes variations in the corresponding input which can cause errors in the output of the circuit. For example, suppose a switch makes transition from 1 to 0. But before going to final value 0, it oscillates between 0 and 1. This chattering may lead the sequential circuit to enter into undesired state and produce undesired outputs.
- Therefore, it is required that the effect switch bouncing is to be nullified at the output. Out of the various techniques available for this, one is to use bounce elimination switch.
- The bounce elimination switch using $\bar{S}\bar{R}$ latch is as shown in Fig. 4.33.

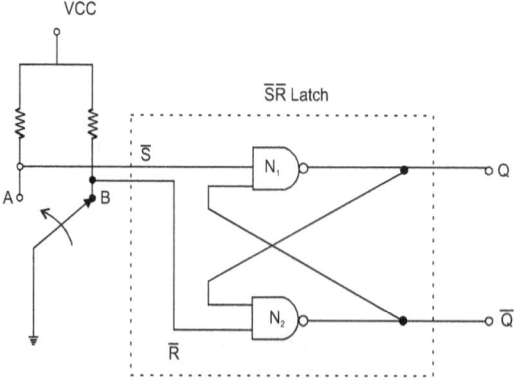

Fig. 4.33: Bounce Elimination Switch

- Initially, the switch is at position B, therefore $\bar{R} = 0$ and $\bar{S} = 1$. As $\bar{R} = 0$, output of N_2 is 1 ($\bar{Q} = 1$) which makes both inputs of N_1 logic 1 and its output $Q = 0$. So initially when the switch is at position B, output of $\bar{S}\bar{R}$ latch is stable i.e. $Q = 0$ and $\bar{Q} = 1$. It is shown in the form of waveforms in Fig. 4.33.

- At instant $t = t_1$, the switch is thrown from position B to A. Certain delay is associated with the switch, therefore it reaches at A at $t = t_2$. Between the instants t_2 and t_1, both $\bar{S}$, $\bar{R}$ are at logic 1. But still the output of the latch is stable i.e. $Q = 0$ and $\bar{Q} = 1$ as shown in Fig. 4.33

- When the switch makes contact at A for the first time at instant t_2, $\bar{S}$ becomes 0 and $\bar{R}$ becomes 1. As $\bar{S} = 0$ output of N_1 i.e. $Q = 1$. It makes both inputs of N_2 logic 1 and its output $\bar{Q} = 0$. Thus at instant t_2 when the switch makes contact at A for the first time, the output of $\bar{S}\bar{R}$ latch moves to another stable state i.e. $Q = 1$ and $\bar{Q} = 0$. It is as shown in Fig. 4.33.

- After the instant t_2, the switch chatters and therefore $\bar{S}$ swings between 0 and 1 at instants t_4, t_4, t_5 as shown. Though $\bar{S}$ swings between 0 and 1, it does not affect the output of N_1, it remains same i.e. $Q = 1$.

- Thus, the mechanical switch has the drawback that it chatters, but it is when combined with $\bar{S}\bar{R}$ latch, it becomes a chatterless switch.

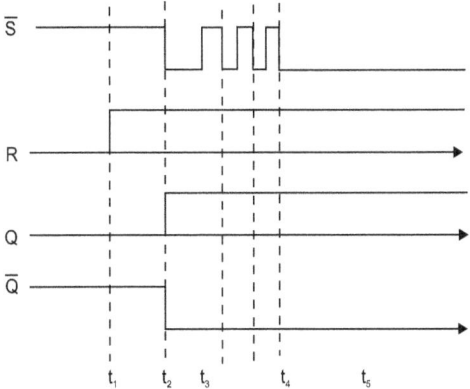

Fig. 4.34

4.18 REGISTERS

- Registers are used for storing the digital information. A register that stores N-bit information is called as N-bit register.
- Flip-flops are used for the construction of registers. As flip-flop can store 1-bit information, a N-bit register consists of N flip-flops.
- D type flip-flops are most widely used in the registers. Also JK flip-flop and SR flip-flop when converted to D flip-flop can be used in the registers.
- A 4-bit register is shown in Fig. 4.35.

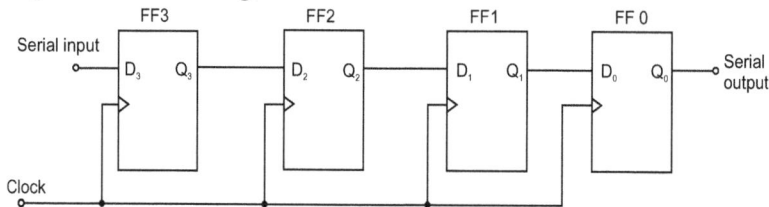

Fig. 4.35 : 4-bit register

- As shown in Fig. 4.35 four positive edge triggered D type flip flops are used.
- The data to be stored in the register must be available in serial form in this case.
- The serial data is applied at the serial input bit by bit starting from least significant bit along with the clock pulses.
- As Q_4 is connected to D_2, Q_2 is connected to D_1 and Q_1 is connected to D_0, the data gets shifted from one flip-flop to another. After four clock pulses the 4-bit information gets stored in the register.

4.19 BUFFER REGISTER

- An 'n' bit registers has group of 'n' flip flop and capable to store any binary information, which contains 'n' numbers of bits.
- This type of register is also called storage registers.
- These are used for temporary storage of data.

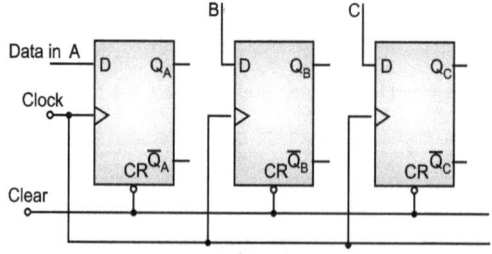

Fig. 4.36 : Buffer register

4.20 SHIFT REGISTER

- The data can be entered in serial or parallel form and can be retrieved in the serial or parallel form. The serial form means bit by bit (one bit at time) and parallel means all the bits are simultaneously retrieved. On the basis of data entered (write) and retrieved (read), the registers are classified as,
- Serial In Serial Out
- Serial In Parallel Out
- Parallel In Serial Out
- Parallel In Parallel Out
- Registers, in which data are entered or/and retrieved in serial form, are referred to as shift register.

4.20.1 Serial In Serial Out Shift Register

> Q. Draw and explain the circuit diagram of 4 bit shift register with serial left shift.
> [May 05, 4 M]

- In serial in serial out shift register, data is entered and retrieved in serial fashion with clock.
- The logic diagram of 4-bit serial in serial out shift register using J-K flip-flop is shown Fig. 4.37.

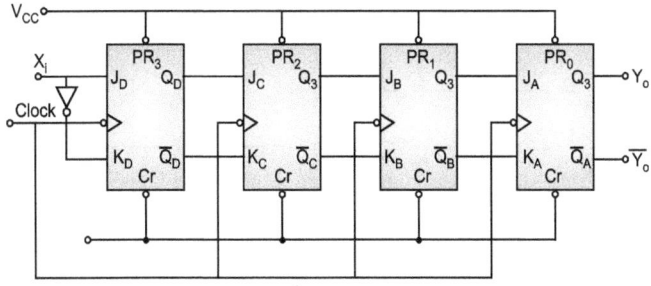

Fig. 4.37

- In Fig. 4.37, X_i is input and Y_o is output of serial in serial out shift register.
- The process of entering the digital data starts with the least significant bits. The data input is entered with falling edge of clock pulse, hence number of clock pulses required to enter the data is equal to the length of digital data or size of shift register. The data is read, bit by bit at output Y_o with clock pulse.

- Let us consider the data 0111 is applied to the input. How the data was entered in shift register is given in Table 4.21 and waveforms of shift register for serial input are shown in Fig. 4.38.

Table 4.21

CLK No.	X_i	Q_D	Q_C	Q_B	Q_A
0	1 (LSB)	0	0	0	0
1	1	1	0	0	0
2	1	1	1	0	0
4	0	1	1	1	0
4		0	1	1	1

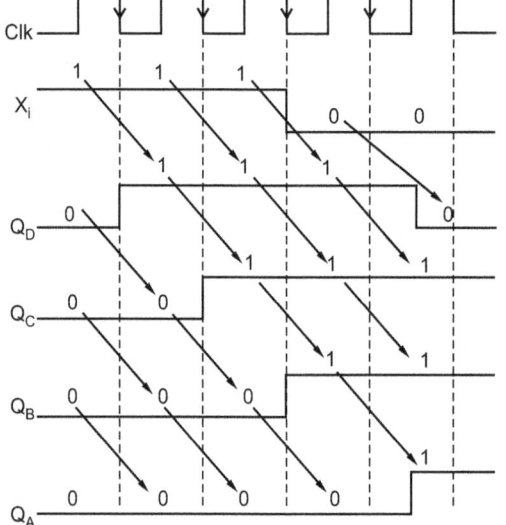

Fig. 4.38

Operation :

The input of flip-flop D is X_i, flip-flop of C is Q_D, flip-flop of B is Q_C and flip-flop of A is Q_B. All flip-flops operate as D flip-flop and input applied is 0111.

Initially shift register is cleared.

$$Q_D\ Q_C\ Q_B\ Q_A = 0000 \text{ and input } X_i = 1$$

4.20 SHIFT REGISTER

- The data can be entered in serial or parallel form and can be retrieved in the serial or parallel form. The serial form means bit by bit (one bit at time) and parallel means all the bits are simultaneously retrieved. On the basis of data entered (write) and retrieved (read), the registers are classified as,
- Serial In Serial Out
- Serial In Parallel Out
- Parallel In Serial Out
- Parallel In Parallel Out
- Registers, in which data are entered or/and retrieved in serial form, are referred to as shift register.

4.20.1 Serial In Serial Out Shift Register

> **Q.** Draw and explain the circuit diagram of 4 bit shift register with serial left shift.
> **[May 05, 4 M]**

- In serial in serial out shift register, data is entered and retrieved in serial fashion with clock.
- The logic diagram of 4-bit serial in serial out shift register using J-K flip-flop is shown Fig. 4.37.

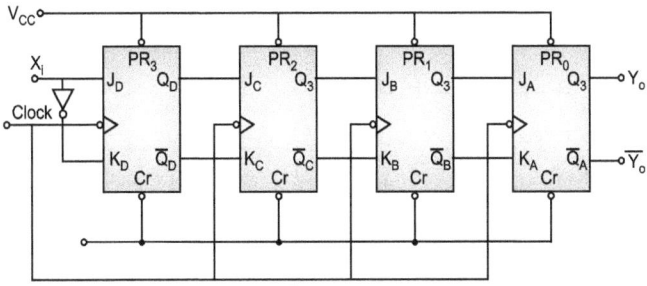

Fig. 4.37

- In Fig. 4.37, X_i is input and Y_o is output of serial in serial out shift register.
- The process of entering the digital data starts with the least significant bits. The data input is entered with falling edge of clock pulse, hence number of clock pulses required to enter the data is equal to the length of digital data or size of shift register. The data is read, bit by bit at output Y_o with clock pulse.

- Let us consider the data 0111 is applied to the input. How the data was entered in shift register is given in Table 4.21 and waveforms of shift register for serial input are shown in Fig. 4.38.

Table 4.21

CLK No.	X_i	Q_D	Q_C	Q_B	Q_A
0	1 (LSB)	0	0	0	0
1	1	1	0	0	0
2	1	1	1	0	0
4	0	1	1	1	0
4		0	1	1	1

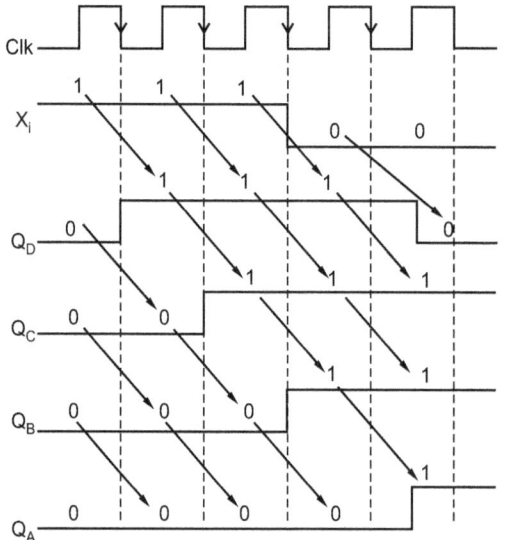

Fig. 4.38

Operation :

The input of flip-flop D is X_i, flip-flop of C is Q_D, flip-flop of B is Q_C and flip-flop of A is Q_B. All flip-flops operate as D flip-flop and input applied is 0111.

Initially shift register is cleared.

$$Q_D\ Q_C\ Q_B\ Q_A = 0000 \text{ and input } X_i = 1$$

DIGITAL ELECTRONICS LOGIC DESIGN (S.E. COMP.)   SEQUENTIAL LOGIC

- At negative edge of first clock pulse, the input data is entered into the flip-flop and at the end of first clock pulse,

$$Q_D\ Q_C\ Q_B\ Q_A = 1000 \text{ and input } X_i = 1$$

- At negative edge of second clock pulse, the inputs are entered and at the end of second clock pulse,

$$Q_D\ Q_C\ Q_B\ Q_A = 1100 \text{ and input } X_i = 1$$

- At negative edge of third clock pulse, the inputs are entered and at the end of third clock pulse,

$$Q_D\ Q_C\ Q_B\ Q_A = 1110 \text{ and input } X_i = 0$$

- At negative edge of fourth clock pulse, the inputs are entered and at the end of fourth clock pulse,

$$Q_D\ Q_C\ Q_B\ Q_A = 0111$$

Disadvantages :
- n clock pulses are required to enter the n-bit data.
- n clock pulses are required to read the n-bit data.
- Once the data is read, it will be lost.

4.20.2 Serial in Parallel Out Shift Register

- In serial in parallel out shift register, data is entered into the register in serial fashion same as serial in serial out shift register and read from the shift register in parallel fashion. In serial output shift register, clock pulses are required to read the data and once the data is read, it will be lost, but in parallel out shift register, clock pulse(s) is not required to read the data and data is not lost after the read operation.
- The logic diagram of four-bits serial in parallel out shift register using D flip-flop is shown in Fig. 4.39.

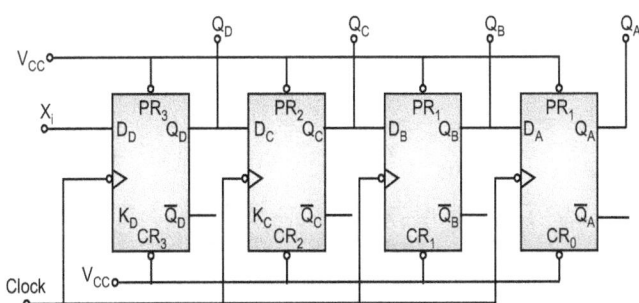

Fig. 4.39

where X_i is serial input for shift register and $Q_D\ Q_C\ Q_B\ Q_A$ are the parallel outputs of shift register.

4.20.3 Parallel In Serial Out Shift Register

Q. Draw and explain the circuit diagram of 4 bit shift register with the following facility parallel in serial out and reset. **[Dec. 08, 6 M]**

Q. Explain with a neat diagram working of parallel in serial out 4-bit shift register. Draw necessary timing diagram. **[May 10, 6 M]**

Q. How will you design parallel in serial out 4bit register having both shift right and shift left facility. **[Dec. 07, 8 M]**

- In parallel in serial out shift register, the data is entered in parallel fashion and data is read in serial fashion. There are two types of parallel loading :
    1. Asynchronous loading,
    2. Synchronous loading.

1. Asynchronous loading :

- In asynchronous loading, the preset inputs are used to load the data simultaneously. The logic diagram of four bit parallel in serial out shift register with asynchronous loading is shown in Fig. 4.40.

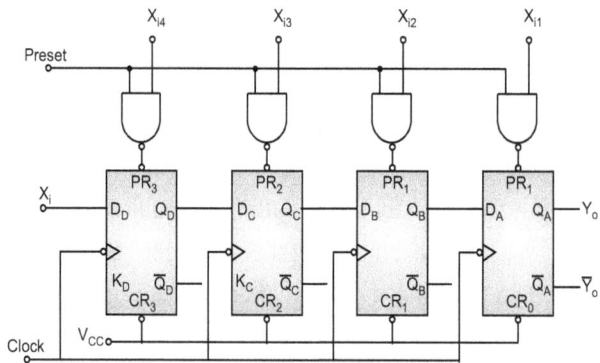

Fig. 4.40

- Initially, connecting the clear input to ground clears the flip-flops. The inputs are given to the parallel inputs (X_{i1}, X_{i2}, X_{i4} and X_{i4}) and preset is connected to logic '0', the output of NAND gate is complement of input, the preset input is active low, flip-flop is set for '0' and unchanged for '1'. The data are written into the registers. The inputs are written into the registers without clock pulse. Such parallel loading is known as asynchronous loading. The data is read from output lines Y_O bit by bit by applying the clock pulse. Once, data is read, it will be lost.

- For example, let us assume the data stored in a shift register is 0101 and it will be read from the output line Y_O. How the data is read from the shift register is given in Table 4.22 and waveforms of shift register for serial out are shown in Fig. 4.41

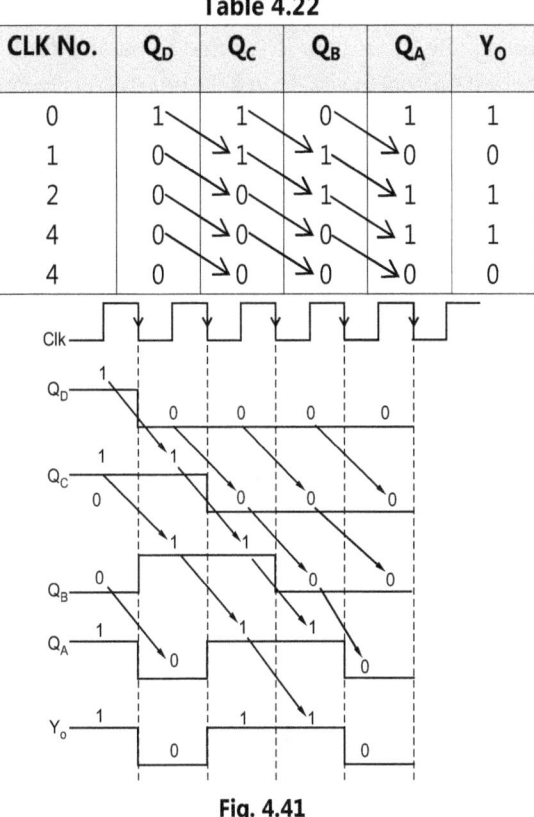

Fig. 4.41

Operation :

The input of flip-flop D is '0', flip-flop of C is Q_D, flip-flop of B is Q_C and flip-flop of A is Q_B. All flip-flops operate as D flip-flop.

Initially data stored in a shift register is 1101.

$Q_D\ Q_C\ Q_B\ Q_A$ = 1101 and output Y_O = 1

- At negative edge of first clock pulse,

    $Q_D\ Q_C\ Q_B\ Q_A$ = 0110 and output Y_O = 0

- At negative edge of second clock pulse,

    $Q_D\ Q_C\ Q_B\ Q_A$ = 0011 and output Y_O = 1

- At negative edge of third clock pulse,

    $Q_D\ Q_C\ Q_B\ Q_A$ = 0001 and output Y_O = 1

- At negative edge of fourth clock pulse,

    $Q_D\ Q_C\ Q_B\ Q_A$ = 0000 and output Y_O = 0

In n-bit parallel in parallel out shift register, n clock pulses are required to read the data and once the data is read, it will be lost.

2. Synchronous loading :

- In synchronous loading, the input data is entered in parallel form with clock pulse. The logic diagram of four bit parallel in serial out shift register in synchronous mode is shown in Fig. 4.42.

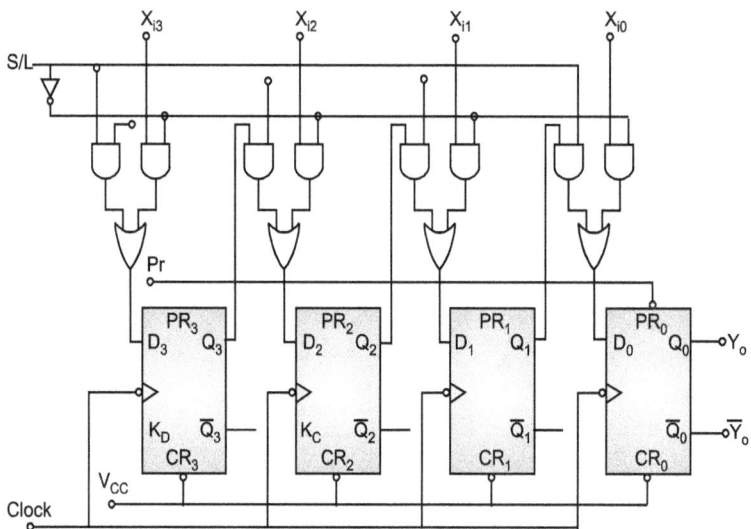

Fig. 4.42

- $\overline{\text{Shift/ Load}}$ control signal is used to control the operation of the shift register. When $\overline{\text{Shift/ Load}}$ is at logic '1', the data is read from Y_0 bit-by-bit with clock pulse. When $\overline{\text{Shift/ Load}}$ is at logic '0', the data inputs X_{i1}, X_{i2}, X_{i4} and X_{i4} load simultaneously with clock pulse. Such type of loading is referred as synchronous loading.
- For example : Consider data inputs are 0101.
- When $\overline{\text{Shift/ Load}}$ signal is 0, the outputs of gates G_1, G_4, G_5 and G_7 are 0 and outputs of gates G_2, G_4, G_6 and G_8 are same to the inputs 0101. The outputs of OR gates are 0101, and these are inputs to D flip-flops. It is loaded into register with falling of the clock pulse.
- When $\overline{\text{Shift/ Load}}$ is 0, the outputs of gates G_2, G_4, G_6 and G_8 are 0 and the outputs of gates G_1, G_4, G_5 and G_7 are 0 Q_4 Q_2 Q_1. The outputs of OR gates are 0 Q_4 Q_2 Q_1, and these are the input to D flip-flops. It is loaded into the register with falling edge of clock pulse. It shows that data is shifted in register and we get output at Y_0.

4.20.4 Parallel In Parallel Out Shift Register

- In parallel in parallel out shift register, data is entered as well as read in parallel fashion. There are two types of parallel loading : (1) Asynchronous loading and (2) Synchronous loading. The logic diagram of four-bit asynchronous loading parallel in and parallel out is shown in Fig. 4.43 and synchronous loading parallel in parallel out is shown in Fig. 4.44.

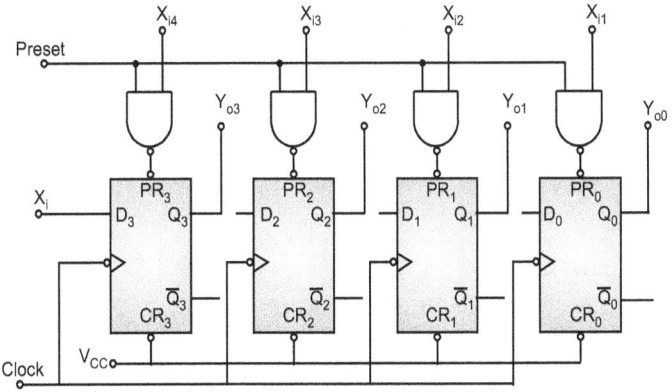

Fig. 4.43

Fig. 4.44

4.20.5 Bi-directional Shift Register

Q. Draw and explain 4 bit bidirectional shift register.	[Dec. 11, 8 M]
Q. Draw the circuit of 4-bit bidirectional shift register.	[Dec. 05, 6 M]
Q. Draw and explain 4-bit shift register having shift and right. Explain any one application of such register.	[May 06, 6 M]

- In bi-directional shift register, the data is shifted to left as well as to right direction. The direction is controlled by the control input $R/\overline{L}$. The four-bit bi-directional shift register is shown in Fig. 4.45

- When R/L̄ control signal is high, the gates G_1, G_4, G_5 and G_7 are enabled. The output of flip-flop A is input for flip-flop B, the output of flip-flop B is input for flip-flop C, the output of flip-flop C is input for flip-flop D and X_{iR} is input for flip-flop. Data is shifted right with clock pulse.

- When R/L̄ control signal is low, the gates G_2, G_4, G_6 and G_8 are enabled. The output of the flip-flop D is input for flip-flop C, the output of the flip-flop C is input for flip-flop B, the output of the flip-flop B is input for flip-flop A and X_{iL} is input for flip-flop D. Data is shifted left with clock pulse.

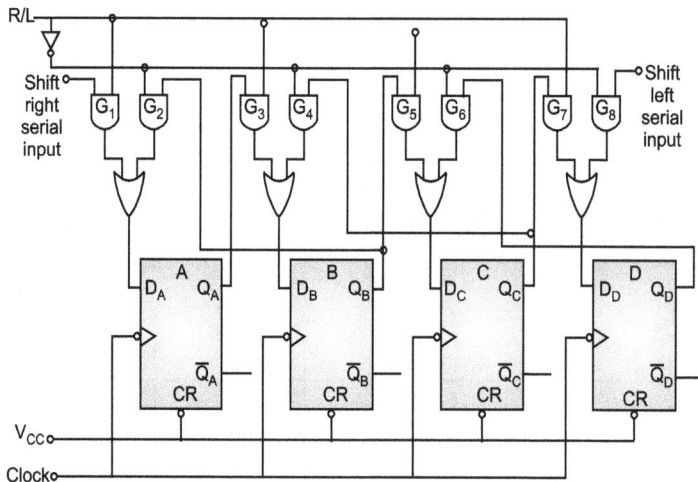

Fig. 4.45

Application of Bi-Directional Shift Register :

- The bi-directional shift register is used to multiply or divide the number by 2^n, provided that '1' is not shifted out of register. For the multiplication of number by 2^n, the data is shifted in left side by the amount of n bits with $X_{iL} = 0$.

- For example : Consider the number is loaded in shift register 0001 and we have to multiply number by $4 = 2^2$.

$$0 0 0 1$$
$$0 0 0 1 \times 2 = 0 0 1 0 \text{ shifted left by 1 bit with } X_{iL} = 0$$
$$0 0 0 1 \times 2^2 = 0 1 0 0 \text{ shifted left by 2 bits with } X_{iL} = 0$$

- In this process the most significant bit is lost.

- For the division of number by 2^n, the data is shifted in right by the amount of n bits with $X_{iR} = 0$. For example, consider the number is loaded in shift register 1000 and we have to divide the number by 2^2.

$$1000$$
$$1000/2 = 0100 \quad \text{shifted right by 1 bit with } X_{iR} = 0$$
$$1000/2^2 = 0010 \quad \text{shifted right by 2 bits with } X_{iR} = 0$$

In this process the least significant bit is lost.

4.20.6 Universal Register

- The universal shift register operates in all possible four modes (SISO, SIPO, PISO, PIPO) and also as bi-directional shift registers. Logic diagram of four-bit shift register operates in all four modes as shown in Fig. 4.46.

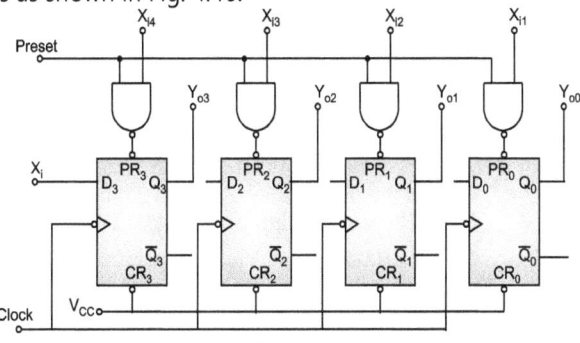

Fig. 4.46

where, X_i is serial input of shift register

$X_{i4}, X_{i2}, X_{i1}, X_{i0}$ are four parallel inputs of shift register

Y_O is serial output of shift register

$Y_{O4}, Y_{O2}, Y_{O1}, Y_{O0}$ are four parallel outputs of shift register.

4.20.7 4-bit Bidirectional Universal Shift Register (74HC194)

- The 74HCI194 is a universal Bidirectional Universal Shift Register it has both serial and parallel input and output capability.

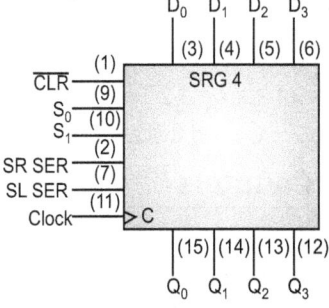

Fig. 4.47 : The 74HCI194 4-bit directional universal register

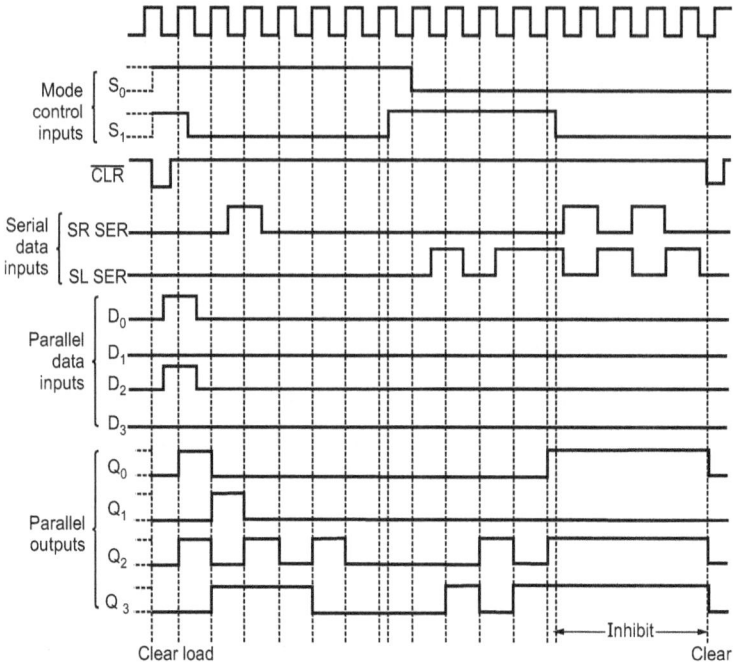

Fig. 4.48 : The timing diagram of 741HC 194

4.21 COUNTERS

- Counter are used for counting the number of events occurred.
- A circuit that counts electrical pulses, applied as input to it is known as counter.
- In practice these circuits are used as event counters i.e. to count number of event occurred. Electrical pulses are generated corresponding to the occurrence of an event and these pulses are given as input to the counters.
- Flip-flops are used for the construction of counters an N-bit counter consists of N flip-flops.
- A counter with n flip-flops has 2^n possible states. Therefore a 4 bit up counter can count from 0 to 7 while 4-bit down counter can count from 15 down to 0.
- Number of distinct states in the operation of counter is known as modulus of that counter and that counter is called mod 2^n counter.
  e.g. 4-bit counter, the number of states is 2^4 = 8. Thus modulus of three bit counter is 8 and it is also called as modulo 2^4 i.e. mod 8 counter.

4.21.1 Classification of Counters

- Basically counters are divided into types
- **(a) Synchronous counter :** In synchronous counters all the flip-flops receive the external clock pulse simultaneously e.g. ring and Johnson counter.

(b) Asynchronous counter : For asynchronous counters the external clock signal is applied to one flip-flop and then the output of preceding flip-flop is connected to the clock of next flip-flop.

- Based upon output sequence the counters are also classified into three categories.

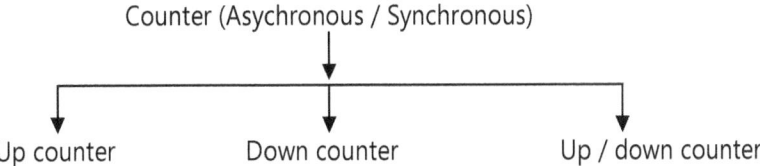

- **Up counter-** If the decimal equivalent of the counter output increases with successive clock pulses, it is called as up counter. For example in a three bit up counter output goes from 0 to 7.
- **Down counter-** If the decimal equivalent of the counter output decreases with successive clock pulses, it is called as down counter. For example in a four bit down counter output goes from 15 down to 0.
- **Up/Down counter-** A counter which can count in any direction i.e. up or down, depending upon direction control input is called as up/down counter.

4.22 ASYNCHRONOUS (RIPPLE) COUNTERS

- A two-bit asynchronous counter is shown in Fig. 4.49 (a). The external clock is connected to the clock input of the first flip-flop (FF_0) only. So, FF_0 changes state at the falling edge of each clock pulse, but FF_1 changes only when triggered by the falling edge of the Q output of FF_0.
- Because of the inherent propagation delay through a flip-flop, the transition of the input clock pulse and a transition of the Q output of FF0 can never occur at exactly the same time. Therefore, the flip-flops cannot be triggered simultaneously, producing an asynchronous operation.

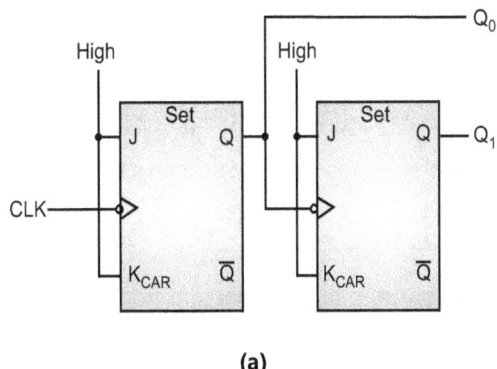

(a)

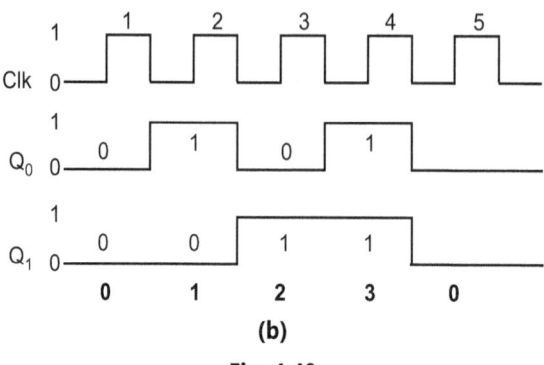

Fig. 4.49

- Note that for simplicity, the transitions of Q_0, Q_1 and CLK in the timing diagram above are shown as simultaneous even though this is an asynchronous counter. Actually, there is some small delay between the CLK, Q_0 and Q_1 transitions.

- Usually, all the CLEAR inputs are connected together, so that a single pulse can clear all the flip-flops before counting starts. The clock pulse fed into FF_0 is rippled through the other counters after propagation delays, like a ripple on water, hence the name Ripple Counter.

- The 2-bit ripple counter circuit above has four different states, each one corresponding to a count value. Similarly, a counter with n flip-flops can have 2 to the power n states. The number of states in a counter is known as its mod (modulo) number. Thus a 2-bit counter is a mod-4 counter.

- A mod-n counter may also described as a divide-by-n counter. This is because the most significant flip-flop (the furthest flip-flop from the original clock pulse) produces one pulse for every n pulses at the clock input of the least significant flip-flop (the one triggers by the clock pulse).

4.22.1 4-Bit Asynchronous Up (Ripple) Counter

Q. Draw and explain 4-bit asynchronous up-counter. Also draw the necessary timing diagram. [May 07, Dec. 12, 6 M]
Q. Draw 4-bit asynchronous counter. Explain with timing diagram. [Dec.09, 8 M]

- For the implementation of 4-bit counter, three flip flops are required.
- The number of distinct states in the operation of this counter is 2^3 = 8. Therefore, it is also called as mod-8 counter.
- In case of 4-bit up counter, the output goes from 0 to 7.
- Let Q_2, Q_1 and Q_0 be the outputs of the three flip flops used for the design. The count sequence is as shown in the table 4.23.

Table 4.23 : Count sequence of 4-bit up counter

Q_2	Q_1	Q_0	State of the counter
0	0	0	0
0	0	1	1
0	1	0	2
0	1	1	4
1	0	0	4
1	0	1	5
1	1	0	6
1	1	1	7

- From the table 4.23 it is clear that the output Q_0 of the least significant flip flop changes for every clock pulse applied to it. So it can be implemented using a T type flip flop with $T_0 = 1$.

- Also, the output Q_1 changes from 0 to 1 or 1 to 0, only when in the corresponding states Q_0 changes from 0 to 1. So it can be implemented using a T-type flip flop with $T_1 = 1$ and Q_0 is connected as its clock input.

- Similarly the output Q_2 changes only when Q_1 changes from 0 to 1. So it can be implemented using a T-type flip flop with $T_2 = 1$ and Q_1 is connected as its clock input. This completes the design and the resulting circuit is as shown as Fig. 4.50(a).

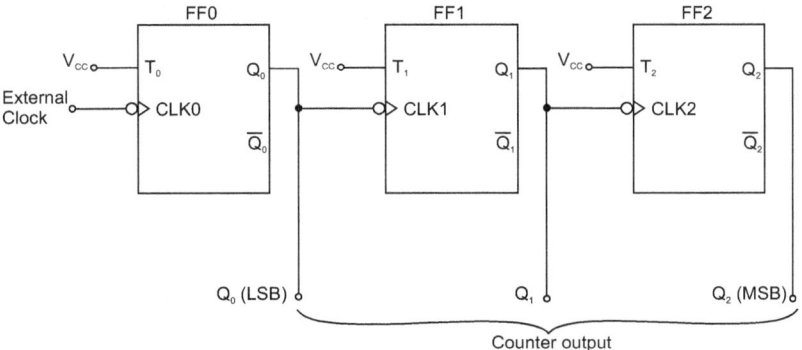

Fig. 4.50 (a) : 3-bit ripple up counter

- The waveforms of the outputs are shown in Fig. 4.50(b).

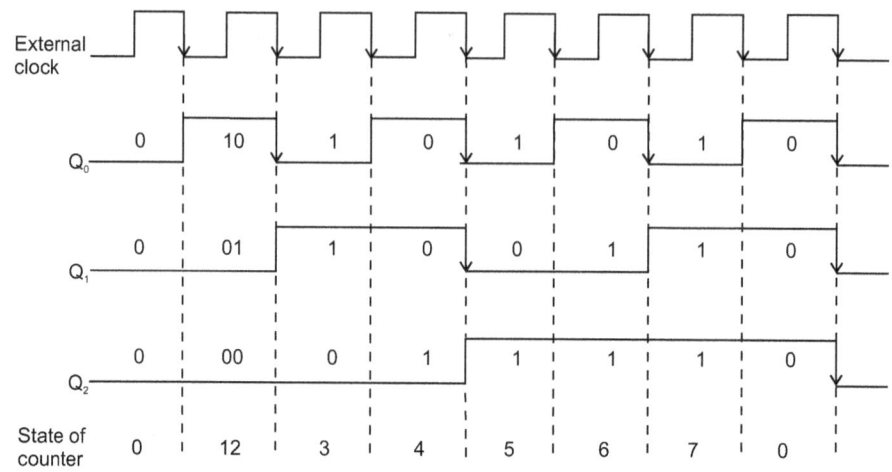

Fig. 4.50 (b) : Waveforms/Timing diagram of 4 bit ripple up counter

- From the waveform of external clock and Q_0, it is clear that two clock periods are required for the completion of one cycle of Q_0. Therefore, clock frequency is twice to that of Q_0 output. In other words the Q_0 is the divide by 2 ($\div$ 2) output with respect to clock frequency. Similarly Q_1 is the divide by 4 ($\div$ 4) output and Q_2 is divide by 8 ($\div$ 8) output with respect to clock frequency.
- Therefore this mod - 8 counter is also known as divide by 8 ($\div$ 8) counter.

4.22.2 4-Bit Asynchronous Up Counter

> Q. Draw 4-bit asynchronous counter. Also explain timing diagram for the same.
> Q. Draw and explain 4-bit binary up counting with this concept. Also draw the necessary timing diagram. Is there any frequency division concept in it? Comment on frequency generated at the output of each flip-flop. **[May 08, 4 M]**

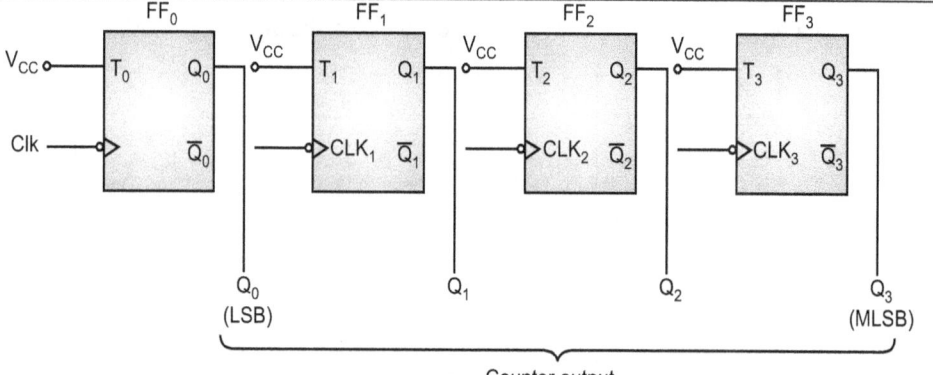

Fig. 4.51 : 4-bit (asynchronous ripple) counter

Fig. 4.51 shows the circuit diagram of 4-bit asynchronous counter using the T flip-flops.

- Since it is 4 bit asynchronous up counter, we need to use four flip-flops number of distinct states in the operation of this counter is 2^4 = 16.

DIGITAL ELECTRONICS LOGIC DESIGN (S.E. COMP.)　　　　　　　　　　SEQUENTIAL LOGIC

Therefore, it is called as mod-16 counter.
- Let Q_0, Q_1, Q_2 and Q_4 be the outputs of the three flip-flops used for the design. The count sequence is as shown in the table.
- Table 4.24 count sequence of 4-bit up counter.

Table 4.24

Q_4	Q_2	Q_1	Q_0	State of the counter
0	0	0	0	0
0	0	0	1	1
0	0	1	0	2
0	0	1	1	4
0	1	0	0	4
0	1	0	1	5
0	1	1	0	6
0	1	1	1	7
1	0	0	0	8
1	0	0	1	9
1	0	1	0	10
1	0	1	1	11
1	1	0	0	12
1	1	0	1	14
1	1	1	0	14
1	1	1	1	15

- From the table it is clear that the output Q_0 of the least significant flip-flop changes for every clock pulse applied to it. So it can be implemented using at type flip-flop with $T_0 = 1$.
- Also the output Q_1 changes from 0 to 1 or 1 to 0, only when in the corresponding states Q_0 changes from 0 to 1. So it can be implemented using a T-type flip flop with $T_1 = 1$ and Q_0 is connected as its clock input.
- Similarly the output Q_2 changes only when Q_1 changes from 0 to 1 so it can be implemented using a T-type flip-flop with $T_2 = 1$ and Q_1 is connected as its clock input.
- Similarly the output Q_4 changes only when Q_2 changes from 0 to 1 so it can be complemented using at type flip-flop with $T_4 = 1$ and Q_2 is connected as its clock input.
- Waveform of output shown below for 4 bit asynchronous (ripple) counter.

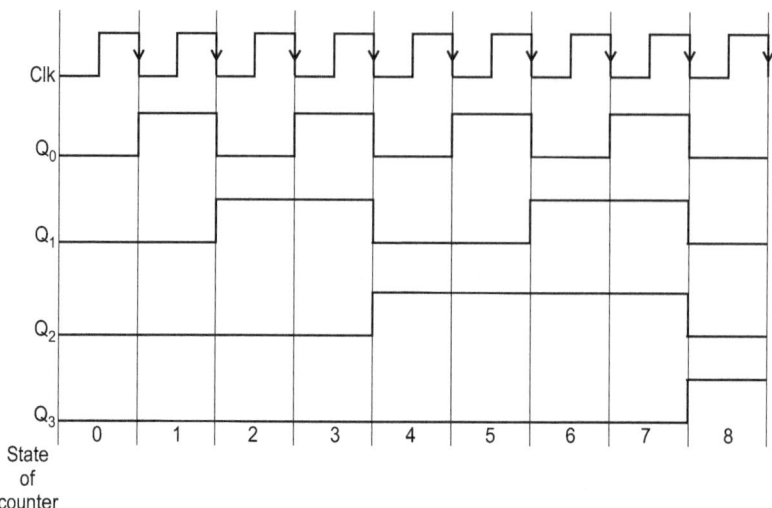

Fig. 4.52

4.22.3 3-bit Asynchronous Down Counter

Example 4.3 : Design 4 bit down ripple counter. Draw waveforms.   [Dec. 2007, 4 M]

Solution :

- 4 bit ripple down counter requires three flip flops. The counter output goes from 7 down to 0. The count sequence is as shown in table 4.25.

Table 4.25 : Count sequence of 4-bit down counter

Q_2	Q_1	Q_0	State of the counter
1	1	1	7
1	1	0	6
1	0	1	5
1	0	0	4
0	1	1	4
0	1	0	2
0	0	1	1
0	0	0	0

- As like previous example, the least significant stage can be implemented using T flip flop with $T_0 = 1$.
- Output Q_1 changes whenever there is 0 to 1 transition of Q_0, in the corresponding states. So we can realize it with a flip flop which is positive edge triggered. The Q_0 output needs to be connected to the clock input and $T_1 = 1$.

- When Q_0 makes transition from 0 to 1, $\bar{Q}_0$ changes from 1 to 0. So we can realize the second stage by using a negative edge triggered flip flop as shown in Fig. 4.53 with $T_1 = 1$. $\bar{Q}_0$ output needs to be connected as clock input.
- Similarly, the most significant stage can be realized with a negative edge triggered T flip flop with $T_2 = 1$ and $\bar{Q}_1$ connected as its clock input. This completes the design and the resulting circuit is as shown in Fig. 4.53. Also the waveforms of the outputs are shown in Fig. 4.54.

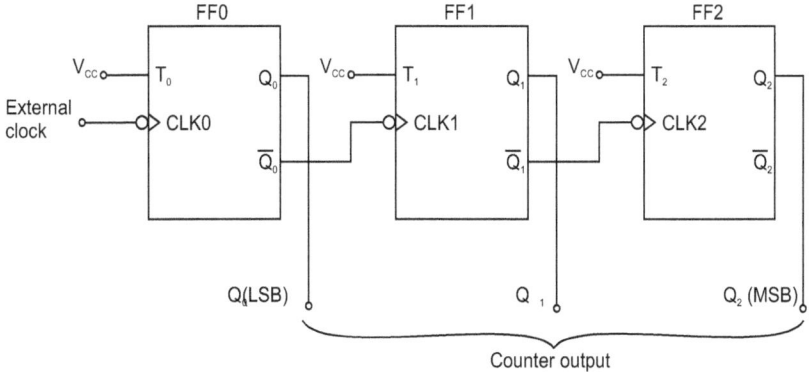

Fig. 4.53 : 3 bit ripple down counter

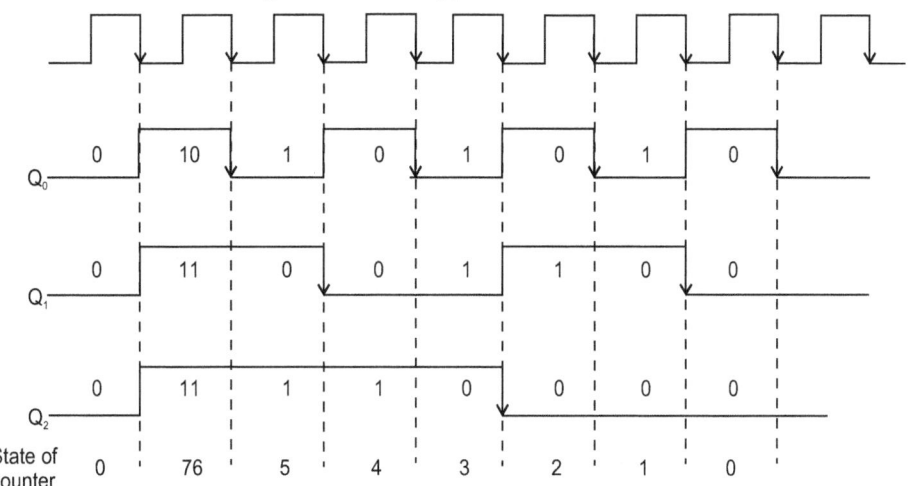

Fig. 4.54 : Waveforms/Timing diagram of 4 bit ripple down counter

4.22.4 4-bit Up / Down Ripple Counter

Example 4.4 :

Design a 4-bit binary Up/Down ripple counter with a control for Up/Down counting. Also draw timing diagram. [Dec. 2004, 8 M]

Solution :

- A ripple up counter Q output of the preceding stages are to be connected to the clock inputs of next stages.

- Similarly from example we know that for a ripple down counter $\bar{Q}$ outputs of preceeding stages are to be connected to the clock input of next stages.

- Therefore to design a Up/Down counter, AND-OR gates are used between flip flops as shown in Fig. 4.55.

- The upper AND gates are enabled when UP/Down input is at logic 1 which connect Q outputs to the inputs. While the lower AND gates are enabled when UP/Down input is 0 which connect $\bar{Q}$ outputs to the clock inputs. For 4-bit counter, 4 four flip flops are required.

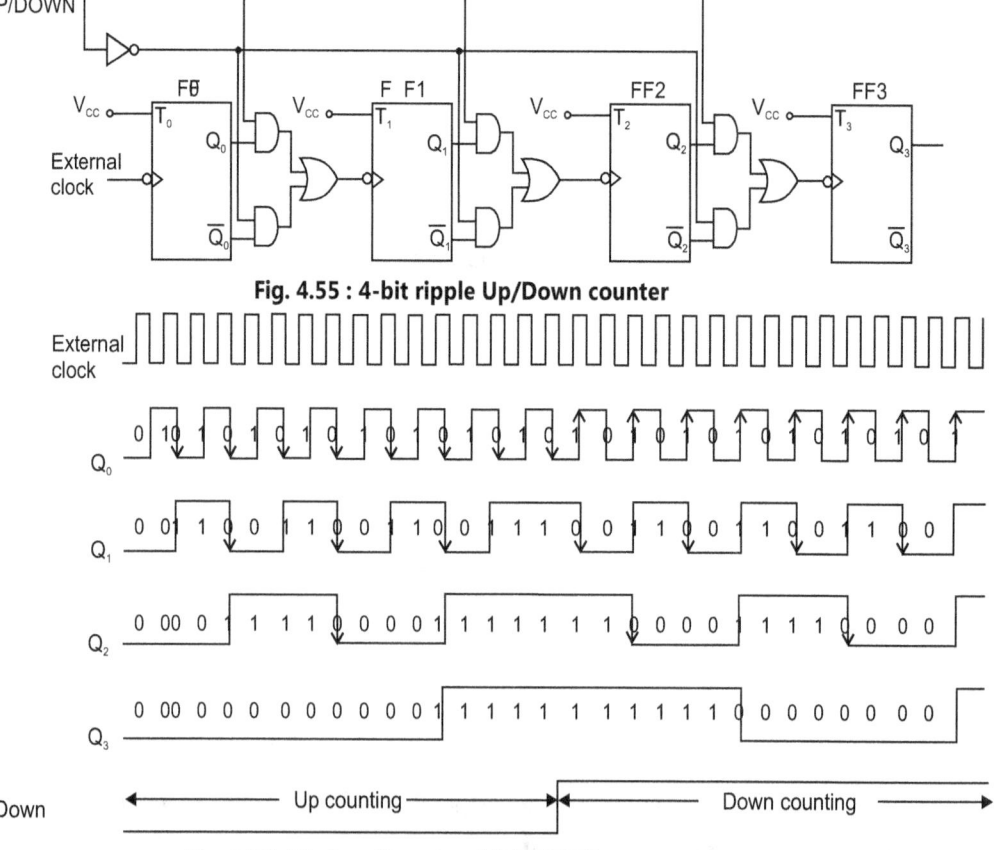

Fig. 4.55 : 4-bit ripple Up/Down counter

Fig. 4.56 : Timing diagram of 4-bit Up/Down counter

4.22.5 MOD-N counter (Modulus of the counter)

Q. What is Mod counter ?

- N bit ripple counter is called as modulus N counter.

- Modulus of counter = 2^n
- From the modulus we can conclude the number of states of counter.

Table 4.26

Sr. No.	Counter type	Modulus
1	2 bit	MOD – 4
2	4 bit	MOD – 8
4	4 bit	MOD - 16

Example 4.5 : Design mod 5 ripple up counter.

Solution :

- It is given that modulus of counter is 5. So number of distinct states in the operation of the counter are 5. The number of flip flops required can be obtained using the following ineqality.

$$2^N \geq \text{Modulus of counter} \quad \ldots(4.9)$$

Where N = number of flip flops.

For N = 1 & N = 2 the inequality is not satisfied.

Putting N = 4, we get,

$$2^3 \geq 5$$
$$\Rightarrow 8 \geq 5$$

- The inequality is satisfied. Therefore for the implementation of mod 5 counter three flip flops are required.
- As ripple up counter is to be designed, we have to use three T flip flops with the T inputs connected to V_{CC}. Also Q_0 and Q_1 outputs are to be connected as the clock input of the respective next stages.
- The count sequence is shown in table 4.27.

Table 4.27 : count sequence of mod 5 ripple up counter

Q_2	Q_1	Q_0	State of the counter
0	0	0	0
0	0	1	1
0	1	0	2
0	1	1	4
1	0	0	4
0	0	0	0

- The counter output goes from 0 to 4. Therefore, it is a truncated counter. So we need to design 'reset logic'.

- From the table it is clear that after the state 4 the counter should be resetted i.e. The state 5 should not occur.

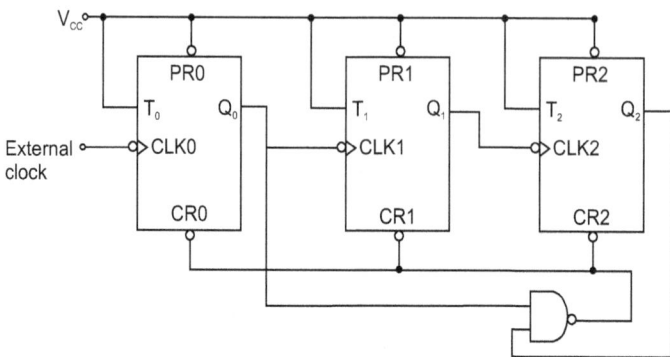

Fig. 4.57: Mod-5 ripple up counter

- For state 5, $Q_2 Q_1 Q_0 = 101$. Therefore whenever both Q_2 & Q_0 become 1, at that instant the counter should be resetted. It can be achived with a simple 2 input NAND gate. The output of the NAND gate must be connected to the clear input of all flip flops, so that the counter gets resetted after the state 4. The resulting circuit diagram is as shown in Fig. 4.57.

4.22.6 Frequency Division

Q. What is frequency division

- The feature of the D-type flip-flop is as a binary divider, for frequency division or as a "divide-by-2" counter. Here the inverted output terminal Q (NOT-Q) is connected directly back to the Data input terminal D giving the device "feedback" as shown below.
- **Divide-by-2 Counter**

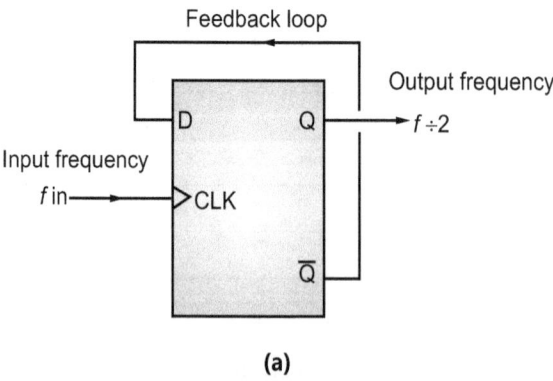

(a)

Fig. 4.58

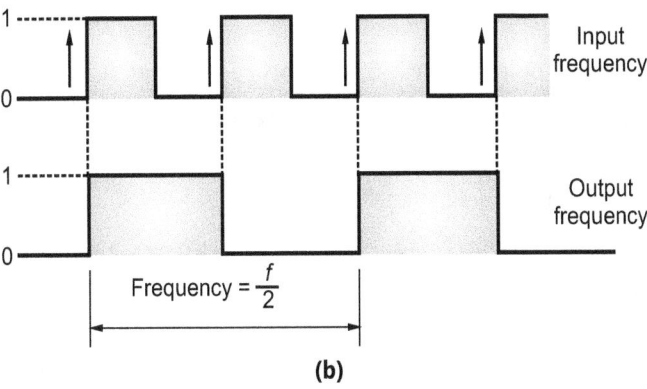

(b)
Fig. 4.58

- It can be seen from the frequency waveforms above, that by "feeding back" the output from Q to the input terminal D, the output pulses at Q have a frequency that are exactly one half ($f \div 2$) that of the input clock frequency. In other words the circuit produces frequency division as it now divides the input frequency by a factor of two (an octave).
- This then produces a type of counter called a "ripple counter" and in ripple counters, the clock pulse triggers the first flip-flop whose output triggers the second flip-flop, which in turn triggers the third flip-flop and so on through the chain producing a ripple effect (hence their name) of the timing signal as it passes through the chain.

Frequency Division using Toggle Flip-flops

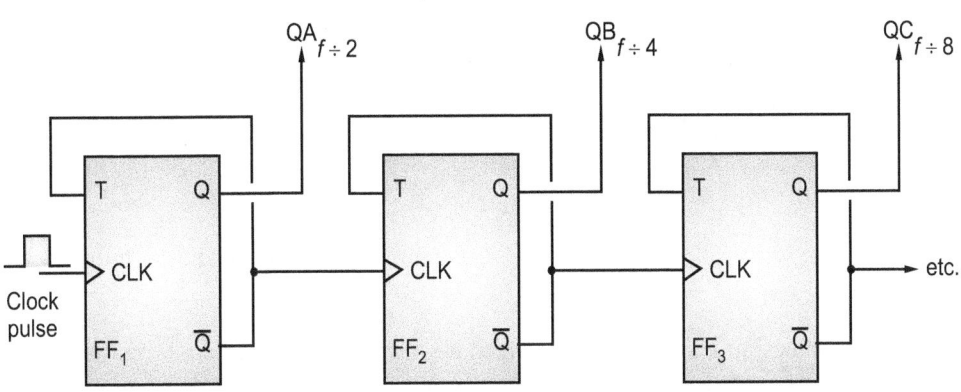

Fig. 4.59

- This type of counter circuit used for frequency division is commonly known as an Asynchronous 4-bit Binary Counter as the output on QA to QC, which is 4 bits wide, is a binary count from 0 to 7 for each clock pulse. In an asynchronous counter, the clock is applied only to the first stage with the output of one flip-flop stage providing the clocking signal for the next flip-flop stage and subsequent stages derive the clock from the previous stage with the clock pulse being halved by each stage.

Example 4.6 :

A certain counter is being pulsed by a 256 kHz clock signal. The output frequency from the last flip flop is 2 kHz : (i) Determine the mod of counter (ii) Determine the counting range.

[May 2005, 2 M]

Solution :

- Input clock frequency is 256 kHz & the output frequency from last flip flop is 2 kHz.
- Therefore it is divide by (256/2=128) counter ($\div$ 128).
- As it is a divide by 128 counters, the modulus of counter is also 128. Therefore it is a mod-128 counter.
- The counting range in case of up counter will be from 0 to 127 i.e. the binary output will go from 0000000 to 1111111.
- Similarly, the counting range in case of down counter will be from 127 down to 0 ie. the binary output will go from 1111111 to 0000000.

4.22.7 4 bit Asynchronous BCD Ripple Counter

Example 4.7 :

Design BCD ripple counter. [Dec. 2007, 4 M]

Solution :

- We know that, binary coded decimal (BCD) is in the range from 0 to 9. Therefore modulus of counter is 10.
- For N = 1, N = 2 & N = 4 the inequality 2.9 is not satisfied.
- Putting N=4 in the inequality 2.9 we get,

$$2^4 \geq 10$$
$$\Rightarrow \quad 16 \geq 10$$

- The inequality is satisfied. Therefore for the implementation of BCD counter four flip flops are required.
- Here we shall design a up counter, for which we require four T flip flops with the T inputs connected to V_{CC}. Also Q_0, Q_1 & Q_2 outputs are connected as the clock inputs of the respective next stages.
- In BCD counter the state $Q_4 Q_2 Q_1 Q_0$ = 1010 should not occur i.e. when Q_4 & Q_1 both become 1, at the same instant the counter should be resetted. Therefore we require a 2 input NAND gate as reset logic for BCD counter. The resulting circuit diagram is shown in Fig. 4.60.

DIGITAL ELECTRONICS LOGIC DESIGN (S.E. COMP.) — SEQUENTIAL LOGIC

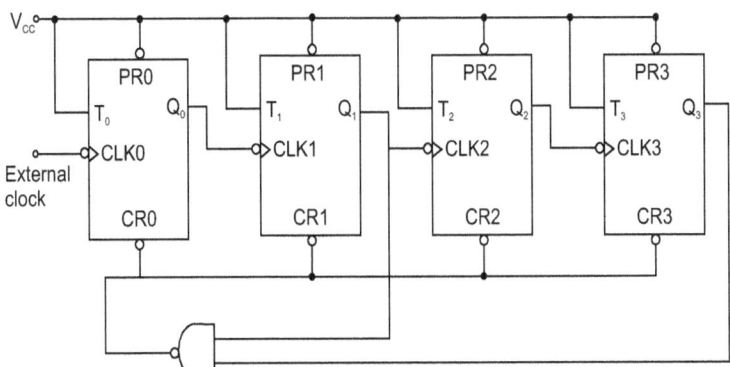

Fig. 4.60 : BCD ripple up counter

4.22.8 Drawbacks of Ripple Counter [Dec. 2007, 4 M]

Q. What are drawbacks of ripple counter?

- Observe the timing diagram of 4 bit ripple up counter shown in Fig. 4.49.
- Upon application of clock pulse, the count sequence proceeds from 7 to 0. That is the output changes from $Q_2 Q_1 Q_0 = 111$ to $Q_2 Q_1 Q_0 = 000$.
- This change from 111 to 000 does not take place simultaneously. As shown in Fig. 4.49 external clock applied to FF0 will change the output Q_0 from 1 to 0 first. Further the 1 to 0 change in Q_0 acts as trigger for FF1 and its output also change from 1 to 0. Now this 1 to 0 transition in Q_1 triggers FF2 to change its output from 1 to 0. In this manner the next state 000 is obtained from the present state 111.
- As explained above, the carry ripples through the circuit, like the ripple in water. Therefore asynchronous counters are known as ripple counters.
- Let us assume that each flip flop shown in Fig. 4.49 has propogation delay of 50 nS duration, the output Q_0 will change from 1 to 0. After another 50 nS duration Q_1 will change from 1 to 0, i.e. after 50 + 50 = 100 nS duration since the clock pulse is applied to FF0. Similarly FF2 will take separate 50 ns duration for the change from 1 to 0. So Q_2 will change after 50+50+50=150 nS duration since the clock pulse is applied to FF0.
- This time period will increase as the numbers of flip flops are increased. This limits the frequency of operation of ripple counters.
- In short, 4 bit ripple up counter requires 150 nS duration to change from state 111 to 000 while in case of synchronous counter shown in Fig. 4.46 as all the flip flops are clocked simultaneously, it takes 50 nS duration for the same change. Also this duration is constant for any number of flip flops.
- Thus asynchronous counters are slower than synchronous counters.

- Another drawback of asynchronous counters is that they can generate straight binary sequences in up or down direction while synchronous counters can be designed for any count sequence.
- Also we have to use JK or T flip flops only in the design of asynchronous counters.

4.23 Study of IC 7490

Q. Which IC is useful for Mod 10 counter?

- IC 74C90 is also known as decade counter IC or MOD-10 counter IC as number of distinct states in its operation are ten.
- It consists of two separate asynchronous counters such as MOD-2 and MOD-5.
- MOD-2 counter is build with a single flip flop known as FF A.
- It can accept clock signal externally at input A and has the output.
- MOD-5 counter is built internally with three flip flops - FF B, FF C and FF D. It also can accept clock signal externally at input B and has the outputs Q_B, Q_C, Q_D.
- Thus, there are four flip flops in the IC 74C90, which are negative edge triggered.
- When MOD-2 and MOD-5 counters are cascaded, it acts as a MOD (2 × 5) = MOD 10 counter.
- The IC has two reset inputs R_1, R_2 and two set inputs S_1, S_2 which are active high inputs. When R_1, R_2 both are connected to all flip flops are cleared i.e. $Q_D Q_C Q_B Q_A$ = 0000. When S_1, S_2 both are connected to logic 1 the counter output is = 1001. The internal structure of IC 74C90 is as shown in Fig. 4.28.

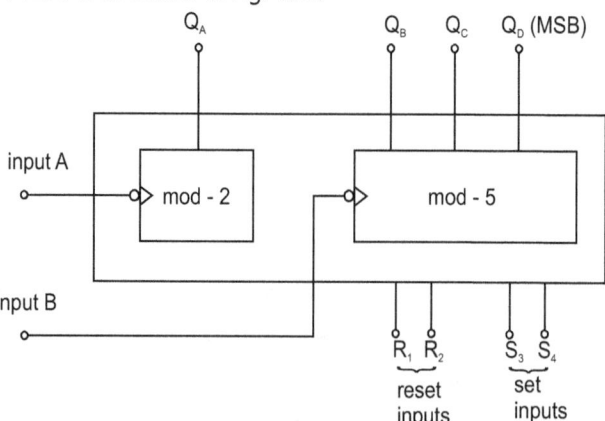

Fig. 4.61 : Internal structure of IC74C90

- As shown in Fig. 4.61 MOD - 2 and MOD - 5 counters can work separately with respect to clock signal applied at input A and input B respective.
- If we connect the output of MOD-2 counter as to input B i.e. as clock signal of MOD-5 counter then it becomes a MOD-10 counter. The count sequence is given in table 4.28.

Table 4.28

Flip-flop Outputs				State of the counter
Q_D	Q_C	Q_B	Q_A	
0	0	0	0	0
0	0	0	1↘0	1
0	0	1	0	2
0	0	1	1↘0	4
0	1	0	0	4
0	1	0	1↘0	5
0	1	1	0	6
0	1	1	1↘0	7
1	0	0	0	8
1	0	0	1	9

- As the external clock signal is applied at input A, output of MOD 2 counter changes at the negative edge of every clock pulse.
- Further MOD-5 counter changes from 0 to 4 (Q_D Q_C Q_B = 000 to Q_D Q_C Q_B = 100) only when the Q_A output changes from 1 to 0 as shown in table 4.28.
- MOD-10 counter using IC 74c90 is as shown in Fig. 4.62.

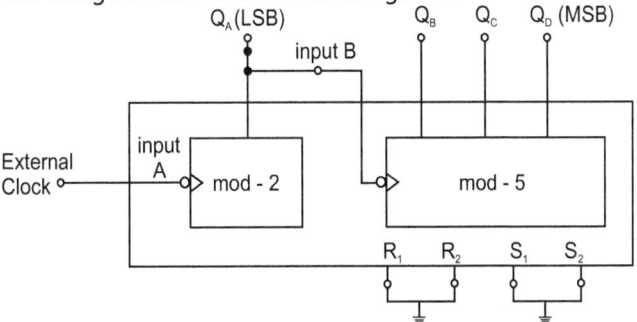

Fig. 4.62 : MOD-10 counter using 74C90

- As shown in Fig. 4.62, for normal operation the set and reset inputs are disabled by connected them to ground.

Example 4.8 :

Design MOD-8 counter using 74C90   [May 2007, 4 M]

Solution :

- For MOD-8 counter, we first connect the IC 74C90 as MOD-10 counter as shown in Fig. 4.63.

- In MOD-8 counter, there are 8 distinct states and output varies from 0000 to 0111 i.e. when the state 1000 is required the counter must be resetted.

- For the state 1000, output $Q_D = 1$ Study of IC 7490. Therefore, Q_D is to be connected to the reset inputs R_1 & R_2 and

- As soon as the circuit reaches to state 1000, Q_D becomes 1 and immediately the counter is reset to 0000. Fig. 4.63 shows the MOD-8 counter.

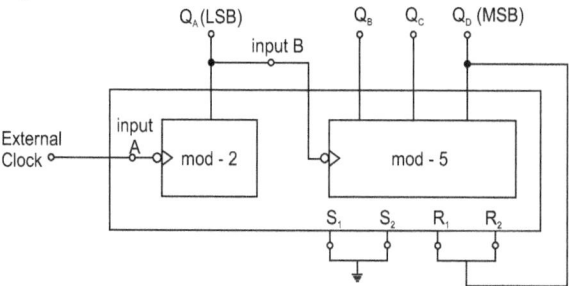

Fig. 4.63 : MOD - 8 counter using IC 74C90

Example 4.9 :

Design divide by 94 counter using IC 74C90.

Solution :

- For divide by 94 or MOD-94 counter we first correct the two ICs 74C90 as MOD -100 counter as shown in Fig. 4.64.

- In MOD 94 counter 9 is the ten's digit & 4 is the one's digit. There are 94 distinct states and output varies from 0000 to 0010 ie. when the state 1001 0011 is reached the counter must be resetted.

- For the state 1001 0011, the outputs Q_D, Q_A of ten's digit IC and the outputs Q_B, Q_A of one's digit IC are 1.Therefore the respective outputs need to be AND ed together and connect them to the reset inputs of both ICs. It is shown in Fig. 4.64.

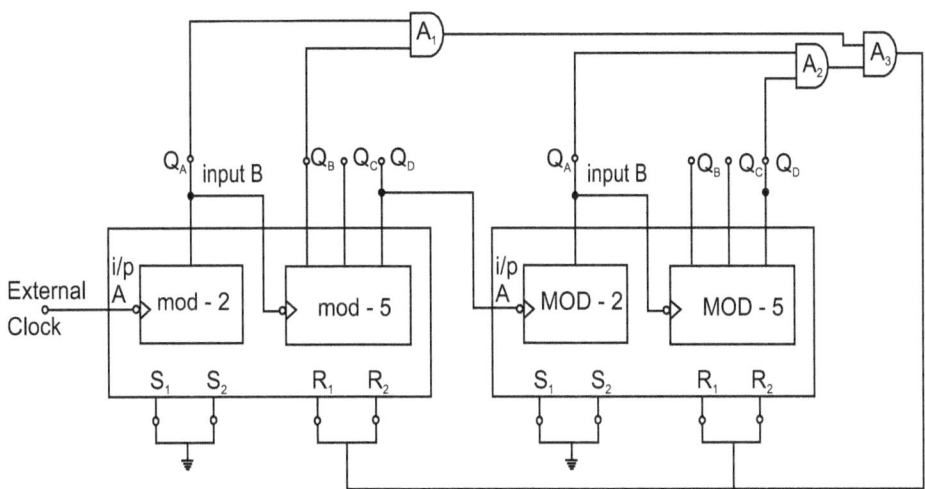

Fig. 4.64 : MOD 94 counter

- As shown in Fig. 4.64, when the circuit reaches to state 1001 00011, the outputs of all AND gates A_1, A_2, A_4 become 1 and as outputs of A_4 is connected to reset inputs of both ICs, immediately the counter is reset to 0000 0000.

Example 4.10 :

In 7490, if Q output is connected to input A & pulses are applied at input B, find counter sequence. **[Dec. 2007, 4 M]**

Solution :

- The circuit is as shown in Fig. 4.65.
- When the clock pulses are applied at input B, the output of the MOD-5 counter changes from 0 to 4 (from Q Q Q =000 to Q Q Q =100) with the application of successive pulses.
- As Q output is connected to input A, the output QA will make transition when Q changes from 1 to 0. The count sequence is as shown in table 4.29.

Table 4.29

Flip-flop Outputs				State of the counter
Q_D	Q_C	Q_B	Q_A	
0	0	0	0	0
0	0	1	0	2
0	1	0	0	4
0	1	1	0	6
1	0	0	0	8
0	0	0	1	1

0	0	1	1		4
0	1	0	1		5
0	1	1	1		7
1	0	0	1		9
0	0	0	0		0

- Though the states of counter are not in straight binary form, the number of distinct states are ten, therefore it is also a MOD-10 counter.

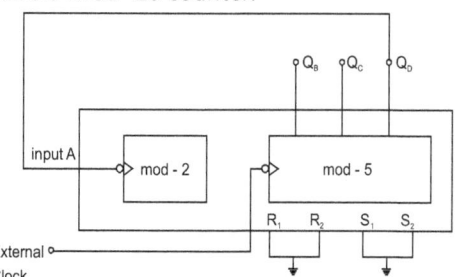

Fig. 4.65

4.24 SYNCHRONOUS COUNTER

Q. What is synchronous counter?

- The Synchronous Counter, the external clock signal is connected to the clock input of every individual flip-flop within the counter so that all of the flip-flops are clocked together simultaneously (in parallel) at the same time giving a fixed time relationship.
- In the synchronous counter the individual output bits changing state at exactly the same time in response to the common clock signal with no ripple effect and therefore, no propagation delay.
- Synchronous Counters use edge-triggered flip-flops that change states on either the "positive-edge" (rising edge) or the "negative-edge" (falling edge) of the clock pulse on the control input resulting in one single count when the clock input changes state.
- Synchronous counters count on the rising-edge which is the low to high transition of the clock signal and asynchronous ripple counters count on the falling-edge which is the high to low transition of the clock signal.

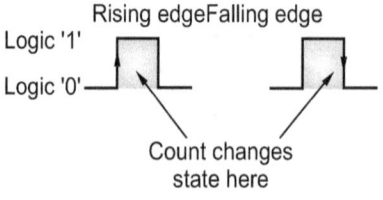

Fig. 4.66

DIGITAL ELECTRONICS LOGIC DESIGN (S.E. COMP.) — SEQUENTIAL LOGIC

- It may seem unusual that ripple counters use the falling-edge of the clock cycle to change state, but this makes it easier to link counters together because the most significant bit (MSB) of one counter can drive the clock input of the next.
- This works because the next bit must change state when the previous bit changes from high to low – the point at which a carry must occur to the next bit. Synchronous counters usually have a carry-out and a carry-in pin for linking counters together without introducing any propagation delays.

Design steps of synchronous counter

- In synchronous counter all the flip flops are clocked simultaneously. Therefore it is faster in operation.
- It can be designed for any count sequence which need not be always straight binary.
- For the design of synchronous counter, first find out the number of flip flops required.
- Then prepare a table consisting of present state, next state and determine the flip flop inputs which must be present to obtain the next state using the excitation table of the flip flop.
- Prepare k-map for each flip flop input and obtain the simplified expressions from which complete the circuit diagram.

4.24.1 3-bit Synchronous Counter

Example 4.11 :
Design 4-bit synchronous counter using JK flip flop and explain.   **[May 2006, 8 M]**

Solution :

- We know that for 4 bit counter three flip flops are required.
- The table consisting of present state, next state and the required inputs of flip flop is as shown in table 4.30. Here Q_2, Q_1 and Q_0 represent the present state variables with Q'_2 Q'_1 and Q'_0 represent the next state variables.

Table 4.30

Present state			Next state			Flip flip inputs					
Q_2	Q_1	Q_0	Q'_2	Q'_1	Q'_0	J_2	K_2	J_1	K_1	J_0	K_0
0	0	0	0	0	1	0	×	0	×	1	×
0	0	1	0	1	0	0	×	1	×	×	1
0	1	0	0	1	1	0	×	×	0	1	×
0	1	1	1	0	0	1	×	×	1	×	1
1	0	0	1	0	1	×	0	0	×	1	×
1	0	1	1	1	0	×	0	1	×	×	1
1	1	0	1	1	1	×	0	×	0	1	×
1	1	1	0	0	0	×	1	×	1	×	1

- Observe the first row of the table 4.41. Present state is $Q_2 Q_1 Q_0 = 0\ 0\ 0$ and next state $Q'_2 Q'_1 Q'_0 = 0\ 0\ 1$. For flip flop 2, $Q_2 = Q'_2 = 0$. Therefore, from first row of excitation table of JK flip flop we get the $J_2 K_2$ input combination as 0 X.
- Similarly for flip flop 1 as $Q_1 = Q'_1 = 0$, the $J_1 K_1$ input combination is 0 X.
- For flip flop 0, present state = $Q_0 = 0$ while the next state = $Q'_0 = 1$. Therefore from the second row of excitation table of JK flip flop we get $J_0 K_0$ input combination as 1 X.
- This completes the first row of the table 4.30. Proceeding in a similar manner, the remaining rows of the table are completed.
- Now we represent each individual input in a k map and obtain the simplified expressions.

K-map for $J_2 \Rightarrow$

Q_2 \ Q_1Q_0	00	01	11	10
0	0	0	1	0
1	X	X	X	X

$\therefore\ J_2 = Q_1 Q_0$

K-map for $K_2 \Rightarrow$

Q_2 \ Q_1Q_0	00	01	11	10
0	X	X	X	X
1	0	0	1	0

$\therefore\ K_2 = Q_1 Q_0$

K-map for $J_1 \Rightarrow$

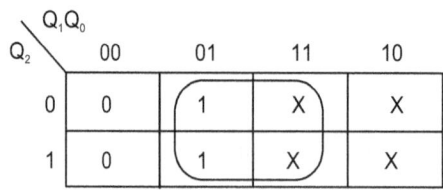

$\therefore\ J_1 = Q_0$

K-map for $K_1 \Rightarrow$

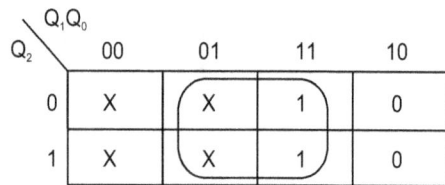

$\therefore\ K_1 = Q_0$

K-map for $J_0 \Rightarrow$

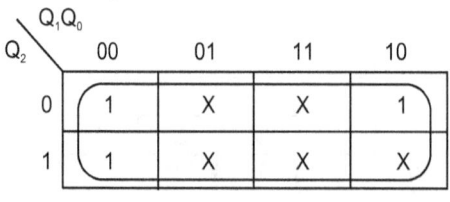

$\therefore\ J_0 = 1$

K-map for $K_0 \Rightarrow$

Q_2 \ Q_1Q_0	00	01	11	10
0	X	1	1	X
1	X	1	1	X

$\therefore\ K_0 = 1$

- Based on above expressions, the resulting circuit diagram is drawn in Fig. 4.67.

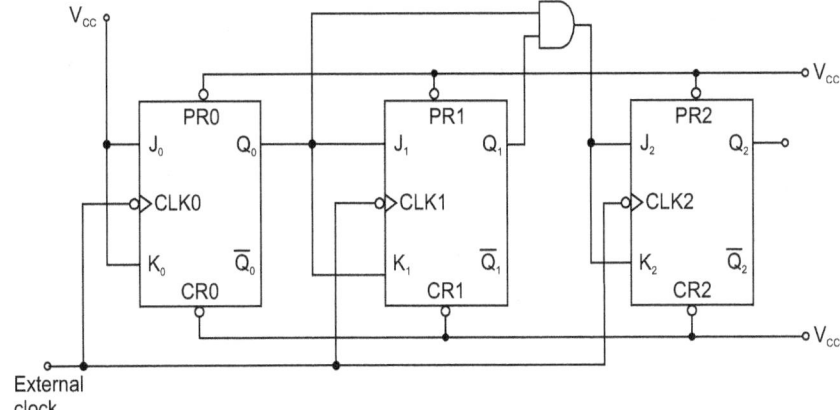

Fig. 4.67 : 3-bit synchronous up counter

4.24.2 4-bit Synchronous Counter

It can be seen that the external clock pulses (pulses to be counted) are fed directly to each J-K flip-flop in the counter chain and that both the J and K inputs are all tied together in toggle mode, but only in the first flip-flop, flip-flop A (LSB) are they connected HIGH, logic "1" allowing the flip-flop to toggle on every clock pulse. Then the synchronous counter follows a predetermined sequence of states in response to the common clock signal, advancing one state for each pulse.

The J and K inputs of flip-flop B are connected to the output "Q" of flip-flop A, but the J and K inputs of flip-flops C and D are driven from AND gates which are also supplied with signals from the input and output of the previous stage.

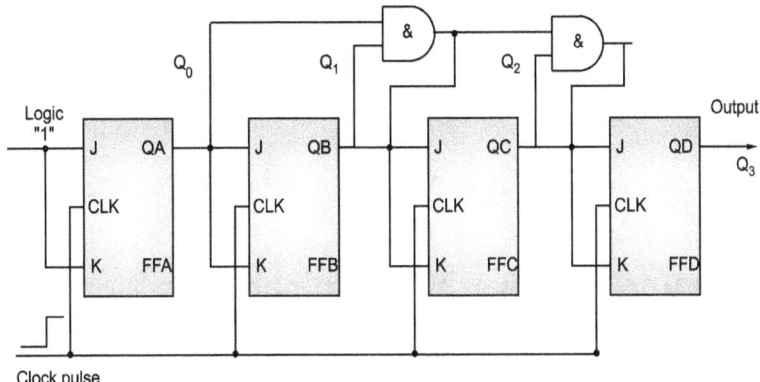

Fig. 4.68

- If we enable each J-K flip-flop to toggle based on whether or not all preceding flip-flop outputs (Q) are "HIGH" we can obtain the same counting sequence as with the asynchronous circuit but without the ripple effect, since each flip-flop in this circuit will be clocked at exactly the same time.

Then as there is no inherent propagation delay in synchronous counters, because all the counter stages are triggered in parallel at the same time, the maximum operating frequency of this type of frequency counter is much higher than that for a similar asynchronous counter circuit.

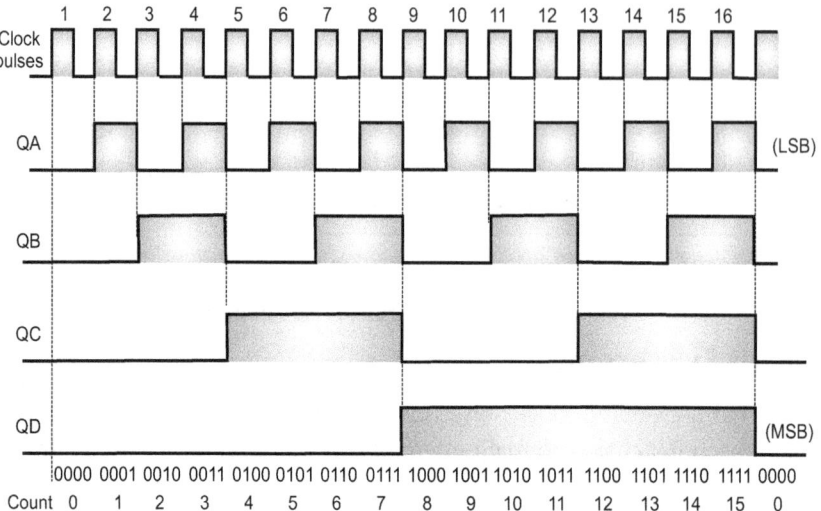

Fig. 4.69 : 4-bit synchronous counter waveform timing diagram

Because this 4-bit synchronous counter counts sequentially on every clock pulse the resulting outputs count upwards from 0 ("0000") to 15 ("1111"). Therefore, this type of counter is also known as a 4-bit Synchronous Up Counter.

- As synchronous counters are formed by connecting flip-flops together and any number of flip-flops can be connected or "cascaded" together to form a "divide-by-n" binary counter, the modulo's or "MOD" number still applies as it does for asynchronous counters so a Decade counter or BCD counter with counts from 0 to 2n-1 can be built along with truncated sequences.

4.24.3 4-bit Up/Down Synchronous Counter

Q. Design and implement 4-bit up/down synchronous counter using MS-JK flip-flop with its truth table. Also draw timing diagram. **[Dec. 08, 12 M]**
Q. Explain with a neat diagram working of 4-bit up-down synchronous counter. Draw necessary timing diagram. **[May 10, 10 M]**

- We know that for 4 bit counter four flip-flop are required.

DIGITAL ELECTRONICS LOGIC DESIGN (S.E. COMP.)   SEQUENTIAL LOGIC

- The table consisting of present state, next state and the required inputs of flip-flop is as shown in table. Here Q_2, Q_1 and Q_0 are present state variable and Q_2', Q_1' and Q_0' represents the next state variables.

Table 4.31

Mode control M	Present state			Next state			Flip-flop inputs		
	Q_2	Q_1	Q_0	Q_2'	Q_1'	Q_0'	T_2	T_1	T_0
0	0	0	0	0	0	1	0	0	1
0	0	0	1	0	1	0	0	1	1
0	0	1	0	0	1	1	0	0	1
0	0	1	1	1	0	0	1	1	1
0	1	0	0	1	0	1	0	0	1
0	1	0	1	1	1	0	0	1	1
0	1	1	0	1	1	1	0	0	1
0	1	1	1	0	0	0	1	1	1

Table 4.32 : For down counting

Mode control M	Present state			Next state			Flip-flop inputs		
	Q_2	Q_1	Q_0	Q_2'	Q_1'	Q_0'	T_2	T_1	T_0
1	0	0	0	1	1	1	1	1	1
1	0	0	1	0	0	0	0	0	1
1	0	1	0	0	0	1	0	1	1
1	0	1	1	0	1	0	0	0	1
1	1	0	0	0	1	1	1	1	1
1	1	0	1	1	0	0	0	0	1
1	1	1	0	1	0	1	0	1	1
1	1	1	1	1	1	0	0	0	1

- Now we represent each individual input in a Kmap and obtain the simplified expression.

$$T_2 = \overline{M}Q_1Q_0 + M\,\overline{Q_1}\overline{Q_0}$$

$$T_1 = \overline{M}Q_0 + M\overline{Q_0}$$

$$T_1 = 1$$

- So logic diagram for 4-bit synchronous up down counter is given below :

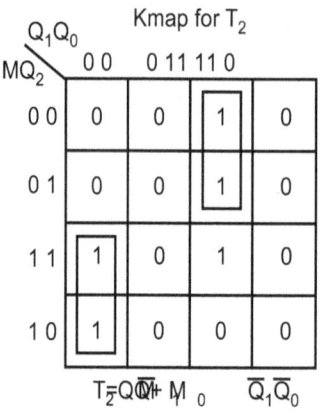
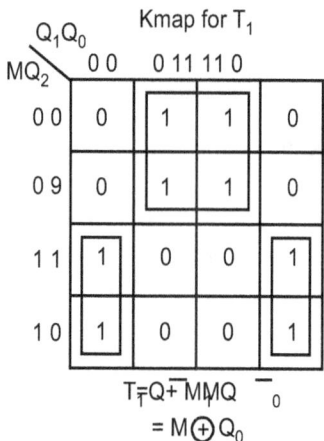
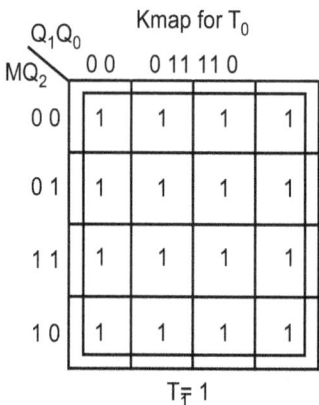

Fig. 4.70 : K-map for 4-bit synchronous up / down counter

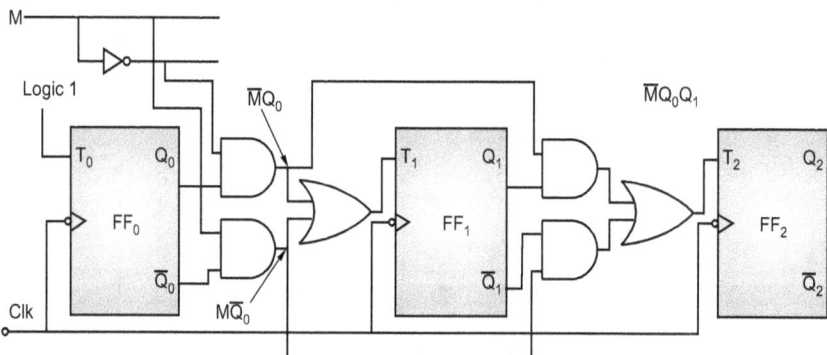

Fig. 4.71 : 4-bit synchronous up / down counter

4.24.4 Modulo N Synchronous Counter

Decade 4-bit Synchronous Counter
- A 4-bit decade synchronous counter can also be built using synchronous binary counters to produce a count sequence from 0 to 9.

- A standard binary counter can be converted to a decade (decimal 10) counter with the aid of some additional logic to implement the desired state sequence.
- After reaching the count of "1001", the counter recycles back to "0000". We now have a decade or Modulo-10counter.

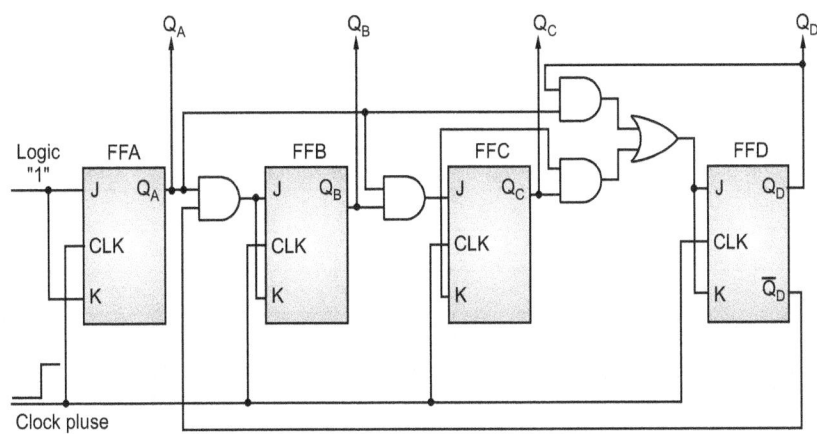

Fig. 4.72 : decade 4-bit synchronous counter

- The additional AND gates detect when the counting sequence reaches "1001", (Binary 10) and causes flip-flop FF4 to toggle on the next clock pulse. Flip-flop FF0 toggles on every clock pulse. Thus, the count is reset and starts over again at "0000" producing a synchronous decade counter.
- We could quite easily re-arrange the additional AND gates in the above counter circuit to produce other count numbers such as a Mod-12 counter which counts 12 states from"0000" to "1011" (0 to 11) and then repeats making them suitable for clocks, etc.

Example 4.12 :

Design mod-12 synchronous counter using D flip flop. **[May 2008, 8 M]**

Solution :

- For the implementation of MOD-12 counter four D flip flops are required.
- It is also a truncated counter. 0 to 11 are used states while 12 to 15 are unused states.
- Next state of unused state is unknown. Let it be don't care. Therefore the corresponding flip flop input is also don't care.
- The table 4.33 consist of present state, next state & the required input of flip flop.

Table 4.33

Present state				Next state				Flip flop input			
Q_4	Q_2	Q_1	Q_0	Q'_4	Q'_2	Q'_1	Q'_0	D_4	D_2	D_1	D_0
0	0	0	0	0	0	0	1	0	0	0	1
0	0	0	1	0	0	1	0	0	0	1	0
0	0	1	0	0	0	1	1	0	0	1	1
0	0	1	1	0	1	0	0	0	1	0	0
0	1	0	0	0	1	0	1	0	1	0	1
0	1	0	1	0	1	1	0	0	1	1	0
0	1	1	0	0	1	1	1	0	1	1	1
0	1	1	1	1	0	0	0	1	0	0	0
1	0	0	0	1	0	0	1	1	0	0	1
1	0	0	1	1	0	1	0	1	0	1	0
1	0	1	0	1	0	1	1	1	0	1	1
1	0	1	1	0	0	0	0	0	0	0	0

- Now we represent each individual input in a K-map & obtain the simplified expressions.

K-map for D_4 ⇒

Q_3Q_2 \ Q_1Q_0	00	01	11	10
00	0	0	0	0
01	0	0	1	0
11	X	X	X	X
10	1	1	0	1

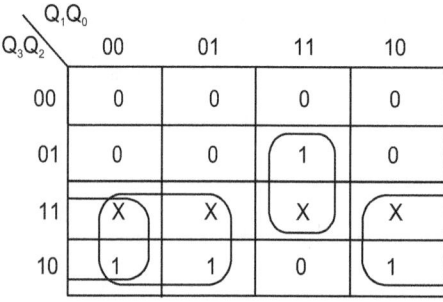

$$D_4 = Q_4\bar{Q}_1 + Q_4\bar{Q}_0 + Q_2Q_1Q_0$$

K-map for D_2 ⇒

Q_3Q_2 \ Q_1Q_0	00	01	11	10
00	0	0	1	0
01	1	1	0	1
11	X	X	X	X
10	0	0	0	0

$$D_2 = Q_2\bar{Q}_1 + Q_2\bar{Q}_0 + \bar{Q}_4\bar{Q}_2Q_1Q_0$$

K-map for D_2 ⇒

Q_3Q_2 \ Q_1Q_0	00	01	11	10
00	0	1	0	1
01	0	1	0	1
11	X	X	X	X
10	0	1	0	1

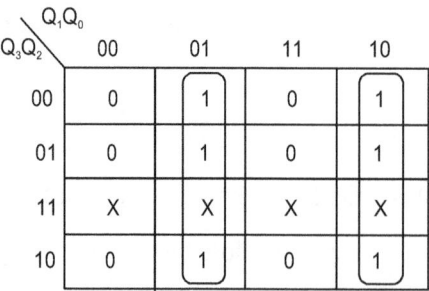

$$D_1 = \bar{Q}_1Q_0 + Q_1\bar{Q}_0 = Q_1 \oplus Q_0$$

K-map for D_0 ⇒

Q_3Q_2 \ Q_1Q_0	00	01	11	10
00	1	0	0	1
01	1	0	0	1
11	X	X	X	X
10	1	0	0	1

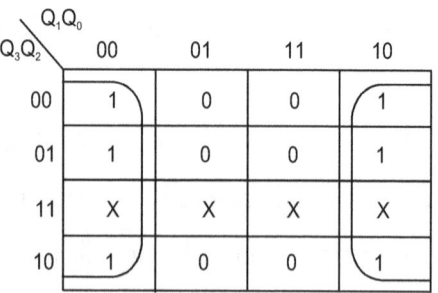

$$D_0 = \bar{Q}_0$$

- Based on above expressions the resulting circuit diagram is shown in Fig. 4.73.

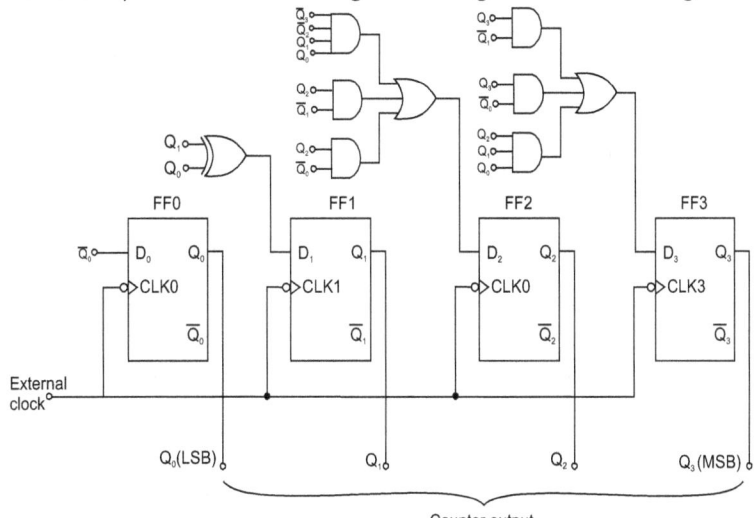

Fig. 4.73

4.24.5 BCD Synchronous Counter

Example 4.13 :
Design and implement synchronous BCD counter using T flip flops.   **[May 2005, 8 M]**
Solution :
- From example, we know that a BCD counter requires four flip flops.
- BCD counter is a truncated counter. In BCD up counter 0 to 9 are used states while 11 to 15 are unused states. Next state of unused state is unknown. Let it be don't care. Therefore the corresponding flip flop input is also don't care.
- The table 4.34 consist of present state, next state & the required input of flip flop.

Table 4.34

Present state				Next state				Flip flip input			
Q_4	Q_2	Q_1	Q_0	Q'_4	Q'_2	Q'_1	Q'_0	T_4	T_2	T_1	T_0
0	0	0	0	0	0	0	1	0	0	0	1
0	0	0	1	0	0	1	0	0	0	1	1
0	0	1	0	0	0	1	1	0	0	0	1
0	0	1	1	0	1	0	0	0	1	1	1
0	1	0	0	0	1	0	1	0	0	0	1
0	1	0	1	0	1	1	0	0	0	1	1
0	1	1	0	0	1	1	1	0	0	0	1
0	1	1	1	1	0	0	0	1	1	1	1
1	0	0	0	1	0	0	1	0	0	0	1
1	0	0	1	0	0	0	0	1	0	0	1

- Now we represent each individual input in a K-map and obtain the simplified expressions.

K-map for $T_4 \Rightarrow$

$Q_3Q_2 \backslash Q_1Q_0$	00	01	11	10
00	0	0	0	0
01	0	0	1	0
11	X	X	X	X
10	0	1	X	X

$\therefore T_4 = Q_4 Q_0 + Q_2 Q_1 Q_0$

K-map for $T_2 \Rightarrow$

$Q_3Q_2 \backslash Q_1Q_0$	00	01	11	10
00	0	0	1	0
01	0	0	1	0
11	X	X	X	X
10	0	0	X	X

$\therefore T_2 = Q_1 Q_0$

K-map for $T_1 \Rightarrow$

$Q_3Q_2 \backslash Q_1Q_0$	00	01	11	10
00	0	1	1	0
01	0	1	1	0
11	X	X	X	X
10	0	0	X	X

$\therefore T_1 = \bar{Q}_4 Q_0$

K-map for $T_0 \Rightarrow$

$Q_3Q_2 \backslash Q_1Q_0$	00	01	11	10
00	1	1	1	1
01	1	1	1	1
11	X	X	X	X
10	1	1	X	X

$\therefore T_0 = 1$

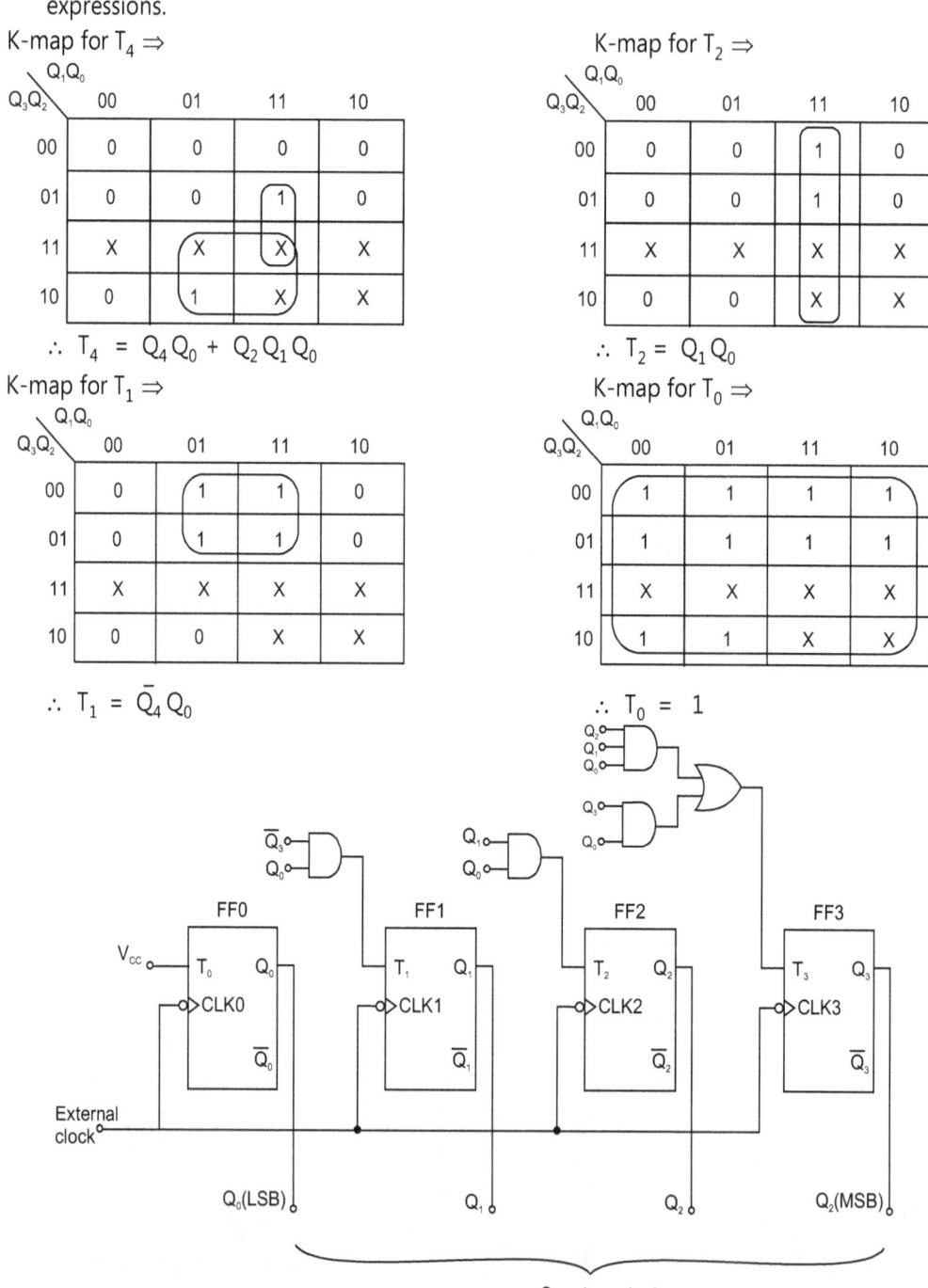

Fig. 4.74

Based on the above expressions the resulting circuit diagram is shown in Fig. 4.74

DIGITAL ELECTRONICS LOGIC DESIGN (S.E. COMP.) — SEQUENTIAL LOGIC

4.24.6 Ring counter

Q. Write short note on Ring counter. [Dec. 08]

Q. Explain ring counter design having initial state 01011 from initial state explain all possible states in the ring. [Dec. 10, 10 M]

Q. Explain Ring counter design having initial state 10110. [May 11, 4 M]

- The shift register acts as ring counter, if the serial output is connected back to the serial input as shown in Fig. 4.75.

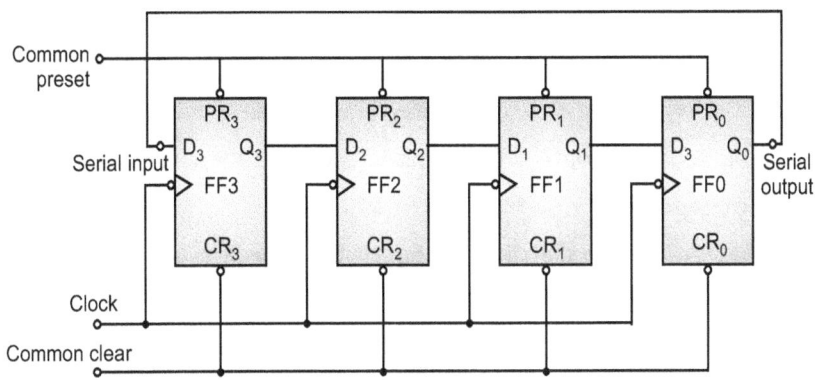

Fig. 4.75 : Ring counter

- Let us consider the initial state of the circuit as $Q_4 Q_2 Q_1 Q_0 = 1000$.
- The output of each flip flop after every clock pulse will be as shown in the table 4.35.

Table 4.35

Clock pulse Number	Q_4	Q_2	Q_1	Q_0
Initially	1	0	0	0
1	0	1	0	0
2	0	0	1	0
4	0	0	0	1
4	1	0	0	0

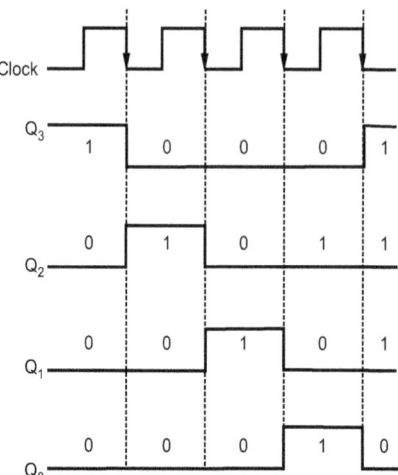

Fig. 4.76 : Waveforms of ring counter

- The n-bit ring counter counts n clock pulses, therefore the circuit shown in Fig. 4.76 counts four clock pulses.
- From table 4.35 it is clear that the number of distinct states in the operation of this counter is four. Therefore, it is a mod - 4 counter. In general n-bit ring counter is mod- n counter. The waveforms are as shown in Fig. 4.76.
- From the waveforms it is clear that, frequency of pulses obtained at any output is equal to frequency of clock pulses divided by four. Therefore this counter is a divide by four ($\div$ 4) counter.
- In general n-bit ring counter is a divide by n ($\div$ n) counter.
- The outputs Q_4, Q_2, Q_1 & Q_0 are sequential non-overlapping pulses which can be used to excite the stepper motor.

Example 4.14 :

Explain ring counter design having initial state 01011.

- There are 5 bits in the given initial state, so we have to use 5 flip flops as shown in Fig. 4.36.
- When apply clear (CLR) pulse then flip flop will preset to 1 output and 4 and 2 are reset to 0 output.

$$Q_4 \ Q_4 \ Q_2 \ Q_1 = 01011$$

Fig. 4.77 shows the arrangement of 5 bit ring counter.

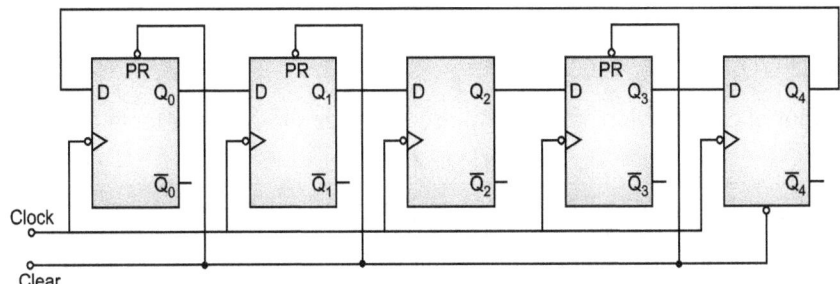

Fig. 4.77

Table 4.36 : 5-bit ring counter table

CLR	CLK	Q_0	Q_1	Q_2	Q_4	Q_4
0	1	1	1	0	1	0
1	1	0	1	1	0	1
1	1	1	0	1	1	0
1	1	0	1	0	1	1
1	1	1	0	1	0	1
1	1	1	1	0	1	0

4.24.7 Johnson counter

Q. Explain the Johnson's counter design for initial state 0110. From initial state explain and draw all possible state. **[Dec. 09, 8 M]**

- It is also known as twisted ring counter or moebius counter.
- The shift register acts as a Johnson counter if the $\bar{Q}_0$ output is connected to the serial input as shown in Fig. 4.78.

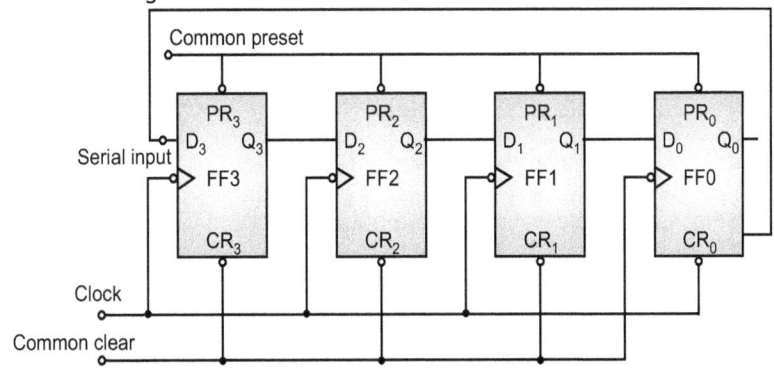

Fig. 4.78 : Johnson counter

- Initially all the flip flops are cleared using the common clear input ie. the initial state of the circuit is $Q_4 Q_2 Q_1 Q_0 = 0000$.
- The output of each flip flop after clock pulse will be as shown in the table 4.37.

Table 4.37

Clock pulse Number	Q_4	Q_2	Q_1	Q_0
Initially	0	0	0	0
1	1	0	0	0
2	1	1	0	0
4	1	1	1	0
4	1	1	1	1
5	0	1	1	1
6	0	0	1	1
7	0	0	0	1
8	0	0	0	0

- From table 4.37 it is clear that the number of distinct states in the operation of this counter is eight. Therefore it is a mod 8 counter. In general, every n-bit Johnson counter is a mod 2n counter. The waveforms are as shown in Fig. 4.79.

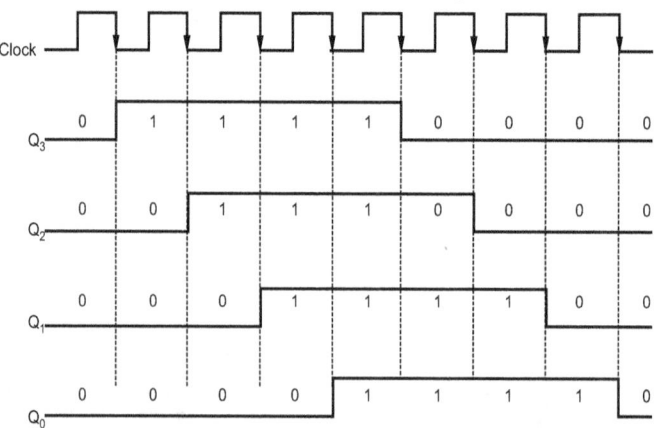

Fig. 4.79 : Waveforms of Johnson counter

- As shown in Fig. 4.79 square waveforms are obtained at each flip flop output.
- Also for completion of one cycle, each output requires eight clock pulses therefore it is a divide by 8 ($\div$ 8) counter.
- In general, n-bit Johnson counter is a divide by 2n ($\div$ 2n) counter.

Example 4.15 :

Design Johnson counter using 2-bit shift register.

Draw waveforms. [PU 2007, 4 M]

Solution :

- A 2-bit Johnson counter can be designed using two flip flops. When the output of FF0 is connected to the D_1 input of FF1 as shown in Fig. 4.80 we get the 2 bit Johnson counter.

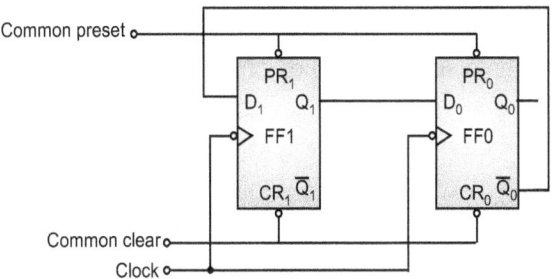

Fig. 4.80 : 2-bit Johnson counter

- The waveforms are shown in Fig. 4.81.

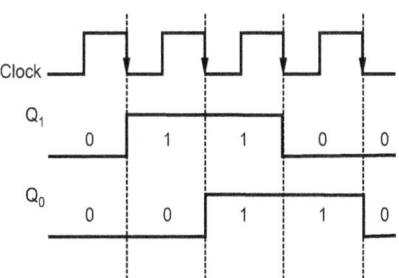

Fig. 4.81 : Waveforms of 2-bit Johnson counter

4.24.8 Unused States and Lock Out Condition

> **Q.** Design sequence generator to generate '11010' sequence using MSJK flip flops. How to avoid lockout condition in sequence generator?
> [May 2006, 4 M, 2007, 4 M, Dec 11, 10M]

Unused states :

- In example 4.20, 1, 4, 4 and 7 states are known as unused states, while 0, 2, 5 & 6 states are known as used states. Upon application of successive clock pulses the counter output goes from 0 to 2, 2 to 5, 5 to 6, 6 to 0 and then the cycle repeats. Therefore these are known as used states.
- Counter output never goes to 1, 4, 4 and 7 states, therefore they are known as un used states.

Lock out condition :
- If the counter output goes to unused state and the next state of it is also another unused state & it repeats again & again so that counter never goes to used state, then that counter is said to be in lock out condition.
- In example 4.20 suppose the counter goes to unused state 1 & upon application of successive clock pulses it goes through a series of unused states as shown below.

$$1 \rightarrow 4 \rightarrow 4 \rightarrow 7$$
           ↑_____|

Then it is said that the counter is in lock out condition.
- If the counter goes into lock out condition, then it becomes useless as it can not generate correct output.
- Lock out condition can be avoided by assigning next state as used state, for every unused state. So whenever counter finds itself in one of the unused state then upon application of clock pulse automatically it will come to the used state & will produce the correct output.

Example 4.16 :

Using JK flip flops design a synchronous counter that has the following sequence.

$$\text{-----} 0 \rightarrow 2 \rightarrow 5 \rightarrow 6 \rightarrow 0 \text{-------}$$

Unused states 1, 4, 4, 7 must always go to 0 on the next clock pulse. **[PU 2005, 10 M]**

Solution :
- From the given sequence it is clear that number of states are 8. Therefore three JK flip flops are required to design the counter.
- The table consist of present state, next state and the required inputs of the flip.

Table 4.38

Present state			Next state			Flip flop inputs					
Q_2	Q_1	Q_0	Q'_2	Q'_1	Q'_0	J_2	K_2	J_1	K_1	J_0	K_0
0	0	0	0	1	0	0	×	1	×	0	×
0	0	1	0	0	0	0	×	0	×	×	1
0	1	0	1	0	1	1	×	×	1	1	×
0	1	1	0	0	0	0	×	×	1	×	1
1	0	0	0	0	0	×	1	0	×	0	×
1	0	1	1	1	0	×	0	1	×	×	1
1	1	0	0	0	0	×	1	×	1	0	×
1	1	1	0	0	0	×	1	×	1	×	1

- Now we represent each individual input in a k-map & obtain the simplified expressions.

K-map for $J_2 \Rightarrow$

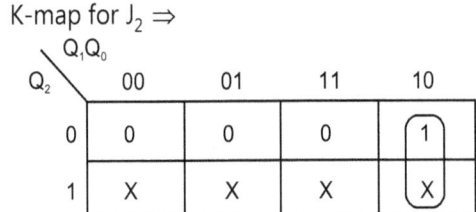

$$\therefore J_2 = Q_1 \bar{Q}_0$$

K-map for $J_1 \Rightarrow$

Q_2 \ Q_1Q_0	00	01	11	10
0	1	0	X	X
1	0	1	X	X

$$\therefore J_1 = \bar{Q}_2 \bar{Q}_0 + Q_2 Q_0 = \overline{Q_2 \oplus Q_0}$$

K-map for $J_0 \Rightarrow$

Q_2 \ Q_1Q_0	00	01	11	10
0	0	X	X	1
1	0	X	X	X

$$\therefore J_0 = \bar{Q}_2 Q_1$$

K-map for $K_2 \Rightarrow$

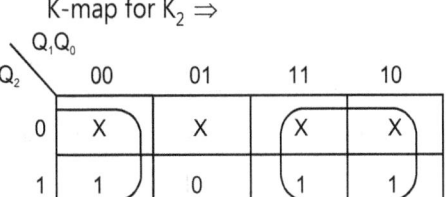

$$\therefore K_2 = Q_1 + \bar{Q}_0$$

K-map for $K_1 \Rightarrow$

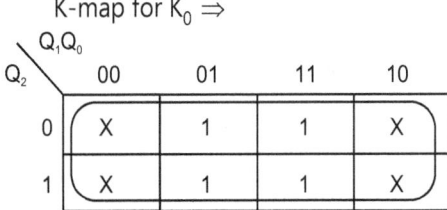

$$\therefore K_1 = 1$$

K-map for $K_0 \Rightarrow$

Q_2 \ Q_1Q_0	00	01	11	10
0	X	1	1	X
1	X	1	1	X

$$\therefore K_0 = 1$$

Based on above expressions the resulting circuit diagram is shown in Fig. 4.82.

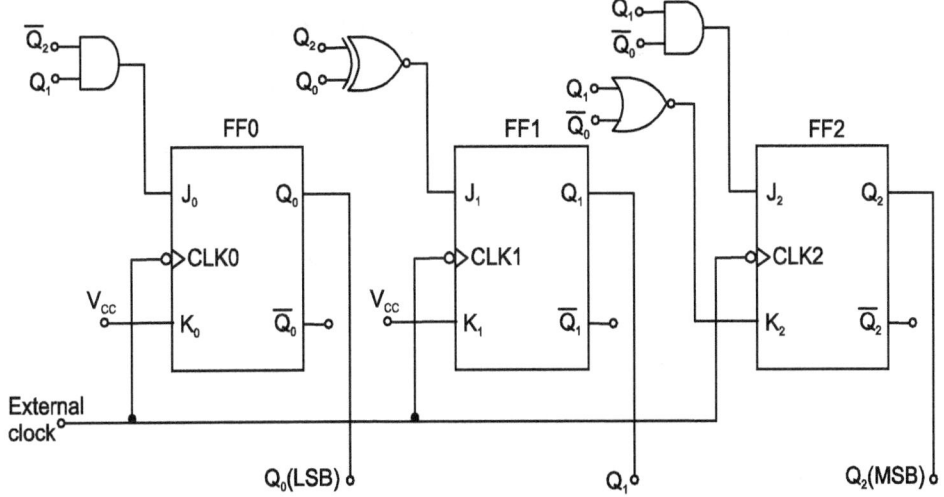

Fig. 4.82

4.25 DIFFERENCE BETWEEN SYNCHRONOUS AND ASYNCHRONOUS COUNTERS

Sr. No.	Asynchronous counters	Synchronous counters
1.	In this type of counter flip-flops are connected in such a way that output of first flip-flop drives the clock for the next flip-flop.	In this type there is no connection between output of first flip-flop and clock input of the next flip-flip.
2.	Main drawback of these counters is their low speed as the clock is propagated through number of flip-flips before it reaches last flip-flop.	As clock is simultaneously given to all flip-flop there is no problem of propagation delay. Hence they are high speed counters and are preferred when number of flip-flop increase in the given design.
4.	Logic circuit is very simple even for more number of states.	Design involves complex logic circuit as number of state increases.
4.	As the flip-flops are not clocked simultaneously.	All the flip-flops are clocked simultaneously.

4.26 PSEUDO RANDOM SEQUENCE GENERATOR

- A random sequence is one which can not be described with a mathematical relationship.
- As the name suggests, a pseudo random is not a completely random sequence or it is a false random sequence as it is a periodic sequence. (periodic random sequence).
- 'Noise' is an example of random sequence, therefore the Pseudo Random (PR) sequence is also known as Pseudo Noise (PN) sequence.
- One important application of the shift register is pseudo random sequence generator.
- The pseudo random sequence generator consists of a number of flip-flops and a combinational circuit for providing a suitable feedback.
- Ex-OR, Ex-NOR gates are used as combinational circuit.

K-map for $J_2 \Rightarrow$

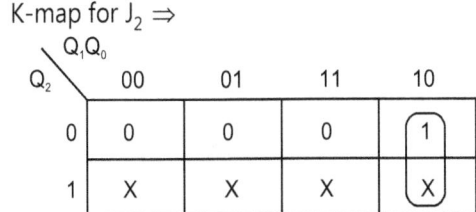

$$\therefore J_2 = Q_1 \bar{Q}_0$$

K-map for $J_1 \Rightarrow$

Q_2 \ Q_1Q_0	00	01	11	10
0	1	0	X	X
1	0	1	X	X

$$\therefore J_1 = \bar{Q}_2 \bar{Q}_0 + Q_2 Q_0 = \overline{Q_2 \oplus Q_0}$$

K-map for $J_0 \Rightarrow$

Q_2 \ Q_1Q_0	00	01	11	10
0	0	X	X	1
1	0	X	X	X

$$\therefore J_0 = \bar{Q}_2 Q_1$$

K-map for $K_2 \Rightarrow$

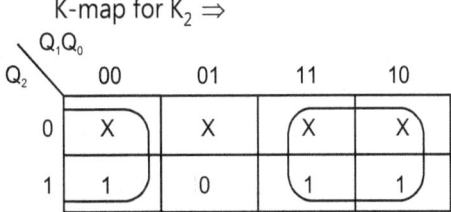

$$\therefore K_2 = Q_1 + \bar{Q}_0$$

K-map for $K_1 \Rightarrow$

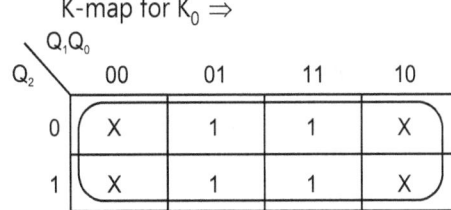

$$\therefore K_1 = 1$$

K-map for $K_0 \Rightarrow$

Q_2 \ Q_1Q_0	00	01	11	10
0	X	1	1	X
1	X	1	1	X

$$\therefore K_0 = 1$$

Based on above expressions the resulting circuit diagram is shown in Fig. 4.82.

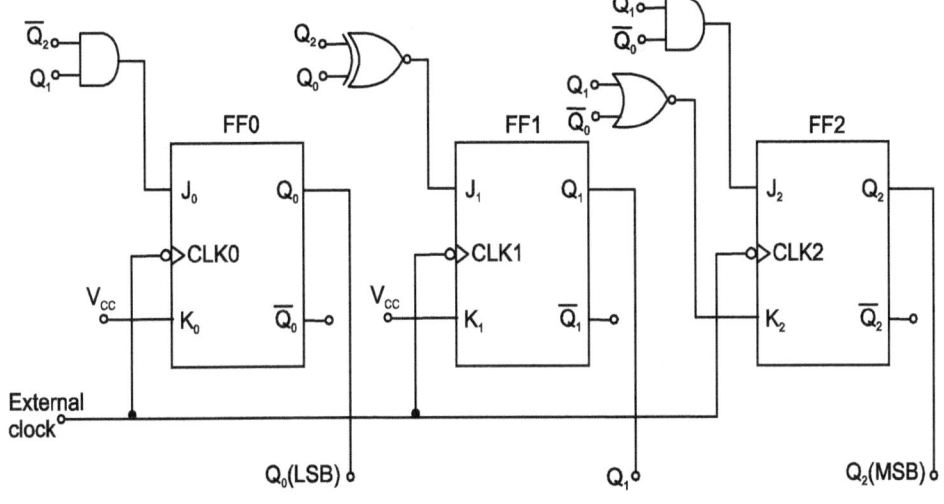

Fig. 4.82

4.25 DIFFERENCE BETWEEN SYNCHRONOUS AND ASYNCHRONOUS COUNTERS

Sr. No.	Asynchronous counters	Synchronous counters
1.	In this type of counter flip-flops are connected in such a way that output of first flip-flop drives the clock for the next flip-flop.	In this type there is no connection between output of first flip-flop and clock input of the next flip-flip.
2.	Main drawback of these counters is their low speed as the clock is propagated through number of flip-flips before it reaches last flip-flop.	As clock is simultaneously given to all flip-flop there is no problem of propagation delay. Hence they are high speed counters and are preferred when number of flip-flop increase in the given design.
4.	Logic circuit is very simple even for more number of states.	Design involves complex logic circuit as number of state increases.
4.	As the flip-flops are not clocked simultaneously.	All the flip-flops are clocked simultaneously.

4.26 PSEUDO RANDOM SEQUENCE GENERATOR

- A random sequence is one which can not be described with a mathematical relationship.
- As the name suggests, a pseudo random is not a completely random sequence or it is a false random sequence as it is a periodic sequence. (periodic random sequence).
- 'Noise' is an example of random sequence, therefore the Pseudo Random (PR) sequence is also known as Pseudo Noise (PN) sequence.
- One important application of the shift register is pseudo random sequence generator.
- The pseudo random sequence generator consists of a number of flip-flops and a combinational circuit for providing a suitable feedback.
- Ex-OR, Ex-NOR gates are used as combinational circuit.

SEQUENTIAL LOGIC

- As stated earlier the pseudo random sequence is a periodic sequence with period $2^N - 1$, where N is the number of flip-flops in the shift register. Thus the sequence repeats after $2^N - 1$ clock cycles.

- We know that, with B flip-flops, maximum possible combinations are 2^N while the maximum length of the pseudo random sequence with N flip flips is $2^N - 1$. This is because, 000 ... 0 (all as) or 111 ... 1 (all 1s) state must be avoided while working with the shift registers.

- Circuit diagram of pseudo random sequence generator using 4-bit shift register is as shown in Fig. 4.83

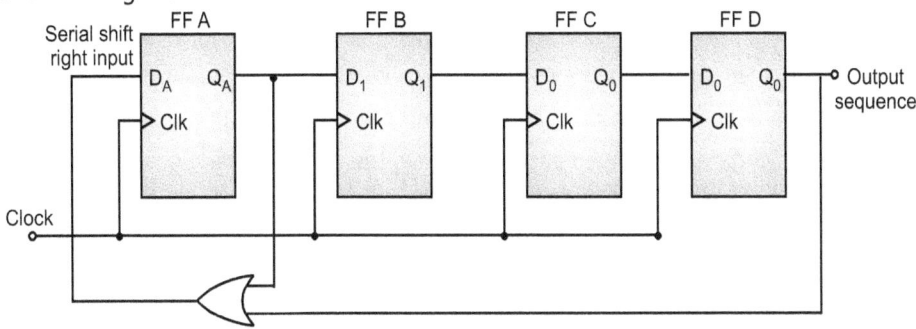

Fig. 4.83 : Pseudo random sequence generator

- 4-bit shift register consist of four D flip-flops as shown in Fig. 4.83. Therefore, the maximum possible length of the PR sequence is $2^4 - 1 = 15$.

- As shown in the Fig. 483. EX-OR gate is used for providing the feedback. Q_A, Q_D are connected as input to the EX-OR gate and its output is connected at serial shift right input of the shift register.

- Table 4.39 indicates the state of the circuit, output of EX-OR gate and individual outputs of the flip-flops.

Table 4.39

Sr. No.	$Q_A \oplus Q_D$	Q_A	Q_B	Q_C	Q_D	State of Circuit
1.	1	0	0	0	1	1
2.	1	1	0	0	0	8
4.	1	1	1	0	0	12
4.	1	1	1	1	0	14
5.	0	1	1	1	1	15
6.	1	0	1	1	1	7

7.	0	1	0	1	1	11
8.	1	0	1	0	1	5
9.	1	1	0	1	0	10
10.	0	1	1	0	1	14
11.	0	0	1	1	0	6
12.	1	0	0	1	1	4
14.	0	1	0	0	1	9
14.	0	0	1	0	0	4
15.	0	0	0	1	0	2
	1	0	0	0	1	1

- The initial state of the shift register is assumed to be 0001. Therefore, $Q_A \oplus Q_D = 0 \oplus 1 = 1$. Which is then written in the corresponding column. Upon application of the clock pulse, the data gets shifted in right direction and the new state 1000 is written. Again the output of EX-OR gate is obtained and is written in the corresponding column. Proceeding in the similar manner the table 4.39 is completed.

- The PR sequence can be obtained at any of the outputs Q_A, Q_B, Q_C or Q_D. In Fig. is shown at Q_D output.

- As shown in Table 4.39, 0000 state is absent as the EX-OR gate is used in the feedback path.

- As stated earlier we can use EX-NOR gate also, in the feedback path but in that case the 1111 state must be excluded.

- The PR sequence will change with the following conditions.

    (1) Number of flip-flops used.

    (2) Type of gate used in the feedback path (EX-OR/EX-NOR).

    (4) Number of gates used,

    (4) Number of inputs to the gate (s).

    (5) Type of inputs to the gate (S), (Q_A, Q_B, Q_C, or Q_D).

    Thus, PR sequence depends upon many factors therefore the term 'random' appears in its name.

Applications of PR sequence:

- We know that PR sequence is also known as PN (Pseudo Noise) sequence and it can be used to test the noise immunity of the system under test.

- Also it is used in data encryption system which protects data from hackers. Valid receiver which knows the exact five conditions listed above will be able to extract information from the encrypted data.

4.27 SEQUENCE GENERATOR

- Sequence generator circuits can be built with shift registers or flip flops. The two methods are discussed here.

4.27.1 Sequence Generator using Shift Registers

- A circuit that generates prescribed sequence of bits upon application of clock pulses is known as sequence generator.
- For this type of sequence generator shift register is used as the basic building block. The block diagram of it is as shown in Fig. 4.84.

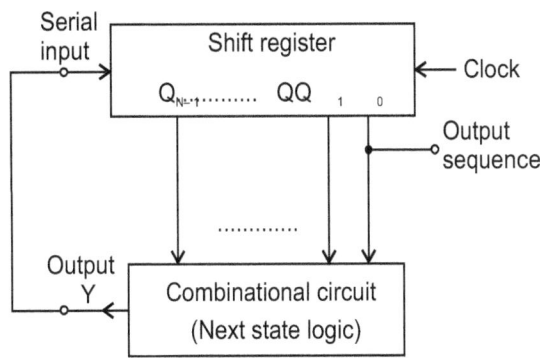

Fig. 4.84 : Block diagram for sequence generator

- As shown in Fig. 4.84, a serial in parallel out (SIPO) shift register is used.
- Depending upon requirement outputs of one or more flip flops of the shift register are connected as input to the combinational circuit which is also known as next state logic. Further the output Y of the combinational circuit is connected as the serial input of the shift register.
- Here main task is to design the combinational circuit that decides the serial input of the flip flop.
- The desired bit pattern (output sequence) is available at the individual output of all flip flops.
- The design procedure is as below.

1. Decide minimum number of flip flops N in the shift register from the length of the sequence L using the relationship.

$$L \leq 2^N - 1 \qquad \qquad \ldots(*)$$

2. Write down the desired sequence under the output of flip flop corresponding to the MSB of the shift register and delay it by one or more clock pulses till the LSB. Write the states of the circuit and check all states are distinct or not.

4. If any state is repeating, increase the count of flip flops by one and repeat the above procedure till distinct states are obtained.

4. Prepare the column of output Y and then represent it in a K-map to get the simplified expression.

5. Built the combinational circuit from the simplified expression and connect its output as serial input of shift register.

Example 4.17 :

Design and implement the following sequence generator using shift register.

------ 1010 ------   [PU 2006, 4 M]

Solution :

- The length of the given sequence is two. Therefore minimum number of flip flops N can be obtained from equation.

$$L \leq 2^N - 1$$

For N = 1; $2 \leq 2^1 - 1$

The inequality is not satisfied

For N = 2; $2 \leq 2^2 - 1$

The inequality is satisfied.

Therefore number of flip flops required = N = 2

- Now we prepare the state table 4.40.

Table 4.40

Q_1	Q_0	State of the circuit
1	0	2
0	1	1

- The desired sequence is written under the output Q_1 (MSB) & is delayed by one clock pulse for Q_0 (LSB). As shown the states of the circuit are distinct, therefore the given sequence generator can be implemented using two flip flops.

- Now we prepare another table 4.41 showing the state of the circuit and output Y of the combinational circuit.

Table 4.41

State of circuit	Q_1	Q_0	Y
2	1	0	0
1	0	1	1
2	1	0	0

- As shown in Fig. 4.85 the output Y of the combinational circuit is connected as the serial input of the shift register. In this example, output Y is to be connected to D1 input of FF1. The output Y applied at D1 will become Q1 after application of the clock pulse. Therefore whatever state of Q1 is required during the next clock cycle, the same must be generated by the combinational circuit during the present clock cycle.

- Based on this, the column for output Y is completed. In the second row of table 4.41, $Q_1 = 0$ therefore, in the first row of column Y, 0 is written as indicated with arrow. Similarly, in the second row of column Y, 1 is written.

- Now we prepare a K-map for Y in terms of Q_1 & Q_0.

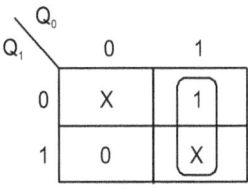

Fig. 4.85

∴ $Y = Q_0$

- As other two combinations of Q_1, Q_0 such as 00 & 11 do not occur, 'X' is written in the corresponding cell of K-map.
- Based on the above expression and the block diagram shown in the Fig. 4.86, the circuit diagram is drawn as shown in Fig. 4.86.

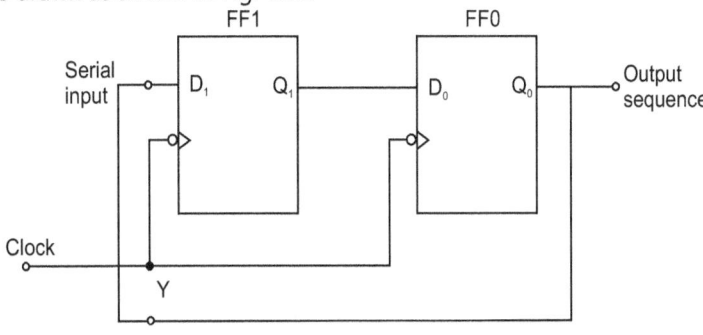

Fig. 4.86

- As shown in Fig. 4.86, as $Y = Q_0$, combinational circuit is a simple connection between output Q_0 and serial input D_1. The desired output sequence is available at both outputs Q_1 and Q_0 with the application of successive clock pulses.

Example 4.18 :
Design sequence generator using Shift register to generate sequence 1101. **[PU 2007, 4 M]**

Solution :
- The length of the given sequence is four. Therefore minimum number of flip flops N can be obtained from equation.
$$L \leq 2^N - 1$$
- Putting N = 2,
$$4 \leq 2^2 - 1$$
The inequality is not satisfied.
Putting N = 4,
$$4 \leq 2^4 - 1$$
The inequality is satisfied
Therefore, number of flip flops required = N = 4.
- Now we prepare the state table 4.42.

Table 4.42

Q_2	Q_1	Q_0	State of the circuit
1	1	0	6
1	1	1	7
0	1	1	4
1	0	1	5

- The desired sequence is written under the output Q_2 (MSB) and is delayed by one clock pulse upto Q_0 (LSB). As shown, the states of the circuit are distinct, therefore the given sequence generator can be implemented using three flip-flops.
- Now we prepare table 4.43 shows the state of the circuit and output Y of the combinational circuit.

Table 4.43

State of circuit	Q_2	Q_1	Q_0	Y
6	1	1	0	1
7	1	1	1	0
4	0	1	1	1
5	1	0	1	1

- From table 4.43, the k-map for output Y is prepared.

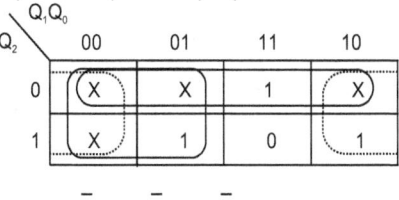

∴ $Y = \bar{Q}_2 + \bar{Q}_1 + \bar{Q}_0$

- Based on the above expression and the block diagram shown in Fig. 4.86, the circuit diagram is drawn as shown in Fig. 4.87.
- As shown in Fig. 4.87, the combinational circuit consists of 4 input OR gate and its output Y is connected to the serial input D_2 of the shift register. The desired output sequence is available at any of the outputs Q_2, Q_1 and Q_0 with the application of successive clock pulses.

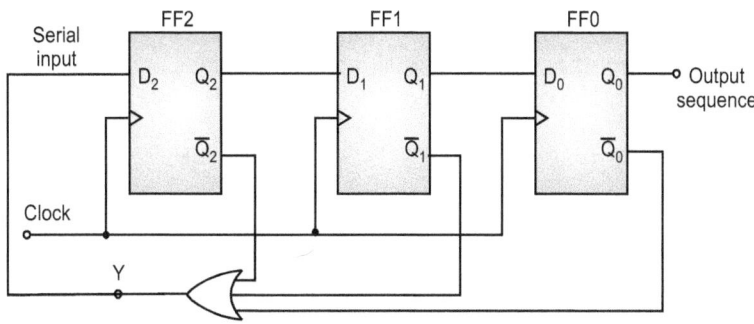

Fig. 4.87

4.27.2 Sequence Generator using Flip-Flops

- The sequence generator using flip flops is same as that of design of a synchronous counter.
- The sequence generator using flips flops can be designed to avoid the lock out condition by assigning the next state as used state for every unused state.

Example 4.19 :
Design the circuit to generate the sequence :

$0 \rightarrow 2 \rightarrow 5 \rightarrow 4 \rightarrow 7 \rightarrow 4$. [PU 2006, 8 M]

Solution :

- From the given sequence it is clear that three flip flops are required for the implementation of the circuit. We shall use D flip flop for the design of the circuit.
- First the table 4.44 consisting of present state of the circuit, next state of the circuit and flip flop input is prepared using the excitation table of D flip flop as shown

Table 4.44

Present state			Next state			Flip flop input		
Q_1	Q_2	Q_0	Q'_1	Q'_2	Q'_0	D_1	D_2	D_0
0	0	0	0	1	0	0	1	0
0	0	1	0	0	0	0	0	0
0	1	0	1	0	1	1	0	1
0	1	1	0	0	0	0	0	0
1	0	0	1	1	1	1	1	1
1	0	1	1	0	0	1	0	0
1	1	0	0	0	0	0	0	0
1	1	1	0	1	1	0	1	1

- We now prepare the K-maps for individual input of flip flops and obtain the simplified expressions.

K-map for $D_2 \Rightarrow$ 　　　　　　　　　　　K-map for $D_1 \Rightarrow$

$Q_2 \backslash Q_1Q_0$	00	01	11	10
0	0	0	0	1
1	1	1	0	0

$$\therefore D_1 = Q_2 \bar{Q}_1 + \bar{Q}_2 Q_1 \bar{Q}_0$$

$Q_2 \backslash Q_1Q_0$	00	01	11	10
0	1	0	0	0
1	1	0	1	0

$$\therefore D_1 = \bar{Q}_1 \cdot \bar{Q}_0 + Q_2 Q_1 Q_0$$

K-map for $D_0 \Rightarrow$

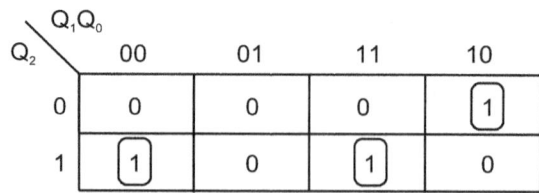

$Q_2 \backslash Q_1Q_0$	00	01	11	10
0	0	0	0	1
1	1	0	1	0

$$\therefore D_0 = Q_2 \bar{Q}_1 \bar{Q}_0 + Q_2 Q_1 Q_0 + \bar{Q}_2 Q_1 \bar{Q}_0$$

- Based on the above expressions the circuit diagram can be constructed as shown in Fig.4.88.

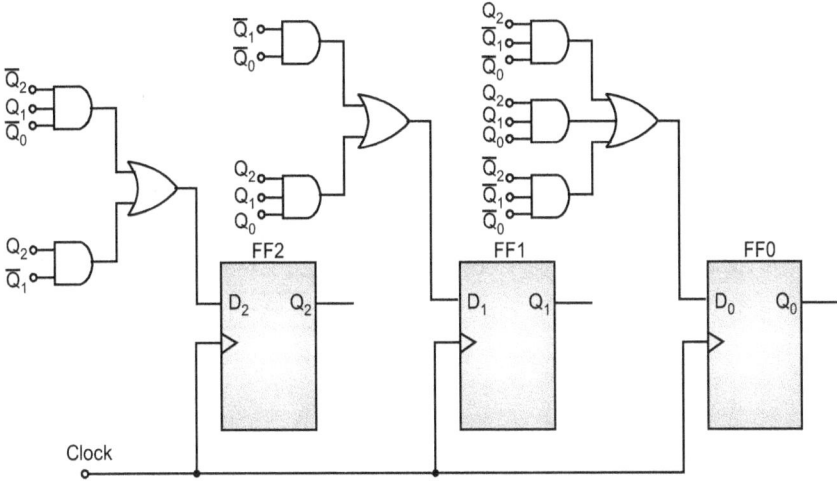

Fig. 4. 88

4.28 THE GENERAL FORM OF A SEQUENTIAL CIRCUIT

- Divide circuit into combinational logic and state.
- Localize feedback loops and make it easy to break cycles.
- Implementation of storage elements leads to various form of sequential circuits.

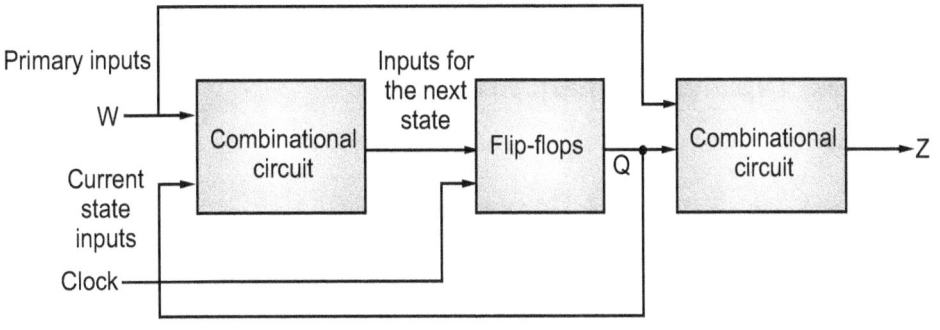

Fig. 4.89

4.28.1 Forms of Sequential Logic

- **Asynchronous** – state changes occur whenever state inputs change (Memory elements may be simple wires or delay elements).
- **Synchronous** – state changes occur in lock step across all storage elements (using a clock).

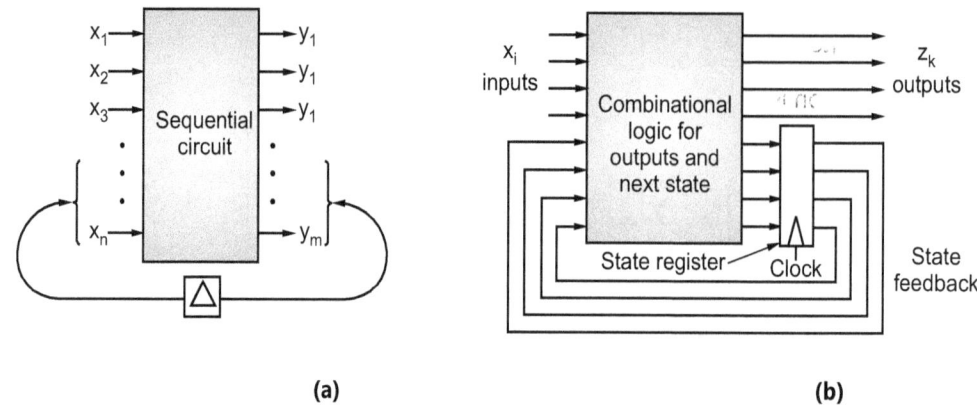

(a)   (b)

Fig. 4.90

4.29 SEQUENCE DETECTOR

- The circuit which detects the occurrence of a particular pattern of the input applied to it, is known as sequence detector.
- The design steps for a sequence detector are same as that of the design steps for a sequential circuit as sequence detector is an example of sequential circuit.
- As there are finite numbers of states in the operation of sequence detector, it is a finite state machine (FSM) and it can be of types – Moore or Mealy.
- The output of the sequence detector becomes 1 when the entire sequence is detected.

4.29.1 Two Types of Sequence Detector

- **Moore machine :** Outputs depend only on the current state.

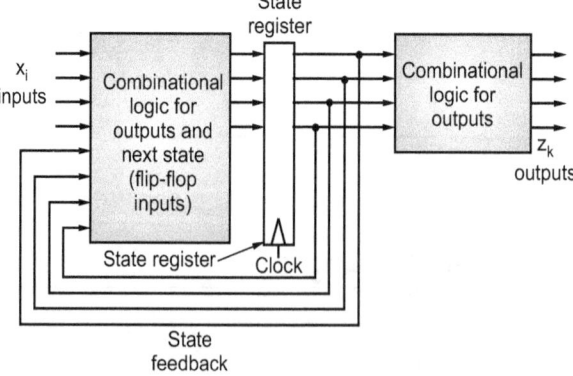

Fig. 4.91

- **Mealy machine :** Outputs depend on both the current state and the primary inputs.

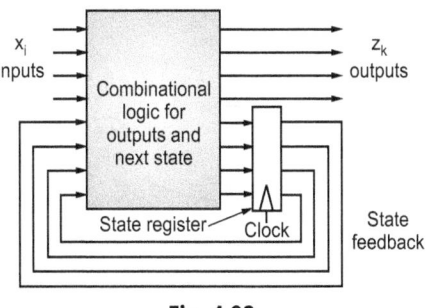

Fig. 4.92

Example 4.20 :

Draw state diagram and state table for sequence detector to detect sequence 110.

[PU 2007, 4M]

Solution :

- As the type of machine is not specified we shall design Moore type machine.
- We select one state as the starting state (reset state). The circuit should enter in this state when the power is turned on or a reset signal is applied. Let this state be 'a'. It can be shown with a node and name of the state is specified inside the node. Also the output Z = 0 is also specified inside the node.
- When in state 'a' as long as the input W = 0 the circuit should remain in the same state. It can be shown with an arc starting and terminating at same state 'a' with label W = 0.
- In state 'a' when the input W = 1 the circuit should recognize this as the first bit of the sequence to be detected and make transition to another state say 'b'. It can be shown with an arc starting at node 'a' and terminating at node 'b' with label W = 1.
- When the circuit is in state 'b' the output Z = 0 as only the first bit of the sequence is detected and not the entire sequence. As in earlier case, there are two possibilities of the input. For input W = 0 the input sequence becomes 10 and comparing it with the first two bits of desired sequence the circuit can neither proceed to the next state (as the sequence is not 11) nor it can remain in the same state (as the last input is 0 and not 1). Therefore, the circuit goes back to state 'a'. It can be shown with an arc from 'b' to 'a' with label W = 0. For input W = 1, the input sequence become 11 which is exactly similar to the first two bits of the sequence to be detected. Therefore, the circuit moves to the next state say 'c' and it can be shown with an arc from 'a' to 'c' with label W = 1.
- Proceeding in this manner upto the state 'd' we can construct the state diagram for the sequence detector as shown in Fig. 4.93.

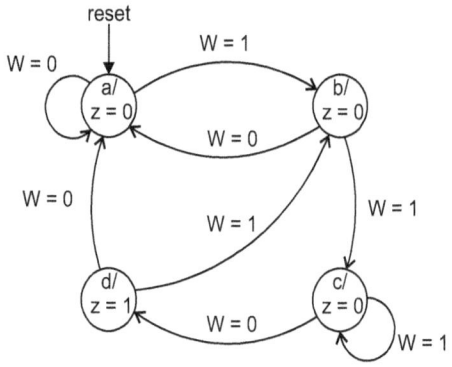

Fig. 4.93

- As shown in Fig. 4.93, there are four states as the length of the sequence to be detected is three. The output Z = 1 in state 'd'.
- The information contained in the state diagram of Fig. 4.93 can be represented in tabular form as shown in the state table 4.45.

Table 4.45

Present State	Next State		Output
	W = 0	W = 1	
a	a	b	0
b	a	c	0
c	d	c	0
d	a	b	1

- When the circuit enters state 'd' output Z = 1, as the sequence 110 has been detected. When instate 'd' if the input W = 0 then the circuit moves to the reset state 'a' and will start detecting the new sequence. If the input W = 1 then the circuit moves to the state 'b' and we say that the circuit has already started detecting the new sequence and the first bit of it has been detected.

Example 4.21 :

Draw the state diagram, write state transition table and design Moore state machine using D flip-flop to detect the given sequence 1011. **[PU 2008, 8 M]**

Solution :

- The length of the sequence to be detected is four so there are five states in the Moore type machine.

Let W be the input and Z be the output of the circuit.

- We select the starting state 'a' in which the circuit enters when the power is turned on or reset signal is applied.
- If input W = 1 then the circuit moves to the next state 'b' otherwise it remains in the same state.
- When in state 'b' the circuit moves to the next state 'c' if the input W = 0. For input W = 1 it remains in the same state 'b' and waits for next input 0 so that it can move to the next state 'c'.
- When in state 'c' the circuit moves to the next state 'd' if the input W = 1. For input W = 0 the input sequence so far is 100. Comparing it with first three bits of desired sequence i.e. 101 we say that the circuit can not proceed to the next state 'd' for input W = 0.
- Now we compare the last two inputs so far i.e. 0 with the first two bits of the desired sequence. As it is not matching we say that the circuit can not remain in same state 'c'.
- Now we compare the last input i.e. 0 with the first bit of the desired sequence. As it is also not matching we say that the circuit can not go back to state 'b'.
- The only option is to go back to state 'a'. Thus, when in state 'c' and the input W = 0 the circuit goes back to state 'a'.
- In a similar manner the behaviour of the circuit can be described for the remaining two states 'd' and 'e'. Based on that the state diagram is constructed as shown in Fig. 4.42.
- As shown in Fig. 4.94 in states 'a', 'b', 'c' and 'd' the output Z is 0 as the entire sequence is not detected in these states. While as the sequence is detected in state 'e' the output Z = 1.
- When in state 'e' if the input W = 0 the input sequence so far is 10110. Comparing last two inputs of this sequence with the first two bits of the desired sequence, we find a match. Therefore, the circuit goes to state 'c' from state 'e' with W = 0 as shown. Here we can say that the circuit starts detecting the input sequence 1011 second time while the first time detection is in progress. Similarly the circuit moves to state 'b' from state 'e' with input W = 1.

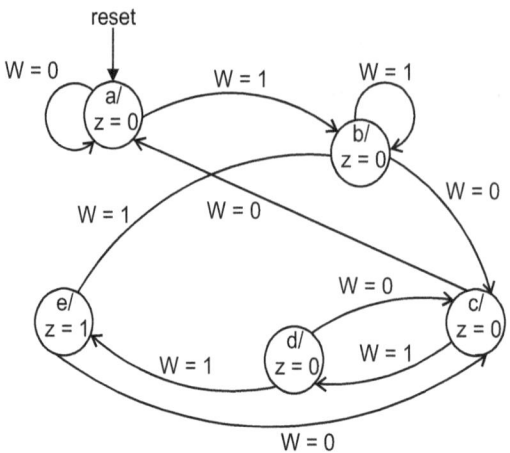

Fig. 4.94

- The information contained in the state diagram of Fig. 4.94 can be represented in tabular form as shown in state table 4.46 which is also known as state transition table.

Table 4.46

Present state	Next State		Output
	W = 0	W = 1	
a	a	b	0
b	c	b	0
c	a	d	0
d	c	e	0
e	c	b	1

- As the number of states are five at least three state variables are required for the representation of the states.
- Eight possible combinations of the three state variables are from 000 to 111. One possible assignment is shown in table 4.47.

Table 4.47

Name of state	Assignment
a	000
b	001
c	010
d	011
e	100

- Based on the assignment shown in table 4.47, we prepare state assignment table 4.48.

SEQUENTIAL LOGIC

Table 4.48

Present state			Next state						Output
			W = 0			W = 1			
U_2	U_1	U_0	U_2	U_1	U_0	U_2	U_1	U_0	Z
0	0	0	0	0	0	0	0	1	0
0	0	1	0	1	0	0	0	1	0
0	1	0	0	0	0	0	1	1	0
0	1	1	0	1	0	1	0	0	0
1	0	0	0	1	0	0	0	1	1

- As shown in table 4.48, U_2, U_1, U_0 are the next state variables and u_2, u_1, u_0 are the present state variables.
- Now, we represent the column of output Z in the k-map and obtain the simplified expression.

K - map for Z ⇒

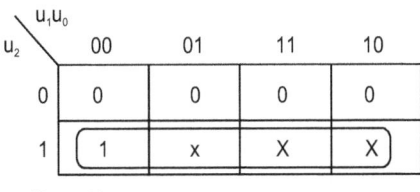

∴   Z = U_2

- As shown in table 4.48, the remaining combinations of the state variables from 101 to 111 are not used. Therefore the output Z for those combinations is shown don't care in the k - map.
- From the table 4.48 and the excitation table of D flip flop the truth table 4.49 is prepared.

Table 4.49

Input	Present State			Next State			Flip flop Inputs		
W	u_2	u_1	u_0	U_2	U_1	U_0	D_2	D_1	D_0
0	0	0	0	0	0	0	0	0	0
0	0	0	1	0	1	0	0	1	0
0	0	1	0	0	0	0	0	0	0
0	0	1	1	0	1	0	0	1	0
0	1	0	0	0	1	0	0	1	0
0	1	0	1	X	X	X	X	X	X
0	1	1	0	X	X	X	X	X	X
0	1	1	1	X	X	X	X	X	X

1	0	0	0	0	0	1	0	0	1
1	0	0	1	0	0	1	0	0	1
1	0	1	0	0	1	1	0	1	1
1	0	1	1	1	0	0	1	0	0
1	1	0	0	0	0	1	0	0	1
1	1	0	1	X	X	X	X	X	X
1	1	1	0	X	X	X	X	X	X
1	1	1	1	X	X	X	X	X	X

- For the unused combinations of the state variables, the next state as well as flip inputs are don't care as shown in table 4.52.
- Now we represent the flip–flop inputs in the K - maps and obtain the simplified expressions.

K - map for D_2 ⇒

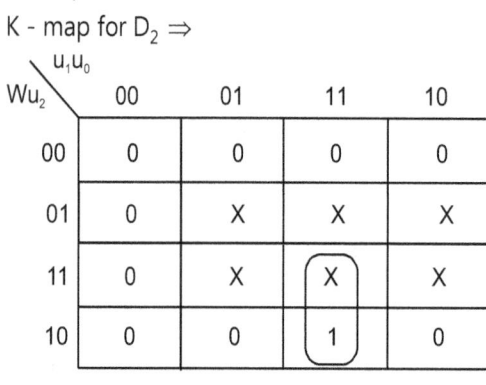

∴ $D_2 = Wu_1 u_0$

K - map for D_1 ⇒

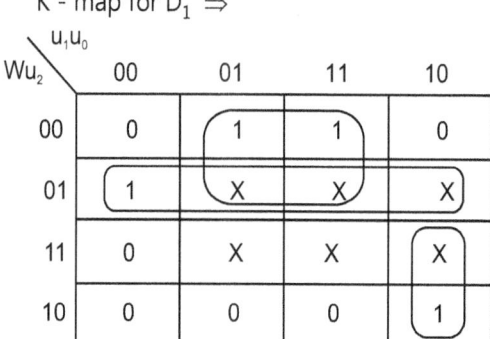

∴ $D_1 = \overline{W}u_2 + \overline{W}\,u_0 + W\,u_1\,\overline{u}_0$

∴ $D_1 = \overline{W}(u_2 + u_0) + Wu_1\overline{u}_0$

K - map for D_0 ⇒

Wu₂ \ u₁u₀	00	01	11	10
00	0	0	0	0
01	0	X	X	X
11	1	1	0	1
10	0	X	X	X

∴ $D_0 = W\overline{u}_1 + W\,\overline{u}_0$

$$\therefore \quad D_0 = W\left(\bar{u}_1 + \bar{u}_0\right)$$

- Based on the above expressions we construct the circuit diagram as shown in Fig. 4.95.

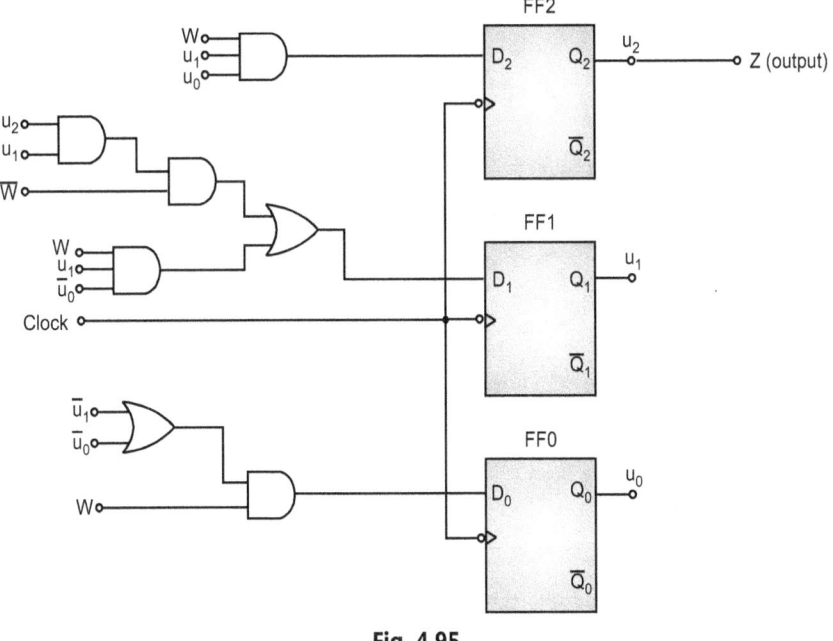

Fig. 4.95

Example 4.22 :

Design a sequence detector to detect the following sequence using JK flip–flops : .... 110 .... (Use Mealy machine) **[PU 2004 - 10 M]**

Solution :

- The length of the sequence to be detected is three, so there are three states in the Mealy type machine.
- Let W be the input and Z be the output of the circuit.
- As in the earlier examples, we select the starting state 'a' in which the circuit enters when the power is turned on or reset signal is applied.
- If input W = 1, then the circuit moves to the next state 'b', otherwise it remains in the same state. In both cases the output Z = 0.
- When in state 'b' the circuit moves to the state 'c' if the input W = 1. For input W = 0 it goes back to the state 'a'. Again in both cases the output Z = 0.
- When in state 'c' if the input W = 1, the circuit remains in the same state 'c' and waits for next input 0. So that the desired sequence is detected. In this case, output Z = 0.
- When in state 'c' if the input W = 1 the circuit remains in the same state 'c' and waits for next 0 so that the desired sequence is detected. In this case output Z = 0.

- When in state 'c', if the input W = 0, the output Z = 1 as the desired sequence is dected. The circuit goes back to state 'a' and will start detecting the new sequence.
- The state diagram is as shown in Fig. 4.96.

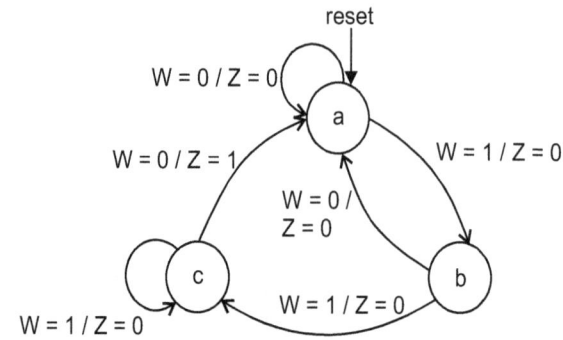

Fig. 4.96

- The information contained in the state diagram of Fig. 4.96 can be represented in tabular form as shown in state table 4.50.

Table 4.50

Present state	Next State		Output	
	W = 0	W = 1	W = 0	W = 1
a	a	b	0	0
b	a	c	0	0
c	a	c	1	0

- As the number of states are three, at least two state variables are required for the representation of the states.
- Four possible combinations of the two state variables are 00, 01, 10 and 11. One possible assignment is shown in table 4.51.

Table 4.51

Name of state	Assignment
a	00
b	01
c	11

- As indicated in table 4.51 the combination 10 is not used for this particular assignment. The assignment may vary therefore we say that the possible assignment is as shown.

- Based on the assignment shown in table 4.51 we prepare state assignment table 4.52.

Table 4.52

Present state	Next State		Output	
	W = 0	W = 1	W = 1	W = 0
$u_1 u_0$	$U_1 U_0$	$U_1 U_0$	Z	Z
00	00	01	0	0
01	00	11	0	0
11	00	11	1	0

- From table 4.54 and the excitation table of JK flip–flop the truth table 4.55 is prepared.
- For the unused combination of the state variable (10), the next state, inputs of the flip–flops and output of the circuit are don't care as shown in table 4.52.
- As shown in table 4.53, $U_1 U_0$ are the next state variables and u_1, u_0 are present state variables.

Table 4.53

Input	Present state		Next state		Flip-flop inputs				Output
W	u_1	u_0	U_1	U_0	J_1	K_1	J_0	K_0	Z
0	0	0	0	0	0	×	0	×	0
0	0	1	0	0	0	×	×	1	0
0	1	0	×	×	×	×	×	×	×
0	1	1	0	0	×	1	×	1	1
1	0	0	0	1	0	×	1	×	0
1	0	1	1	1	1	×	×	0	0
1	1	0	×	×	×	×	×	×	×
1	1	1	1	1	×	0	×	1	0

- Now we represent the flip– flop inputs and the output in the separate K - maps and obtain the simplified expressions.

K - map for $J_1 \Rightarrow$

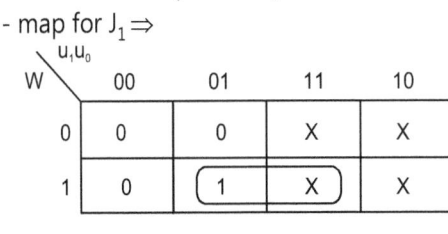

$\therefore J_1 = Wu_0$

K - map for $K_1 \Rightarrow$

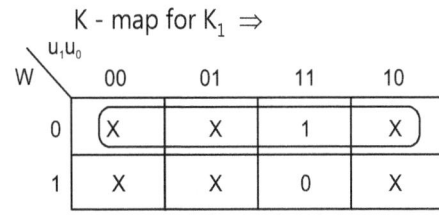

$\therefore K_1 = \overline{W}$

K - map for J_0 ⇒

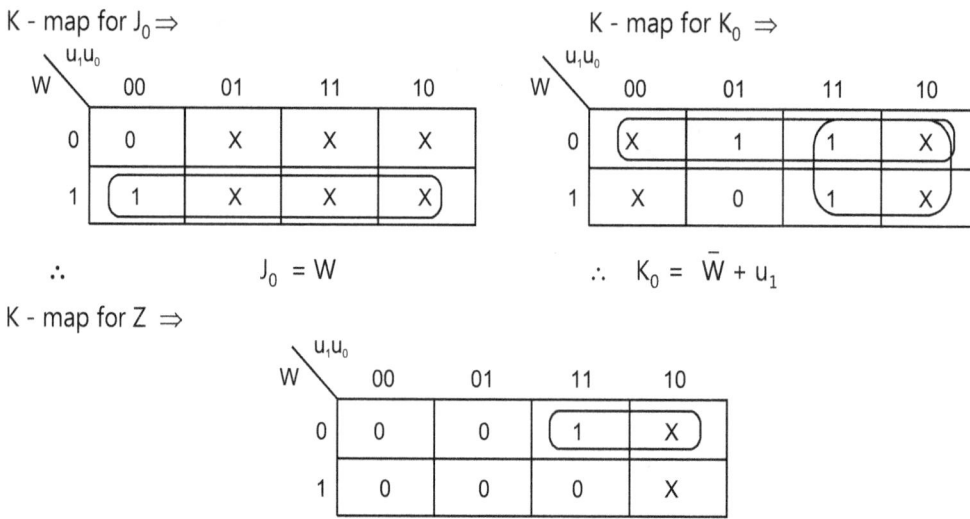

∴ $J_0 = W$

∴ $K_0 = \overline{W} + u_1$

K - map for Z ⇒

W \ u_1u_0	00	01	11	10
0	0	0	1	X
1	0	0	0	X

∴ $Z = \overline{W} u_1$

- Based an above expressions we construct the circuit diagram as shown in Fig. 4.97.

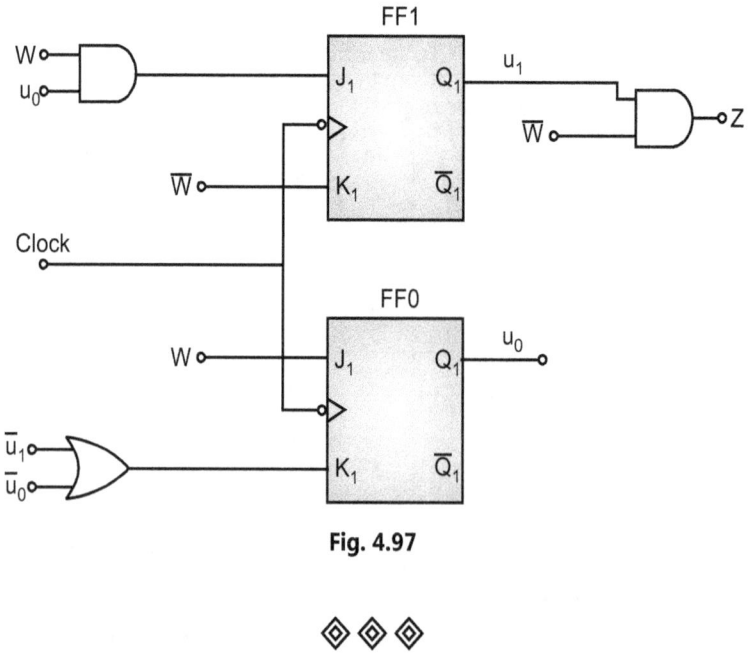

Fig. 4.97

Unit - V

ASM & VHDL

5.1 INTRODUCTION

Q. What is the ASM chart ? **[Dec. 08, May 11, 11 M]**
Q. Given feature of ASM. **[May 12, 2 M]**
Q. Explain ASM techniques designing the sequential circuit in detail. **[May 12, 4 M]**

- Sequential circuits with finite number of states are known as finite state machines (FSMs) state diagram and state table are used for the description of the behaviour of the FSMs.
- FSMs have less number of inputs and outputs. For larger machines having greater number of inputs and output a different form of representation, called as algorithmic state machine (ASM) chart is used.
- ASM charts are just like flow charts and equivalent of nested if–then–else statements.
- The ASM charts were pioneered at Hewlett- Packard Laboratories by Thomas Osborne and were further developed by Christopher Clare.

5.2 ASM CHART NOTATIONS

Q. State and explain basic components of ASM chart. **[Dec. 11, 6 M]**

- As said earlier, ASM charts are similar to flow charts. There elements used in ASM charts are (1) State box, (2) Decision box and (3) Conditional output box.

(1) State Box :
- A rectangular box in a ASM chart is known as state box. It is as shown in Fig. 5.1.

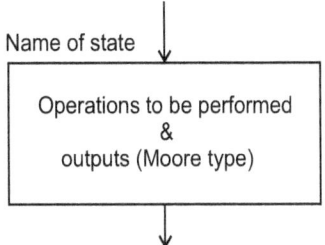

Fig. 5.1 : State box

- A state box represents the state of the machine. It is equivalent to a node in the state diagram or a row in a state table.

- When the machine is in a particular state, certain operations need to be performed. For example, decrement count by one, shift the content of a register to left by one bit position etc. These operations to be performed are listed inside the state box as shown in Fig. 5.1.
- We know that in Moore type machine outputs are decided only by the present state of the machine. Such outputs along with their status are also listed inside the state box.
- As shown in Fig. 5.1 the name of the state is indicated outside the box in the top left corner.

(2) Decision Box :

- A diamond shaped box in a ASM chart is known as decision box. It is as shown in Fig. 5.2.
- A diamond box indicates that the stated condition is to be evaluated. Based on the evaluation, the exit path I or exit path II is selected.
- The condition to be evaluated may be just to check the status of a input (whether it is 1 or 0) or may be an expression formed with more than one inputs.

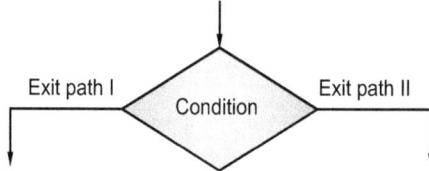

Fig. 5.2 : Decision box

(3) Conditional Output Box :

- An oval shaped box in a ASM chart is known as conditional output box. It is as shown in Fig. 5.3.

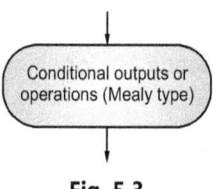

Fig. 5.3

- We know that, in a Mealy type machine, outputs are decided by the present state of the machine and the inputs applied to the machine. Such outputs along with their status are specified inside the conditional output box.
- The conditional output box is always at one of the exit paths of the decision box.
- Therefore, a condition is first evaluated in a decision box and then the outputs are generated as listed inside the conditional output box.
- The operations to be performed, based on the particular condition are also listed inside this box.

Example 5.1 :

Draw ASM chart for the sequence detector 11 of Moore type.

Solution :

- The length of the sequence to be detected is two. Therefore, number of states are three for a More type machine.
- Let W be the input to the circuit and Z be the output of the circuit which becomes1 when the sequence is detected.
- Upon power on or application of reset signal, the circuit enters into the first state 'a'.
- As shown in Fig. 5.4 it is represented with the state box. Name of the state is written outside the box at top left corner and the status of the output i.e. Z = 0 is written inside the box.
- When in state 'a' the input W can be 0 or 1. If W = 0 the circuit remains in state 'a' while if W = 1 it moves to the next state 'b'.
- As shown in Fig. 5.4 the condition of the input W is tested in a decision box. If W = 0, the exit path from a decision box leads to state 'a' and for W = 1 there is a transition from state 'a' to state 'b'.
- Similarly when in state 'b', with input W = 1, there is a transition from state 'b' to state 'c' and for input W = 0, there is a transition from state 'b' to state 'a'.
- When the circuit enters state 'c' the output Z = 1 as shown in Fig. 5.4. For input W = 1 in state 'c' the circuit does no transition while for input W = 0 it goes back to state 'a'.
- The ASM chart is as shown in Fig. 5.4.

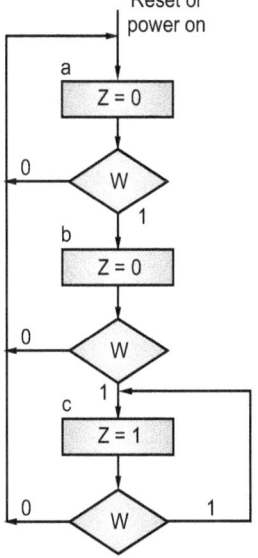

Fig 5.4 : ASM chart for sequence detector 11 - Moore type

Example 5.2 :

Repeat example for a Mealy type machine.

Solution :

- The length of the sequence to be detected is two. Therefore, numbers of states are two for a Mealy type machine.
- Let W be the input of the circuit and Z be the output of the circuit which becomes 1 when the sequence is detected.
- Upon power on or application of the reset signal the circuit enters into the first state 'a'.
- As shown in Fig. 5.5 it is represented with a state box. Name of the state is written outside the box at top left corner and the status of then output i.e. Z = 0 is written inside the box.
- When in state 'a' the input W can be 0 or 1. If W= 0, the circuit remains in same state 'a' while if W= 1, it moves to the next state 'b'.
- As shown in Fig. 5.5 the condition of the input W is tested in a decision box. If W= 0 the exit path from a decision box leads to state 'a' and for W = 1, there is a transition from state 'a' to state 'b'.
- When the circuit is in state 'b' and input W = 1, the output Z = 1 as the sequence gets detected. In this case the circuit remains in the same state 'b'.
- As shown in Fig. 5.5 the condition of the input W is tested in a decision box. At the exit path corresponding to W = 1, a conditional output t box is shown and inside it the status of output Z = 1 is written. It leads to the same next state 'b'.
- Also, when in state 'b', the circuit goes to state 'a' if the input W = 0. At the another exit path corresponding to W = 0 a transition to state 'a' is shown.
- The ASM chart B as shown in Fig. 4.40.

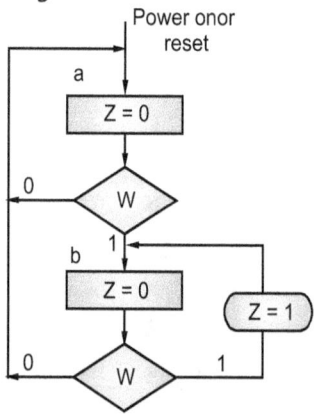

Fig. 5.5 : ASM chart for sequence detector 11 – Mealy type

Example 5.3 :

Draw ASM chart for a synchronous counter that goes through following states.

.... 0 – 4 – 2 – 6 – 1 – 5 – 3 – 7 – 0 – 4 ....

Solution :

- There are eiop Moore type, so there is no conditional output box.
- As shown in Fig. 5.6 the ASM chart consists of only state boxes representing the various states of the circuit and the transition from one state to another takes place with respect to the clock pulse.

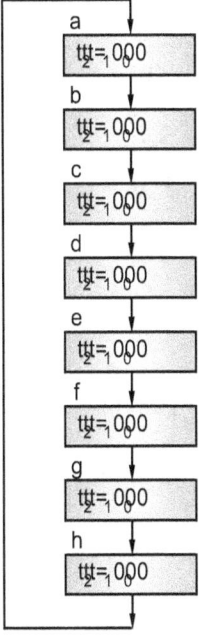

Fig. 5.6

Example 5.4 :

Draw the ASM chart for mod 4 up counter with the condition that there exist an input signal W, and if W = 1 the count is incremented by 1 otherwise it remains same.

Solution :

As modulus of counter is four, there are same number of distinct states in the operation of it.

- Let 'a', 'b', 'c' and 'd' be the names of the states associated with each count 0, 1, 2 and 3 respectively.

- It is given that the count is incremented by one if the input W = 1. Thus the transition from state 'a' to state 'b', from 'b' to 'c' from 'c' to 'd' and from 'd' to 'a' is possible only when input W = 1, otherwise the circuit remains in the same state.
- Thus it is required that, in each state the status of W must be checked in a decision box and accordingly the next state is decided as shown in Fig. 5.7
- Also the four states are represented with the state boxes in the ASM chart shown in Fig. 5.7.

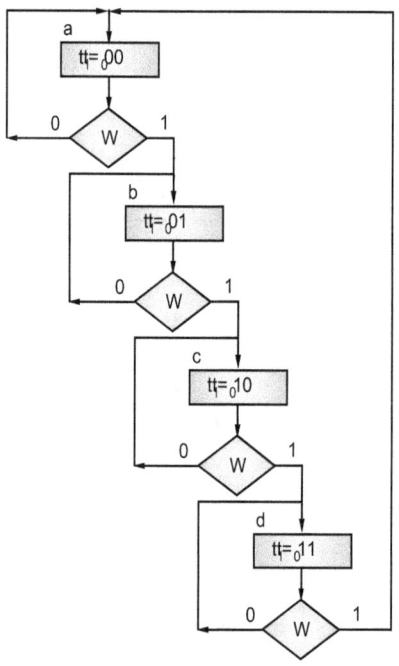

Fig. 5.7

Example 5.5 :

Draw ASM chart for a 2 - bit up /down counter with the mode control input M. For M = 1 it acts as up counter otherwise down counter.

Solution :

- For a 2 - bit counter there are four distinct states in the operation of it.
- Let 'a', 'b', 'c', and 'd' be the names of the states associated with each count 0, 1, 2 and 3 respectively.

- For mode control input M = 1, it acts as a up counter. Thus, there is a transition from state 'a' to state 'b', from 'b' to 'c', from 'c' from 'c' to 'd' and from 'd' to 'a' when M = 1.
- For mode control input M = 0, it acts as a down counter. Thus there is a transition from state 'a' to state 'd', from 'd' to 'c', from 'c' to 'b' and from 'b' to 'a' when M = 0.
- Thus as shown in Fig. 5.8 after every state the mode control input M is checked and the next state is decided.

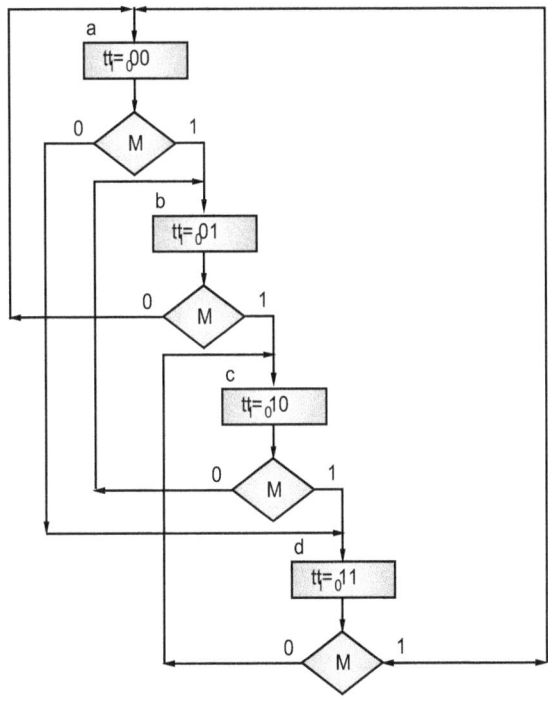

Fig. 5.8

5.3 CONTROLLER FOR ASM USING MULTIPLEXERS

- From the block diagram of sequential circuits shown in Fig. 5.9 it is clear that the flip flop inputs are derived from the combinational circuit.
- Up till now the block next state decoder i.e. combinational circuit we realized with the logic gates.
- In the design of controller for ASM, we now use multiplexers instead of the logic gates as shown in the Fig. 5.9

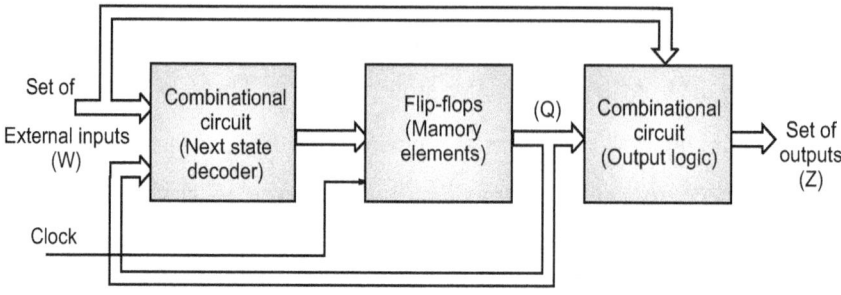

Fig. 5.9

- The flip flops used in this method are of D type.
- Also the output of flip flops i.e. present state of the circuit acts as select inputs of the multiplexers.

Example 5.6 :

Draw ASM chart for the sequence detector 11 (Moore type) and design controller using multiplexers.

Solution :

The ASM chart for the sequence detector 11 (Moore type) is as shown in Fig. 5.10.

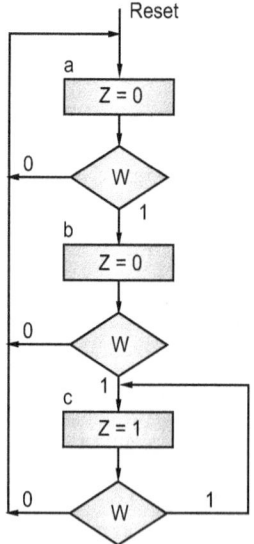

Fig. 5.10

- From the ASM chart shown in Fig. 5.10 we prepare the state table 5.1.

Table 5.1

Present State	Next State		Output
	W = 0	W = 1	Z
a	a	b	0
b	a	c	0
c	a	c	1

- As there are three states number of state variables required are two. Let the state assignment be as shown in table 5.2.

Table 5.2

Name of State	Assignment
a	00
b	01
c	10

- Therefore two flip flops are required for implementation. As number of multiplexers are equal to number of flip flops, two multiplexers are required.
- Also, number of states are three, therefore we require a multiplexer with at least three inputs i.e. 4 : 1 multiplexer is required.
- We construct table 5.3 consisting of multiplexer input number, present state, next state, condition for transition and output of the circuit as shown.

Table 5.3

Multiplexer Input Number	Present State $t_1 t_0$	Next State $T_1 T_0$	Condition for Transition	Output
0	00	00	w = 0	0
0	00	01	w = 1	0
1	01	00	w = 0	0
1	01	10	w = 1	0
2	10	00	w = 0	1
2	10	10	w = 1	1

- Let multiplexers M and N generate the next state variables T_1 and T_0 respectively. We now prepare the expressions for the inputs of mux M and mux N.
- **0th Input of Mux M :** Observe the first two rows of the table 5.3. The next state variable $T_1 = 0$ in both rows irrespective of what is the status of input w. Therefore 0th input of Mux M is given by,

$$\text{Mux M (0)} = 0$$

- **0th Input of Mux N :** The state variable T_0 in first two rows is same as that of input W. Therefore it is given by,

  Mux N (0) = W

- Proceeding in the similar manner, we write the expressions for the remaining inputs of multiplexers,

  Mux M (1) = W

  Mux M (2) = W

  Mux N (1) = 0

  Mux N (2) = 0

- The expression for output Z is obtained from the K-map.

K-map for Z ⇒

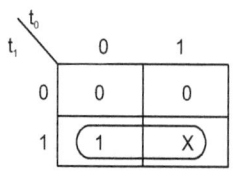

∴ Z = t_1

- Based on above expressions we construct the circuit diagram as shown in Fig. 5.11.

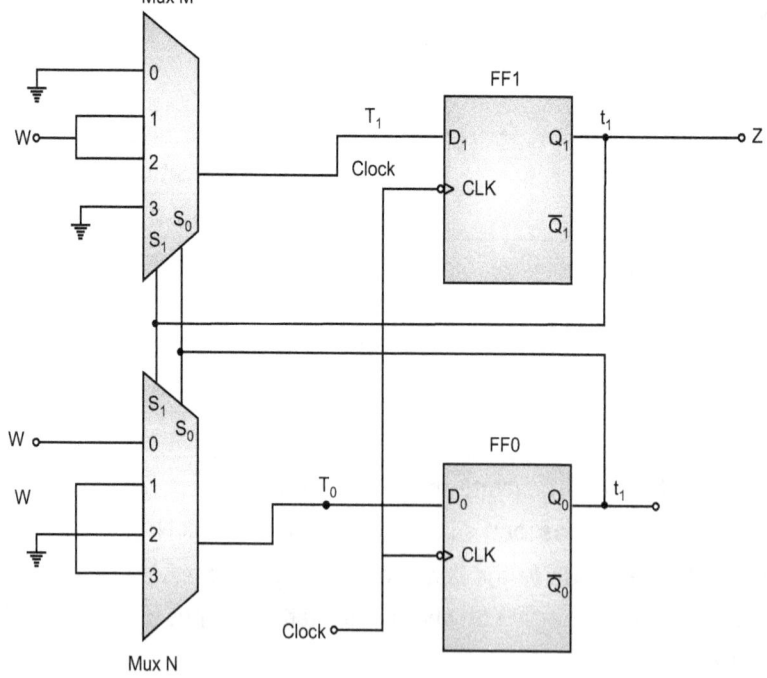

Fig. 5.11

Example 5.7 :

Draw ASM chart for sequences detector 110 (Moore machine) and design controller circuit for the same.

Solution :

The ASM chart for the sequence detector 110 (Moore machine) is as shown in Fig. 5.12.

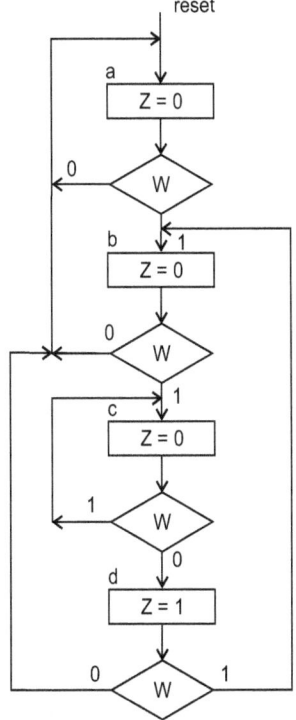

Fig. 5.12

- From the ASM chart shown in Fig. 5.12 we prepare the state table 5.4.

Table 5.4

Present State	Next State		Output
	W = 0	W = 1	Z
a	a	b	0
b	a	c	0
c	d	c	1
d	a	b	1

- As there are four states, number of state variables required are two. Let the state assignment be as shown in table 5.5.

Table 5.5

Name of State	Assignment
a	00
b	01
c	10
d	11

- Therefore two flip flops are required for implementation.
- Also two multiplexers are required for which number of inputs are four.
- Based on Table 5.4 and 5.5 we construct table 5.6 consisting of multiplexer input number, present state, next state, condition for transition and output of the circuit as shown.

Table 5.6

Multiplexer Input Number	Present State $t_1 t_0$	Next State $T_1 T_0$	Condition for Transition	Output
0	00	00	W = 0	0
0	00	01	W = 1	0
1	01	00	W = 0	0
1	01	10	W = 1	0
2	10	11	W = 0	0
2	10	10	W = 1	0
3	11	00	W = 0	1
3	11	01	W = 1	1

- The expression for output Z is obtained from K-map.

K-map for Z ⇒

t_1 \ t_0	0	1
0	0	0
1	0	1

∴ $Z = t_1 \cdot t_0$

- Let multiplexers M and N generate the next state variables T1 and T0 respectively. The expressions for the inputs of them are :

$$\text{mux M (0)} = 0 \qquad \text{mux N (0)} = W$$
$$\text{mux M (1)} = W \qquad \text{mux n (1)} = 0$$
$$\text{mux M (2)} = 1 \qquad \text{mux N (2)} = \overline{W}$$
$$\text{mux M (3)} = 0 \qquad \text{mux N (3)} = W$$

- Based on above expressions we construct the circuit diagram as shown in Fig. 5.13.

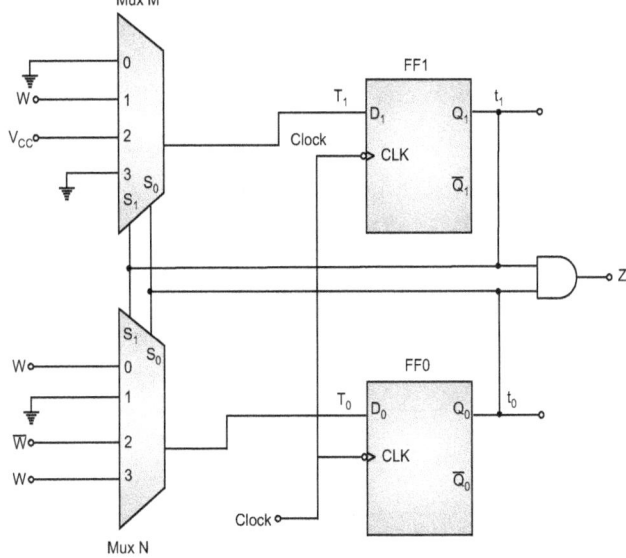

Fig. 5.13

Example 5.8 :

Draw ASM chart for sequence detector 11 (Mealy type) and design controller for it.

Solution :

- The ASM chart for sequence detector 11 (Mealy type) is as shown in Fig. 5.14.

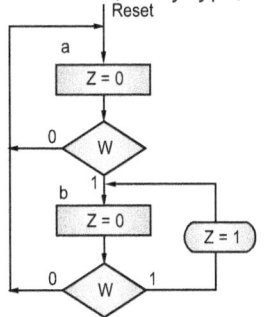

Fig. 5.14

- From the ASM chart shown in Fig. 5.14 we prepare the state table 5.7.

Table 5.7

Present State	Next State		Output	
	W = 0	W = 1	W = 0	W = 1
a	a	B	0	0
b	a	B	0	1

- As there are only two states, one state variable is required.
- Let the assignment be a = 0 and b = 1.
- Therefore, one flip flop and one multiplexer with two inputs is required for implementation.
- Based on Table 5.7, we construct Table 5.8 consisting of multiplexer input number, present state, next state, condition for transition and output of the circuit as shown.

Table 5.8

Multiplexer Input Number	Present State (t)	Next State (T)	Condition for Transition	Output (Z)
0	0	0	w = 0	0
0	0	1	w = 1	0
1	1	0	w = 0	0
1	1	1	w = 1	1

- The expression for output Z is obtained from the k-map.

K-map for Z ⇒

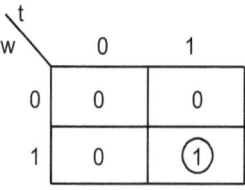

$$\therefore Z = w \cdot t$$

- Let the multiplexer A generate the next state variable T.
The expressions for its inputs are

$$\text{mux M (0)} = W$$
$$\text{mux M (1)} = W$$

- Based on above expressions, we construct the circuit diagram as shown in Fig. 5.15.

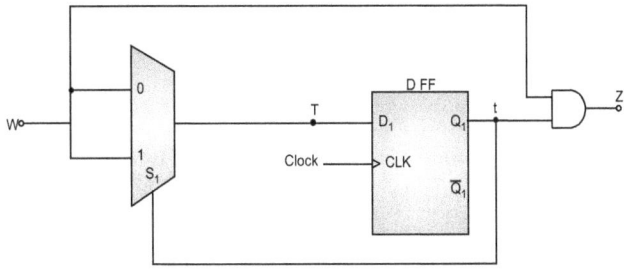

Fig. 5.15

5.4 INTRODUCTION TO VHDL

- In this unit we discuss Library, Entity, Architecture, Modelling styles, Data objects, concurrent and Sequential statements, Design examples, using VHDL for basic combinational and sequential circuits, Attributes.
- We know that, any digital circuit consists of only a few basic circuits; AND, OR, and NOT gates, a memory element flip-flop, irrespective of the size and complexity of the circuit. The digital circuits can be designed using manual methods, such as simplification of Boolean expressions using Boolean algebraic theorems, graphical methods, tabular methods, using available SSI and MSI devices (mux/demux, registers, counters etc). These design (synthesis) methods or tools are well for design of systems which are small in size and are not complex enough in today's context.
- However, the increasing size and the complexity of digital systems require design methods with the use of computers. These methods are known as Computer Aided Design (CAD) methods. The number of CAD tools have been developed for this purpose.
- CAD tools made it possible to design modern complex logic circuits, and also made the design work much easier. Many tasks in the design process are performed automatically by the CAD tools resulting in faster and efficient design.
- A number of Hardware Description Languages (HDLs) have been developed for describing the structure and behavior of complex digital circuits and number of HDL based CAD tools have been developed for the design of digital systems.

5.5 VLSI DESIGN

Q. What is the VLSI technology ? Give classification of IC technology. **[4 M]**

- VLSI stands for Very Large Scale Integration. It is the process of integrating milion of transistors on tiny silicon chips. VLSI circuit technology is one of the basic components of today's high technology. VLSI device are found in all varieties of applications from simple home appliances to complex space crafts. The main benefits are complex functionality in very small package.

Classification of IC technology :

Type	Device	Year	Function
SSI	1-100	1960	Gates, op-amps
MSI	100-1k	1965	Filters
LSI	1k-10k	1970	Microprocessor, ALU
VLSI	> 10k	1975	Memory, DSP

5.6 COMPARISON OF VHDL AND VERILOG

Q. Give comparison between VHDL and Verilog.
Q. What is VHDL ? [Dec. 10, 12, 2 M]

VHDL	Verilog
1. It is somewhat difficult and complex than verilog.	1. Relatively simple especially for 'c' language users.
2. It result in slower simulation.	2. Results in fast simulation.
3. It is superior in higher system level designs.	3. It has a very good acceptance in ASIC.
4. Procedures and functions may be placed in a package. So that they, can be used for any design.	4. There is no concept of package in VERILOG.
5. A library is a store for complied VHDL code.	5. No concept of a liabrary.
6. VHDL allows concurrent procedure calls.	6. VERILOG does not allow concurrent task calls.

5.7 LEVELS OF ABSTRACTION

Q. Explain levels of abstraction in detail.

- Different styles are adopted for writing VHDL code. Abstraction defines how much detail about the design is specified in a particular description. There are four main levels of abstraction.

(i) Layout level :
- It is lowest level of abstraction. It specifies actual layout of design on silicon. Detailed timing information, analog effects are specified.

(ii) Logic level :
- A model is described by the logic gates and the connection between logic gates. This design has information about function, architecture, technology, detailed timing. Layout information and analog effects are ignored.

(iii) Register transfer level :
- This model describes the flow of data between registers and how a design processes the data. The design is specified using register and the logic in between.

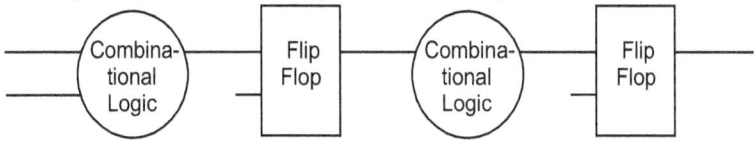

Fig. 5.16

- Design contains architecture information, no details of technology, no specification of absolute timing delays.
- Entire code is partitioned between clocked and combinational processes.

(iv) Behavioral level :
- The model is specified by describing functionality of the design using HDL's without specifying the architecture of registers.
- It contains timing information required to represent a function.

e.g. Behavioral model of an AND gate with A and B inputs, and C as output.

```
process (A, B)
   begin
      if  (A = '1' and B = '1') then
            C <= '1';
      else
            C <= '0';
         end if;
         end process;
```

5.8 DATA OBJECTS

Q. With the help of suitable example explain data objects
(i) constant (ii) variable (iii) signal (iv) file **[May 09, 12, 8 M]**
Q. Explain data objects in detail. **[May 10, 8 M]**
Q. Give different types of data object.
Q. Write a note on data types of VHDL.

A VHDL object consist of one of the following :
- Constant
- Variable
- Signal

- **Constant :**

Constant objects are names assigned to specific values of a type. Constant is an object whose value cannot be changed once defined for the design. By use of constant, model becomes more readable and easy to update.

The syntax is

   constant constant_name : type_name := value ;

The value specification is optional

e.g. constant PI : real := 3.1414 ;

   constant WIDTH : integer := 8 ;

   constant delay : time := 10 ns ;

- **Variable**

A Variable is an object with single current value. The value of variable may change. Variables are used for local storage in process statements and subprograms. All value assignments to variable occur immediately.

The variable declaration syntax is

   variable variable_name : type_name := initial value ;

e.g. variable P, Q : bit ;

   variable DELAY : time ;

   Variable WIDTH : std_logic_vector (7 downto 0) ;

- **Signal**

Signal objects are used to connect entities together to form models. Signals are communication media between entities. Signals are nothing but the wires (which connect two or more components) lying inside an IC.

Signals can be declared in entity declaration section, architecture declaration section, and package declarations. Signals declared in packages can be shared among entities and called global signals.

The syntax is

   signal signal_name: signal _type := initial value ;

   The value specification is optional.

e.g. signal VCC : bit := '1' ;

   signal GROUND : std_logic := '0' ;

   signal INT_BUS : bit_vector(7 downto 0) ;

   signal CONTROL : std_logic_vector(15 downto 0) ;

Signals declared in entity declaration section are global to any architecture for that entity. Signals declared in architecture can only be referenced in that architecture only.

- **Variable Vs Signal**

Variable	Signal
1. The value of variable is updated immediately, after the execution of variable assignment statement.	1. The value of signal is updated after an amount of time or after a delta delay, after the execution of signal assignment statement.
2. Variables are declared in the process.	2. Signals are declared in architecture before begin statement.
3. A variable has only two properties attached to it : Type and Value.	3. A signal has three properties attached to it : Type, Value, and Time.
4. During simulation, variables occupy less storage than signal.	4. During simulation, signals occupy more storage than variables.
5. Variable assignment is ': =' i.e. Y : = A OR B	5. Signal Assignment is '< =' i.e. Y < = A OR B

5.9 VHDL COMPONENT

Q. Write short note on VHDL component. [2 M]

  1. Entity

  2. Architecture

Q. Write short note on Entity. [Dec. 11, 2 M]

Q. Describe the main component of a VHDL description. [Dec. 11, 2 M]

A component is a very important concept in VHDL. A component can be a complete design or a small part of a system.

VHDL component has two parts :
1. Entity
2. Architecture

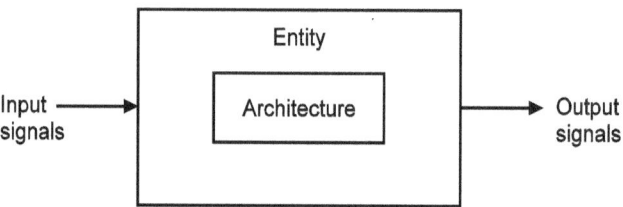

Fig. 5.17 : A VHDL component

Entity : It is actually used for port declaration for inputs and outputs. An entity is the most basic building block in VHDL. So, entity acts as a black box, which gives the external view of the design. Entity does not know about the internal behaviour of the component.

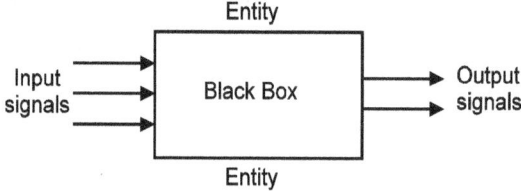

Fig.5.18 : Entity

Entity name is the same as the component name.

For example, the entity of full adder looks like as shown in Fig. 5.19.

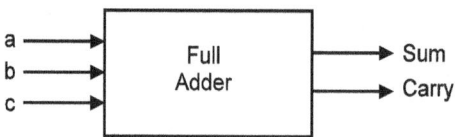

Fig. 5.19 : Entity for Full Adder

5.9.1 Entity

| Q. Explain entity in detail with one example. | [6 M] |
| Q. Explain entity in detail. | [4 M] |

- The entity describes the design's interface to the external circuit. It is equivalent to pin configuration of an IC. Entity declaration defines the input and output ports of the design. Each port in the port list must be given a name, data flow direction and a type. Entity can be used as a component in other entities after being compiled into a library.

- The syntax for entity declaration is :

  entity ENTITY_NAME is

  port (Port list) ;

  end ENTITY_NAME ;

e.g entity OR_ GATE is

  port (A1, A2, A3, A4: in bit ;

     B1, B2, B3, B4: in bit ;

     Y1, Y2, Y3, Y4: out bit) ;

     end OR_GATE ;

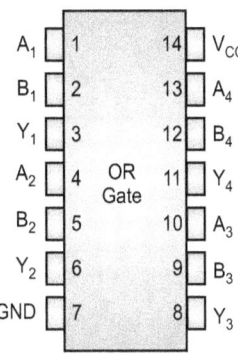

Fig. 5.20

- Entity declaration starts from keyword entity and ends with keyword end. Between this ports are defined with keyword port. Ports are declared with their name, mode and type.
- Mode specifies the direction of ports. Four types of modes are defined in VHDL as follows.

Mode in – value can be read but not assigned. i.e. input port.

Mode out – value can be assigned but not read. i.e. output port.

Mode inout – value can be read and assigned. i.e. input/output port. (bidirectional signals)

Mode buffer – output port with internal read capability.

- In above example, entity OR_GATE is declared for an IC of OR gate as shown. Ports A1, A2, A3, A4, B1, B2, B3, B4 are defined as an input port of bit type.

  Y1, Y2, Y3, Y4 are declared as output ports. There is no semicolon after last line in port list.
- Every VHDL code must start with entity. VHDL design description must include only one entity and at least one corresponding architecture.

Buffer :

- Once a port is declared as mode buffer, it is similar to a port which is declared as mode out, but out mode does not allow for internal feedback.
- Mode buffer is used for ports, which are readable within the entity, such as for counter outputs. In counter, present state used to determine the next state, so the value of counter must be in the feedback loop, therefore counter outputs are declared as buffer.

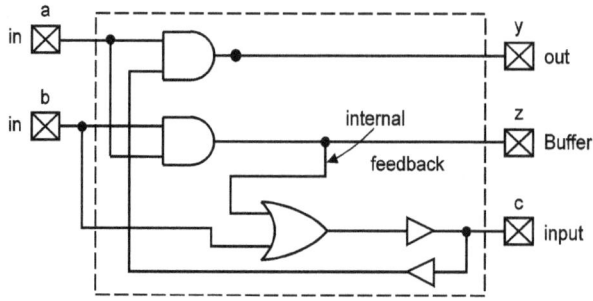

Fig. 5.21 : Modes and their signal sources

As shown in Fig. 5.21, signals a and b act only as the input, signal y acts only as output. Signal z is declared as buffer, therefore, it can be reread internally. Signal c acts as the bidirectional signal; i.e. input or output.

Examples of entity :

Q. Write entity for an IC, ALU. [4 M]

Example 5.9 : Write entity for an IC shown in Fig. 5.22.

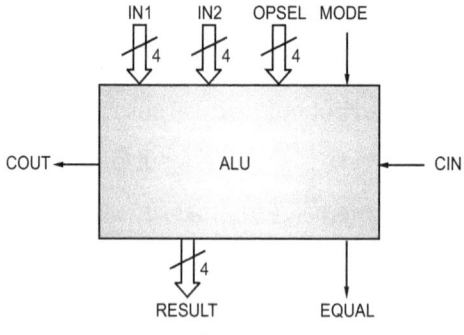

Fig. 5.22

Solution :

    entity ALU is
        port (IN1, IN2, OPSEL : in bit_ vector (3 downto 0) ;

```
        MODE, CIN : in bit ;
        COUT, EQUAL : out bit ;
        RESULT : out bit_vector (3 downto 0)) ;
    end ALU ;
```

Example 5.10 :
Write the entity construct for the R-S flip flop circuit as shown below.

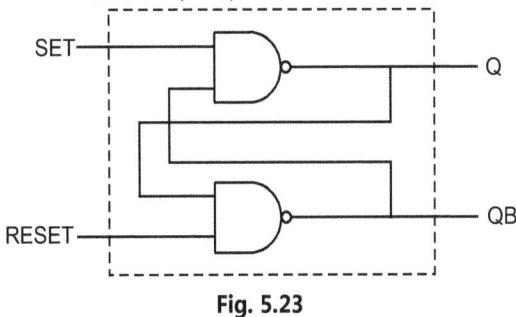

Fig. 5.23

Solution :
Let the name of the entity be RSFF. It has two input ports SET and RESET and two bidirectional ports Q and QB. Then entity construct will be

```
    entity RSFF is
    port    (SET, RESET: in bit ;
            Q, QB: buffer bit) ;
    end     RSFF;
```

5.9.2 Architecture

Q. Explain architecture component of VHDL in detail. [4 M]

- Architecture describes a design's behavior and functionality (internal behaviour of entity). Architecture specifies behavior, function, interconnections, relationship between inputs and output of an entity.
- Architecture can contain only concurrent statement. An entity can have more than one architecture. There can be no architecture without an entity.
- The syntax of architecture body is

    architecture ARCHITECTURE_NAME of ENTITY_NAME is
        [declarative part]
    begin
    [Statement part]
    end ARCHITECTURE_NAME ;

    The words architecture, of, is, begin and end are keywords in VHDL.

Architecture_Name

- Architecture must be given a name consisting of a text string which should be assigned by a designer in a way meaningful to the design.

ENTITY_NAME

Must write the name of entity for which the architecture is to be written.

Declarative part

It appears before the keyword begin. It can be used to declare signals, user_defined types, constants, components, subprogram etc.

Statement part

It is contained between the keywords begin and end. All the statements are executed concurrently (simultaneously).

The functionality of the design can be expressed in terms of following styles which are called styles of modeling.

1. Data flow
2. Behavioral
3. Structural

Example 5.11 :

Write the VHDL code for the circuit shown in Fig. 5.24.

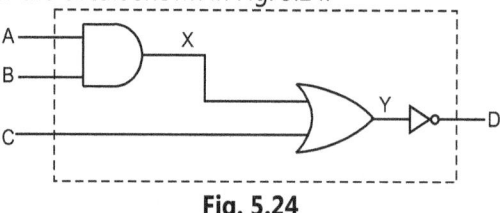

Fig. 5.24

Solution :

This circuit is having three inputs A, B, C and one output D. To express D in terms of A, B, C, we have to consider intermediate wires X and Y. Inputs A, B, C and output D must be defined in entity declaration.

The intermediate wires (wires running inside an IC) X, Y should be declared as signal in declarative part of architecture body.

        entity ANDORNOT is

          port (A, B, C: in bit ;

             D: out bit) ;

          end ANDORNOT ;

      architecture ANDORNOT_ARCH of ANDORNOT is

```
            signal X,Y: bit ;
                begin
                    X <= A and B ;
                    Y <= X or C ;
                    D <= not Y ;
        end ANDORNOT_ARCH ;
```
The sequence of statement is not important.

> **Q.** Consider a simple example of half adder. How will you write a VHDL entity declaration for half adder ? Also write an architecture of half adder ? Also write an architecture of half adder in structural style of modeling and data flow style of modeling. **[Dec. 10, 8 M]**

Example 5.12 :
Write the VHDL code to design half adder.

Solution :
The truth table and circuit of half adder is as shown.

Input		Output	
IN1	IN2	Sum	Carry
0	0	0	0
0	1	1	0
1	0	1	0
1	1	0	1

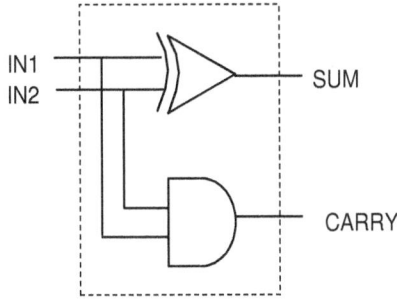

Fig. 5.25 : Half adder

Half adder is having two inputs IN1, IN2 and two outputs SUM, CARRY.

No need of signal declaration.

    entity HALFADDR is

```
    port (IN1, IN2: in bit ;
        SUM, CARRY: out bit) ;
end HALFADDR ;
architecture HALFADDR_ARCH of HALFADDR is
begin
    SUM < = IN1 xor IN2 ;
    CARRY < = IN1 and IN2 ;
end HALFADDR_ARCH ;
```

5.10 CONCURRENT STATEMENTS

Q. Give classification of different types of concurrent statement   [2 M]

A VHDL architecture body consists of a set of interconnected concurrent statements. Concurrent statement in a design executes simultaneously. All concurrent statements describe the functionality of multiplexer structure. It is not possible to design storage elements like flip-flop using concurrent statements only.

The concurrent statements defined in VHDL are :

- Concurrent signal assignment
- Block statement
- Component Instantiation statement
- Generate statement
- Process statement

5.10.1 Concurrent Signal Assignment

Q. Explain concurrent signal assignment with example.   [4 M]
Q. Describe the types of concurrent signal Assignment.   [6 M]

(i) Simple Concurrent Signal Assignment

The syntax is

    Target <= expressions ;

i.e. Target signal receives the value of an expression. A signal assignment is defined by '<='

    e.g.   Z <= A and B ;

The logical AND of A and B is assigned to Z. This statement is executed whenever either A or B has an event occurred on it. An event on a signal is a change in the value of that signal. [Whenever value of A or B changes, statement will execute].

A signal assignment statement is said to be sensitive to changes on any signal that are to the right of the <= symbol. The above statement is sensitive to A and B.

Signal assignment statement creates the driver. Z <= A and B statement will create one AND gate with A and B inputs and Z as output.

i.e. It has created driver for Z.

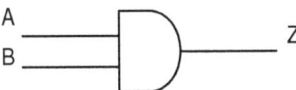

Let, X <= Y; It will connect nodes X and Y. Driver for X will be created like.

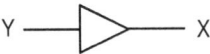

In concurrent statements, there are no implied registers.

(ii) Conditional Concurrent Signal Assignment

The syntax is

    target <= Boolean expression1 when condition

        else

        expression2 ;

when statement can also be nested.

While executing when statement,

Each condition is tested in the order in which it is written.

The value of that expression whose associated condition is true will be assigned to the target.

If none of the conditions are true, the value of expression associated with last else is assigned to the target.

e.g.   Z < = A when ASSIGN_A = '1'

                          else

                          B when ASSIGN_B = '1'

                          else

                          C;

ASSIGN_A is tested; if it is '1', then the value of A will be assigned to Z.

If ASSIGN_A is not equal to '1', then condition ASSIGN_B is tested, if it is '1' then Z will be equal to B.

If ASSIGN_B is not equal to '1' then the value of C will be assigned to Z.

(iii) Selected Concurrent Signal Assignment

The syntax is

    with choice_ expression select

```
target <= expression1 when choice1,
         expression2 when choice2,
         expressionN when choiceN,
         expression when others ;
```

'with_select' statement evaluates choice_expression and compares that value to each choice value in the order in which they are written. The value of that expression where match is found is assigned to the target. If no match is found, expression associated with others will be assigned to target.

- No two choices can overlap.
- All possible choices must be enumerated.
- Each choice can be either a static expression (such as 3) or a static range (such as 1 to 3).
- Each value in the range of the choice expression type must be covered by one choice.
- "others" clause is optional.
- All choices for the expression must be included, otherwise "others" clause must be the last choice.

Example 5.13 :

Write VHDL code for 2 bit comparator.

Solution :

For 2 bit comparator, there are two, 2 bit inputs A, B and three outputs Y0, Y1, Y2.

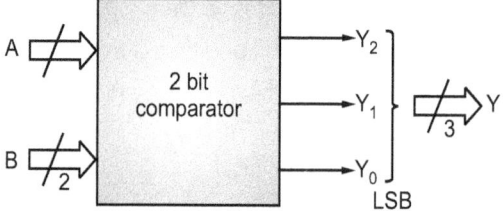

Fig. 5.26 : 2 bit comparator

Truth table :

If A = B then Y2 = 0, Y1 = 0, Y0 = 1   i.e. Y = 001
If A > B then Y2 = 0, Y1 = 1, Y0 = 0   i.e. Y = 010
If A < B then Y2 = 1, Y1 = 0, Y0 = 0   i.e. Y = 100

From truth table itself, we can describe the relationship between input and output and hence no need of gate circuitry for this design.

```
entity COMP1 is
    port (A, B,: in bit_vector (1 downto 0) ;
    Y: out bit_vector (2 downto 0) ;
end COMP1 ;
    architecture COMP1_ARCH of COMP1 is
```

```
                begin
    Y <= "001" when A = B
        else
            "010" when A > B
        else
            "100" when A < B ;
    end COMP1_ARCH ;
```

- Single bit value must be specified in single quotes i.e. '1', '0'.
  Multi bit value must be specified in double quotes i.e. "100", "1010".
- Let Y = Y2 Y1 Y0

If declared as Y: out bit_vector (2 downto 0) ; then Y0 is considered as LSB and Y2 as MSB.

If declared as Y: out bit_vector (0 to 2) ; then Y2 is considered as LSB and Y0 as MSB.

5.10.2 Block Statement

Q. Explain the Block statement with syntax.	[4 M]

Main purpose of block statement is organizational only. It constructs only separate part of the code without adding any functionality. It allows the designer to logically group areas of the model.

Each block represents a self-contained area of the model. Signals, types, constants etc. declared in the block are local to that block and can not be referenced outside of that block.

The syntax is

```
        label: block
        [block declarative item]
        begin
            concurrent statements              optional
        end block [label] ;
```

label → is required to name the block.

e.g. ALU: block
　　　signal QBUS: bit_vector (31 downto 0) ;
　　　begin
　　　　　C <= A add B ;
　　　　　C <= A sub B ;
　　　end block ;

Block can also be nested.

e.g. BLK1: block

```
    signal QBUS: bit_ vector (31 downto 0) ;
    begin
      BLK2: block
        signal QBUS: bit_ vector (31 downto 0) ;
        begin
            -- BLK2 statements
        end block BLK2 ;
            -- BLK1 statements
      end block BLK1 ;
```

In this example, signal QBUS is declared in two blocks. One block is contained in the other. BLK1 is the parent block of BLK2. The QBUS signal from BLK1 has been overridden by a declaration of the same name in BLK2.

Example 5.14 :

Write VHDL code to design D-latch using Block statement.

Solution :

The pin configuration of D-latch is as shown in Fig. 5.27.

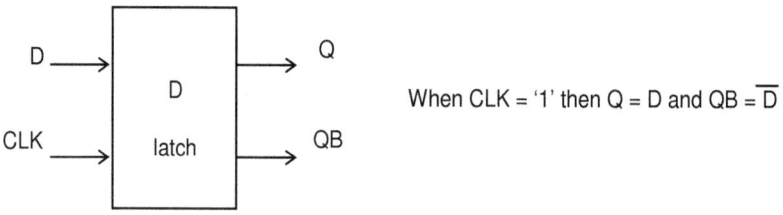

When CLK = '1' then Q = D and QB = $\overline{D}$

Fig. 5.27

```
    entity DLATCH is
        port (D, CLK: in bit ;
              Q, QB: out bit) ;
    end DLATCH ;
    architecture DLATCH_ARCH of DLATCH is
    begin
        B1: block (CLK = '1')          -- guard expression
            begin
                Q <= guarded  D ;       -- statement 1
                QB <= guarded  not ( D ) ;  -- statement 2
            end block B1 ;
    end  DLATCH_ARCH ;
```

- When CLK is equal to '1' then value of D and its complement will be assigned to Q and QB respectively.

When CLK is not equal to '1' then statement 1 and statement 2 (guarded statement) will disable or turned off (does not execute).

5.10.3 Component Instantiation Statement

Q. Explain component instantiation statement. [4 M]

Component is predesigned, preanalyzed, precompiled entity_architecture pair (VHDL model). Components are normally placed in design library. Component specifies a subsystem, which can be instantiated in another architecture leading to a hierarchical specification.

The component can be defined in package, design entity, architecture, or block declarations. Components must be declared before *begin* statement of architecture, if it is declared in architecture. A component must be declared before it is instantiated. e.g. Suppose VHDL code for half adder is written, compiled and verified, and placed either in design library or in working directory, then for full adder design, we can use half adder as component because full adder can be designed using two half adders and one OR gate.

The syntax for component declaration is :

    component   component_name
        port (port_list) ;
    end component;

e.g.   component HALFADDR
        port (IN1, IN2: in bit ;
            SUM, CARRY: out bit) ;
        end component ;

Component_name should be same as entity name of VHDL code which is using as component. In port list copy the port list of entity (entity of VHDL code which is using as component).

Component Instantiation :

It is selecting a compiled specification of component in the library and linking it with the architecture where it will be used.

Component Instantiation statement is used to build a net list in VHDL by referencing a previously defined hardware component in current design.

It introduces a subsystem declared elsewhere as a component in current design.

The syntax for component instantiation is :

    Instance_name: component_name

        port map ([port_name =>] expression

            [port_name =>] expression.);

Instance_name is name of the instance of the component.

Component_name is name of the component to be instantiated.

Port map connects each port of this instance of component_name to a signal valued expression in the current entity.

Ports can be mapped to signals by 'named' or 'positional' notation.

Ports of the component are called formal ports. Ports of top_level entity (entity of main design) are called actual ports. Named association is port maps by names are preferred because it makes the code more readable and pins can be specified in any order.

All positional port mapping should be placed before any named port mapping.

Example 5.15 :

Write VHDL code for NAND gate and write VHDL code for the logic circuit shown in Fig. 5.28 by using NAND gate design as component.

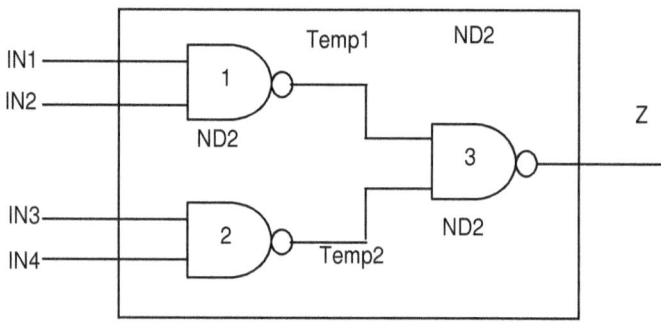

Fig. 5.28 (a)

Solution :

(a) Design of NAND gate

Let

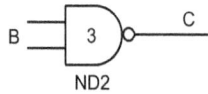

Fig. 5.28 (b)

    entity ND2 is

        port (A, B: in bit ;

            C: out bit) ;

        end ND2 ;

```
architecture ND2_ARCH of ND2 is
begin
   C <= A nand B;
end ND2_ARCH;
```

If we save the VHDL file, it will save with its entity name.

i.e. This file will save as ND2.VHDL. Now if this file is compiled, verified and placed either in design library or in working directory, then this VHDL code can be used as component in design of any other circuit.

(b) Design of given circuit (Structural Model)

```
entity COMPND2 is
    port ( IN1, IN2, IN3, IN4 : in bit;
    Z: out bit );
end COMPND2;
architecture COMPND2_ARCH of COMPND2 is
component ND2
    port   ( A, B : in bit;
    C: out bit );
    end component;
    signal TEMP1, TEMP2 : bit;
begin
I1: ND2 port map ( IN1, IN2, TEMP1 );              -- Positioned port mapping
I2: ND2 port map ( A => IN3, B => IN4, C => TEMP2 );    -- Named port mapping
I3: ND2 port map ( TEMP1, TAMP2, C=> Z );          -- Mixed port mapping
end COMPND2_ARCH;
```

ND2 design is declared as component in architecture before begin statement. Signals TEMP1 and TEMP2 are declared. Three component instantiation statements I1, I2, and I3 are written.

I1 instance creates one copy of ND2 design i.e. NAND gate1 with two inputs mapped IN1, IN2 and one output named TEMP1.

Similarly, I2 instance creates NAND gate2 with input named IN3, IN4 and an output TEMP2.

I3 instance creates NAND gate3 with input TEMP1 which gets connected to the output of NAND gate1 and TEMP2 connected to the output of NAND gate2 and output Z

5.10.4 Generate Statement

Q. Explain the generate statement in detail with example.	[6 M]
Q. Explain the forms of generate statement.	

Generate statement is used to select concurrent statements conditionally or to replicate concurrent statements. It is used to create multiple copies of components, processes, or blocks i.e. it provides a compact description.

Generate statement has two forms :

    (i) for...generate   (ii) if...generate

(i) for...generate

It creates multiple copies of components, processes, or block i.e. it executes concurrent statements number of times.

The syntax is :

    label: for identifier in range generate

        {concurrent statements}

    end generate [label] ;

Number of copies is determined by a discrete range. Range must be computable integer, in either of following forms :

integer_expression to integer_expression

integer_expression downto integer_expression

Each integer_expression evaluates to an integer

for_generate statement declares a new local integer variable with the name identifier. Identifier is assigned the first value of range, and each concurrent statement is executed once. Identifier is then assigned next value in range, and each concurrent statement is executed once more. This is repeated until identifier is assigned the last value in range. Each concurrent statement is then executed for the last time and execution continues with the statement following *end generate* statement. The loop identifier is then deleted.

(ii) if...generate

It made zero or one copy, conditionally.

The syntax is

    label : if expression generate

        {concurrent statement}

        end generate [label] ;

If expression is true, then concurrent statements are executed once, otherwise no execution of concurrent statements.

e.g.   CKO : if K=0 generate

    DFF : D_FLIP port map (COUNT, CLOCK, QCK) ;

    end generate CKO;

Example 5.16 :

Design 4 bit full adder with 1 bit full adder as a component using generate statement.

Solution :

Refer Example 6.7.

Where four copies of one bit full adder are created by instantiating component full adder four times. For this four instances, (FA0, FA1, FA2, FA3) are written.

Same can be done by writing one instance and using for-generate statement as follows :

```
entity ADDRGEN is
    port ( A, B : in  bit_ vector ( 3 downto 0 ) ;
            CIN : in  bit ;
             S : out  bit_vector (3  downto  0 ) ;
            COUNT : out bit) ;
end ADDRGEN ;


architecture ADDRGEN_ARCH of ADDRGEN is
    component  FULLADDR
        port ( A, B, CIN : in  bit  ;
                S, C : out  bit ) ;
    end component ;
    signal  TEMP :  bit_vector (4  downto  0 ) ;
begin
        TEMP(0) <= CIN ;
        GK: for K in 0 to 3 generate
            FA : FULLADDR  port map (A(K), B(K), TEMP(K), S(K), C(K+1) ) ;
        end generate GK ;
        COUT <= TEMP(4) ;
end ADDRGEN_ARCH ;
```

5.10.5 Process Statement

Q. Explain the process statement in detail. [6 M]

In VHDL, process statement contains only sequential statement.

Process is the primary concurrent VHDL statement used to describe sequential behavior (i.e. sequential statements). All the statements in the process, are executed sequentially, hence order of statements is important. All process in an architecture executes concurrently.

Signals to which some value is assigned within a process are not updated with their new values until the process suspends.

The syntax for process declaration is :
    process (sensitivity list)
            Declaration part
    begin
            Sequential statements
    end process;

In declaration part, types, variables, constants, subprograms can be declared. Statement part contains only sequential statement.

Process never stops, it repeats forever, unless suspended.
To suspend the process, either sensitivity list or wait statements are used.

- **Sensitivity list**

Sensitivity list is a list of signals to which process is sensitive. Sensitivity list defines the signals that cause the statements inside the process statement to execute whenever one or more elements of the list changes its value.

Process executes when any one of the signals in the sensitivity list changes. A process with a sensitivity clause must not contain an explicit wait statement. Process should either have a sensitivity list or wait statement at the end. Only static signal names are allowed in the sensitivity list.

Wait Statement

Wait statement is only used in the process statement. This statement provides an alternate way to suspend the execution of a process.

A process can be suspended by means of a sensitivity list, i.e. when a process has a sensitivity list it always suspends after executing the last sequential statement in the process. For example, given in listing. This process executes, when there is an event on a or c and suspends after executing the last statement.

e.g. process statement with sensitivity list.
    process (a, c)
    begin
        if a > c then
            y <= '1';
        else
            y <= '0';
        end if;
    end process;

The alternate way to suspend the process is by using a wait statement.
listing ----- process statement with wait statement.
    process
    begin

```
        if a > c then
            y <= '1';
        else
            y <= '0';
        end if;
        wait on a, c;
    end process;
```

The wait statement is placed at the end of a process. If wait statement was the last statement in the process, the process resumes execution from the first statement in the process.

There are basically **three types** of wait statements.

1. wait on sensitivity_list;
2. wait until Boolean_expression;
3. wait for time_expression;

We can also combine these statements into a single statement as,

wait on sensitivity_list until boolean_expression for time_expression;

Examples of wait statements are

1. **Wait until Clk = '1'**

It means that for the wait condition to be satisfied and execution of the code to continue, there must be an event on signal Clk, i.e. change in value and that value of Clk must be equal to '1' i.e. a rising edge for Clk.

2. **Wait on x, y, z**

In this the execution of wait statement causes the enclosing process to suspend and then wait for an event to occur on signals x, y or z. When there is an event on x, y or z, the process resumes execution from the next statement onwards after the wait statement. If the wait statement is the last statement in the process, the process resumes execution from the first statement.

3. **Wait for 12 ns**

This wait statement causes the enclosing process to suspend for 12 ns, and when the simulation time advances to T + 12 ns, the enclosing process resumes execution from the statement following the wait statement. We can also use the command as

    constant period : time := 12 ns;
    wait for 3 period;

4. **Wait on clock for 15 ns**

The execution of wait causes the enclosing process to suspend and then wait for an event to occur on clock for a time_out interval of 15 ns. If there is no event on clock within 15 ns, the process resumes execution with the statement following the wait.

5. Wait until answer > 80 for 10 ms

When wait statement executes, it suspends the process. The boolean condition (answer > 80) is evaluated every time there is an event on answer. If the answer > 80, (after the event on answer) then it will resume the execution of the next statement.

If there is no event on answer or if the boolean condition is false, then it will wait for maximum 10ns 10 ms and resumes the execution of the next statement.

6. Wait on clock until answer > 80

When this wait statement executes, it suspends the execution of process. It checks the boolean condition only after there is an event on clock, if the boolean condition is true, then only go to the next statement, otherwise continue to wait.

7. Wait for 0 ns

It means to wait for one delta time. This statement is useful when we want the process to be delayed so that delta-delayed signal assignments within a process can take effect. For example,

    process
    begin
        wait on a;
        y <= a;
        wait for 0 ns;
        z < = y;
    end process;

Process takes very less time to execute (less than delta delay). If signal a changes at 20 ns, y is scheduled to get the new value of a at 20 ns + 1 delta. The wait statement (wait for 0 ns) causes the process to suspend for one delta. Signal y gets updated with it's new value. Process resumes at 20 ns + 1Δ, z gets the new value of y at 20 ns + 2Δ.

If the "wait for 0 ns" statement was not present, then both the statements (y <= a and z <= y) get executed sequentially at time 20 ns and in that case, y gets the new value of a, but z gets the old value of y i.e. logic '0'.

It is an error if both a sensitivity list and a wait statement are present within a process.

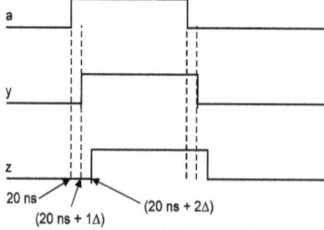

Fig. 5.29 : Effect of 'wait for 0 ns'

It is permissible to have several wait statements, inside the same process.

Example 5.17 :
```
process
begin
    --
    wait until clock = '0';
    --
    wait until clock = '0';
    --
    wait until clock = '0';
end process;
```
The wait is actually a sequential command. The wait command can not be used in functions, but wait can be used in procedures and processes.

5.11 SEQUENTIAL STATEMENTS

Q. Explain the following statements used in VHDL with suitable example.
   (i) Process (ii) case (iii) if then else (iv) signal assignment   **[May 13, 8 M]**
Q. What is the difference between concurrent and sequential statement of VHDL ?
   [May 10, Dec. 09, 12, 6 M]
Q. Compare if and case statement ?
Q. Explain the types of sequential statements.   **[6 M]**

Sequential statements are executed one after the another, in the order in which they are written. Sequential statements can appear only in process or subprograms. Only sequential statements can use variables.

5.11.1 If Statement

The syntax is :
```
if condition then
sequential statements end if ;
```
If condition is true then statements will execute.

if _else statement

The syntax is
```
if condition then
        statement1 ;
else
        statement2 ;
end if ;
```

If condition is true then statement 1 will execute, otherwise statements compact 2 will execute.

Nested if_else

The syntax is
```
   if  condition1 then
              statement1 ;
   elseif condition2 then
             statement2 ;
   else
             statements3 ;
   end if ;
```

If condition 1 is true then statement 1 will execute. Then it checks condition 2, if it is true, statements 2 will execute. Otherwise statement 3 will execute.

if statement evaluates each condition in order. It generates a priority structure. It is same as concurrent statement when_else.

Use of if statement is suitable or easy upto three or four levels (conditions).

e.g.
```
   process ( A,B,C,X )
   begin
   if ( X = "0000") then
           Z <= A ;
   elsif ( X <= "0101") then
           Z <= B ;
   else
       Z <= C ;
      end if ;
   end process ;
```

5.11.2 Case Statement

> Q. Explain the case statements in detail.

The syntax is :
```
   case expression is
       when choice1  => statement1 ;
       when choice2  => statement2 ;
       when choiceN  => statementN;
       when others   => statements;
   end case ;
```

e.g.
```
process ( A,B,C,X )
begin
    case X is
        when  0 to 4  => Z <= B;
        when  5       => Z <= C;
        when  6 to 9  => Z <= A;
        when  others  => Z <= '0';
    end case ;
end process ;
```
"case" statement selects for execution, one of the number of alternative sequence of statements. Statements following each "when" clause is executed, only if the choice value matches the expression value. Each choice can be either a static expression (such as 4) or a static range (such as 1 to 5).

Every possible value of the case expression must be covered in one and only one when clause i.e. no choices can overlap.

It corresponds to "with_select " in concurrent statement.

"case" statement produces parallel logic whereas "if " statement produces priority encoded logic.

Example 5.18 :

Design 8:1 multiplexer using case statement

Solution :

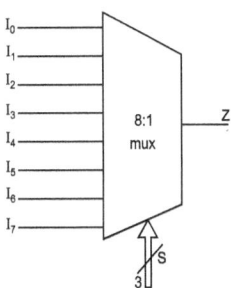

Fig. 5.30 : 8 : 1 Multiplexer

```
entity  MUX81 is
    port ( I0, I1, I2, I3, I4, I5, I6, I7 : : in bit ;
              S : in  bit_vector (2  downto 0);
           Z : out  bit );
end MUX81 ;
```

```
architecture MUX81_ARCH of MUX81 is
begin
    process ( I0, I1, I2, I3, I4, I5, I6, I7, S )
    begin
    case S is
        when "000"  =>  Z<= I0 ;
        when "001"  =>  Z<= I1 ;
        when "010"  =>  Z<= I2 ;
        when "011"  =>  Z<= I3 ;
        when "100"  =>  Z<= I4 ;
        when "101"  =>  Z<= I5 ;
        when "110"  =>  Z<= I6 ;
        when "111"  =>  Z<= I7 ;
        when others =>  Z<= '0';
    end case ;
    end process ;
end MUX81_ARCH ;
```

5.11.3 Null Statement

null statement does not perform any action. It can be used to indicate that when some condition is met, no action is to be performed.

e.g.
```
    case S is
        when "00"   => Z<= '1' ;
        when "01"   => Z<= '0' ;
        when others => Z<= null
    end case ;
```

5.11.4 Loop Statement

loop statement is used to execute sequence of sequential statements repetitively.

while loop statement

The syntax is :
```
    loop_label : while condition loop
        Sequence_of_statements
    end loop loop_label ;
```
Sequence of statement will execute till condition is true.

e.g.
```
    process (A)
    begin
```

```
L1 : while P <= 4 loop
    Z (I) <= A( I+4 );
        I = I +1;
    end loop L1;
end process;
```
It has a Boolean iteration scheme. Condition is evaluated before execution.

for loop statement

The syntax is :

```
loop_label: for loop_parameter in range loop
            sequence_of_statements
            end loop loop_label;
```

The loop is executed once for each value in the range. Range determines number of execution of loops. The range is tested at the beginning of loop execution.

The loop parameter is a constant, which may be used but not altered. Loop counter only exists within the loop.

e.g. FACTORIAL := 1;

```
L1: for NUMBER in 2 to10 loop
        FACTORIAL := FACTORIAL * NUMBER;
    end loop L1;
```

5.11.5 Next Statement

The syntax are :

(i) next;

(ii) next loop_label when condition;

"next" statement is used only inside a loop. "next" statement skips the remaining statement in the current iteration of the loop and execution starts from the first statement of the next iteration of the loop.

e.g.
```
    for X in 1 to 10 loop
        SUM := SUM +5;
        if (SUM =100) then
            next;
        else
            null;
        end if;
        Y := Y + 1;
    end loop;
```

The next statement also cause an inner loop to be existed.

    L1: for X in 10 downto 1 loop

        Statement group 1 ;

    L2 : loop

      Statement group 2 ;

      next loop L1 when flag = '1' ;

      Statement group 3 ;

      end loop L2 ;

    Statement group 4 ;

    end loop L1 ;

When flag = '1', statement group 3 and 4 are skipped and execution starts from the first statement of loop L1 and L2 was terminated.

5.11.6 Exit Statement

"exit" statement entirely terminates the execution of the loop in which it is located.

The syntax are :

(i) exit ;

(ii) exit loop_ label when condition ;

e.g. 1

    exit L1_LOOP when (I < 5) ;

This statement completes the execution of the loop labelled L1_LOOP when the expression (I < 5) is true.

The exit statement provides a quick and easy method of exiting a loop statement when all processing is finished or an error or warning condition occurs.

e.g. 2

    SUM :=1 ; J := 0 ;

    L3: loop

      J := J + 21 ;

      SUM := SUM * 10 ;

      If (SUM > 100) then

          exit L3 ;

        end if ;

    end loop L3 ;

Loop L3 will execute till condition SUM > 100 is false. When SUM > 100 becomes true, execution of loop L3 will completely terminate.

5.11.7 Report Statement

The syntax is :

report string-expression ;

   [severity expression] ;

"report" statement is used to print or display the specified string and the severity level to be reported to the simulator for appropriate action.

The severity is specified in the STANDARD package and contains following values.

        note,   warning,   error,   failure

Default value is note.

Normally, report statement is used with assertion statement.

Assert Statement :

It is basically used for Error Management in VHDL. With Assert statement, it is possible to test function and time constraints on a model inside a VHDL component.

If the condition for an **assert** is not met (false) during simulation of a VHDL code, a **message** of a certain **severity** is sent to the user (to the simulator).

Syntax :

   Assert <condition>

   Report <message>

   Severity <error_level>

If the condition is not met (condition is false), the report statement is executed and gives the message to the simulator. Also there are four different severity levels for the message (error_levels). These are

- Note is the Default severity level.
- Warning
- Error
- Failure

The message and severity level are displayed in the VHDL simulator's command window.

An Assert is both a sequential and a concurrent command.

We will see an example of a concurrent assertion statement used in SR flip-flop model. The code is written to ensure that the input signals R and S are never simultaneously zero. The VHDL code is given below. As shown, in the assert command, when both, S and R are '0', at that time, Assert command becomes false. As "not   (S='0' and R='0')", is false when both S and R are '0' simultaneously, then the message is given as "R and S are both low, not valid inputs".

   library ieee;

   use ieee.std_logic_1164.all;

```vhdl
entity SRFlip_Flop is
    for (S, R : in std_logic; Q, Qbar : out std_logic);
end SRFlip_Flop;
architecture SR_arch of SRFlip_Flop is
begin
    assert not (S = '0' and R = '0')
Report "S and R are both low, not valid input"
severity ERROR;
end SR_arch;
```

Similarly, the equivalent process statement for above example is given below :

```vhdl
process
begin
    assert not (S = '0' and R = '0')
    report "S and R are both low, not valid inputs";
    severity ERROR;
    wait on S, R;
end process.
```

Next, we will see a program, to check that the simulator time does not exceed, 1000 ns. The code is given below.

Now is a predefined function that returns the current simulation time.

```vhdl
process (clk)
begin
    assert now < 1000 ns
    report "simulator time exceeds 1000 ns"
    severity Failure;
end process;
```

Next, we will see a program of Rising edge triggered D-flip-flop. It uses assertion statement to check for setup and hold times.

```vhdl
library ieee;
use ieee.std_logic_1164.all;

entity D-Flipflop is
    port (D, clk : in Bit ; Q, Qbar : out Bit);
end D-Flipflop;
```

```vhdl
architecture DFF_arch of D-Flipflop is
constant Hold_Time : TIME := 4 ns;
constant Setup_Time : TIME := 3 ns;
begin
process (D, clk)
    variable LastEventonD, LastEventonclk : TIME;
begin
    -- check for hold time
    if D'Event then
            assert Now = 0 ns or (Now - LastEventonD) > = Hold_Time;
            report "Hold Time is too short";
            severity ERROR;
            LastEventonD : = Now;
    end if;
    -- check for setup time
    if clk = '1' and clk'Event then
            assert Now = 0 ns or (Now - Last EventonD) >= Setup_Time;
            report "Setup time is too short"
                severity Error;
            LastEventonclk := Now;
    end if;
                    -- Behavior of FF
    if clk = '1' and clk event then
                Q <= D;
                Qbar <= not D;
            end if;
        end process;
    end DFF_arch;
```

The hold time is the minimum time the data must remain stable **after** the clock changes.

The setup time is the minimum time the data input must be stable **before** the clock changes as shown in Fig. 5.31.

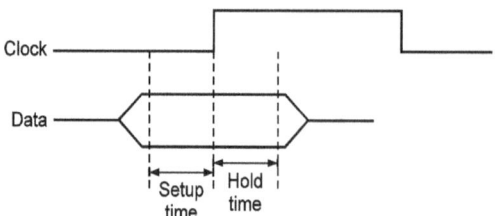

Fig. 5.31 (a) : Set up and Hold time

As already discussed, Now is a function which returns the current simulation time. All processes are executed until they suspend during the initialisation phase. To prevent misleading message appearing during initialisation phase of simulation, the expression "Now = 0 ns" is used in the assertion statement. In the DFF example, as shown already when there is an event on signal D or clk, the process executes. The first if statement is executed when there is an event on D. The assertion statement

    (Now = LastEventonclk) >= Hold_time

checks for the Hold_time. The difference between the current simulation time and the last time an event occurred on signal clk is greater than a constant Hold_time. If this statement is false, it means the Hold_time is short and it prints the message.

Similarly, the setup time is checked. The last if statement describes the latch behavior of the D type flip-flop.

We will see one more example to check spikes at the input of a buffer.

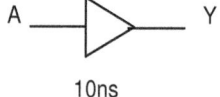

Fig. 5.31 (b)

The buffer has 10 ns propagation delay. If the spike has width of 5 ns or less, then print the message as "spike is detected".

    library ieee;
    use ieee.std_logic_1164.all;
    package PACK is --- package to store propagation delay and min-pulse
        constant min_pulse : TIME := 5 ns;
        constant propagation_delay : TIME : = 10 ns;
    end PACK;
    library ieee;
    use ieee.std_logic_1164.all;
    use work.PACK.all;
    entity buffer is

```
port (A : in bit;
        Y : out bit);
end buffer;
architecture buffer_arch of buffer is
begin
    process (A)
        variable LastEventonA : TIME := 0 ns;
    begin
        assert Now = 0 ns or (Now–LastEventonA) >= min_pulse;
        report "spike detected on input of buffer";
        severity WARNING;
        LastEventonA := Now;
        Y <= A after propagation_delay;
    end process;
end buffer_arch;
```

5.12 STYLES OF MODELING

Q. Explain the types of sequential statements.	[6 M]
Q. Write short note on architecture with modeling styles.	[Dec. 11, 4 M]
Q. Describe different modeling styles of VHDL with suitable examples.	[May 10, 12, 8 M]

The styles or ways in which functionality of design is described are called styles of modeling. Three modeling styles are

- Data flow
- Behavior
- Structural

5.12.1 Data Flow Modeling

Q. Explain the concept of data flow modeling.	[May 10, 12, 8 M]

In this modeling, the flow of data through the entity is expressed using concurrent signal assignment statements, i.e. it has a set of concurrent assignment statements. Each statement is executed when any of its input signal changes its value. This modeling needs Boolean equations as design specification.

e.g.   Design of AND gate
        entity AND1D is
            port (A, B : in bit ;

```
            C : out bit );
    end AND1D;
    architecture AND1D_ARCH of AND1D is
    begin
            C <= A and B;
    end AND1D_ARCH;
```

Example 5.19 :

Write down VHDL code for the given AND_OR network using structural modeling.

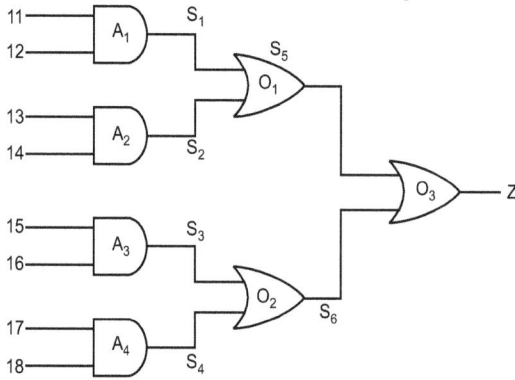

Fig. 5.32

Solution :

Assume AND1 and OR1 entity_architecture pair are precompiled, verified and are available in working directory.

```
    entity STRUCT is
        port ( I1, I2, I3, I4, I5, I6, I7, I8 : in bit ;
                Z : out bit );
    end STRUCT ;
    architecture STRUCT_ARCH of STRUCT is
            component AND1
            port ( A, B : in bit ;
                    C : out bit );
        end component ;
            component OR1
            port ( P, Q : in bit ;
                    R : out bit );
    end component ;
        signal S1, S2, S3, S4, S5, S6 : bit ;
```

```
begin
    A1  :  AND1  port map ( I1, I2, S1 );
    A2  :  AND1  port map ( I3, I4, S2 );
    A3  :  AND1  port map ( I5, I6, S3 );
    A4  :  AND1  port map ( I7, I8, S4 );
    O1  :  OR1   port map ( S1, S2, S5 );
    O2  :  OR1   port map ( S3, S4, S6 );
    O3  :  OR1   port map ( S5, S6, Z );
end STRUCT_ARCH ;
```

5.13 PACKAGE AND LIBRARY

5.13.1 Package

Package is a collection of commonly used subprograms, data types, constants etc. A package is common storage area. Packages are used to hold the data to be shared among a number of entities. The data declared inside a package can be referenced by other entities.

A package consists of two parts :

(i) Package declaration   (ii) Package body

(i) Package declaration

It defines the interface for the package (similar to entity).

The package declaration section can contain the following declarations.

- Subprogram declaration
- Type subtype declaration
- Constant, deferred constant declaration
- Signal declaration creates a global signal
- File declaration
- Alias declaration
- Component, attribute declaration
- Use clause.

All the items declared in the package declaration section are visible to any design unit that uses the package with a use clause.

The constants whose name and types are declared in the package declaration section, but actual values specified in the package body section are called as deferred constant.

The syntax for package declaration is

    package package_name is
            declarations ;
    end [package] package_name ;

e.g.   package P1 is
        constant RISE, FALL : time ;
        end P1;

RISE and FALL are deferred constants.

(ii) Package body

Package body is used to define the values for deferred constants, to specify the subprograms bodies for subprogram declared in package declaration.

Package body also contains

- Subprogram declaration
- Subprogram body
- Type, subtype declaration
- Constant, file, alias declaration
- Use clause.

It specifies the actual behavior of the package (similar to architecture).

A package declaration can have only one package body, both having the same name.(contrast to entity_architecture).

Writing of package body is optioned.

It contains the hidden details of a package (i.e. package body is not visible).

The syntax for package body is

    package body Package_name is
        Declarations ;
      subprograms body ;
    end Package_name ;

e.g. package body P1 is
        RISE := 5 ns ;
        FALL :=10 ns ;
    end P1;

Packages are stored in libraries for convenience purposes. User-created packages by default stored in work library.

"use" statement is used to access a package from a library and "library" keyword is used to access particular library.

The syntax is

    library Library_name;

    use Library_name. package_name. particular_name;

    e.g.

    library BLIB ;   -- allows your design to access library BLIB

    use BLIB.P1.all ;   -- allows your design to use entire P1 package from library BLIB.

    use BLIB.P1.NAND2; -- allows your design to use only component NAND2 from package P1 which is kept in library BLIB.

5.13.2 Design Libraries

A design library is an area of storage in the file system of the host environment. The management of the design libraries is not defined by the language and is tool - implementation - specific.

Generally, there are three types of libraries in VHDL :

1. Library IEEE
2. Library WORK
3. Library STD

When a VHDL component is compiled, it is saved in the work library as default. The work library is not the name of a directory on the PC, on which the compilation is being done, but a logical name.

VHDL tools usually define the work library automatically when the tool is started up. This means that different work libraries will be obtained depending on where the VHDL compiler is started. All compiled components are stored in a library. Packages too are usually stored in a library. The VHDL standard is defined in such a way that the Work and STD libraries are always visible. These two libraries do not, have to be specified in the VHDL code. The following invisible lines are always included in every VHDL code.

Library work;

Library std;

use std.standard.all;

The std library has the package named standard. In standard package itself, data types such as bit, bit_vector, character, time and integer are defined.

STD library has two packages predefined, these are standard and TextIO.

Package standard is a predefined package that contains the definitions for the predefined types and functions of the language. This package contains the following types – Boolean, Bit, character, severity_level, integer, real, time, string, file_open_kind and file_open_status.

Standard package also contains the following subtypes such as : Delay_length (from type time), natural (from type Integer), positive (from type Integer). Standard package also contains the function Now.

Package TEXTIO

It contains declarations of types and subprograms that support formatted I/o operations on text files.

TEXTIO package contains types such as LINE, TEXT, SIDE, WIDTH. It has standard text files such as Input and output. It has input procedures such as Readline and Read, and output procedure write.

Library IEEE

It contains the package STD_Logic_1164, which defines a nine value logic type and its associated overloaded functions and other utilities.

Package STD_LOGIC_1164 :

This package shall be compiled into a design library. It contains the following :

type STD_ULOGIC is ('U' – Uninitialized

        'X' – Forcing unknown

        '0' – Forcing '0'

        '1' – Forcing '1'

            'Z' – High impedance

            'W' – Weak unknown

            'L' – Weak 0

            'H' – Weak 1

            '–' – don't care

            );

It also contains STD_ULOGIC_VECTOR as type,

function RESOLVED, subtype STD_LOGIC.

subtype STD_LOGIC is Resolved STD_ULOGIC,

    -- STD_LOGIC is Resolved from STD_ULOGIC

type STD_LOGIC_VECTOR is array (Natural range < >)

    of STD_LOGIC;

This package also contains subtypes such as, X01, X01Z, UX01, UX01Z etc.

There are also functions available. These functions are and, nand, or, nor, xor, xnor, not.

The conversion functions are To_BIT, To_BITVECTOR, To_STDULOGIC, To_STDLOGICVECTOR, To_STDULOGICVECTOR.

Edge detection functions such as RISING_EDGE, FALLING_EDGE etc.

Library Clause :

The library clause makes visible the logical names of design libraries. The format is library TTL, CMOS;

Above statement makes the logical names TTL and CMOS visible in the design unit.

The library clause

    library STD, work;

is implicitly declared for every design unit.

Use Clause :

Two forms of use clause

        use library_name . primary_unit_name;

        use library_name . primary_unit_name.item;

If all items within a primary unit are to be made visible, the keyword all can be used. For example,

        use IEEE.STD_LOGIC_1164.all;

If we need to use TEXTIO package, then it must be declared in the VHDL code,

        use STD.TEXTIO.all;

5.14   VHDL CODES

5.14.1 Mux Code

1. Mux using with statement

```vhdl
library ieee;
    use ieee.std_logic_1164.all;
entity mux_using_with is
    port (
        din_0  :in  std_logic;-- Mux first input
        din_1  :in  std_logic;-- Mux Second input
        sel    :in  std_logic;-- Select input
        mux_out :out std_logic -- Mux output
    );
    end entity;
architecture behavior of mux_using_with is
begin
    with (sel) select
    mux_out din_0 when '0',
            din_1 when others;
end architecture;
```

2. Mux : using when statement

```
entity mux_using_when is
    port (
        din_0  :in  std_logic;-- Mux first input
        din_1  :in  std_logic;-- Mux Second input
        sel    :in  std_logic;-- Select input
        mux_out :out std_logic -- Mux output
        );
end entity;
architecture behavior of mux_using_when is
begin
mux_out <= din_0 when    (sel = '0') else
          din_1
end architecture;
```

3. Mux : using if statement

```
library ieee;
    use ieee.std_logic_1164.all;
entity mux_using_if is
    port (
        din_0  :in  std_logic;-- Mux first input
        din_1  :in  std_logic;-- Mux Second input
        sel    :in  std_logic;-- Select input
        mux_out :out std_logic -- Mux output
        );
end entity;
architecture behavior of mux_using_if is
begin
    MUX:
    process (sel, din_0, din_1) begin
        if (sel = '0') then
            mux_out <= din_0;
        else
            mux_out <= din_1;
        end if;
end process;
end architecture;
```

4. Mux : Using case statement

```vhdl
library ieee;
use ieee.std_logic_1164.all;
entity mux_using_case is
    port (
        din_0  :in  std_logic;-- Mux first input
        din_1  :in  std_logic;-- Mux Second input
        sel    :in  std_logic;-- Select input
        mux_out :out std_logic -- Mux output
    );
end entity;
architecture behavior of mux_using_case is
begin
    MUX:
    process (sel, din_0, din_1) begin
        case sel is
            when '0'    => mux_out <= din_0;
            when others => mux_out <= din_1;
        end case;
    end process;
end architecture;
```

5.14.2 Binary Adder VHDL Code

1. Program for 4-bit binary adder

```vhdl
library IEEE;
use IEEE.STD_LOGIC_1164.all;
entity adder_4bit is
    port(
    a : in STD_LOGIC_VECTOR(3 downto 0);
    b : in STD_LOGIC_VECTOR(3 downto 0);
    carry : out STD_LOGIC;
    sum : out STD_LOGIC_VECTOR(3 downto 0)
    );
end adder_4bit;
architecture adder_4bit_arc of adder_4bit is
```

```vhdl
Component fa is
   port (a : in STD_LOGIC;
      b : in STD_LOGIC;
      c : in STD_LOGIC;
      sum : out STD_LOGIC;
      carry : out STD_LOGIC
      );
end component;
signal s : std_logic_vector (2 downto 0);
begin
   u0 : fa port map (a(0),b(0),'0',sum(0),s(0))
   u1 : fa port map (a(1),b(1),s(0),sum(1),s(1));
   u2 : fa port map (a(2),b(2),s(1),sum(2),s(2));
   ue : fa port map (a(3),b(3),s(2),sum(3),carry);
end adder_4bit_arc;
```

2. Program for N bit binary adder

```vhdl
entity BitAdder2 is
generic (N: natural :=2);
   Port ( X : in std_logic_vector(N-1 downto 0);
      Y : in std_logic_vector(N-1 downto 0);
      SUM : out std_logic_vector(N-1 downto 0);
      CARRY : out std_logic);
end BitAdder2;
architecture Behavioral of BitAdder2 is
signal result: std_logic_vector(N downto 0);
begin
      result <= ('0' & X)+('0' & Y);
      SUM <= result(N-1 downto 0);
      CARRY <= result(N);
end Behavioral
```

5.14.3 Counter VHDL Code

1. 4-bit unsigned up counter with Asynchronous clear

```vhdl
library ieee;
   use ieee.std_logic_1164.all;
   use ieee.std_logic_unsigned.all;
```

```vhdl
entity counter is
    port(C, CLR : in  std_logic;
        Q : out std_logic_vector(3 downto 0));
end counter;
architecture archi of counter is
    signal tmp: std_logic_vector(3 downto 0);
    begin
        process (C, CLR)
            begin
            if (CLR='1') then
                tmp <= "0000";
            elsif (C'event and C='1') then
                tmp <= tmp + 1;
            end if;
        end process;
        Q <= tmp;
end archi;
```

2. 4-bit unsigned down counter with synchronous set

```vhdl
library ieee;
use ieee.std_logic_1164.all;
use ieee.std_logic_unsigned.all;

entity counter is
    port(C, S : in  std_logic;
        Q : out std_logic_vector(3 downto 0));
end counter;
architecture archi of counter is
  signal tmp: std_logic_vector(3 downto 0);
  begin
    process (C)
      begin
      if (C'event and C='1') then
          if (S='1') then
          tmp <= "1111";
          else
```

```vhdl
          tmp <= tmp - 1;
        end if;
      end if;
    end process;
    Q <= tmp;
end archi;
```

3. 4-bit unsigned up counter with asynchronous load from primary input

```vhdl
library ieee;
use ieee.std_logic_1164.all;
use ieee.std_logic_unsigned.all;

entity counter is
  port(C, ALOAD : in  std_logic;
       D : in std_logic_vector(3 downto 0);
       Q : out std_logic_vector(3 downto 0));
end counter;
architecture archi of counter is
  signal tmp: std_logic_vector(3 downto 0);
  begin
    process (C, ALOAD, D)
      begin
        if (ALOAD='1') then
          tmp <= D;
        elsif (C'event and C='1') then
          tmp <= tmp + 1;
        end if;

    end process;
    Q <= tmp;
end archi;
```

4. 4-bit unsigned up counter with synchronous load with a constant

```vhdl
library ieee;
use ieee.std_logic_1164.all;
use ieee.std_logic_unsigned.all;
entity counter is
```

```vhdl
    port(C, SLOAD : in  std_logic;
         Q : out std_logic_vector(3 downto 0));
end counter;
architecture archi of counter is
  signal tmp: std_logic_vector(3 downto 0);
  begin
    process (C)
      begin
        if (C'event and C='1') then
          if (SLOAD='1') then
            tmp <= "1010";
          else
            tmp <= tmp + 1;
          end if;
        end if;
      end process;
    Q <= tmp;
end archi;
```

5. 4-bit unsigned up counter with asynchronous clear and clock enable

```vhdl
library ieee;
use ieee.std_logic_1164.all;
use ieee.std_logic_unsigned.all;

entity counter is
  port(C, CLR, CE : in std_logic;
       Q : out std_logic_vector(3 downto 0));
end counter;
architecture archi of counter is
  signal tmp: std_logic_vector(3 downto 0);
  begin
    process (C, CLR)
      begin
        if (CLR='1') then
          tmp <= "0000";
        elsif (C'event and C='1') then
```

```vhdl
      if (CE='1') then
        tmp <= tmp + 1;
      end if;
    end if;
  end process;
  Q <= tmp;
end archi;
```

6. 4-bit unsigned up/down counter with asynchronous clear

```vhdl
library ieee;
use ieee.std_logic_1164.all;
use ieee.std_logic_unsigned.all;
entity counter is
  port(C, CLR, UP_DOWN : in std_logic;
       Q : out std_logic_vector(3 downto 0));
end counter;
architecture archi of counter is
  signal tmp: std_logic_vector(3 downto 0);
  begin
    process (C, CLR)
      begin
        if (CLR='1') then
          tmp <= "0000";
        elsif (C'event and C='1') then
          if (UP_DOWN='1') then
            tmp <= tmp + 1;
          else
            tmp <= tmp - 1;
          end if;
        end if;
    end process;
    Q <= tmp;
end archi;
```

7. 4-bit signed up counter with asynchronous reset

```vhdl
library ieee;
use ieee.std_logic_1164.all;
use ieee.std_logic_signed.all;
```

```vhdl
entity counter is
  port(C, CLR : in  std_logic;
       Q : out std_logic_vector(3 downto 0));
end counter;
architecture archi of counter is
  signal tmp: std_logic_vector(3 downto 0);
  begin
    process (C, CLR)
      begin
        if (CLR='1') then
          tmp <= "0000";
        elsif (C'event and C='1')  then
          tmp <= tmp + 1;
        end if;
    end process;
    Q <= tmp;
end archi;
```

5.14.4 Shift Register VHDL Code

1. Design of 4 Bit serial in - Serial out shift register using behavior modeling style.

```vhdl
library ieee;
use ieee.STD_LOGIC_1164.all;
entity siso_behavior is
    port(
        din : in STD_LOGIC;
        clk : in STD_LOGIC;
        reset : in STD_LOGIC;
        dout : out STD_LOGIC
        );
end siso_behavior;
architecture siso_behavior_arc of siso_behavior is
begin
    siso : process (clk,din,reset) is
    variable s : std_logic_vector(3 downto 0) := "0000" ;
    begin
      if (reset='1') then
        s := "0000";
```

```vhdl
        elsif (rising_edge (clk)) then
            s := (din & s(3 downto 1));
        dout <= s(0);
        end if;
    end process siso;
end siso_behavior_arc;
```

2. 8-bit shift-left register with positive-edge clock, serial in, and serial out

```vhdl
library ieee;
use ieee.std_logic_1164.all;
entity shift is
  port(C, SI : in  std_logic;
       SO : out std_logic);
end shift;
architecture archi of shift is
  signal tmp: std_logic_vector(7 downto 0);
  begin
    process (C)
      begin
        if (C'event and C='1') then
          for i in 0 to 6 loop
            tmp(i+1) <= tmp(i);
          end loop;
          tmp(0) <= SI;
        end if;
    end process;
    SO <= tmp(7);
end archi;
```

3. 8-bit shift-left register with negative-edge clock, clock enable, serial in, and serial out

```vhdl
library ieee;
use ieee.std_logic_1164.all;
entity shift is
  port(C, SI, CE : in  std_logic;
       SO : out std_logic);
end shift;
architecture archi of shift is
  signal tmp: std_logic_vector(7 downto 0);
  begin
```

```vhdl
  process (C)
    begin
      if (C'event and C='0') then
        if (CE='1') then
          for i in 0 to 6 loop
            tmp(i+1) <= tmp(i);
          end loop;
            tmp(0) <= SI;
        end if;
      end if;
    end process;
    SO <= tmp(7);
end archi;
```

4. 8-bit shift-left register with positive-edge clock, asynchronous clear, serial in, and serial out

```vhdl
library ieee;
use ieee.std_logic_1164.all;
entity shift is
  port(C, SI, CLR : in std_logic;
       SO : out std_logic);
end shift;
architecture archi of shift is
  signal tmp: std_logic_vector(7 downto 0);
  begin
    process (C, CLR)
      begin
        if (CLR='1') then
          tmp <= (others => '0');
        elsif (C'event and C='1') then
          tmp <= tmp(6 downto 0) & SI;
        end if;
    end process;
    SO <= tmp(7);
end archi;
```

5. 8-bit shift-left register with positive-edge clock, synchronous set, serial in, and serial out

```vhdl
library ieee;
use ieee.std_logic_1164.all;
```

```vhdl
entity shift is
  port(C, SI, S : in  std_logic;
       SO : out std_logic);
end shift;
architecture archi of shift is
  signal tmp: std_logic_vector(7 downto 0);
  begin
    process (C, S)
      begin
        if (C'event and C='1') then
          if (S='1') then
            tmp <= (others => '1');
          else
            tmp <= tmp(6 downto 0) & SI;
          end if;
        end if;
      end process;
    SO <= tmp(7);
end archi;
```

6. 8-bit shift-left register with positive-edge clock, serial in, and parallel out

```vhdl
library ieee;
use ieee.std_logic_1164.all;
entity shift is
  port(C, SI : in  std_logic;
       PO : out std_logic_vector(7 downto 0));
end shift;
architecture archi of shift is
  signal tmp: std_logic_vector(7 downto 0);
  begin
    process (C)
      begin
        if (C'event and C='1') then
          tmp <= tmp(6 downto 0)& SI;
        end if;
      end process;
    PO <= tmp;
end archi;
```

7. 8-bit shift-left register with positive-edge clock, asynchronous parallel load, serial in, and serial out

```
library ieee;
use ieee.std_logic_1164.all;
entity shift is
  port(C, SI, ALOAD : in std_logic;
       D : in std_logic_vector(7 downto 0);
       SO : out std_logic);
end shift;
architecture archi of shift is
  signal tmp: std_logic_vector(7 downto 0);
  begin
    process (C, ALOAD, D)
      begin
        if (ALOAD='1') then
          tmp <= D;
        elsif (C'event and C='1') then
          tmp <= tmp(6 downto 0) & SI;
        end if;
      end process;
    SO <= tmp(7);
end archi;
```

8. 8-bit shift-left register with positive-edge clock, synchronous parallel load, serial in, and serial out

```
library ieee;
use ieee.std_logic_1164.all;
entity shift is
  port(C, SI, SLOAD : in std_logic;
       D : in std_logic_vector(7 downto 0);
       SO : out std_logic);
end shift;
architecture archi of shift is
  signal tmp: std_logic_vector(7 downto 0);
  begin
    process (C)
      begin
        if (C'event and C='1') then
          if (SLOAD='1') then
```

```
        tmp <= D;
      else
        tmp <= tmp(6 downto 0) & SI;
      end if;
    end if;
  end process;
  SO <= tmp(7);
end archi;
```

9. 8-bit shift-left/shift-right register with positive-edge clock, serial in, and parallel out

```
library ieee;
use ieee.std_logic_1164.all;

entity shift is
port(C, SI, LEFT_RIGHT : in std_logic;
    PO : out std_logic_vector(7 downto 0));
end shift;
architecture archi of shift is
  signal tmp: std_logic_vector(7 downto 0);
  begin
    process (C)
      begin
        if (C'event and C='1') then
          if (LEFT_RIGHT='0') then
            tmp <= tmp(6 downto 0) & SI;
          else
            tmp <= SI & tmp(7 downto 1);
          end if;
        end if;
    end process;
    PO <= tmp;
end archi;
```

Unit - VI

PROGRAMMABLE LOGIC DEVICES

6.1 PLD OVERVIEW

- Programmable Logic Devices (PLD) are standard ICs that are available in standard configurations. PLDs are configured (programmed) to create a part customized to a specific application, and so they also belong to family of ASICs. PLDs use different technologies to allow programming of the device. PLDs are available as erasable or mask-programmed.

The features of PLDs are

- No customized mask layers or logic cells
- Fast design turnaround time.
- A signal large block of programmable interconnect.

Types of PLDs

- Simple Programmable Logic Devices (SPLDs)
- Complex Programmable Logic Devices (CPLDs)
- Field Programmable Gate Arrays (FPGAs)

Simple Programmable Logic Devices

SPLDs are also known as :

- PAL (Programmable Array Logic)
- GAL (Generic Array Logic)
- PLA (Programmable Logic Array)
- PLD (Programmable Logic Device)
- SPLDs are the smallest and consequently the least expensive form of programmable logic. An SPLD is typically comprised of 4 to 22 macro cells and can typically replace a few 7400 series TTL devices.

6.1.1 SPLD (Simple PLD)

> **Q.** State the limitations of SPLD.

- A SPLD-architecture based device consists of two or more vendor-specific macrocells to realize the logic functions.

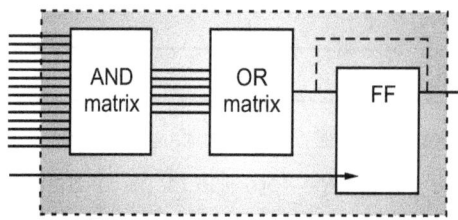

Fig. 6.1 : Simplified SPLD macrocell

Significant characteristics for the SPLD-architecture :

- one macrocell per output
- minimum two macrocells per device
- typically all macrocells identical
- one product term per macrocell
- product term typically generated by a AND-matrix and OR-matrix
- minimum one matrix (AND/OR) programmable
- dedicated flip-flop (FF) per macrocell

Main-advantages :

- predictable timing
- easy to develop

Main-disadvantages :

- inefficient resource utilization
- only for simple logic functions

6.1.2 GAL (Generic Array Logic)

- GAL offered CMOS electrically erasable PROM (EPROM, E2PROM) variations on the PAL concept. GAL architecture has reprogrammable AND array, a fixed OR array and reprogrammable output logic.

- GAL is similar to PAL with output logic macrocells (OLMCs), which provide more flexibility. Output logic macrocell can be configured either for a combinational output of for a registered output. GAL can be erased and reprogrammed and usually replace a whole set of different PALs.

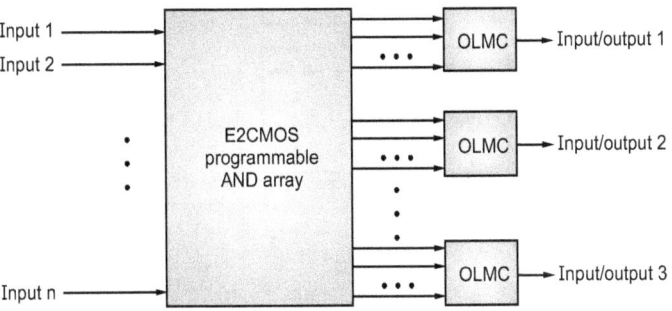

Fig. 6.2

- The reprogrammable array is essentially a grid of conductors forming rows and columns with an electrically erasable CMOS (E2CMOS) cell at each cross-point, rather than a fuse as in a PAL. Each column is connected to the input of an AND gate, and each row is connected to an input variable or its complement.
- Any combination of input variables or complements can be applied to an AND gate to form any desired product term by programming each E2CMOS cell These configurations correspond to the various types of I/O configurations found in the PAL devices that the GAL is designed to replace.

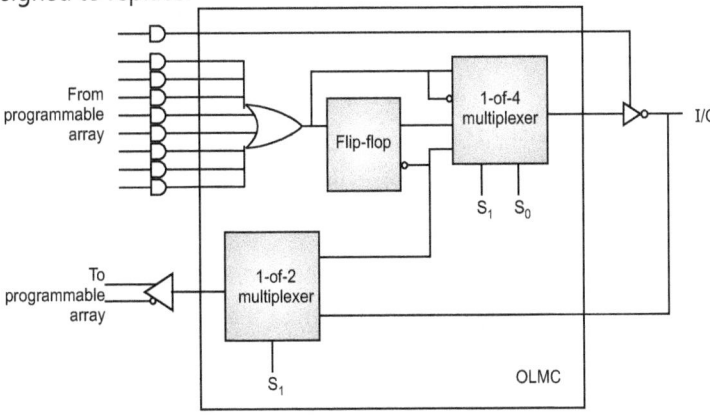

Fig. 6.3

6.1.3 Read only Memory (ROM) as a PLD

- A ROM can store an array of binary data. Data stored in the ROM can be read out whenever required, but cannot be changed under normal operating condition. Fig. 6.4 shows a ROM that has n input lines and m output lines. It contains an array of 2^n words and each word is m bits long. The input line serves as an address to select one of the 2^n words.
- ROM consists of a decoder and a memory array. When binary input is applied to the decoder inputs, only one of the 2^n decoder outputs is 1, which selects one of the words in the memory array, and the binary data stored in this word is transferred to the memory output lines. A $2^n \times m$ ROM can realize m function of n variables. ROM can store a truth table with 2^n rows and m columns.

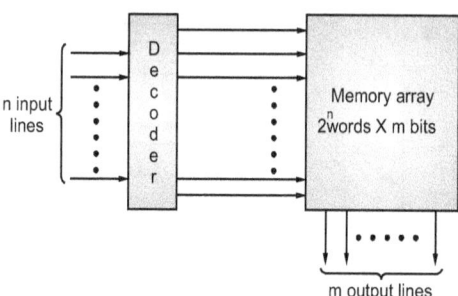

Fig. 6.4 : Basic ROM structure

- Mask-programmable ROMs and erasable programmable ROMs (called EPROMs) are the basic types of ROM.

- Data is permanently stored in a mask-programmable ROM at the time of manufacture. Use of Mask-programmable ROMs is economical only if large quantities are required with the same data entry. If only a small quantity of ROMs are required with a given data array, EPROMs may be used.

- During the development phase, it is needed to modify the data stored in a ROM, so EPROMs are used instead of mask-programmable ROM. By using PROM programmer, data stored in EPROM can be changed. Data is erased using an ultraviolet light. The electrically erasable PROM (EEPROM) is a more recent development. EEPROM is similar to EPROM, except that, stored data is erased using electrical pulses instead of ultraviolet light.

- Flash memories have built-in programming and erase capability so that data can be written to a flash memory placed in a circuit without the need of separate programmer.

6.1.3.1 ROM organization

- A 16 bit ROM array is shown in Fig. 6.5. To select any one of the 16 bits, a 4 bit address (A_3 A_2 A_1 A_0) is required. The lower order two bits (A_1 A_0) are decoded by the decoder D_L which selects one of the four rows whereas the higher order two bits (A_3 A_2) are decoded by the decoder D_H which activates one of the four column sense amplifiers.

- The output is enabled by applying logic 1 at the chip select (CS) input. Programming a ROM means to selectively open and close the switches in series with the diodes.

- For example, if the switch of diode D_{21} is in closed position and if the address input is 0110, row 2 is activated connecting it to column 1. Also the sense amplifier of column 1 is enabled which gives logic 1 output if the chip is selected (CS = 1). This shows that a logic 1 is stored at the address 0110. If the switch of the diode D_{21} is open, logic 0 is stored at the address 0110.

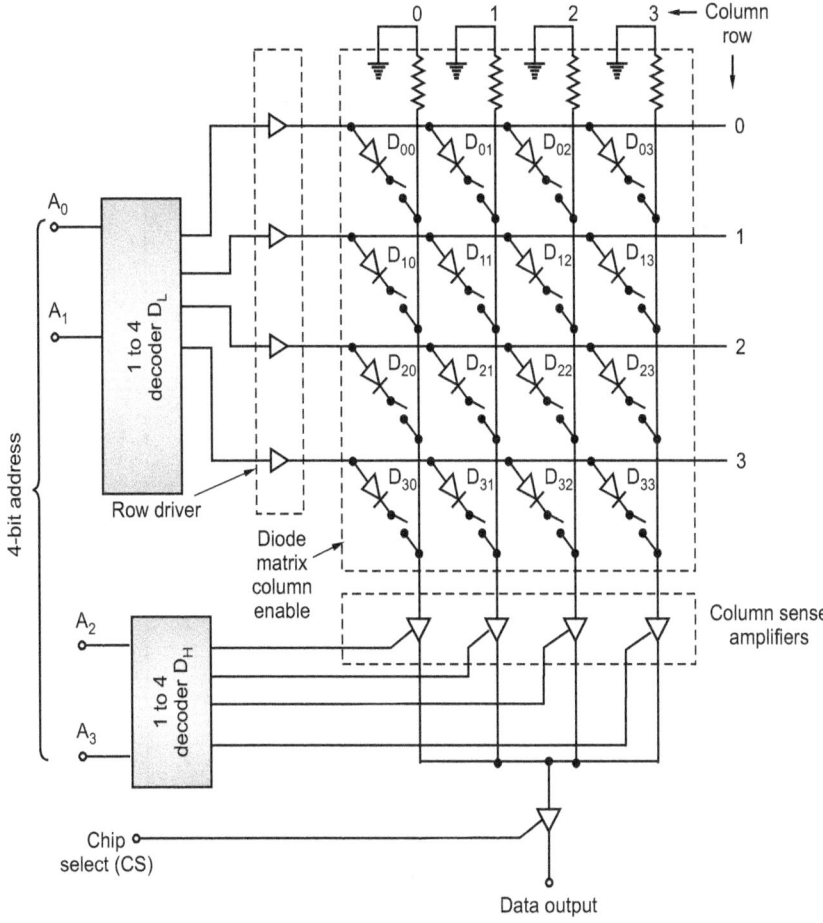

Fig. 6.5 : 16 bit ROM array

A ROM consists of an array of bipolar junction transistor or field effect transistors are also available.

6.1.3.2 Circuit realization using ROM

Example 6.1 :

Using ROM, implement the circuit represented by the following conditions.

$$Y_1 = \overline{x4}$$

$$Y_2 = x1\,x3 + \overline{x2}\,x4$$

$$Y_3 = \overline{x1}\,x2 + x2\,\overline{x3}$$

$$Y_4 = x1\,x2\,x3\,x4$$

Solution :

First make the ROM program table that represents the conditions given by the equations.

x1	x2	x3	x4	Y1	Y2	Y3	Y4
0	0	0	0	1	0	0	0
0	0	0	1	0	1	0	0
0	0	1	0	1	0	0	0
0	0	1	1	0	1	1	0
0	1	0	0	1	0	1	0
0	1	0	1	0	0	1	0
0	1	1	0	1	0	1	0
0	1	1	1	0	0	1	0
1	0	0	0	1	0	0	0
1	0	0	1	0	1	0	0
1	0	1	0	1	1	0	0
1	0	1	1	0	1	0	0
1	1	0	0	1	0	1	0
1	1	0	1	0	0	1	0
1	1	1	0	1	1	0	0
1	1	1	1	0	1	0	1

The ROM implementation is shown in Fig. 6.6.

In Fig. 6.6, BL is the bit line and WL is the world line. No physical contact is there between WL and BL line. When BL line is grounded irrespective of the value on WL line, a, 0 is stored. When high voltage is applied on WL line, the diode is forward biased and 1 is considered to be stored. Thus if a diode is present, 1 is considered to be stored and if there is no diode, 0 is stored.

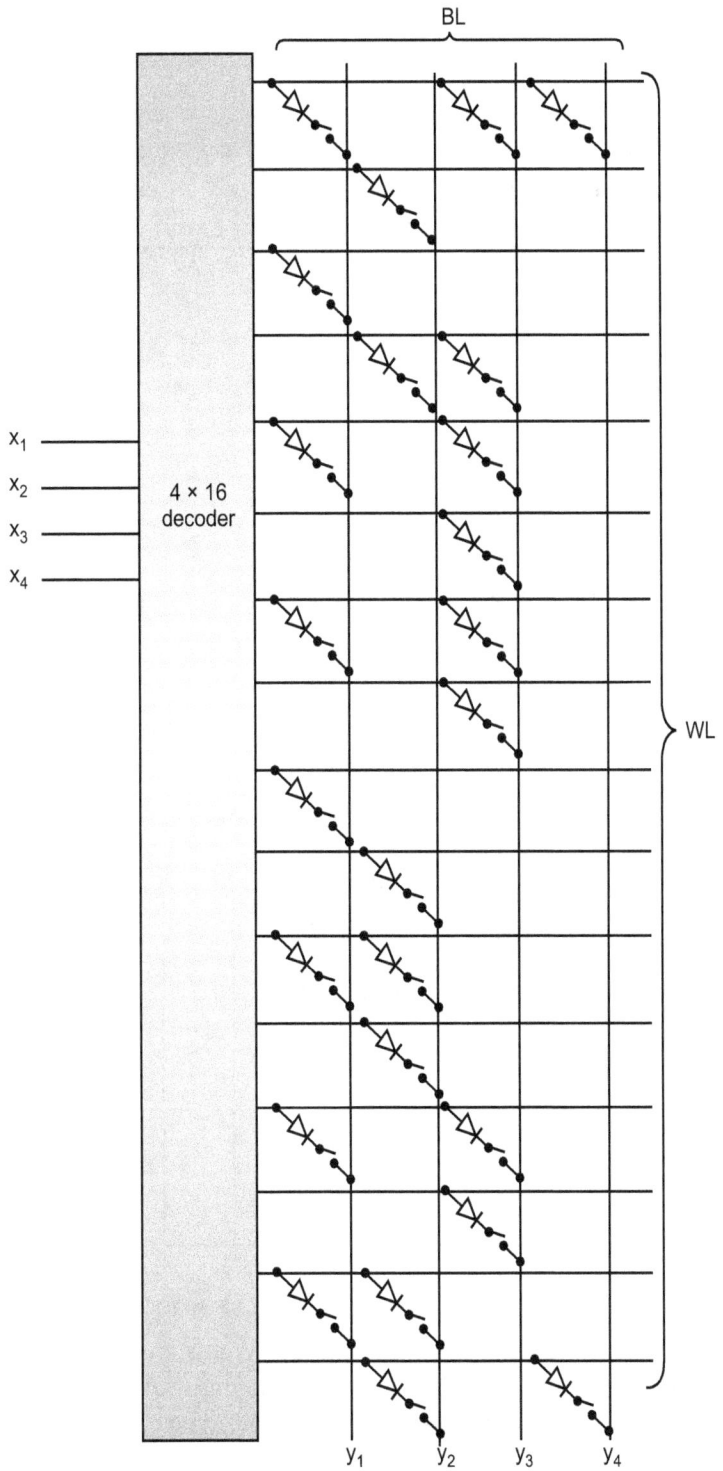

Fig. 6.6 : ROM implementation

Example 6.2 :
Implement the full adder circuit in ROM.
Solution :
Make the ROM program table that represents the Boolean equations for sum and carry outputs from the full adder.

A	B	Cin	Sum	Carry
0	0	0	0	0
0	0	1	1	0
0	1	0	1	0
0	1	1	0	1
1	0	0	1	0
1	0	1	0	1
1	1	0	0	1
1	1	1	1	1

The Boolean equations for sum and carry are

$$\text{Sum} = \bar{A}\bar{B}\,\text{Cin} + \bar{A}B\,\overline{\text{Cin}} + A\bar{B}\,\overline{\text{Cin}} + AB\,\text{Cin}$$
$$\text{Carry} = AB + B\,\text{Cin} + A\,\text{Cin}$$

The ROM implementation is as shown in Fig. 6.7.

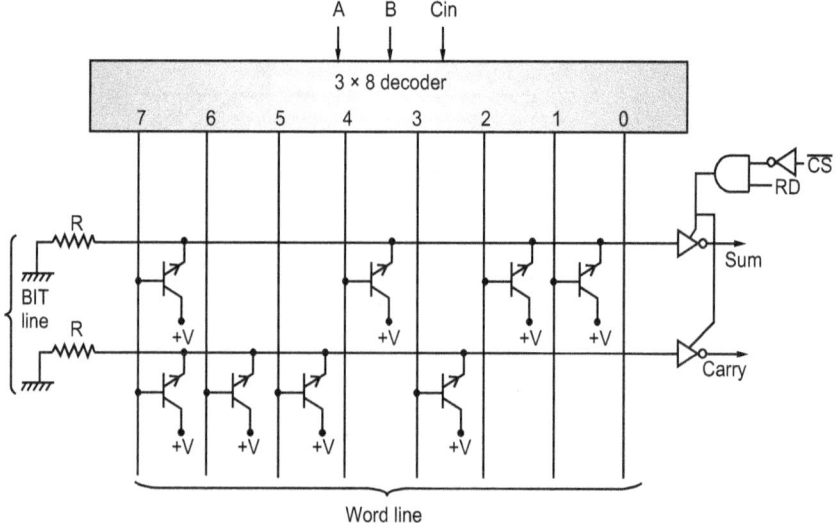

Fig. 6.7 : Implementation of full adder in ROM

- The ROM used contains bipolar junction transistor. Words are programmed by joining the intersections using n-p-n transistor. If a connection exists, transistor is present when the word line is addressed, the bit line goes HIGH. The tristate gates are enabled when CS is LOW and RD is HIGH.

- A PROM structure includes fusible links (See Fig. 6.8) between the emitters of the npn (n-p-n) and the bit lines. To program the device, current pulses are passed through the links until the fuses are blown.

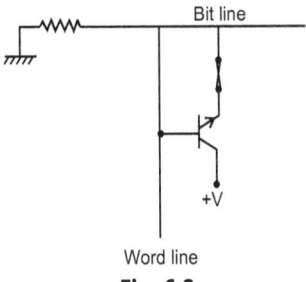

Fig. 6.8

6.2 PROGRAMMABLE LOGIC ARRAYS (PLAs)

Q. Explain PLA. [Dec. 08, 2 M]
Q. Explain brief the internal architecture of a PLA. [Dec. 05, 4 M]

The first PLDs were Programmable Logic Arrays (PLAs). A programmable logic array device contains basically an array of AND-OR functions.

6.2.1 Architecture of PLA

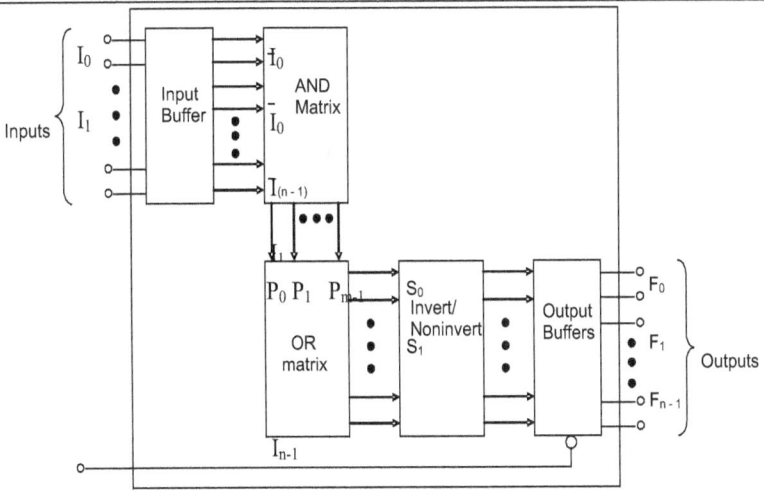

Fig. 6.9 : Block diagram of PLA device

- A PLA consists of two level AND – OR circuits on a single chip. The number of AND and OR gates and their inputs are fixed for a given PLA chip.

The AND gates provide the product terms and OR gates ORs their product terms and generate a SOP (sum of products) expression.

The block diagram for internal architecture of PLA is shown in Fig. 6.9.

(a) Input buffer

- Input buffer produces inverted as well as non-inverted inputs at the output as shown in Fig. 6.10 for one input. There are similar buffers for each one of the n inputs. Input buffers are required to limit loading of the sources that drive the inputs.

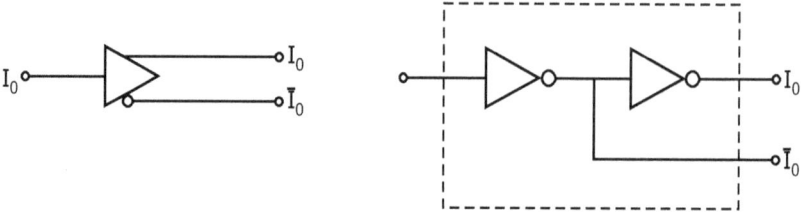

Fig. 6.10 : Input buffers

(b) AND Matrix

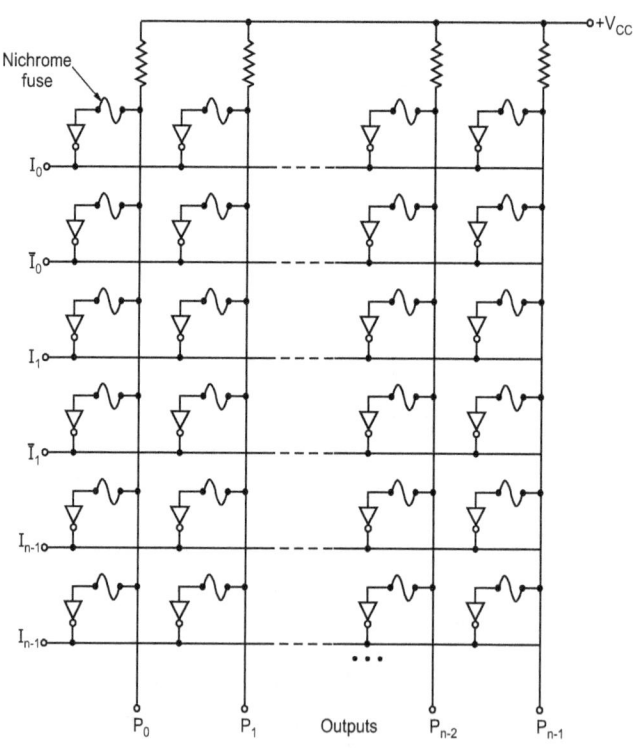

Fig. 6.11 : An AND matrix

- An AND matrix is used to form product terms. A typical AND matrix is shown in Fig. 6.11. It has M AND gates. 2n (I0 to In-1 and $\overline{I_0}$ to $\overline{I_{n-1}}$) inputs and M (P0 to Pm-1) outputs of

AND matrix. Each AND gate has all the input variables (2n). Nichrome fuse link is connected in series with each diode. All the links are closed in an unprogrammed PLA device and logic 0 is stored.

- Each AND gate generates one product term which is given by

$$P = I_0 \cdot \overline{I_0} \cdot I_1 \cdot \overline{I_1} \ldots I_{n-1} \cdot \overline{I_{n-1}}$$

By using a programmer device, unwanted links are opened, to generate required product term.

- The gate representation for P0 output is shown in Fig. 6.11.

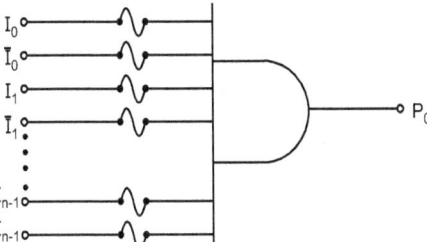

(c) OR matrix

- The OR matrix is used to produce the logical sum of the product terms (outputs of AND matrix). Fig. 6.12 shows an OR matrix using transistor. An OR gate consists of parallel connected transistors with a common emitter load. S_0 to S_{m-1} are the outputs of an OR matrix. All the fuse links are closed in an unprogrammed device. The S_0 output is given by

$$S0 = P0 + P1 + \text{----} \ Pm\text{-}1$$

- The unwanted fuse links can be opened to generate required sum terms.

  For example, if P_0 and P_1 fuse links are closed and all others are blown off (opened) for the output S_0, then

$$S0 = P0 + P1$$

- The logic symbol for one OR gate is shown in Fig. 6.12.

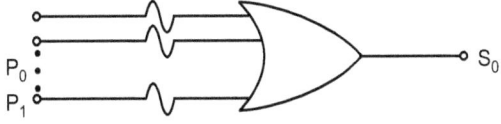

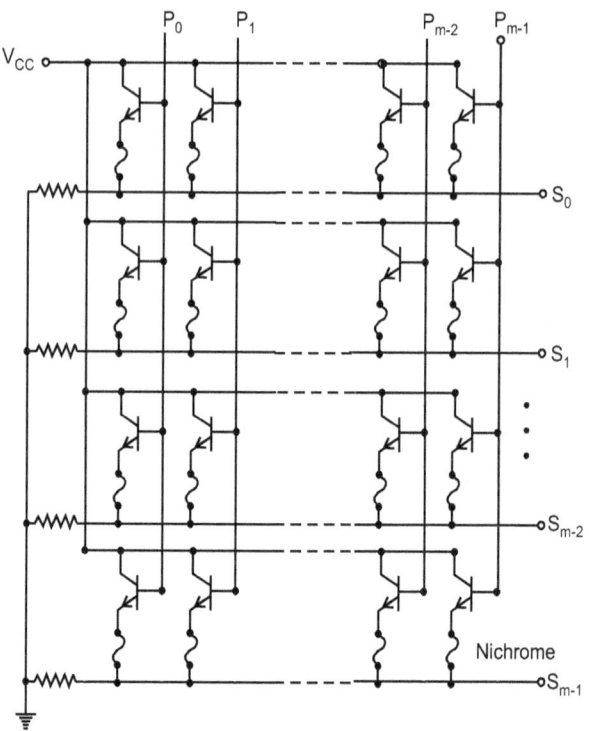

Fig. 6.12 : An OR matrix

(d) Invert/Non-Invert matrix

- This is a programmable buffer. This is used to generate active low or active high outputs. Typical circuits for this operation are shown in Fig. 6.13.

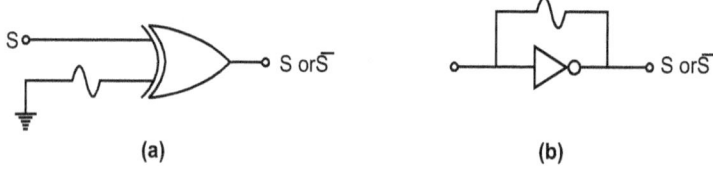

Fig. 6.13 : Inverting/Non-Inverting Buffer

When fuse link is closed, the output is S and output is $\bar{S}$ when fuse is blown off (opened).

(e) Output buffer

- To increase the driving capability of the PLA, output buffers are required. Usually, the outputs are TTL compatible. Fig. 6.14 shows the three-state output buffers.

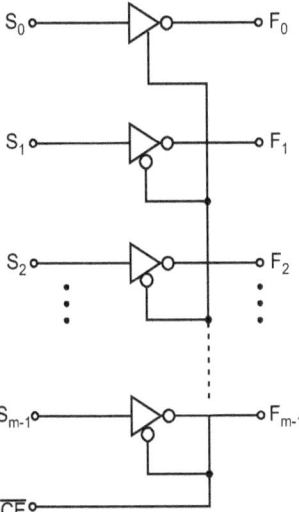

Fig. 6.14 : Output Buffers

(f) Output through flip-flop and Buffers

- The output of the OR gate can be connected to the input of flip-flops. The device output can be available through tristate buffers. The PLA device with Output flip-flops and Buffers are suitable for state machine application.

- The PLA can be represented by AND and OR arrays as shown in Fig. 6.15.

- A PLA device can be programmed similar to the programming of ROM. For a mask programmable device, the data pattern is to be specified by the customer. The appropriate masks are designed by the manufacturers and the data pattern are built in during the manufacturing process.

- An FPLA (Field Programmable Logic Array) has all its nichrome links intact at the time of manufacturing. The unwanted links are electrically open circuited during programming. The links to be opened are accessed by applying voltages at the inputs and outputs of the device. The FPLAs are not reprogrammable.

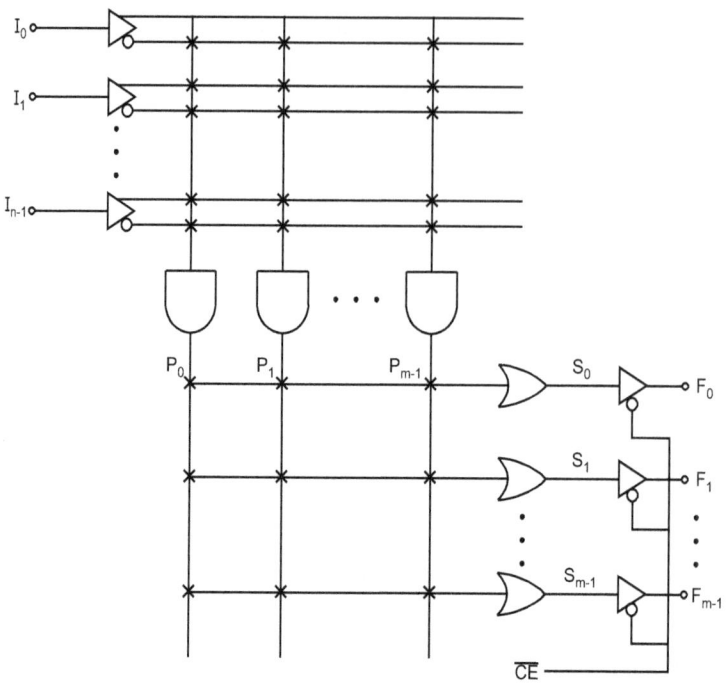

Fig. 6.15 : Representation of PLA

6.2.2 Circuit Realization using PLA

Example 6.3 :

Realize the following functions using PLA.

$$F0 = \Sigma\, m\,(0, 1, 4, 6)$$
$$F1 = \Sigma\, m\,(2, 3, 4, 6, 7)$$
$$F2 = \Sigma\, m\,(0, 1, 2, 6)$$
$$F3 = \Sigma\, m\,(2, 3, 5, 6, 7)$$

Solution :

If we minimize each function separately, the result is

$$F_0 = \bar{A} \cdot \bar{B} + A\bar{C}$$
$$F_1 = B + A\bar{C}$$
$$F_2 = \overline{AB} + B\bar{C}$$
$$F_3 = AC + B$$

Fig. 6.16 shows an NMOS PLA that realizes the above functions.

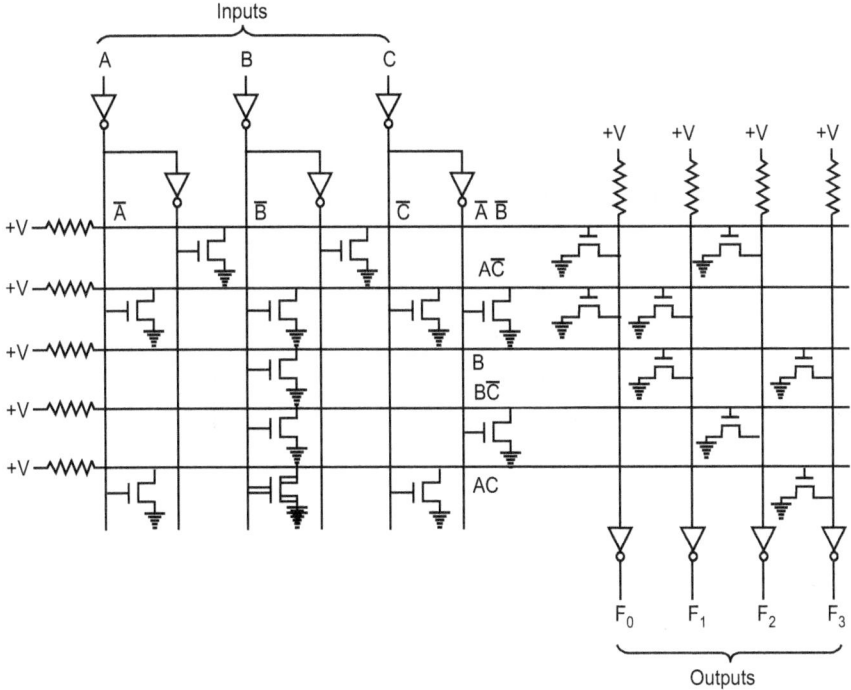

Fig. 6.16 : PLA realization

Logic gates are formed in the array by connecting NMOS switching transistor between the column lines and row lines. The transistors act as switches, so if the gate input is a logic 0, the transistor is off. If the gate input is a logic 1, the transistor provides a conducting path to ground. Transistors connected in AND and OR array act as NOT gates. If there is a transistor between row and column line, then that bit is considered.

For example, consider Fig. 6.17 (a).

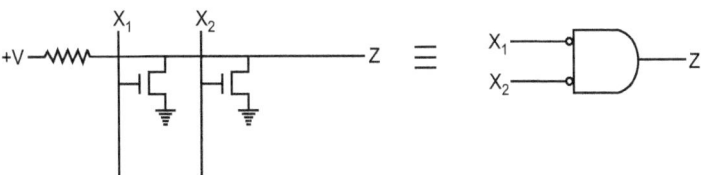

Fig. 6.17 (a)

If X1 and X2 = 0, both transistors are off, and the pull up resistor brings the Z output to a logic 1 level (+v). If either X1 or X2 is 1, the corresponding transistor is turned on, and Z = 0.

Thus $\overline{X1 + X2} = \overline{X1}\,\overline{X2}$ which corresponds to a NOR gate.

The AND-OR array equivalent of Fig. 6.17 (a) is shown in Fig. 6.17 (b).

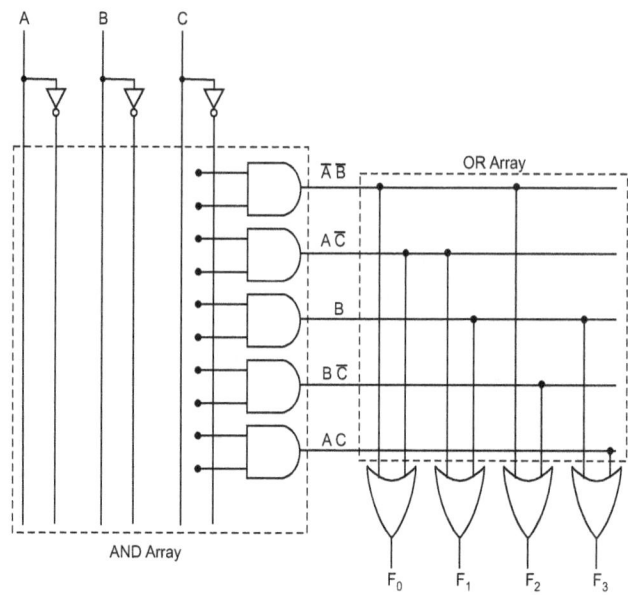

Fig. 6.17 (b) : AND-OR array equivalent of Fig. 6.17 (a)

Example 6.4 :

Implement BCD to gray code converter using PLA or Explain in brief design model of PLA for any code conversion example. [Dec. 10, 8 M]

Solution :

The following table shows BCD numbers and their equivalent gray code.

Table 6.1

BCD Code				Gray Code			
B_3	B_2	B_1	B_0	G_3	G_2	G_1	G_0
0	0	0	0	0	0	0	0
0	0	0	1	0	0	0	1
0	0	1	0	0	0	1	1
0	0	1	1	0	0	1	0
0	1	0	0	0	1	1	0
0	1	0	1	0	1	1	1
0	1	1	0	0	1	0	1
0	1	1	1	0	1	0	0
1	0	0	0	1	1	0	0
1	0	0	1	1	1	0	1

From the table, we can get

$$G3 = B3$$
$$G2 = B2 \oplus B3 = \overline{B2}\,B3 + B2\,\overline{B3}$$
$$G1 = B1 \oplus B2 = \overline{B1}\,B2 + B1\,\overline{B2}$$
$$G0 = B0 \oplus B1 = \overline{B0}\,B1 + B0\,\overline{B1}$$

PLA with 4 inputs, 7 product terms and 4 outputs is shown in Fig. 6.18.

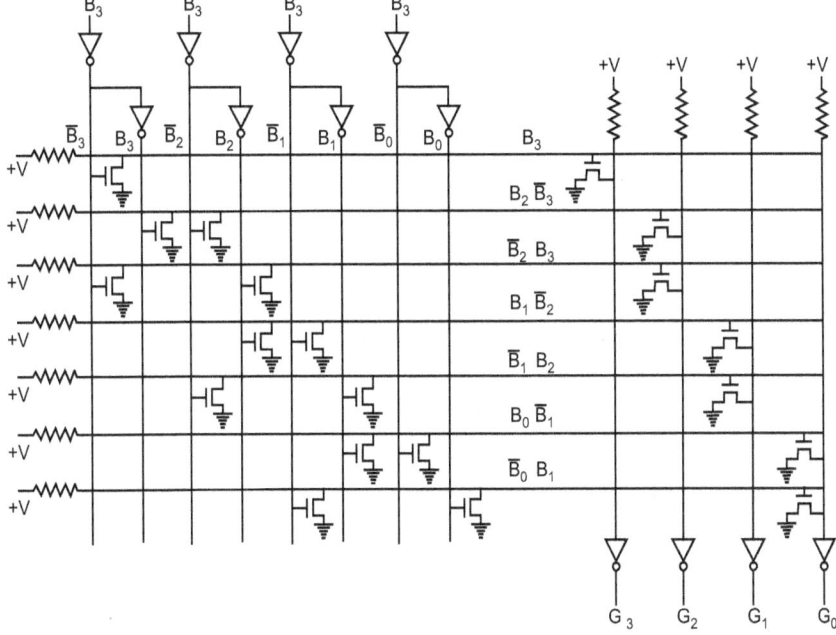

Fig. 6.18 : PLA realization

The AND-OR array equivalent of Fig. 6.18 is shown in Fig. 6.19.

- From Fig. 6.19, it can be noticed that PLA utilizes less space as compared to ROM. A more better way of utilization of empty space in PLA can be done by allowing two or more input lines to share the same column, or to let the product lines share the same row or by both. This sharing is known as folding.

- In PLA, both AND and OR arrays are programmable. Hence PLA devices are more flexible than PAL devices. Thus the same AND output can be sent to any number of OR gates.

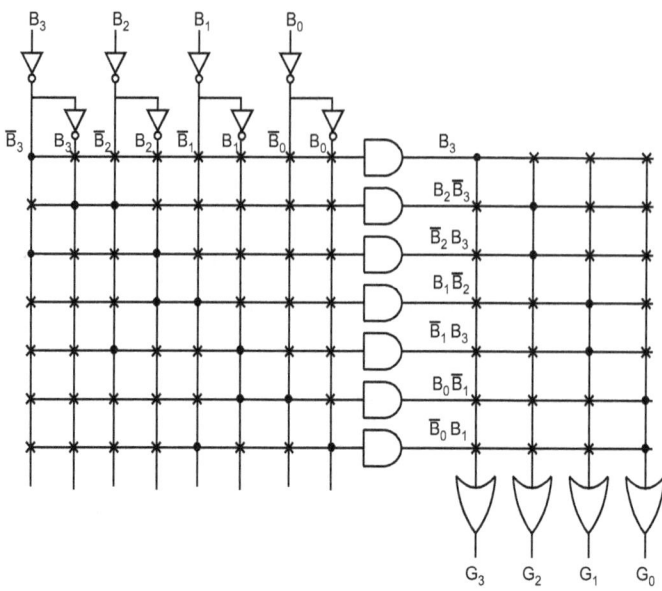

Fig. 6.19: AND-OR Array Equivalent of Fig. 6.18

6.3 PROGRAMMABLE ARRAY LOGIC (PAL)

Q. Explain PAL [Dec. 08, 4 M]
Q. Explain the design model of PAL. [May 11, 8 M]

- In programmable array logic, the AND array is programmable and the OR array is fixed. The basic structure of the PAL is the same as PLA. PAL is less expensive than PLA because only the AND array is programmable.

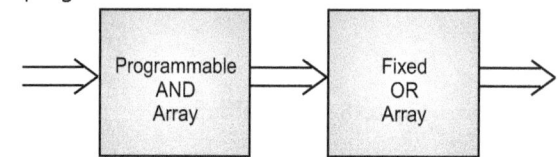

(a) Structure of PAL

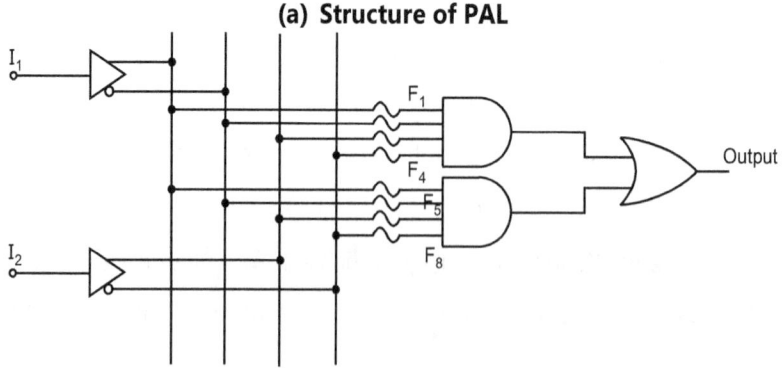

Fig. 6.20 : (b) Unprogrammed PAL segment

Fig. 6.20 represents a segment of an unprogrammed PAL. The symbol

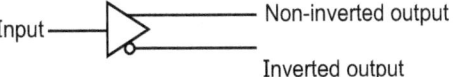

represents an input buffer, with inverted and non-inverted outputs. A buffer is used to drive many AND gate inputs. When the PAL is programmed, the fusible links (F1, F2 - - F8) are selectively blown to leave the desired connections to the AND gate inputs. Connections to the AND gate inputs in a PAL are represented by 'X's, as shown here.

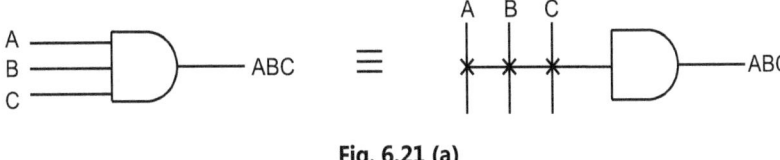

Fig. 6.21 (a)

As an example, Fig. 6.21 (b) shows the realization of the function $I1\ \bar{I_2} + \bar{I_1}\ I_2$ by using PAL segment.

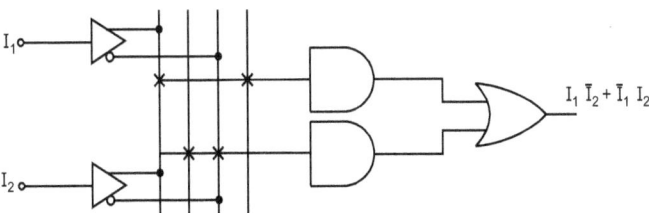

Fig. 6.21 (b) : Programmed PAL segment

The 'X's indicate that the I_1 and $\bar{I_2}$ lines are connected to the first AND gate, and the $\bar{I_1}$ and I_2 lines are connected to the other AND gate.

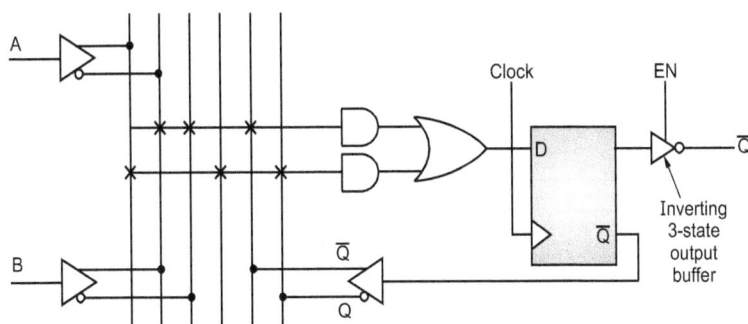

Fig. 6.22 : Sequential PAL segment

- Typical PALs have from 10 to 20 inputs and from 2 to 10 outputs. 2 to 6 AND gates driving each OR gate. PALs are also available that contain D flip-flop with inputs driven from the programmable array logic. Such PALs provide a convenient way of realizing sequential networks. Fig. 6.14 shows a segment of sequential PAL. The D flip-flop is driven from an OR gate, which is fed by two AND gates. The flip-flop output is fed back to the programmable AND array through a buffer. Thus the AND gate inputs can be connected to A, $\bar{A}$, B, $\bar{B}$, Q or $\bar{Q}$. The 'X's on the diagram shows the realization of the next-state equation.

$$Q+ = D = \bar{A}B\bar{Q} + \bar{A}BQ$$

The flip-flop output is connected to an inverting tristate buffer, which is enable when EN = 1.

> **Q.** Implement the following function using PLA
>
> $$F_1(A, B, C) = \Sigma m(1, 2, 4, 6)$$
> $$F_2(A, B, C) = \Sigma m(0, 1, 6, 7)$$

Example 6.5 :

Implement the following output function using suitable PLA

$$f(A, B, C, D) = \Sigma m(3, 4, 5, 7, 10, 14, 15)$$

Solution :

To implement a combinational circuit using PLA, first we need to convert the function in their sum of products form. Also, we can find the common product terms among the K-maps of the outputs.

K – map is

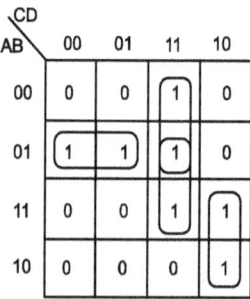

Fig. 6.23

$$f(A, B, C, D) = \bar{A}B\bar{C} + \bar{A}C\bar{D} + BCD + AC\bar{D}$$

Now, in the above equation, there are 4 product terms. Therefore, we need minimum 4 inputs, 1 output and 4 product terms.

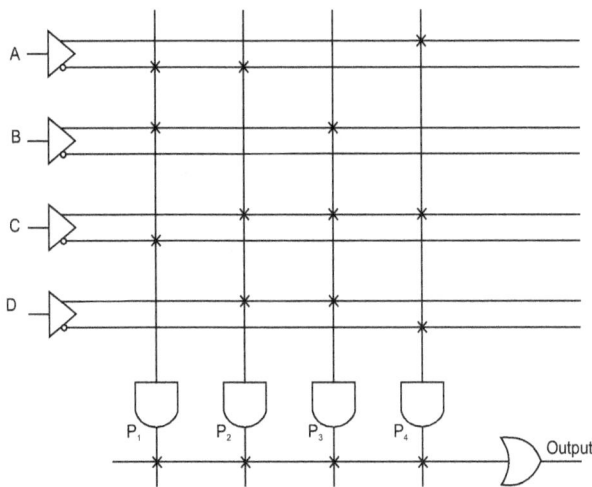

Fig. 6.24 : Programmed PLA for example 6.5

Example 6.6 :

Implement Full Adder Circuit Using PLA.

Solution :

Now, we will first draw the Truth Table of Full Adder

Table 6.2 : Truth table of Full Adder

Inputs			Outputs	
A	B	C	Sum	Carry
0	0	0	0	0
0	0	1	1	0
0	1	0	1	0
0	1	1	0	1
1	0	0	1	0
1	0	1	0	1
1	1	0	0	1
1	1	1	1	1

From the above truth table, we can write the equations for sum and carry as.

$$\text{Sum} = \Sigma m\ (1, 2, 4, 7)$$
$$\text{Carry} = \Sigma m\ (3, 5, 6, 7)$$

The K-maps are used to simplify the above equations.

K - map for sum

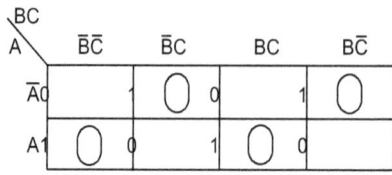

Fig. 6.25

We can write the SOP as

$$\text{Sum} = \bar{A}\bar{B}C + \bar{A}B\bar{C} + A\bar{B}\bar{C} + ABC$$

Similarly, the K-map for carry is

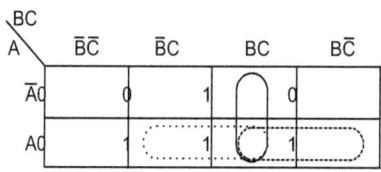

Fig. 6.26

SOP for carry is   Carry = AC + AB + BC

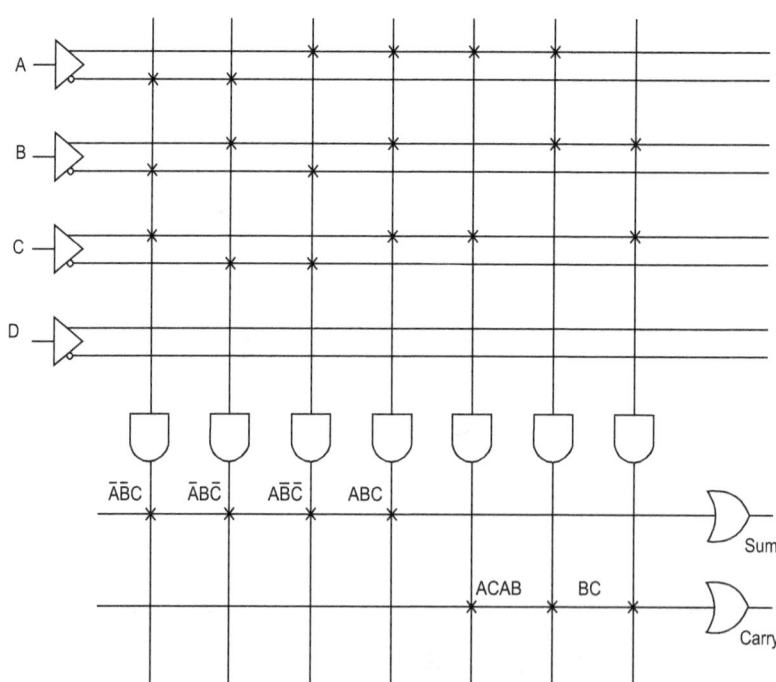

Fig. 6.27 : Programmed PLA

Example 6.7 :

Implement the following output function using PAL.

$$f_1(x, y, z) = \Sigma m\ (0, 1, 3, 6, 7)$$

$$f_2(x, y, z) = \Sigma m\ (1, 2, 4, 6)$$

Solution :

In PAL, the OR array is fixed and AND array is programmable. Since the OR array is fixed the number of product terms per OR gate cannot be changed. In PALs, unlike the PLAs, a product term cannot be shared among two or more OR gates. First, we need to simplify the functions f_1 and f_2 using k - map.

K-map for f_1

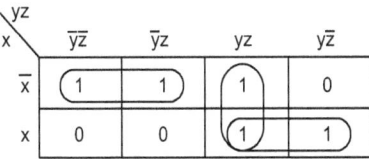

Fig. 6.28

∴ $f_1 = \bar{x}\bar{y} + yz + xy$

K -map for f_2

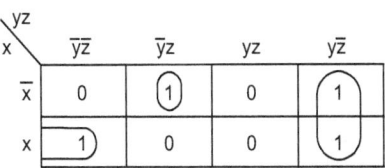

Fig. 6.29

$f_2 = \bar{x}z + y\bar{z} + x\bar{y}\,z$

From above equations, we require 3 inputs, 2 outputs and maximum 3 product terms per OR gate.

Now, we will prepare a PAL program table.

Table 6.3 : PAL Program Table

Product Terms		AND Inputs			Outputs
		x	y	z	
$\bar{x}\bar{y}$	1	0	0	–	
yz	2	–	1	1	$f_1 = \bar{x}\bar{y} + yz + xy$
xy	3	1	1	–	
$x\bar{z}$	4	1	–	0	
$y\bar{z}$	5	–	1	0	$f_2 = x\bar{z} + y\bar{z} + \bar{x}\bar{y}z$
$\bar{x}\bar{y}z$	6	0	0	1	

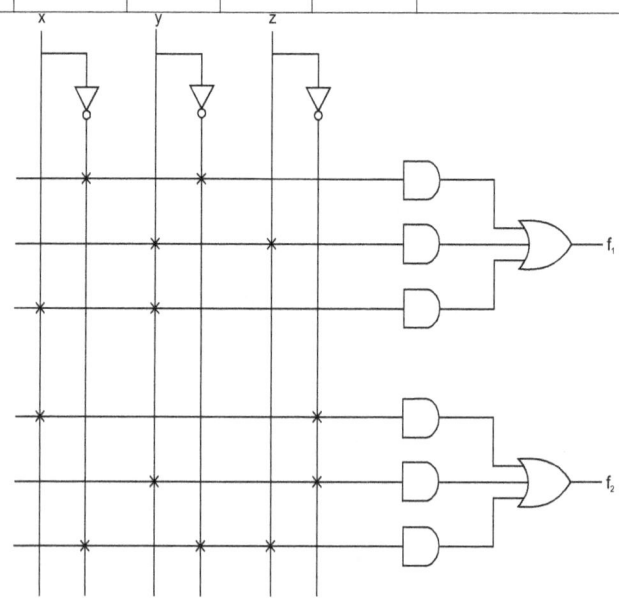

Fig. 6.30 : Programmed PAL

6.4 CPLD : COMPLEX PROGRAMMABLE LOGIC DEVICE

Q. Draw and explain the general architecture of CPLD.
Q. Draw and explain the block diagram of CPLD. Explain features of CPLDCX 95 72.

- PLAs and PALs are useful for implementing a wide variety of small digital circuits. Each device can be used to implement circuits that do not require more number of inputs, product terms and outputs that are provided in the particular chip.
- These chips are limited to fairly modest sizes, typically supporting a combined number of inputs plus outputs of not more than 32. For implementation of circuits that require more

inputs and outputs either multiple PALs or PALs can be employed or a more sophisticated type of chip called a Complex Programmable Logic Device (CPLD) can be used.

- A CPLD comprises multiple circuit blocks on a single chip, with internal wiring resources to connect the circuit blocks. Each circuit block is similar to a PAL or a PLA. These PAL like blocks are connected to a set of interconnection wires. Each PAL like block is also connected to a sub circuit labelled input block, which is attached to a number of the chips input and output pins. The interconnection wiring contains programmable switches that are used to connect the PAL-like blocks.

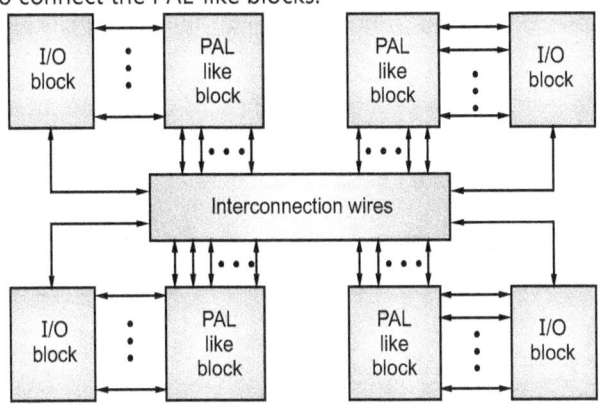

Fig. 6.31 : CPLD

- Packages: PLCC (Plastic Lead Chip Carrier)
  QFP (Quad Flat Pack)

Like a PLCC package, QFP has pins on all the four sides, but whereas the PLCC's pins wrap around the edges of the package, the QFP's pins extend outward from the package, with a downward-curve shape. The QFP's pins are thinner than those on a PLC which means that the package can support a large number of pins; QFP's are available with more than 200 pins, whereas PLCC's are limited to a few 100 pins.

6.4.1 XC9500 CPLD Family

6.4.1.1 Features Of Xc9500 Series

1. High-performance device due to 5 ns pin-to-pin logic delays on all pins and fCNT upto 125 MHz.
2. Large density range having 36 to 288 macro cells with 800 to 6400 usable gates.
3. 5 V in-system programmable.
4. Endurance of 10,000 program/erase cycles.
5. Global and product term clocks, output enables, set and reset signals.
6. Slew rate control on individual blocks.
7. User programmable ground pin capability.
8. High drive 24 mA outputs.

9. 3.3 V to 5 V input/output capabilities.
10. Advanced CMOS 5 V Fast Flash technology.
11. Supports parallel programming of multiple XC9500 devices.
12. Extension IEEE std. 1149.1 boundary scan (JTAG) support.

6.4.1.2 Architecture of XC9500

- Each XC9500 device is consisting of multiple function blocks (FBs) and I/O blocks (IOBs) fully interconnected by the fast connect II switch matrix.
- The input/output block (IOB) provides buffering for device input and output. Each function block provides programmable logic capability with extra wide 54 inputs and 18 outputs.
- The fast connect II switch matrix connects all functions blocks output and input signals to the Function Block inputs. For each Function Block, upto 18 outputs (depending on package pin count) and associated output enable signals drive directly to the IOBs.

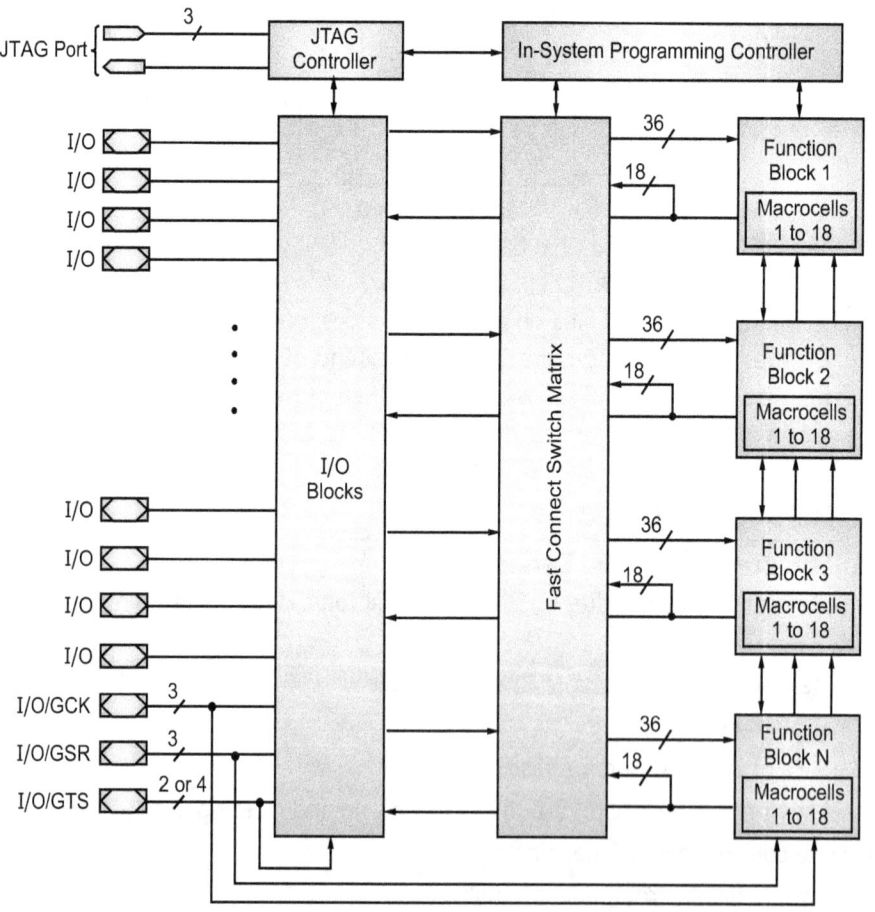

Fig. 6.32 : XC9500 architecture

(A) Function block (FB)

- Each function block is comprised of 18 independent macro cells, each capable of implementing a combinational or registered function. The function block also receives global clock, output enable and their corresponding output enable signals also drive the IOB. The function block generates 18 outputs that drive the fast connect switch matrix. These 18 outputs and their corresponding output enable signals also drive the IOB.

- Each function block supports local feedback paths that allow any number of function block outputs to drive into its own programmable AND-array without going outside the function block. These paths are used for creating very fast counters and state machines where all state registers are within the same Function Block.

(B) Macrocell

- A macrocell is the CPLD logic cell which is made of gates only. A macrocell can implement both combinational and registered equations. Five direct product terms from the AND-array are available for use as primary data inputs to implement combinational functions or as control input including clock, set/reset and output enable.

- The product term allocator associated with each macrocell selects how the five direct terms are used. Macrocell register can be used as D-type or T-type flip-flop or it may be bypassed for combinational operation. Each register supports both asynchronous set and reset operations.

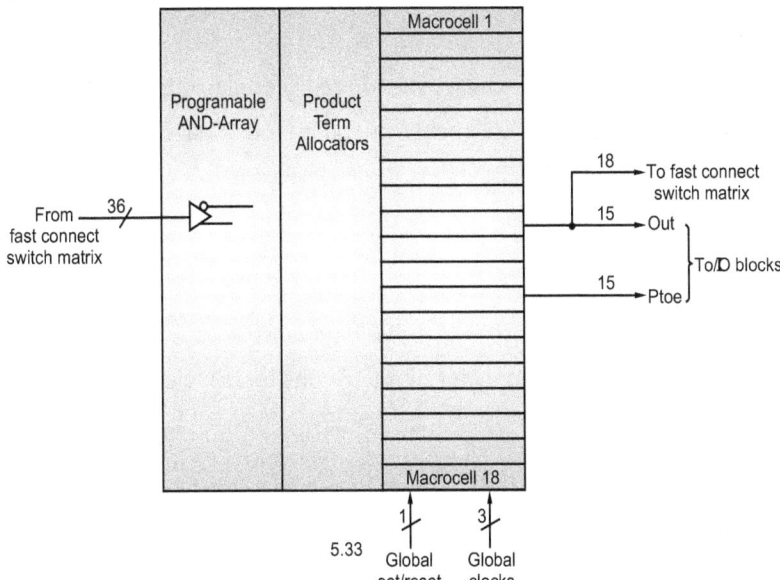

Fig. 6.33 : XC9500 function block

(C) Fast connect switch matrix

- To fast connect switch matrix connects signals to the FB inputs. The fast connect matrix is capable of combining multiple internal connections into a single wired. AND output before driving the destination FB. This provides additional capability and increases the effective logic fan-in of the destination FB without any additional timing delay. All the IOB outputs and all the FB outputs drive the Fast Connect matrix.

(D) Input/output block (IOB)

- It is interface between the internal logic and the device user input/output pins. It includes an input buffer, output driver, output enable selection multiplexer and user programmable ground control. Each IOB is providing slew rate control.
- The rise and fall times of the output signals can be set to be fast or slow. Each IOB provides user programmable ground pin capability. This allows device I/O pins to be configured as additional ground pins.
- By strategically locating programmable ground pins to external ground connection, system noise generated from large numbers of simultaneously switching outputs may be reduced. Each IOB provides a bus-hold circuitry which eliminates the need to tie unused pins either high or low by holding the last known state of the input until the next input signal is present.

6.4.1.3 CPLD XC 9572

He XC9500XL family has some of the cheapest and readily available CPLDs. This development boads from Dangerous Prototypes will help you build your first custom logic chip using simple schematic entry, Veliog, or VHDL.

- XC9572XL CPLD with 72macrocells
- 5volt tolerant inputs
- On-board 3.3 volt power supply for core and pins
- Selectable 3.3 volt or external supply for pins (1.8 volts to 3.3 volts)
- LEDs for output
- Push button for input
- Populated JTAG header
- Easy to program with the Bus pirate
- Open source (CC-BY-SA)

6.5 FPGA : FIELD PROGRAMMABLE GATE ARRAY

Q. Draw and explain structural diagram of FPGA.	[May 07, 08, Dec. 05, 4 M]
Q. What is LUT in FPGA.	[Dec. 07, May 06, 2 M]
Q. Write short note on FPGA.	[Dec. 11, 6 M]
Q. Draw and explain Basic architecture of FPGA. State difference between PLA and FPGA.	[May 13, 8 M]
Q. What is mean by FPGAD. Explain internal structure of FPGA.	[May 08, 12, 10 M]

- Each FPGA vendor has its own FPGA architecture. But in general term they all are variations of that as shown in Fig. 6.34.

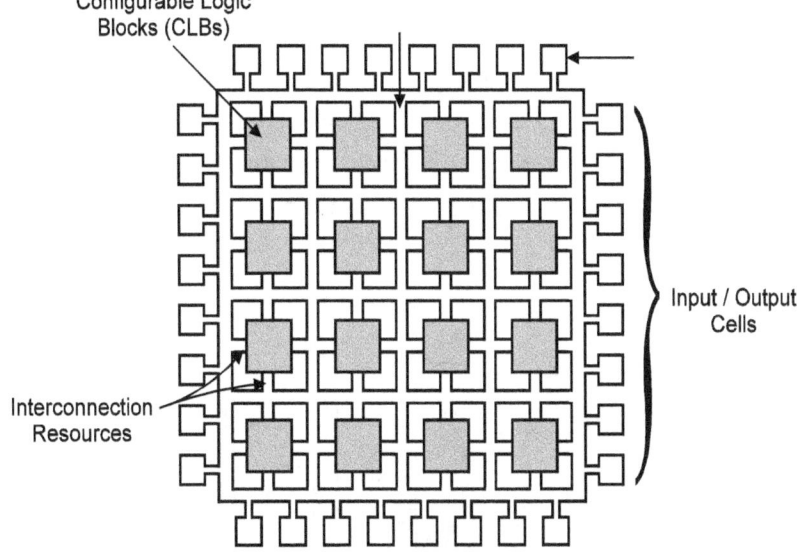

Fig. 6.34 : General architecture of an FPGA

- The architecture consists of configurable logic blocks, configurable I/O blocks and programmable interconnects. Also, there will be clock circuitry for driving the clock signals to each logic block, and additional logic resources.

- It is a programmable logic device that supports implementation of relatively large logic circuits. They do not contain AND or OR planes. It contains three main types of resources : logic blocks, I/O blocks for connecting to the pins of the package and inter connection wires and switches.

   ☐ Logic blocks

   ☐ Inter connection switches.

Fig. 6.35 : FPGA

- The logic blocks are arranged in a two dimensional array and the interconnection wires are organized as horizontal and vertical routing channels between rows and columns of logic blocks. The routing channels contain wires and programmable switches that allows the logic blocks to be interconnected in many ways.
- The FPGAs can be used to implement logic circuits of more than a few hundred thousand equivalent gates in size. The FPGAs are available in four packages : PLCC, QFP, PGA (Pin Grid Array) and BGA (Ball Grid Array).

6.5.1 Details of FPGA Architecture

1. **Configurable Logic Blocks :** Configurable Logic Blocks contain the logic for the FPGA. In a large grain architecture, these CLBs will contain enough logic to create a small state machine. In a fine grain architecture, more like a true gate array ASIC, the CLB will contain only very basic logic. The diagram in Fig. 6.36 would be considered a large grain block. It contains RAM for creating arbitrary combinational logic functions. It also contains flip-flops for clocked storage elements, multiplexers in order to route the logic within the block and to and from external resources. The multiplexers also allow polarity selection and reset and clear input selection.

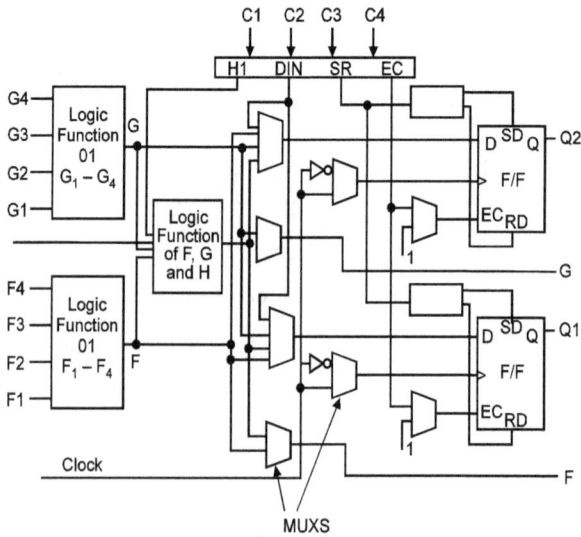

Fig. 6.36 : FPGA configurable logic block

2. **Configurable I/O Blocks :** A configurable I/O block, shown in Fig. 6.37 is used to bring signals onto the chip and send them back off again. It consists of an input buffer and an output buffer with three states and open collector output controls. Typically, there are pull-up resistors on the outputs and sometimes pull-down resistors. The polarity of the

output can usually be programmed for fast or slow rise and fall times. In addition, there is often a flip-flop on outputs so that clocked signals can be output directly to the pins without encountering significant delay. It is done for inputs so that there is not much delay on a signal before reaching a flip-flop which would increase the device hold time requirement.

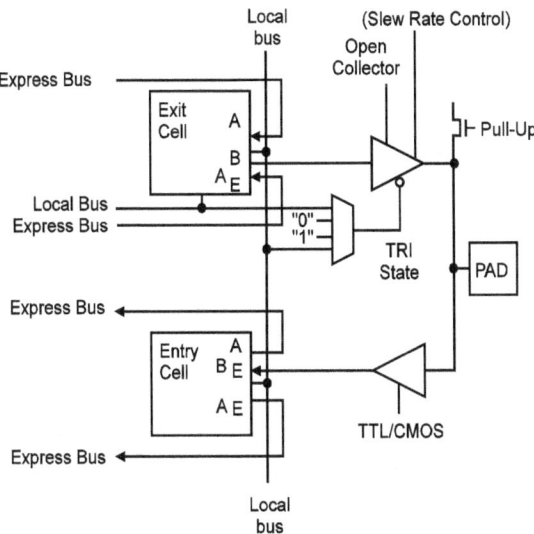

Fig. 6.37 : FPGA configurable I/O block

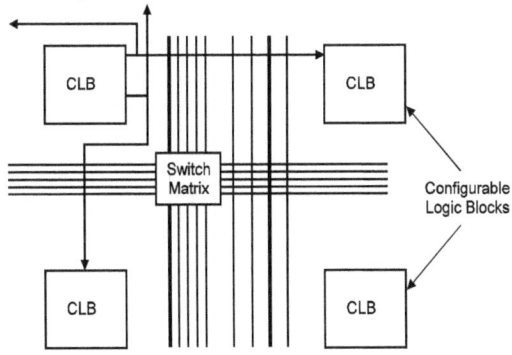

Fig. 6.38 : FPGA programmable interconnect

The interconnect of an FPGA is very different than that of a CPLD, but is rather similar to that of a gate array ASIC. In Fig. 6.38, a hierarchy of interconnect resources can be seen. There are long lines which can be used to connect critical CLBs that are physically far from each other on the chip without inducing much delay. They can also be used as buses within the chip. There are also short lines which are used to connect individual CLBs which are located physically close to each other. There are often one or several switch matrices, like that in a CPLD, to connect these long and short lines together in specific ways. Programmable switches inside the chip allow the connection of CLBs to interconnect lines and interconnect lines to each other and to the switch matrix. Three-state buffers are used to connect many CLBs to a long line, creating a bus. Special long lines, called global clock lines, are specially designed for low impedance and thus fast propagation times. These are connected to the clock buffers and to each clocked element in each CLB. This is how the clocks are distributed throughout the FPGA.

3. Clock Circuitry : Special I/O blocks with special high drive clock buffers, known as clock drivers, are distributed around the chip. These buffers are connected to clock input pads and drive the clock signals onto the global clock lines described above. These clock lines are designed for low skew times and fast propagation times. As we will discuss later, synchronous design is a must with FPGAs, since absolute skew and delay cannot be guaranteed. Only when using clock signals from clock buffers can the relative delays and skew times be guaranteed.

4. LUT : The most commonly used logic block is a Look up Table (LUT) which contains storage cells that are used to complement a small logic function. Each cell is capable of holding a single logic value either 0 or 1. The stored value is produced as the output of the storage cell. LUTs of various sizes may be created, where the size is defined by the number of inputs.

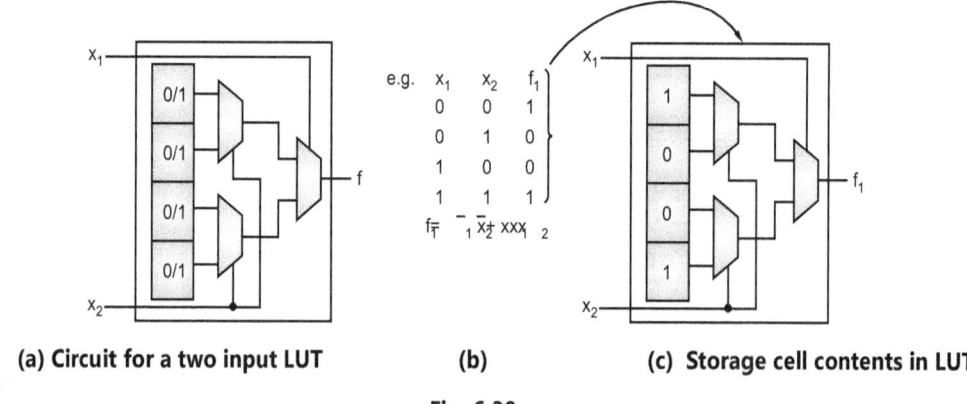

(a) Circuit for a two input LUT   (b)   (c) Storage cell contents in LUT

Fig. 6.39

In commercial FPGA chips, LUTs usually have either four or five inputs, which require 16 and 32 storage cells respectively. FPGAs also have extra circuitry included with their LUTs. FPGAs are configured by using the ISP method. The storage cells in the LUTs in an FPGA are **volatile** which means that they loose their stored contents whenever, the power supply for the chip is turned OFF. Hence, the FPGA has to be programmed every time power is applied. Often a small memory chip that holds its data permanently, called Programmable Read Only Memory (PROM) is included on the circuit board that houses the FPGA. The storage cells in FPGA are loaded automatically from the PROM when power is applied to the chips.

Fig. 6.39 (a) shows the structure of a small LUT. It has two inputs x_1 and x_2 and one output f. It is capable of implementing any logic function of two variables. The two variable truth table has four rows so this LUT will have four storage cells. One cell corresponds to the output value in each row, of the truth table. The input variables x_1 and x_2 are used as the select inputs of three multiplexers. Depending on the values of x_1 and x_2, the content of the one of the four storage cells are selected as the output of the LUT.

Consider the truth table in Fig. 6.39 (b). The function f_1 from the table can be stored in the LUT as shown in Fig. 6.39 (c). The arrangement of multiplexers in the LUT correctly realize the function f_1. When $x_1 = x_2 = 0$, the output of the LUT is driven by the top storage cell, which represents the entry in the truth table for $x_1, x_2 = 00$.

6.6 COMPARISON OF CPLD AND FPGA

Q. Compare CPLD and FPGA.

Sr. No.	CPLD	FPGA
1	PAL like blocks, Switching matrix Fig. 6.40 (a)	IOB, CLB, Large gate array Fig. 6.40 (b)
2	CPLDs are coarse grain devices, which contain large logic blocks with large fan in and –or logic.	FPGAs are fine grain devices, with small logic blocks.
3	Small to medium density.	Medium to very high density, suitable for large complex designs.

4	Time delays are predictable. It provides fast pint to pin performance.	In FPGA, delays are dependent on application.
5	EEPROM/Flash-based architecture.	Use SRAM/Antifuse technology.
6	Less density.	More density.
7	CPLD's are non-volatile	FPGAs are volatile.
8	High power consumption.	Low power consumption.
9	Large and wide blocks with less number of I/O pins.	Blocks and cells are smaller in size, with more number of I/O pins.